Injecting Substance Use, Recovery and Critical Harms

Injecting Substance Use, Recovery and Critical Harms: Understanding the Complexities of the Drug Problem provides an important overview into the history, drivers and consequences of drug injecting, what sustains it and why problems continue to surprise clinicians, policy-makers and politicians. It explores the gritty reality of the harms caused by injecting drugs, and puts the medical, psychiatric and social damage in a contemporary context. Among the many harms resulting from substance use are viral and bacterial epidemics and devastating loss of life. Although no simple solutions are possible, by engaging with the consequences of drug use, the book aims to understand the causes, to prevent worse outcomes.

Drawing on the author's in-depth experiences at the forefront of practice, policy and research in this field, the book provides an extended case study examining drug injecting and the HIV crisis in the Scottish health system. The book shows how trying to get to grips with the "drug problem" is complicated by confusing definitions of what is a drug and where the separation lies between the benefits and harms, Culture and politics, which vary across nations, determine legal status, and consequently penalties and acceptability. In grappling with these complexities, the book aims to develop a strong theoretical framework which examines how substance use is socially constructed within public health policy and practice.

The book should be essential reading for health, medicine and social care students and those with an interest in the consequences of illicit substance use including those studying law, humanities, business and politics. It will also be informative for professionals and policy-makers in the criminal justice, health and education sectors and those responsible for political influence and planning in the public realm. Anyone who thinks that substance use will not throw up new problems and challenges for the health and politics affecting us all in the future just has to consider the roller coaster of the last six decades.

Roy Robertson (James R. Robertson) is Professor of Addiction Medicine at the University of Edinburgh Usher Institute and was a General Practitioner in NW Edinburgh for 40 years. He was a Member of the Home Office, ACMD, for 10 years, Chair of their Shipman Inquiry committee and a member of several Scottish drug advisory committees. He has had a special interest in the politics and harms of HIV/AIDS and injection drug use.

Injecting Substance Use, Recovery and Critical Harms

Understanding the Complexities of the Drug Problem

Roy Robertson

Routledge
Taylor & Francis Group
LONDON AND NEW YORK

Designed cover image: Getty Images

First published 2026
by Routledge
4 Park Square, Milton Park, Abingdon, Oxon OX14 4RN

and by Routledge
605 Third Avenue, New York, NY 10158

Routledge is an imprint of the Taylor & Francis Group, an informa business

British Library Cataloguing-in-Publication Data
A catalogue record for this book is available from the British Library

Library of Congress Cataloging-in-Publication Data
Names: Robertson, Roy (J. Roy) author
Title: Injecting substance use, recovery and critical harms : understanding the complexities of the drug problem / Roy Robertson.
Description: Abingdon, Oxon ; New York, NY : Routledge, 2027. | Includes bibliographical references and index.
Identifiers: LCCN 2026000228 (print) | LCCN 2026000229 (ebook) | ISBN 9781041006596 hardback | ISBN 9781041006183 paperback | ISBN 9781003611097 ebook
Subjects: LCSH: Intravenous drug abuse | Intravenous drug abusers--Diseases | Intravenous drug abuse--Scotland--Edinburgh | Drug abuse--Government policy | LCGFT: Case studies
Classification: LCC RC564 .R63 2027 (print) | LCC RC564 (ebook)
LC record available at https://lccn.loc.gov/2026000228
LC ebook record available at https://lccn.loc.gov/2026000229

ISBN: 9781041006596 (hbk)
ISBN: 9781041006183 (pbk)
ISBN: 9781003611097 (ebk)

DOI: 10.4324/9781003611097

Typeset in Times New Roman
by Deanta Global Publishing Services, Chennai, India

Contents

Acknowledgements

Love and thanks, to Liz and our boys.

I have drawn heavily from the work and companionship of colleagues when sharing research and policy issues. Some of them include Lorraine Copeland, Jim McKenzie, Kennedy Roberts, John Dunn, Pete Shishodia, Hannah Beresford, John Budd, Ray Brettle, Ralph Bouhaidar, David Weller, Brian McKinstry, Andrew Moss, Robert Newman, Martin Plant, Dave Liddle, Andy McAuley, John Strang, Sheila Bird, Matthew Hickman, John Macleod, Catriona Matheson, Saket Priyadarshi and Alison Richardson,

The doctors and staff of Muirhouse Medical Group have provided unwavering support for people with substance use problems (as well as the unfathomable workload that makes up family practice). Specialist care colleagues have shared the complex problems that make up drug and alcohol dependency medicine especially those in psychiatry, alcohol-related diseases, infectious disease services and laboratory colleagues.

Patients, clients or people, and their families, who have substance use problems have shared their stories and information and they are the ones who have experienced the trauma of addiction. I hope this book might help others like them in some way.

1 Introduction

The scope of this book

Addiction and substance use is a worldwide problem with many facets and multiple manifestations. Cultural norms affect local and national practice; cannabis and other plant-based substance use is common in many regions, and drugs such as alcohol are embedded in normal behaviour throughout most countries. Policy and practice vary from place to place and evolve over time. This book is not attempting to cover more than a fraction of this territory but to present an extended case study drawing upon local and national issues in Scotland and the United Kingdom, with implications for other places. It will concentrate on injecting drug use. It will also draw upon policy that affects most countries compliant with national, regional and international organisations such as national governments, European legislation and, of course, United Nations charters which form the basis of many national regulations. The case study of events affecting people in Scotland will hopefully resonate with people who use drugs by injection and policy and clinical practitioners elsewhere.

Background

The enduring fascination of drugs in the academic press, the public media and in literature ensures that the topic is never far from our awareness. Drug taking in the workplace, among celebrities and public figures; drugs in sport; the portrayal of drugs, for good or bad, in films, theatres and schools; and the, realistic and fanciful, claims of the benefits of new and traditional substances create a whirlwind of information and confusion.

To add to the mystique, the word "drugs" means different things to different people. The range of drugs and drug-related issues comes from the lack of specificity of the word "drug". The word itself includes meanings as diverse as a substance that provides benefits of life-saving medication and, alternatively, the materials which exist in the dark and mysterious world of dependency and addiction. Drugs are responsible for cures and comforts and are essential for compassionate treatments. They are associated with spiritual and mystical experiences, bizarre behaviours and, at the same time, incredible damage to tissues and mental health. Drugs occur in art and literature as a creative force but are, in other settings, characterised

DOI: 10.4324/9781003611097-1

as demonic influences. The bad guys in fiction are often depicted as being motivated by the use of drugs or the rewards of their illegal trafficking. The harmful impact of drugs on a large part of the population is reflected in national and international statistics and from personal testimonies. Stories, statistics and opinions about drugs are never far from the public domain.

These ambiguities mean that the word drug is hardly adequate to include all the wonders of modern pharmacotherapies and at the same time the creative force behind literary fiction and plotting, and the devastating effects on the lives of those dependent.

In addition to this, there is the range of substances from the ever-increasing production of the pharmaceutical industry to historically available naturally occurring compounds, some of which are still in use and which generate modern medicines. Throughout history, drugs have been used to provide solace and relief from pain and suffering, but also responsible for the pains and the torment resulting from the harms associated with dependency and addiction.

The word addiction also has multidimensional and multicultural meanings and interpretations. Whether addiction is a disease or a learned behaviour, a voluntary or a compulsory pastime, a self-imposed harm to the user or a malign effect on communities are all active issues in the public and scientific debate. To what extent addiction is culturally specific and whether there is, could or should be, a common approach to management is a challenge to lawmakers and those who support people with dependency problems.

Terminology and definitions are important, and in this book various terms will be used interchangeably as they appear and evolve in the literature and policy documents over time. Some terms are pejorative and stigmatising and have become redundant. Junkie, drug addict and drug user have been largely replaced by people or persons who use drugs, and addiction by the term substance use disorder (SUD). Terms for treatment for people with opiate difficulties vary from Methadone Maintenance Treatment (MMT) to Opiate Substitute Treatment (OST), Opiate Agonist Treatment (OAT), Medically Assisted Treatment (MAT), and Medication Treatment for Opioid Use Disorder (MOUD). Terms such as dependency and occasionally addiction will both be used in this book as they are embedded in the literature and for the same reason drugs, substances, drug user, drug misuser and drug dependent are retained. Occasionally it is necessary to use the term addict instead of the preferred alternative of person who uses drugs (PWUDs) or person/people who inject drugs (PWIDs) as historic texts and references contain all these terms. Things change with enlightened insights and a fashion for clarity.

In the world of self-administering substances outwith a medical prescription or supervision, division exists in defining dependency or addiction. From a simple belief that substance use was aligned to delinquency and criminality, understanding causal factors and the effects of factors outside the individual, new insights have developed.

In his groundbreaking book, Zinberg described a different approach to understanding drug use. For the first time, a wider view of the drivers of substance use included the environment around the individual as an important factor in initiating and sustaining dependency (Zinberg 1984). This and other changes in approach started an unstoppable trend towards a research agenda beginning to make connections between substance use and inequalities, minority populations and multimorbidity, which had been previously commented on but failed to make the transition into public awareness and policy agendas. Many other research contributions around the same time challenged the prevailing view of substance (mainly heroin) use as a behaviour that might be amenable to short-term punitive treatments. The work of others described the progression of people using drugs, including injection of heroin, from dependency to abstinence as they aged and when social and environmental conditions changed. In her study on returning soldiers from the war in Vietnam, Robins found the following, which challenged the prevailing view of addiction being a pervasive and permanent state.

> In his paper on Robins' studies on heroin use in US Vietnam Veterans Hall noted that, high rates of heroin use (34%) and symptoms of heroin dependence (20%) among US soldiers while serving in Vietnam. In the first year after returning to the United States only 1% became re-addicted to heroin, although 10% tried the drug after their return
>
> (Hall 2016)

In his study of ageing heroin users, Charles Winick entered a new perspective on the healing process of ageing, proposing that the majority of people using heroin mature out of drug use and, if they avoid the obvious harms, manage to stop using drugs with or without treatment (Winick 1982).

Dan Waldorf, a sociologist working in California, New York and latterly Guatemala, made it his work to "to attack and demolish myths about drug users and heroin addicts" (Waldorf 1998). Waldorf described "natural recovery" and drew attention to the interacting forces of the social environment around people who use drugs as a factor in initiating drug use and the potential for leaving it.

These contributors, and others, began to overturn the prevailing view in institutions, governments and the media that people who use drugs were consigned to a life of criminality and unrelenting substance dependency.

Reports and research were quickly followed in the era of HIV/AIDS by research, increasingly funded by grant awarding institutions, to explore the clinical impact and epidemiology of dependency and injecting drug use. The urgency to initiate treatment led these to a canon of research findings supporting pragmatic interventions described as "harm reduction" and longer-term opiate agonist treatments and, to a lesser extent, the importance of detoxification and residential rehabilitation.

Although Waldorf and others explored drug use through the development of accessing people with drug experience to describe the personal dimensions, the involvement of lived experience still had some time to come before voices from the substance users themselves would become a direct and important influence (Biernacki 1981). The stigma around drugs and people who use substances and the legal status of substances support groups, personal testimonies were and still are, sensitive and need to be protected carefully. The belief that heroin use is compatible with an otherwise "normal" life and sustained employment took time to reach acceptability. It wasn't until relatively recently that researchers observed that there were different patterns of heroin use. An example of this discovery, previously well known to some in the world of drug use, was an important study in Glasgow that concluded that:

> Drug research should more fully incorporate previously hidden populations to more fully inform theory and practice. The pharmacological properties of specific substances should not be assumed to inevitably lead to addictive and destructive patterns of drug use" (Shewan 2005). Although still resisted as a reality, this evidence of controlled substance use is compatible with the studies of the long-running heroin treatments in the so-called "British System" which allowed treatment with prescribed heroin to continue for many years and for many allowed continuous employment and survival beneath the radar of public scrutiny
>
> (Strang 1989, Berridge 1991, Berridge 2004).

Increasingly, personal testimony and exposure to public view give insights. Kirsten E. Smith, Professor at the US National Institute on Drug Abuse (NIDA), gives us an important insight as a substance user turned author and leading academic into the nature of addiction in her paper "Disease with Decision" in the *Journal of Substance Abuse Treatment* (Smith 2022). In her eloquent description and leading research, she expresses important views on the relative importance of adverse background events and the process of neurological changes in the brain after prolonged exposure to various mind-altering substances. Among her pragmatic and useful conclusions is one directed at guiding treatment policy. As she says, the risks of trying to force a complex set of conditions into a relatively convenient diagnostic label should be avoided.

> I posit that we should not need labels to care about addicted people and make scientifically informed treatment accessible. Addicted people deserve help because they either need or want it, regardless of labels that presume to describe the aetiology or likely trajectory of their problems. I conclude that some labels, even those needed for clinical classification of human behaviour, may be pernicious.

In his book entitled *The Urge: Our History of Addiction*, Carl Erik Fisher, the psychologist, again warns against the view of dependency as a single entity (Fisher 2022).

> It is not that addiction is or is not a brain disease, or a social malady, or a universal response to suffering – it is all of these things and none of them at the same time, because each level has something to add but cannot possibly tell the whole story.

Fisher further clarifies his thoughts under three headings:

- *Don't conflate drug use with addiction or even with harm – heed the research by Lee Robins on Vietnam vets, for example, which showed that most of those who used heroin in that war stopped once they returned to a normal life. Punitively extending the tentacles of drug-testing is harmful, because many will fail at some point, become marginalised and be driven from legal work into crime.*
- *Second, abstinence isn't the only – or even necessarily the safest – goal of treatment. We know this because of the major contribution of methadone and, more recently, buprenorphine to opioid addiction treatment, though neither of them is yet fully utilised.*
- *Third, do not "wage war" on drugs, because that instantly becomes a war on drug users, with poor, non-white and disadvantaged people the most likely victims.*

All these concepts swirl round the policy and treatment agendas which, despite scientific support for interventions, were still dominated by ideological political control opposed to a paradigm shift towards inclusion, human rights and policy movement from criminal justice to health agendas (Berridge 1996). Change of vision in the United Kingdom and Europe has been brought about by the emergence of strong peer support advocacy and growth in the volume of lived experience interest. This has been backed by a more progressive policy including addressing stigma towards dependency and associated problems and a human rights approach to treatment. A new vocabulary is helping describe the subjective world of dependency and the relationship and needs of the caring service sector. "Pathways of Hope", "Dave's Story", "Trauma Informed Care" and "The Recovery Journey" are increasingly part of the terminology of the policy agenda leading to initiatives like Conversation Cafes and "Humanising Healthcare" groups involving people with SUD issues and their families linking in to establish organisations like Alcoholics Anonymous, Cocaine Anonymous and local groups (Pathways of Hope 2025). Self-help, peer support and alternatives to mainstream services are blossoming in the United Kingdom and Europe and changing in their capacity to merge the abstinence focus with harm reduction and long-term support.

To a degree, this mirrors the views and purpose of longstanding grassroots agencies and sectors supported by organisations like Alcoholics Anonymous and Narcotics Anonymous. Ironically, this contemporary grassroots movement in the United Kingdom returned to the policy agenda of the 1980s when government policy was largely non-medical and depended heavily on charitable and non-statutory organisations like Phoenix House, City Roads in London and many other residential rehabilitation units based on the religion-inspired "concept houses".

Management and treatment, whatever modality this might include, must navigate these complexities, often with a pragmatism that accepts the contradictions of behaviours at times both harmful and rewarding. Concentrating on reducing harms may seem like an evasion from the intuitively better ambition of a "cure" based on achieving enduring abstinence, but unfortunately, much of what public health and medical care do is management of symptoms related to drug use. This might, arguably, be similar to management of conditions arising from disease or harms associated with ageing, trauma, unwise behaviours, obesity or environmental or disease processes. The notion of drug dependency as a long-term condition is uncomfortable for some, but although persistence over many years is not inevitable, as we shall explore later, the enduring nature of substance use requires a long view.

Legislation and top-level policy are constantly looking for the piece of the jigsaw that is the most important without recognising that the total picture in individuals and SUD as a whole is a holistic approach encompassing the needs of affected individuals over time and through phases of recovery and attention to enforcement and penalties levied on people with a substance use disorder. A recurring theme is the swing from one policy vision to another and the association of harmful substance use with social disorder (Berridge 2009, The Brixton Disorders 1981).

The management of addiction or substance use disorder (SUD) is, for some, a medical problem and for others, a sociopolitical issue giving rise to many opinions about the pathway leading to a solution. For the past century, as the use of drugs and the harms resulting from their use have expanded exponentially, it is fair to say that societies and governments have struggled to offer solutions or to feel comfortable with change. The manifest injuries caused by drugs, however, demand and require an intervention both short-term and with an eye on longer-term strategy.

In the wide landscape of managing drug problems there are many demands, but injecting substances into the body must account for the most visible, dramatic and expensive set of consequences. The urgency to endorse change, which might give rise to treatments and policies designed to discourage drug injecting or to minimise the potential harms from this practice, must be a political imperative.

Why we struggle with addiction and put it at the bottom of our priority list for research and treatment funding is not immediately clear. Enduring debates over the cause and consequence of addiction problems explore genetic, environmental and moral choices when all these are known to be factors in heart disease, cancer and most known diseases. Unlike most other diseases, including those clearly linked to known risk behaviours such as smoking, excess drinking and dietary choices, addiction continues to be a socially unacceptable condition. This position brings with it attitudes and prejudices that generate many of the harms associated with drug use. Since the mid-20th century, morphine and its derivatives, codeine and heroin have been the basis of most analgesia for use in the relief of pain. In the last twenty years the use of synthetic opiates or opiate-like compounds increasingly adds to the medical pharmacopeia. All this contributes to the difficulty in describing the impact, for good or bad, of "drugs".

The history of drug injecting

The history of injecting substances beneath the skin goes back to experimentation in the 17th century. Among other contenders for the credit, Alexander Wood of Edinburgh and Charles-Gabriel Pravaz from Lyon are known commonly as the inventors of the syringe for subcutaneous injection (Norn 2006). Wood developed a device to inject morphine beneath the skin to alleviate pain, and Pravaz separately designed a syringe in 1853.

While the well-intentioned development of injecting as a way of introducing substances into the body improved access to the circulation and provided a way of managing treatment where other routes were not available, new risks emerged. The ability to introduce drugs, vaccines and fluids was a major step forward in the development of therapeutics and maintaining life. Two areas of difficulties became common over time: the overuse of injections by misguided medical people and the disastrous development and proliferation of self-administered substances by injection.

Some reports suggest that needle sharing was practised by drug abusers as early as 1902 in China and 1914 in the United States (Zule 1997). For medical purposes, as we know it, the invention of a modern syringe and needle began in Europe and North America in the early part of the 19th century since which time their use, and public and professional popularity, has expanded rapidly, as noted by one author;

> The rapid uptake of the hypodermic syringe as a medical technology by physicians in Europe and America since its introduction in the middle of the 19th century has led to a level of medical and public acceptance seldom reached by other therapeutic techniques.

However, the same author draws attention to widespread abuse of injecting and the associated risks, especially in developing countries.

> Presently, the developed world has clear guidelines regarding injection use and safety; in contrast, developing countries are facing the brunt of risks associated with the use of this technology, which was introduced into their societies during the early 20th century. There is now a popular demand for injections, and an alarming number of unnecessary and unsafe injections are being administered.
>
> (Kotwal 2005)

Since then, the risks associated with unsafe injection practices, in medical situations, have been well rehearsed. In this study, reported in the Bulletin of the World Health Organization, an alarming rate of transmission of blood-borne infections is related to unsafe or unnecessary injections:

> ....and children and adults who are ill or hospitalized, including those infected with HIV, are often exposed to 10–100 times as many injections. An average of 95% of all injections are therapeutic, the majority of which were judged to be unnecessary. At least 50% of injections were unsafe in 14 of 19 countries (representing five developing world regions) for which data were available. Eighteen studies reported a convincing link between unsafe injections and the transmission of hepatitis B and C, HIV, Ebola and Lassa virus infections and malaria. Five studies attributed 20–80% of all new hepatitis B infections

> to unsafe injections, while three implicated unsafe injections as a major mode of transmission of hepatitis C.
>
> (Simonsen et al. 1999)

A literature review of the history of injecting drug use found evidence of outbreaks of malaria in Egypt, the United States and China between 1929 and 1937 which were attributed to needle sharing and intravenous injection of opioids. These reports suggest that both needle sharing and intravenous drug use were common by 1937 (Zule 1997). Another communication from the World Health Organization draws attention to the economic burden of "unsafe injections" principally causing hepatitis B and C and HIV:

> Annually more than 1.3 million deaths and US$ 535 million are estimated to be due to current unsafe injection practices. With the global increase in the number of injections for vaccination and medical services, safer injecting technologies such as auto-disable syringes must be budgeted for. Investment in health education and safer disposal will also reduce infections associated with unsafe injecting practices. Safer injecting practices are more expensive than current less safe practices, but the additional cost is more than offset by the reduction in disease that would result.
>
> (Miller 1999)

These examples of the widespread use and misuse of injecting equipment exist at the same time as the rise in illegal drug injecting for non-therapeutic purposes.

The rise of illicit drug injecting

Until recently, heroin was the illegal substance most injected in the United Kingdom, but substance use is constantly evolving. Novel substances emerge, and illegal supply chains take advantage of new opportunities to market traditional drugs in new ways and in new communities.

In the United Kingdom, the number of people using illegal heroin was small in the late 1950s and early 1960s. It seemed that the remarkably common use of opium and related products used in Victorian and Edwardian times, when opium products were marketed widely as a cure for all sorts of conditions, had passed. Laudanum was a 10% solution of opium powder in alcohol, widely used to treat everything from pain and insomnia to moderate pain. It was even used to quieten crying babies. The name laudanum, from the Latin *laudare*, meaning "to praise", was coined by the 16th-century Swiss-German physician Paracelsus. Ironically, in the modern context, his dictum was "only the dose makes the poison".

Early control measures began in the United Kingdom with the Pharmacy Act of 1868. This was the first attempt to introduce regulations relating to poisons and other substances considered to be dangerous. Before this, cocaine derivatives and opium derivatives were widely available. After World War I, a national system of regulation and treatment was introduced resulting from concerns about soldiers returning from the conflict who were using cocaine and other drugs. There was also concern about immigrants and ethnic minorities in London using drugs (Spear 1993). This was the start of the "British system" when licensed doctors could prescribe opiate and cocaine compounds to people with a dependency problem (Strang 1989).

In 1961 the UK Government committee known as the Brain committee concluded that "on the evidence before us the incidence of addiction to dangerous drugs was very small ... there seemed no reason to think that any increase was occurring". At that time there were thought to be between 300 and 400 people addicted to drugs in the United Kingdom, of which about a tenth were using heroin. There was, however, an emerging problem reported by psychiatrists and the Home Office "addicts index" over the next few years which was variously attributed to small importers and the arrival of a group of Canadian people moving as regulations tightened in 1958 in Canada (Bewley. T. 1965, Bewley 1968, Spear H.B. 1971). This new wave of non-medical drug users was more publicly visible and characterised as similar to those using heroin in the USA. In response, the Brain committee was reconvened in 1964, and this time recommended that the prescription of heroin should be allowed but that this should be confined to a new system of regional treatment centres which were subsequently established in 1968. The report instituted controls over the prescription of heroin and cocaine, which was to be allowed only by doctors licensed by the Home Office. Despite the signs of drug-related harms, the urgency visualised by the committee was clearly to control the prescribing of heroin more than the treatment of the dependent patient. By modern standards the definition of who was an "addict" was vague and applied to a variety of individuals deriving from different backgrounds. The large-scale availability of heroin in communities had still not emerged and, as in the USA, most drug injecting was confined to larger urban centres such as New York, San Francisco and London. In a landmark study in the Drug Dependency Unit in Edinburgh, which described the first 100 people referred to the new unit, the majority of people at the clinic were doctors or nurses (Woodside 1973).

Subsequent controls in the United Kingdom are enshrined in the Misuse of Drugs Act 1971. This regulation remains the substantial piece of legislation designed to comply with the United Nations Charter of 1961 and reflects, in outline similar laws enacted in all member states. These defining moments in drug control have dominated public policy, justice system practice and the role of the medical professions since then. Change has, of course, taken place within the tight restrictions of the 1971 Act not least in prescribing policies for people who use opiates and, during the intervening period, the focus has moved from a paradigm based on the need to reduce the supply of drugs prominent in the 1980s to reducing demand for drugs in the 1990s. More recently a policy of reducing the harm caused by drugs has been the underlying approach to management (Bennet and Holloway 2005).

This changing policy environment comes along with the use of terminology which struggles to separate out the benefits and the risks and increasingly tries to accommodate the balance between top-down enforcement and individual rights and opinions. The debate about the medical use and application of drugs finds it hard to differentiate between the science and research findings in the application of medical compounds and the promotion of mind-altering drugs for recreational and personal benefits. This latter force for inclusion and decriminalisation often relies on personal expression of the benefits and, at times, spiritual value of various mind-altering drugs.

The complicated debate involving those who advocate for recreational use of drugs such as psychedelics and cannabis citing evidence for lifestyle choices is sometimes in conflict with the medical and current legal requirement for a different level of evidence of benefit and safety (Zullino 2025). The reality is that a lot of people use drugs of some description and that balencing the harms against the benefits has become increasingly difficult. There are, however, some drugs and perhaps equally important, some modalities of drug use, like injecting a substance, that carry a higher degree of risk than others.

The importance of defining dependency/addiction

The simple issue of quantity used and frequency of use must be one of the markers of increased risk, but defining dependency and separating occasional "non-dependent" or recreational use from harmful dependency has limited the rationale for treatment and the consequent allocation of medical and support resources.

Case definitions as identified by two international systems are the basis of understanding harms and risks. There are two standard international classification systems. The World Health Organization, Geneva-based, International Classification of Diseases, currently in its 11th iteration and the US-based Diagnostic and Statistical Manual of Mental Disorders, (DSM-5) published by the American Psychiatric Association are the most useful publications. (World Health Organization 2024, American Psychiatric Association 2022)

The widely used DSM-5 publication lists several criteria which are needed to make a diagnosis of the presence of what is now referred to as a "substance use disorder". Of the eleven conditions in the list, only two are required to be present to allow for a basic diagnosis of dependency and five to identify a serious problem. This indicates the range and extent of substance use impact. Some of these criteria reflect symptoms of drug use and lack many objective signs but demonstrate the need to recognise dependency as a problem even if the individual is not completely disabled.

The criteria are:

1. Hazardous use: You have used the substance in ways that are dangerous to yourself and/or others, i.e. overdosed, driven while under the influence, or blacked out.
2. Social or interpersonal problems related to use: Substance use has caused relationship problems or conflicts with others.
3. Neglected major roles to use: You have failed to meet your responsibilities at work, school or home because of substance use.

4. Withdrawal: When you stop using the substance, you experience withdrawal symptoms.

5. Tolerance: You have built up a tolerance to the substance so that you have to use more to get the same effect.

6. Used larger amounts/longer: You have started to use larger amounts or use the substance for longer amounts of time.

7. Repeated attempts to control use or quit: You've tried to cut back or quit entirely but haven't been successful.

8. Much time spent using: You spend a lot of your time using the substance.

9. Physical or psychological problems related to use: Your substance use has led to physical health problems, such as liver damage or lung cancer, or psychological issues, such as depression or anxiety.

10. Activities given up to use: You have skipped activities or stopped doing activities you once enjoyed in order to use the substance.

11. Craving: You have experienced cravings for the substance.

Source, American Psychiatric Association (2022)

The WHO International Classification of Diseases has a similar list of criteria and suggests that "a definite diagnosis of dependence should usually be made only if three or more of the following have been present together at some time during the previous year".

1. a strong desire or sense of *compulsion to take the substance.*

2. *difficulties in controlling substance-taking behaviour* in terms of its onset, termination or levels of use

3. a physiological *withdrawal state when substance use has* ceased or been reduced, as evidenced by: the characteristic *withdrawal syndrome for the substance*; or use of the same (or a closely related) substance with the intention of relieving or avoiding withdrawal symptoms

4. *evidence of tolerance*, such that increased doses of the psychoactive substances are required in order to achieve effects originally produced by lower doses (clear examples of this are found in alcohol- and opiate-dependent individuals who may take daily doses sufficient to incapacitate or kill non-tolerant users)

5. *progressive neglect of alternative pleasures* or interests because of psychoactive substance use, increased amount of time necessary to obtain or take the substance or to recover from its effects

6. *persisting with substance use despite clear evidence of overtly harmful consequences*, such as harm to the liver through excessive drinking, depressive mood states consequent to periods of heavy substance use, or drug-related impairment of cognitive functioning; efforts should be made to determine that the user was actually, or could be expected to be, aware of the nature and extent of the harm.

Source: Diagnostic guidelines for drug dependence (ICD 10 1993)

These sources differ in their criteria for the presence of a substance misuse disorder but may be used to direct treatment and classification for other purposes. As tools in treatment, they are helpful in understanding, learning and teaching about the hazards and consequences of substance use, as well as for people who use drugs, to understand their problems. They are also important in recognising change in understanding of dependency disorders. Alongside the traditional markers of dependency, such as increased use, withdrawal symptoms, tolerance to increased doses, repeated attempts at withdrawal and psychological problems associated with use there are changes and additional definition categories. Examples of change in the definitions criteria are the inclusion of definitions of gambling, exercise and eating disorders and inclusion of, in the diagnostic criteria for lifestyle problems, issues such as impact on employment capability and socialisation difficulties as well as "recurrent legal problems". The severity of dependency is also usefully noted in the updated manuals using a system of numbers of criteria included indicating the severity of the disorder (Hasin et al. 2013).

Harmful impact of drug use and the scale of the problem

The United Nations Office on Drugs and Crime, World Drugs Report, in 2024 noted that in 2022 cannabis was the most used drug worldwide with an estimated 292 million users in the last year, equivalent to 6% of the global population aged 15-64 years. This was followed in frequency by 60 million opiate users, 30 million stimulant users (like amphetamines), 23 million cocaine users and 20 million ecstasy users. The report noted that the range of drugs increases all the time and polydrug use is becoming more common. The largest burden of disease continues to be due to opiates, and opiate-related deaths are still increasing in some regions, although harms from other drugs are at an increased percentage (UNODC 2024).

Injecting drugs continues to be the most harmful problem, with increased risks of several issues, including those from blood-borne infections. The largest number of these were in North America and East and Southeast Asia. The subregions with the highest proportions of people who inject drugs (PWID) are North America at 1% and Eastern Europe with 1.3% (UNODC 2024). In England and Wales, approximately 3 million adults (aged 16–59) reported using drugs in the year ending June 2022, accounting for 9.2% of the population (Jones 2022).

In their review of the numbers of people who inject drugs in the world, Degenhardt and colleagues found "*evidence of Injecting Drug Use (IDU) was recorded in 179 of 206 countries or territories, which cover 99% of the population aged 15–64 years*" (Degenhardt et al. 2017).

The European Drug Report for 2024 identifies injecting drug use as a major problem in most European countries with variable levels of treatment services such as needle and syringe provision and opiate agonist treatment services (European Monitoring Centre for Drugs and Drug Addiction 2024). The report notes that there is increasing variation in drug use with other drugs including amphetamines, cocaine, synthetic cathinones, opioid agonist medications and a variety of new psychoactive substances being injected either alone or in combination. Multiple substances are commonly detected in syringe residues, often including both stimulant and opioid drugs, and polydrug use can increase the risk of a drug overdose. The availability of highly potent synthetic opiates such as fentanyl and its derivatives is an additional concern as is the introduction of the benzimidazole opioids (nitazines) which have caused serious overdose outbreaks in several European countries.

When it comes to gender differences, one of the key messages of the World Drugs Report is that "Men make up the large majority of people who use drugs, but women who use drugs face greater harms and more barriers to entering treatment".

Based on data from 18 countries, about 20% of people who inject drugs (PWID) are women, but women are more likely to carry a higher burden of disease as a consequence of injecting drugs. Injecting combinations of drugs, which was a common practice in the Bronx in the late 1970s and 1980s, and now widespread practice, clearly increases the risks (Hartel et al. 1996). Other studies of global prevalence of drug use find that in western countries and Australia, about 30% of the drug injecting population is female, and in Asian countries, this is considerably less, around 3% (Degenhardt et al. 2017).

The World Drugs Report goes on to say about women drug injectors that:

> they are 1.2 times more likely than men to be living with HIV (based on data from 58 countries). The vulnerability of women stemming from conventional gender roles and gender power structures and relations may also increase their vulnerability to unsafe sexual and injecting behaviours. Women who inject drugs are likely to have a male intimate partner who initiated them into drug use; they are also likely to ask their male partner to inject them. Women who use, including those who inject, drugs are also vulnerable to gender-based violence and sexual abuse perpetrated by both their intimate partners and by other people who use drugs around them, law enforcement officers and drug service providers.

In a long list of health conditions with strong claims to be the most neglected in the allocation of resources, mental health continues to achieve top status. In the crowded field of mental health diagnoses, substance use fails on almost all qualifying criteria for priority.

The role of artistic representation of drug use and a case study of injecting drug use

As outlined in later chapters, the domestic and local environment sets the scene for creating conditions leading to harms on a lesser or greater scale. While research and clinical sciences increasingly describe, measure and quantify the impact and effects of drugs, the brutality and indignity of a period, or a lifetime, of injecting drugs is hard to imagine, and the rewards of the euphoric moments must be outweighed by the burden of physical, social and psychological traumas. For clinical practitioners and for the general reader, therefore, the personal and fictional literature is important in telling us about addiction in the same way as a painting has an additional message to a photograph. The combination of insightful fact and fiction is compelling. Thomas De Quincey's accounts of the fantasy world of the effect of opium were combined with a place in the social life of the university area of the city of Edinburgh. De Quincey, once described as the greatest essay writer of our language. (Towill 1971) lived in Lothian Street (now demolished) in the Southside of the city. Charles Darwin and his brother lodged in the same street; Johnson and Boswell dined there at least once (Boswell lived a few streets away in James Court off the Royal Mile). Conan Doyle, during his studies in Edinburgh, was influenced by Dr Joseph Bell, whose skills in using observation to derive conclusions about his patients were renowned. Conan Doyle admitted later that he used this experience to develop the fictitious character of Sherlock Holmes. In more recent times, Irvine Welsh's book, and later film dramatisation, of the lives of heroin "addicts" in the city brought to the common awareness of a reality previously unknown or at least ignored, leading to a modern classic in print and film. *Trainspotting*, which, ironically, did much to destigmatise an increasingly common problem, illuminated a social context in which heroin was becoming commonplace. The local cop hero of Ian Rankin's books sheds another light on the criminal life of Edinburgh. John Rebus, the tough detective, inhabits familiar locations and explores the impact of, amongst other things, the drug subculture. Fiction based on the opiate crisis in the USA gives a different insight such as a description of the crisis in West Virginia. The author of Demon Copperhead, Barbara Kingsolver, informs us of the personal and social impact of opiates without shying away from the profound negative effects. In this way the popular media, film, literature and personal testimony of individuals and celebrities add detail and emotion in a way that science and research fail to, setting things in time, place and person.

Journalistic accounts and autobiography also have important places to play in describing underground activity which is hiding in plain sight. Miles Davis, the legendary jazz musician, describes his heroin experiences around 1949 vividly in his autobiography (Miles Davis 1990):

> I wasn't it in my veins yet, but I was snorting as much as I could get my hands on…when I saw Matinee again, he said. 'Miles don't waste that little money on getting some to snort, because you're still gonna be sick. Go on and shoot it then you'll feel much better.' That was the beginning of a four year horror show.

Davis goes on to describe the community of jazz musicians at the time who injected heroin. It is a lineup of many of the great names at the time in jazz music. This coincided with a community Davis describes as suffering from unbelievable racial prejudice which existed at the time and often living on the edge of poverty.

As a journalistic classic, Randy Shilts's book and film *And the Band Played On* brought to public attention not only the epidemic of HIV/AIDS but also the world of gay sex. He includes injection drug users in the epic denouncement of multiple failures in public health policy, political cover-up and social awareness as a vector of viral transmission into the heterosexual community (Shilts 1987).

The story of events in Edinburgh is small in the global tragedy of drug use and misuse but has importance as a case study and had a disproportionate impact in demonstrating the combination of social and political influences on the harms caused by drugs (Robertson 2025).

Neglect in government, academic and education sectors have created a problem which is the source of some embarrassment in many Scottish institutions.

Despite some focus on the problem over the last few years, the annual figures of death from overdose of illicit drugs continue to cause distress to individuals, families and communities. Characterised as a problem with a disproportional impact in Scotland compared to all other European countries, it remains poorly understood why Scotland is an outlier. Solutions, consequently, are fragmented, and funding arrangements are short-term and temporary and at risk of changing priorities.

Explanations for the staggering numbers of deaths that have some credibility include the systematic gathering of these data by Scottish institutions. Compared to some countries, Scotland does gather, record and report statistics on deaths more accurately than some comparable countries. The historic accumulation of individuals with substance dependency problems who are now reaching an advanced stage with various connected medical problems also contributes to the disproportionate number of drug-related deaths in Scotland (Norman 2011 Parkinson 2018). The reality, however, is more complicated and is discribed in more dertail in subsequent chapters. The illegal drug supply chain is unregulated despite the constant efforts of law enforcement agencies, which constantly wrestle with the moving target of new drugs and complicated international organised crime. The control of illegal drugs into the country and throughout communities is a constant challenge for police and border control authorities.

Problems in other parts of the systems of control and treatment are seen in a stressed and underfunded response from the National Health Service and social services who have to respond to serial crises and an increasing caseload of people suffering not just from the negative effects of drugs but from the linked diseases. Caseloads for pulmonary and cardiac conditions, HIV/AIDS, hepatitis and coexisting alcohol dependency, linked with mental health problems, continue to increase across all specialties. It is easy to see how a lethal combination of medical and environmental circumstances leads to early death in increasing numbers. Over the past three or four decades, Scotland has had outbreaks of HIV/AIDS, anthrax, clostridium and drug deaths among people who use drugs that have required massive investment. There are clearly many causal factors for the mortality burden caused by drugs, and the impact of substances may be much greater than drug-related deaths. People with substance use problems die from many disorders not recorded in the National Records of Scotland drug death figures, and their loss in economic measures of disability rates them higher than most diseases requiring NHS care. Drug deaths are a symptom of a larger malaise, undoubtedly associated with intergenerational inequalities, and are a problem that is clearly neglected in communities where statutory services are increasingly devolving responsibility to the third sector. Without the collaboration needed to manage a multisystem set of disorders, individuals find themselves moving between carers and in and out of emergency departments without a coherent plan.

Solutions range from increased enforcement and control over supply to maximising availability of residential rehabilitation programmes and the rather vague general collection of interventions described as harm reduction. The more strategic and primary prevention perspective draws attention to the enduring concentration of deaths in areas of relative poverty and sees a clear solution in addressing inequalities (McCartney 2017).

We have learned from our colleagues in the alcohol treatment sector that interventions such as education, minimum pricing of alcohol and restricting advertising that public health approaches have a significant benefit. Changing attitudes and investing in support services also have a positive impact. There remains the unfortunate negative influence of the alcohol industry obstructing progress and relentlessly promoting and glamoursing a drinking lifestyle.

The failure of successive governments to recognise the underlying issues and the fragmentation of the care system in the localities that need them most is obvious. Spending on substance use, like mental health disorders, is an area of policy that has neglected research, academic and teaching resources and evidence-based treatment.

People with substance use problems die young and over a shorter lifetime than they should have, they consume a fraction of the cost which most people expect over many more years of acute and chronic requirements for medical and social care. The loss of economic activity and the savings that could be made if the damage caused by drugs could be prevented add to the urgency to take substance problems more seriously. The scale of the damage due to injecting drug use is estimated by Degenhardt and colleagues.

> Globally, we estimate 82·9% (76·6–88·9) of people who inject drugs (PWIDs) mainly inject opioids and 33·0% (24·3–42·0) mainly inject stimulants. We estimate that 27·9% (20·9–36·8) of PWID globally are younger than 25 years, 21·7% (15·8–27·9) had recently (within the past year) experienced homelessness or unstable housing, and 57·9% (50·5–65·2) had a history of incarceration.
>
> (Degenhardt et al. 2017)

Understanding and measuring substance use

A better understanding of the range of use and subsequent harms caused by drugs is helped by clearer definitions included in the International Classification of Diseases and the American Psychiatric Association descriptions of the condition. Lessons from other dependency situations such as alcohol are relevant and the, maybe simplistic, division of types of alcohol abuse into five categories can inform understanding of the condition and ways to intervene. A study on a general public population in the USA, published in 2007, concluded that there were five distinct manifestations and patterns of alcohol use (Moss et al. 2007).

The researchers identified unique subtypes of alcoholism based on respondents' family history of alcoholism, age of onset of regular drinking and alcohol problems, symptom patterns of alcohol dependence and abuse, and the presence of additional substance abuse and mental disorders. The subtypes were allocated into groups.

The largest group were described as the "young adult subtype" (31.5%). These were young adult drinkers with low rates of mental disorders or co-occurring substance use. This group rarely looked for help for their problems. The second largest group were the "young antisocial subtype", which comprised 21% of the population of alcohol-dependent people. This group tended to be in their mid-twenties, had early onset of regular drinking, and alcohol problems. Interestingly, greater than 50% of this group had a family history of alcohol problems and about 50% of the group had a psychiatric diagnosis, including depression, anxiety, personality disorder or psychosis. More than three-quarters had coexisting drug use. The next largest group were described as a "functional subtype". This was 19.5% of US alcoholics population and were typically middle-aged, better educated, with stable jobs and families. About one-third of this group had a family history of alcohol problems and about one-quarter had major depressive illness sometime in their lives. A further 19% of the study population were categorised as the "intermediate familial subtype". This group tended to be more middle-aged and had a family history of alcohol in about half the cases. The prevalence of mental health problems, depression or bipolar illness, was high at about 50%, and smoking and substance use were quite common. Only 25% of this group ever sought treatment for their problem drinking. The smallest group (9%) were the "chronic severe subtype". This group were mostly made up of middle-aged individuals who had early onset of drinking and alcohol problems, with high rates of personality disorder diagnosis and criminality, and almost four out of five had family alcohol disorder problems. This group had the highest rate of other psychiatric disorders, including depression, bipolar disorder and anxiety disorders; high rates of smoking; as well as marijuana, cocaine and opiate dependence. Two-thirds of these alcoholics sought help for their drinking problems, making them the most prevalent diagnostic type of problem drinker in treatment.

This research is relevant for understanding other substance use situations. Almost every approach to reducing drug use and harms depends upon a clear definition of substance use in order for the intervention to be targeted and refined for individuals and populations. Without a clear understanding of the nature of the population to be treated or educated, substance use becomes too big a problem to be easily addressed. There may be individuals who are at an increased risk of substance use and, as in the case of alcohol misuse, there may be groups who have such different characteristics that the prevention and treatments which may be effective are distinctly different. Treatment and education for people with one problem may be conflated with others, potentially causing lack of benefit or even harm. Subsets of people who use drugs might be usefully defined, like the alcohol subsets, by vulnerability and increased risk and behaviours resulting from the substance use. It is, of course, possible or even likely that individuals may progress from one level of use and risk to a greater level, but interventions need to be appropriate for the individual and personalised treatment is essential. A crude categorisation might be based on increased numbers of risk factors such as family history and early life experiences (positive and negative factors), educational attainment and types of drugs used in the present and past. Crucially, the level of risks present, such as comorbid smoking, multiple drugs used and the presence of injecting behaviour, might put an individual in a group or category that requires special, or more urgent, help.

Measuring and diagnosing drug dependence is in some ways more difficult as many of the problems and clinical issues causing harm are generated or exacerbated by the illegal behaviours surrounding the supply and the use of a wide variety of substances. In clinical practice and research projects, several validated assessment instruments are available and are often used to standardise interventions and to compare individuals and groups. Very simple questionnaires for each assessment for alcohol or substance use, such as the CAGE questions for alcohol and the DAST (Drug Abuse Screening Test) for substance use, are available. More detailed and time-consuming measures of the impact of drugs are included in the Addiction Severity Index test, which includes, *"section on family history of alcohol, drug, and psychiatric problems" and "assess route of drug administration; additional illegal activities; emotional, physical, and sexual abuse; quality of the recovery environment; and history of close personal relationships"* (McLellan et al. 1992). Other instruments may be used in formal or specialist treatment settings or research projects, such as the Structured Clinical Interview for DSM-IV Disorders (SCID) or the modified Michigan Alcohol Screening Test (American Psychiatric Association 2022, Westermeyer 2004). A summary of tests commonly used in evaluating the degree of impact of alcohol and/or drugs on the health and quality of life of people affected is available at the National Library of Medicine (National Library of Medicine 2005).

Many situations will require a combination of tests when comorbid psychiatric or behavioural conditions such as depression, psychosis or situational stresses exist. Measuring the severity or complexity of a substance use problem is important to assess not just the urgency of treatment but also the value of the treatment in effecting clinical improvements over time.

For many clinical situations, and for people in treatment, improvement can be subtle and subjective. The simple action of attending a therapist or confiding in a support worker can be hugely changing, and simple improvements like reducing or ceasing the injection of drugs can be an obvious and transformational step.

During the 1980s, the confusion of treatments and theoretical models of addiction was addressed at a series of conferences and publications which tried to rationalise the understanding of addiction or, as the new preferred term suggested, substance use. Recognising commonalities between behaviours such as smoking, excess alcohol use and drugs such as cocaine and heroin was important, and as time went on, additional behavioural difficulties with gambling and sexual compulsions were included. The list goes on, but the early discussions led to a rational model of dependency and progression from remission to relapse and remission described as "models of change" (Prochaska 1986, Miller et al. 2013). This model of understanding the dependency process and the implications for treatment and prognostic estimations has underpinned much of treatment and has been applied and validated in opiate-dependent people as well as other situations (Tejero 1997).

The original model of processes of change is immediately recognisable to people working in the drug or alcohol dependency field and has formed the basis for many treatment projects and the inspiration for the "12 step model" of recovery widely accessed in therapy. The stages according to the original transtheoretical model are precontemplation, contemplation, preparation, action, maintenance, and termination (Prochaska 1986, Macleod 1967).

Treatment and recovery

Much has been written and perhaps the largest part of the treatment and recovery sector is based around psychological interventions. Such a general term encompasses an enormous number of aspects of human behaviours and responses to things that influence change. This ranges from individual self-motivation, therapies designed to promote healthy living, mainstream psychological treatments and less well understood complementary therapy solutions and individual beliefs. Not to be underestimated is the spiritual and religious belief that undoubtedly underpins a lot of recovery from the damaging effects of dependency. As in other human behavioural traits, therapies are not mutually exclusive and, in fact, most of what is broadly termed recovery arises from a combination of self-realisation, life time "events", positive and negative, and formal therapeutic interventions. Sudden and life-changing recovery and abstinence from drugs sometimes happens as an epiphany and dramatic response to an event or self-discovery, but even in these moments some ground preparation has usually been evolving in the consciousness to allow change. More commonly, recovery is cumulative, gradual and emerges over time. Recovery in the narrow definition of abstinence from intoxicating drugs is, for most, a process rather than a single event. In response to therapy or life events, behaviour changes. This can be in a positive or negative direction as often seen in a pattern of remission and relapse. For most people who engage in drug use, their pattern of use changes over time, injecting less, taking less risks with sharing equipment, modifying friendship groups to allow a more mature pattern of drug taking and improving access to support systems. Detailed examination of the importance of phamacological treatements for substance use is outlined in chapter 9.

Policy more recently has recognised the importance of integrated treatment programmes accepting the inevitability of a long recovery process often taking many years and requiring repeated treatment episodes.

A Cochrane review of studies of interventions for primary alcohol use disorder found that clinical linkage to mutual aid recovery support services leads to rates of continuous abstinence and remission that are 20 to 60% higher over 3 years than those achieved with other evidence-based treatments such as cognitive behavioural therapy, further supporting the essential role of clinical and peer support (Kelly 2024, Barnes 2019).

Conclusion

The definition of addiction and the terminology used in describing substances and substance users is important. As drug use has expanded in the 20th and into the 21st centuries, understanding of the causes and effects have evolved and interventions have improved. Describing the addictive phenomenon has moved from the term "addiction" or "addict" to "drug use" or "drug user" and more recently "person who uses drugs" or "person who injects drugs". A preferred term is now substance use disorder (SUD) to further bring it into a less stigmatised arena and inevitably, the realm of a medical condition.

The broader view of addiction as a complex interaction between neurological brain dysfunction and behavioural abnormality is important for drug policy. In his book, Blancarte-Jaber argues that

> the effectiveness of drug policy constructs depends to some degree upon their philosophical conceptions of addicted persons and their behaviour. Biopsychosocial models offer a more holistic approach to the understanding of addiction and integrate a physiological understanding of the brain mechanisms involved in addiction with a socially conscious contextualization of addiction within a particular economic and political environment.
>
> (Blancarte 2025)

A useful source for these observations comes from Buchman and colleagues in their paper which explores the concept: "We propose a 'biopsychosocial systems' model where psychosocial factors complement and interact with neurogenetics. A systems approach addresses the complexity of addiction and approaches free choice and moral responsibility within the biological, lived experience and socio-historical context of the individual" (Buchman 2010, Bennett 2005).

Consultations in social media and at public meetings and professional groups are often associated with frustration with the "authorities" but provide an increasing insight into the success or failure of treatment systems. Occasional mismatches in communications cloud progress and give rise to the sometimes disjointed nature of drug treatment policy at a local, national and international level. This results in widely varying approaches to management or treatments of people who use drugs. An active debate continues on the wisdom of decriminalisation or legalisation of various substances and trials continue to test new initiatives.

For therapists and treatment organisations, dealing with the unexpected, unexplained and unconventional is a fundamental requirement for success. Open access, respect for individual choice and tolerance in the face of setbacks and crises must be built into structures and funding arrangements.

In many western countries, progress has been significant in understanding the nature of dependency and coming to terms with the presence of a significant population of people who use drugs in a controlled or an uncontrolled way. Stigma at all levels, from government institutions to hospital departments and public discourse, has improved but remains a problem, and diplomacy is urgently needed.

Role models of recovery or controlled use are less common than those for people with alcohol problems, as people who use drugs are mostly seen as casualties or victims, and the relentless procession of deaths among the underprivileged as well as the celebrated are largely unnoticed. The noticeable change in attitudes towards injecting drug users has been driven by the rising cost to society of drug taking harms and the recognition of the increasing "normality" in the use of a variety of substances.

In reality, substance users are outlaws in the sense of being outside the usual constraints imposed by society. Literature and the arts convey mixed messages about drugs, presenting a life of drama or criminality, or a heroic struggle for survival. As in the evidence for other marginalised and stigmatised groups over the centuries, improvement comes with political change; inclusion instead of exclusion from societal norms, support and human rights; and research and technological understanding to improve the lives of those in harm's way. Terminology has evolved in a linguistic transference from "Junkie" to drug addict and drug users to the contemporary terms of "people who inject drugs" and "people who use drugs". No doubt further changes will reflect evolving sensitivities and sympathies.

References

American Psychiatric Association, ed. *Diagnostic and Statistical Manual of Mental Disorders, Fifth Edition, Text Revision (DSM-5-TR)*. American Psychiatric Publishing, Washington, DC, 2022.

Barnes DM, Jarlais DD. Feasibility of a simple and scalable cognitive-behavioral intervention to treat problem substance use. *J Subst Use*. 2019;24(6):693–95. https://doi.org/10.1080/14659891.2019.1657190.

Bennett T, Holloway K. *Understanding Drugs, Alcohol and Crime*. Open University Press, Buckingham, 2005.

Berridge V. AIDS and British drug policy: history repeats itself...? in: Whynes DK, Bean PT (eds.) *Policing and Prescribing: The British System of Drug Control*. Palgrave Macmillan UK, London, 1991, pp. 176–99. https://doi.org/10.1007/978-1-349-11451-1_10.

Berridge V. 1986 the drugs issue AIDS rises up the policy agenda. In Berridge V (ed.) *1996 AIDS in the UK. The Making of Policy 1981–1994, Chapter 4.* Oxford University Press, Oxford, 1996.

Berridge V. The "British System" and its history: myth and reality, in: *Heroin Addiction and The British System*. Routledge, London, 2004.

Berridge V. Heroin prescription and history. *N Engl J Med*. 2009;361:820–1. https://doi.org/10.1056/NEJMe0904243.

Bewley T. Heroin addiction in the United Kingdom (1954–1964). *Br Med J*. 1965 Nov 27;2(5473):1284–6. https://doi.org/10.1136/bmj.2.5473.1284.

Bewley TH, Ben-Arie O, James IP. Morbidity and mortality from heroin dependence. 1. Survey of heroin addicts known to home office. *Br Med J*. 1968 Mar 23;1(5594):725–6. https://doi.org/10.1136/bmj.1.5594.725.

Biernacki P, Waldorf D. Snowball sampling: problems and techniques of chain referral sampling. *Sociol Method Res*. 1981;10(2):141–63.

Blancarte-Jaber F. 2025. *In A Transdisciplinary Study of Addiction. A New Framework for Drug Policy Reform*. Routledge, London, 2025.

Buchman DZ, Skinner W, Illes J. Negotiating the relationship between addiction, ethics, and brain science. *AJOB Neurosci.* 2010;1(1):36–45. https://doi.org/10.1080/21507740903508609.

Degenhardt L, Peacock A, Colledge S, et al. Global prevalence of injecting drug use and sociodemographic characteristics and prevalence of HIV, HBV, and HCV in people who inject drugs: a multistage systematic review. *Lancet Glob Health.* 2017 Dec;5(12):e1192–207. https://doi.org/10.1016/S2214-109X(17)30375-3.

European Monitoring Centre for Drugs and Drug Addiction. *European Drug Report 2024: Trends and Developments*, 2024. https://www.emcdda.europa.eu/publications/european-drug-report/2024_en.

Fisher CE. *The Urge: Our History of Addiction.* Penguin Press, London, 2022.

Hall W, Weier M. Lee Robins' studies of heroin use among US Vietnam veterans. *Addiction.* 2016 Jan;112(1):176–80. https://doi.org/10.1111/add.13584.

Hartel DM, Schoenbaum EE, Selwyn PA, Friedland GH, Klein RS, Drucker E. Patterns of heroin, cocaine and speedball injection among Bronx (USA) methadone maintenance patients: 1978–1988. *Add Res.* 1996 Jan 1;3(4):323–40.

Hasin DS, O'Brien CP, Auriacombe M, et al. DSM-5 criteria for substance use disorders: recommendations and rationale. *Am J Psychiatry.* 2013 Aug;170(8):834–51. https://doi.org/10.1176/appi.ajp.2013.12060782.

ICD 10 1993. available at ICD10ResearchDiagnosis.PDF accessed 24/02/26.

Jones P. Drug misuse in England and Wales: Year Ending June 2022 [Internet]. Office for National Statistics; 2022 [cited 2023 Nov 27]. https://www.ons.gov.uk/peoplepopulationandcommunity/crimeandjustice/articles/drugmisusein england and wales/yearendingjune2022#main-points.

Kelly JF, Stout RL. Community recovery support services for opioid use disorder re covery. In: *Responding to the Opioid Epidem IC: A Guide for Public Health Practitioners.* American Public Health Association, Washington, DC, 2024.

Kotwal A. Innovation, diffusion and safety of a medical technology: a review of the literature on injection practices. *Soc Sci Med.* 2005 Mar;60(5):1133–47. https://doi.org/10.1016/j.socscimed.2004.06.044.

McCartney G, Popham F, Katikireddi SV, Walsh D, Schofield L. How do trends in mortality inequalities by deprivation and education in Scotland and England & Wales compare? A repeat cross-sectional study. *BMJ Open.* 2017;7(7):e017590. https://doi.org/10.1136/bmjopen-2017017590.

McLellan AT, Kushner H, Metzger D, Peters R, Smith I, Grissom G, Pettinati H, Argeriou M. The fifth edition of the addiction severity index. *J Subst Abuse Treat.* 1992;9(3):199–213. https://doi.org/10.1016/0740-5472(92)90062-s.

Macleod RM. The edge of hope: social policy and chronic alcoholism 1870–1900. *J Hist Med Allied Sci.* 1967;XXII(3):215–45. https://doi.org/10.1093/jhmas/ XXII.3.215.

Miles the Autobiography. Picador, London, 1990.

Miller WR, Heather N, editors. *Treating Addictive Behaviors: Processes of Change.* Springer Science & Business Media, New York, 2013 Jun 29.

Miller MA, Pisani E. The cost of unsafe injections. *Bull World Health Organ.* 1999;77(10):808–11.

Moss HB, Chen CM, Yi HY. Subtypes of alcohol dependence in a nationally representative sample. *Drug Alcohol Depend.* 2007 Dec 1;91(2–3):149–58. https://doi.org/ed10.1016/j.drugalcdep.2007.05.016.

National Library of Medicine. Substance Abuse Treatment: For Adults in the Criminal Justice System [Internet]. Rockville (MD): Substance Abuse and Mental Health Services Administration (US); 2005. (Treatment Improvement Protocol (TIP) Series, No. 44.) Appendix C, 2005.

Norman P, Boyle P, Exeter D, Feng Z, Popham F. Rising premature mortality in the UK's persistently deprived areas: only a Scottish phenomenon? *Soc Sci Med.* 2011;73(11):1575–84. https://doi.org/10.1016/j.socscimed.2011.09.034.

Office GBH. *Tackling Drug Misuse: A Summary of the Government's Strategy.* Home Office, London, 1985.

Norn S, Kruse PR, Kruse E. Traek af injektionens historie [On the history of injection]. *Dan Medicinhist Arbog.* 2006;34:104–13.

Parkinson J, Minton J, Lewsey J, Bouttell J, McCartney G. Drug-related deaths Scotland 1972013: evidence of a vulnerable cohort of young men living indeprivedareas. *BMC Public Health.* 2018;18(1):357. https://doi.org/10.1186/s12889-018-5267-2

Pathways of Hope. A public Information comic. simplebooklet.com.

Prochaska JO, DiClemente CC. Toward a comprehensive model of change. In: *Treating Addictive Behaviors: Processes of Change*. Springer US, Boston, 1986.

Robertson R, McCartney G. Learning from HIV and drug policy failures: reflections from clinical practice and research in Edinburgh. *Drugs Habits Soc Pol* 2025;26(1):29–42.

Shewan D, Dalgarno P. Evidence for controlled heroin use? Low levels of negative health and social outcomes among non-treatment heroin users in Glasgow (Scotland). *Br J Health Psychol.* 2005 Feb;10(Pt 1):33–48. https://doi.org/10.1348/135910704X14582.

Shilts R. *And the Band Played On*. Penguin Books, London, 1987.

Smith KE. Disease and decision. *J Subst Abuse Treat.* 2022;142:108874. https://doi.org/10.1016/j.jsat.2022.108874.

Simonsen L, Kane A, Lloyd J, Zaffran M, Kane M. Unsafe injections in the developing world and transmission of bloodborne pathogens: a review. *Bull World Health Organ.* 1999;77(10):789–800.

Spear HB, Glatt MM. The influence of Canadian addicts on heroin addiction in the United Kingdom. *Br J Addict Alcohol Other Drugs.* 1971 Sep;66(2):141–9. https://doi.org/10.1111/j.1360-0443.1971.tb02377.x.

Spear HB, Mott J. Cocaine and crack within the "British system": a history of control. In: Bean P (ed.) *Cocaine and Crack: Supply and Use*. The Macmillan Press, London, 1993.

Strang J. 'The British system': past, present and future. *Int Rev Psychiatry* 1989;1(1–2):109–20. https://doi.org/10.3109/09540268909110388.

Tejero A, Trujols J, Hernández E, Perez de los Cobos J, Casas M. Processes of change assessment in heroin addicts following the Prochaska and DiClemente transtheoretical model. *Drug Alcohol Depend.* 1997;47(1):31–37. doi:10.1016/s0376-8716(97)00071-9

The Brixton Disorders. *The Scarman Report: Report of an Inquiry*. Penguin Books, London, 1982.

Towill ES. The Den of the Opium Eater. *The Scotsman Newspaper*, 1971.

UNODC. Vienna 2024 World Drugs Report 2024. WDR24_Key_findings_and_conclusions.pdf.

UNODC. *World Drug Report 2024.* United Nations, Vienna, 2024.

Waldorf D. Misadventures in the drug trade. *Subst Use Misuse*. 1998;33(9):1957–91. https://doi.org/10.3109/10826089809059328.

Westermeyer J, Yargic I, Thuras P. Michigan assessment-screening test for alcohol and drugs (MAST/AD): evaluation in a clinical sample. *Am J Addict.* 2004 Mar–Apr;13(2):151–62. https://doi.org/10.1080/10550490490435948.

Winick. C. 1982. Maturing out of narcotic addiction. *Bull Narc*. 1962;14(1):1–7.

World Health Organization. (2024). Clinical descriptions and diagnostic requirements for ICD-11 mental, behavioural and neurodevelopmental disorders. Geneva: World Health Organization

Woodside M. The first 100 referrals to a Scottish Drug Addiction Treatment Centre. *Br J Addict Alcohol Other Drugs*. 1973 Oct;68(3):231–41. https://doi.org/10.1111/j.1360-0443.1973.tb01250.x.

Zinberg, NE. *Drug, Set, and Setting : The Basis for Controlled Intoxicant Use*. Yale University Press, New Haven, 1984.

Zule WA, Vogtsberger KN, Desmond DP. The intravenous injection of illicit drugs and needle sharing: an historical perspective. *J Psychoactive Drugs*. 1997 Apr–Jun;29(2):199–204. https://doi.org/10.1080/02791072.1997.10400188.

Zullino D. Do not conflate debates on regulating therapeutic use of psychotropic substances with those on the legalization of their non-therapeutic use. *Addiction*. 2025 Feb;120(2):211–2. https://doi.org/10.1111/add.16667.

2 Hepatitis in injecting drug users

Background

The word hepatitis refers to any inflammation of the liver and can be manifested by symptoms such as jaundice, with associated nausea and abdominal pain, or discovered by blood testing for markers of liver disorder. More detailed investigations are carried out using tests such as biopsy or scanning. Hepatitis can cause liver damage resulting from an infectious agent such as a virus or a non-infectious drug, poison or toxin. Probably the most common cause of liver damage in western countries results from prolonged and excessive alcohol use, but obesity and the associated fatty liver changes are also precursors to permanent liver failure. There are several viruses causing liver damage, the main strains of hepatitis viruses being classified as types A, B, C, D and E. Infections like these or other causes of hepatitis can be a short-term and self-limiting illness with complete recovery once the irritant has gone and the virus has been eliminated by the immune system. Often, however, infection can lead on to a more chronic progression and liver damage with fibrotic states and cirrhosis and eventually liver cancer. These later-stage liver disorders are often called end-stage liver disease (ESLD) and hepatoma (liver cancer). As well as these causes of primary cancer of the liver, metastatic deposits are commonly found in the liver secondary to cancer occurring elsewhere in the body. Primary sites giving rise to spread into the liver come principally from bowel, lung, breast, pancreas and stomach but potentially from any other malignancy as stages advance or treatment is delayed.

Symptoms and signs of primary or secondary cancer of the liver may be evident some time after other features of the disease process and may be discovered a part of a planned investigation into signs elsewhere.

For people who inject drugs, the most immediate risk of viral hepatitis comes from transmission through contaminated injecting equipment shared with an infected source. The diseases collectively known as viral hepatitis vary in severity and outcomes. They can all cause symptoms and signs of hepatitis, but their pattern of spread and clinical outcomes vary. Hepatitis A and E are largely spread by the faecal-oral route and can occur in epidemics among people of any age when hygiene is poor. Commonly, symptoms are mild or even subclinical, with recovery without long-term consequences most likely. Exceptions in a small percentage of cases lead to fulminant hepatitis and risk to life and pregnancy. The presence of a coexisting condition giving rise to an immune-compromised state increases the risk of serious damage caused by these viruses.

DOI: 10.4324/9781003611097-2

Hepatitis B, C and D can also be a transitory illness but are also associated with more severe disease and are most commonly caused by contact with contaminated blood or body fluids. The most common causes of transmission of hepatitis B worldwide are sexual or from mother to baby at birth. Other transmission routes include transfusion with an infected product, injecting drug use using shared paraphernalia or from sharp surgical instruments.

Hepatitis A

This form of hepatitis is spread by the faecal-oral route and is less common in recent years in high-income countries. The immunity in the UK population is lower than in previous decades, and the young adult population is therefore susceptible. Vaccination is recommended when travelling to low-income countries and for certain occupations, including drug workers.

The risk of hepatitis A for people who inject drugs has decreased in recent years, but there is an elevated risk for men who have sex with men. There is also a risk of added damage from hepatitis A infection in those people who are already living with liver disease caused by injecting drug use or with active hepatitis C infection. Outbreaks of hepatitis A have also been documented among people who inject drugs in several countries. An outbreak among people who inject drugs in Aberdeen contributed to a major increase in the number of cases in Scotland in 2001 (148 cases), and clusters of this infection have been recorded in injecting drug users and people living in hostels (Roy et al. 2004, O'Donovan et al. 2001, Syed et al. 2003). Several US states have also reported outbreaks mostly among persons reporting drug use or homelessness. Close contact and poor standards of personal hygiene among these groups, with possible faecal contamination of shared injecting equipment or drugs, appears to be the most likely mode of transmission (Hutin et al. 2000, Roy 2004). Consideration should be given to maximising opportunities for vaccination in drug services, prisons and via outreach services in homeless shelters, hostels and anyone in close living situations.

People who inject drugs should be given hepatitis A vaccination along with tetanus, two injections some months apart, or in combination with hepatitis B vaccination.

Hepatitis B

In 1963, an American physician/geneticist working at the discovered what he called the "Australia Antigen" (later designated hepatitis B surface antigen HBsAg) in the serum of an Australian First Nations person (Blumberg et al. 1965). Testing for this marker of hepatitis B infection quickly became an important clinical tool for identifying the cause of otherwise unexplained jaundice and clinical hepatitis. Jaundice, however, only occurs in between 30% and 50% of cases of acute hepatitis B. The development of a test for the hepatitis B virus meant that blood donations could be tested, dramatically reducing the risk of transfusion-associated infections.

The incubation period of hepatitis B ranges from 40 to 160 days. Serological tests indicate different stages of infection; the marker of acute infection is first the presence of the surface antigen HBsAg. This commonly appears between 60 and 90 days after exposure. In most cases, the symptoms resolve spontaneously, and this antigen is no longer found in the blood. In a small proportion of cases, the condition becomes chronic and HBsAg remains present, indicating ongoing virus replication. In some cases, an additional antigen HBeAg is positive. These cases are the most infectious. About 5% or less of cases in adults become chronically infected unless the individuals are compromised immunologically. The risk of chronic infection among those infected at birth is much higher.

Current, active infection can be detected by the presence of HBsAg in the serum. Blood and body fluids from these individuals should be considered to be infectious. In most individuals, infection will resolve and HBsAg disappears from the serum, but the virus persists in some people who become chronically infected with hepatitis B. Chronic hepatitis B infection is defined as persistence of HBsAg in the serum for six months or longer. Among those who are HBsAg positive, those in whom hepatitis B e-antigen (HBeAg) is also detected in the serum are the most infectious. Those who are HBsAg positive and HBeAg negative (usually anti-HBe positive) are infectious but generally of lower infectivity. For those who have eliminated the virus, an antibody is present for life indicating past infection.

Infection with this virus is a worldwide health problem. The burden of infection reported by the World Health Organisation is highest in the Western Pacific and African Regions, where 97 million and 65 million people, respectively, are chronically infected. As for the other WHO Regions, 61 million people are infected in the WHO South East Asia Region, 15 million in the WHO Eastern Mediterranean Region, 11 million in the WHO European Region and 5 million in the WHO Region of the Americas (WHO 2024).

WHO estimates that 254 million people were living with chronic hepatitis B infection in 2022, with 1.2 million new infections each year. Local and regional outbreaks are associated with injecting drug use (Gruer 1991, Robertson 1985)

Hepatitis C

The story of this virus among drug users is one of initial alarm and subsequent success. Discovery of a virus distinctly different from hepatitis A and B viruses was a major breakthrough in the late 1980s and resolved the longstanding question of the nature of the previously named non A non B infection (NANB) (Houghton 2009). Prior to identifying the hepatitis C virus NABB was considered to be the cause of transfusion-associated hepatitis and those cases who had advanced cirrhosis and liver cancer but no previous infection with the already identified strains of hepatitis. The development of a test for hepatitis C in 1990 allowed for the global testing for this infection and hepatitis B in injecting drug users and the revelations of its widespread prevalence (Nelson 2011). The presence of variants of the virus in several studies identified characteristics showing some similarity and suggests spread across continents among people who inject drugs, with a specific emphasis on

London as a hub (Cochrane et al. 2002). The World Health Organisation reported, in 2022, that an estimated 50 million people had chronic hepatitis C with 1 million new infections every year. The death rate from cirrhosis and liver cancer caused by this infection was estimated at 242,000 (Mitchell et al. 2024). The rise in numbers of people injecting drugs had a significant effect on the rapid increase in hepatitis C as demonstrated by phylogenetic analysis of strains 1a and 1b. Injecting drug use is well described amongst soldiers in World War I and it is possible that this could have contributed to early HCV transmission and the impact of drug use had been underestimated (Robson 1999, editorial JAMA 1950). From the time of World War II, the number of medical procedures involving blood products increased rapidly, probably accounting for the rapid spread of hepatitis C infection. The rise in numbers of people injecting drugs and using contaminated equipment rapidly increased in the 1960s, accounting for a further rapid increase in hepatitis C. Interestingly, one study found that the rate of increase slowed prior to the introduction of specific antiviral probably due to an increased awareness of the virus after the introduction of a test in 1990 (Magiorkinis et al. 2009). The use of injecting equipment is graphically described in an important publication which described "The injection century: massive unsterile injections and the emergence of human pathogens". This study covers more than just hepatitis C and reflects on other emerging global epidemics, suggesting that we are in a new era of biological control risks (Drucker et al. 2001).

> The emergence of epidemic HIV and hepatitis C virus in the 20th century suggest that massive unsterile injections can become an important new catalyst for biological change, capable of greatly accelerating the spread of many human pathogens and allowing previously isolated viruses to establish global pandemics. In this way, massive unsterile injecting can profoundly reorder some fundamental biological relations between agent, host, and environment, with unpredicted effects for human parasite ecology and public health.
>
> (Gisselquist 2008)

Hepatitis C is now known to have been around for several centuries (Pybus et al. 2007). Geneticists have demonstrated that historically there were times of rapid spread driven over the last century by injecting drug use, blood transfusion with contaminated blood products and unsafe injections (Smith et al. 1997). With reference to injecting drug users, the epidemic of hepatitis C (and B) depended on increasing numbers of people using heroin by injection, and Pybus and colleagues concluded that

> We estimate that exponential growth began between 1924 and 1953, and one could speculate that this was initiated by introduction of virus into opiate-injecting communities, such as that documented in London during the 1950s.
>
> (Pybus 2004)

In higher income countries the iatrogenic routes have largely disappeared but are probably still important in lower-income economies. Mass vaccination campaigns and other rapid increases in use of injecting products caused a massive rise in hepatitis C worldwide during the 20th century. The tragic infection of a large part of the population in Egypt resulting from contaminated products used during a mass schistosomiasis campaign is one of the few cases where a specific cause can be identified, but speculation about the mass vaccination of troops going to the African theatre of war in World War II remains a possible cause of some of the pandemic spread.

The story continues with evidence of spread of hepatitis in many countries and especially when under stress such as present-day Ukraine, where the displacement of people through conflict leads to conditions of stress and infectious disease transmission (Stroffolini 2012, Yakovleva et al. 2023).

In Scotland, modelling of the hepatitis C epidemic estimated that the number of people who have used drugs or still inject drugs who would develop advanced liver disease and possibly liver cancer would double between 2000 and 2020. The authors wouldn't know at the time that an effective treatment would significantly reduce this problem, but their advocacy for early detection and increased testing for people who may not know that they are or were at risk in the past remains highly relevant (Hutchinson et al. 2005).

The surveillance study carried out in Scotland every two years since 2008 made the following observations in its 2022 report (Public Health Scotland 2022).

> The prevalence of chronic HCV (i.e. active infection) has reduced markedly from 37% in 2015–16 to 19% in 2019–20, contemporaneous with the scale-up of HCV treatment among PWID in community settings. More than half (53%) of participants who would have been eligible for therapy (i.e. with evidence of either current or past chronic infection) reported having been treated for their HCV infection.
>
> Despite the reduction in chronic HCV prevalence, the incidence of infection remains high at 12 new HCV cases per 100 person-years in 2019–20.
>
> (Public Health Scotland 2022)

Injecting drug use continues to be a significant driver of the global hepatitis C epidemic, with WHO estimating that 23% of new hepatitis C infections are attributable to unsafe drug injecting practices. Nearly every second person injecting drugs is living with hepatitis C (an estimated 6.8 million people in 2022). Overall, liver diseases caused by hepatitis C account for more than half the deaths attributed to the use of drugs and is considerably overlooked in poorer populations (World Drugs Report 2024, Ventura-Cots 2022).

The European Union Drugs Agency recently released a report outlining prevention strategies for hepatitis C in people who inject drugs. Eleven case studies in eight member states were used to demonstrate the positive effect of harm minimisation measures (EUDA 2024). Projects ranged from being clinic-based to outreach and peer group contacts and included awareness and educational programmes, testing opportunities and early interventions with treatments for people already infected. The report concluded that innovative outreach programmes were useful in reaching hard-to-reach people and were effective in addressing the aims of the Agency in trying to be inclusive and effective in reducing the incidence of hepatitis C.

Although there is currently no vaccination for hepatitis C, the rapid development of antiviral treatments allows for over 95% successful treatment. Not all cases of hepatitis C require treatment as recovery can take place after acute infection, but all cases of chronic infection require treatment. In high-income countries, the possibility of eliminating the infection is a reality, but in many countries, this requires a huge increase in diagnosis testing and treatment availability. A slightly pessimistic view on progress being made is expressed in a recent publication.

> Assuming high-income countries will maintain current levels of diagnosis and treatment, only 24% are on track to eliminate HCV by 2030, and 60% are off track by at least 20 years. If current levels of diagnosis and treatment continue falling, achieving WHO's 2030 targets will be more challenging. With less than ten years remaining, screening and treatment expansion is crucial to meet WHO's HCV elimination targets.
>
> (Gamkrelidze et al. 2021)

Efforts to help towards elimination targets include screening in accident and emergency departments. In one such trial as part of routine care, patients were randomly assigned to either nontargeted screening, in which HCV testing was offered regardless of risk, or targeted screening, in which testing was offered based on risk assessment. Conclusions include the finding that nontargeted screening was superior to targeted screening. However, only around 20% of both groups with newly diagnosed HCV positive tests progressed to treatment. The authors concluded that there was an urgent need for innovative models of HCV treatment (Haukoos et al. 2025).

Prevention depends on screening transfusion products and education about safer injecting and equipment among people who use drugs.

Reducing the incidence of hepatitis C virus (HCV) infection is a World Health Organization (WHO) elimination goal.

Evidence on whether Scotland has reached the WHO elimination target of ≤ 2 per 100 person-years in their population of people who inject drugs was investigated in 2025 (McDonald et al. 2025).

Over a period when direct-acting antiviral therapy was scaled up in Scotland, major reductions in the incidence of primary infection, reinfection, and total HCV infection were evident, indicating that the WHO target is within reach for this high-risk population.

Hepatitis D

This virus is more enigmatic and systems for testing and monitoring are less well developed worldwide. It is unusual among viruses as it only coexists with hepatitis B and has been described as a satellite or subviral agent as it only infects humans in the presence of hepatitis B. When this additional viral burden occurs, a more damaging liver disease can occur, and "superinfection" can result in a higher fatality rate or progress more likely to a chronic state, liver cirrhosis or cancer. Approximately 30% to 70% of patients with chronic hepatitis D have cirrhosis at diagnosis and more than 50% die of liver disease within 10 years of diagnosis (Makino et al. 1987, Negro et al. 2023 Asselah 2023). In Europe, hepatitis D remains endemic in Romania and Moldova. Hot spots sustained by immigrants and people who inject drugs have been reported in Russia (Rizzetto et al. 2017, Raimondo 1982).

People who inject drugs are the group at highest risk of hepatitis D, and outbreaks are uncommon. Among those tested for hepatitis B, the presence of hepatitis D has declined in Spain, from 30% to 4.2% over the last 20 years (Aguilera et al. 2018). An Italian study of people positive for hepatitis C from 2012 showed only 2.8% of 543 people who had injected drugs were HBsAg positive, making them susceptible to hepatitis D (Stroffolini et al. 2012) In Taiwan, however, the prevalence of hepatitis D among people who had injected drugs was nearly 44%, but many were in an older age group, possibly reflecting a period of greater risk and prior to immunisation against hepatitis B.

A study in the Lancet in 1982 raised alarm about the high prevalence of delta virus in injecting drug-using populations in Italy, 44% (8/18) in Denmark, 33% (11/33) in Switzerland, and 31% (15/49) in Ireland (Raimiondo 1982)

> Rizetto and others, in their 2021 study, concluded that "HDV infection is vanishing in the domestic populations of high-income countries as a secondary effect of long-standing and successful HBV vaccination programmes, leaving behind an ageing cohort of patients with advanced liver fibrosis."
>
> (Rizetto 2017)

Vaccination for hepatitis

The first hepatitis B vaccine was approved in the United States in 1981. A recombinant version came to market in 1986. It is now on the World Health Organization's List of Essential Medicines.

Education, screening of blood products and harm reduction measures have had a dramatic effect on reducing transmission of hepatitis B and C, but as with other infections, vaccination is the best hope for preventing outbreaks and transmission from person to person and reducing global prevalence. Only hepatitis B has a specific vaccine in current use, having been developed first. Early vaccines were developed from heat-treated serum from infected cases, but in 1986, a genetically engineered vaccine was produced using no blood products. Hepatitis B and C are responsible for 80% of all liver cancers, and this form of cancer is the second most common cause of cancer death worldwide. This makes the hepatitis B vaccine the first anti-cancer vaccine.

The World Health Organisation has estimated that 4.5 million deaths could be prevented in low- and middle-income countries by 2030 through vaccination and is developing a strategy to reduce new infections by 90% and deaths by 65% by 2030 (WHO 2024). Liver disese represents a major challenge in many European countries (Cooke 2022).

Among people who use drugs, vaccination against hepatitis B is critically important. Numbers of cases of acute hepatitis B and C have fallen over the last two decades, and outbreaks with significant numbers involved are rare. Laboratory reports of acute hepatitis B fell from a peak of just below 2,000 reports from England and Wales in 1984 to 531 reports in 1992. This is due to a variety of harm reduction measures, including injecting equipment supplies, education and opiate agonist treatment, but vaccination has undoubtedly helped. Unfortunately, from an initial high uptake of voluntary immunisation, this has fallen in recent years, perhaps reflecting a reduction in the perception of the risk of contracting hepatitis B. In England, Wales and Northern Ireland, uptake of hepatitis B vaccination fell from 75% in 2012 to 61% in 2021 (UKHSA 2024).

The hepatitis B vaccines are described in the "Green Book" (UK immunisation schedule) (2022). They may be given separately or in combination with hepatitis A. For infants, it is given in combination with other vaccines. The vaccine can be given as three single doses at 0, 1 and 6 months or an accelerated schedule at 0, 1, 2 and 12 months for pre- or post-exposure prophylaxis.

The hepatitis B vaccine is given as a single or combined product:

- monovalent hepatitis B vaccine (HepB)
- bivalent combination vaccine: hepatitis A and B (HepA/HepB)
- hexavalent combination vaccine containing diphtheria/tetanus/acellular pertussis/inactivated polio vaccine/Haemophilus influenzae type b/hepatitis B (DTaP/IPV/Hib/HepB)

Vaccination against hepatitis B should be given to people who have or may inject drugs and sexual and household contacts of PWIDs. Needlestick injuries where the contact is in a high-risk group need assessment with blood taken before vaccination and consideration of passive immunisation with immunoglobulin.

A report from the UK Government monitoring system concluded the following:

> Self-reported vaccine coverage amongst people who inject drugs has been steadily declining over recent years and measuring uptake amongst other at-risk populations, including migrant populations, people accessing sexual health services (SHSs), people in prison, and patients with chronic kidney disease, remains challenging. Ongoing engagement with stakeholders, including healthcare providers, communities, health commissioners and policymakers, is vital to strengthen data systems, reporting mechanisms and collaborative networks. Data from the UAM survey of people who inject drugs for England indicates that self-reported uptake of at least one dose of hepatitis B vaccine has decreased from 74.6% in 2015 to 60.7% in 2022.
>
> (UKHSA 2024)

Results from the Scottish monitoring project show a similar slow decline in uptake of hepatitis B vaccination among people who inject drugs:

> The proportion of participants who reported vaccination for the hepatitis B virus (HBV) is on a decreasing trend, with 68% reporting receipt of at least one dose in 2019–20 from a high of 77% in 2015–16.
>
> (Public Health Scotland 2020).

A history of Hepatitis among people who inject drugs

The evolution of hepatitis among people who use drugs is closely associated with the development of increased numbers of people involved. Clearly, the very nature of the transmission of a virus like hepatitis B depends upon the numbers involved but also the demographics of these people, whether they travel and use drugs elsewhere from their home environment and critically, whether or not they inject drugs. The descriptions of the drugs used, the people using them and the environment in which people take drugs have changed dramatically over the last seven decades, as descriptions and research reports testify.

The concerns with increased cannabis use were the fundamental problem in the 1950s, particularly in the USA. Many governments' assessments of the numbers of people involved with cannabis were rudimentary, and when they did gather data, numbers were, by today's standards, very small. The following quote from Bewley and others demonstrates the size of the caseload in the United Kingdom in the middle of the last century. At that time, the UK Home Office, which was and remains responsible for drug policy, gathered numbers from reports from medical practitioners about people who were thought to be using controlled drugs. This "Addicts Index" was discontinued in 1980 when it was replaced by more suitable recording systems. This research predates the UK legislation, the Misuse of Drugs Act 1971, which formalised a system of classification and penalties for use of drugs in line with the United Nations Charter of 1961 (Single convention).

> Between 1947 and 1967 1272 cases of heroin addiction were reported to the Home Office. Of these 890 had taken opiates, 89 had died, and of the 293 not known to be taking opiates 189 had been in prison, hospital or a similar institution. The rate of recording new cases had increased, doubling every 16 months. The mortality among "non therapeutic" addicts was 28 times the expected rate and chiefly due to sepsis, suicide or overdose. Of new cases in the last 2 years 40% were under the age of 20. Possibly 800 followed by 1200 will be reported in 1967 and 1968.
>
> (Bewley et al. 1968)

Further exemplifying the early structures and understanding of the drug problem comes from a publication from the editorial team at the Journal of the American Medical Associations which refers to concerns about drugs but has non-specific general observations of increased cannabis use, cocaine increasing in prevalence and only tangentially to opiates and no reference to injecting of heroin. Amongst other suggestions, the editor notes the suggestion from the Expert Committee on Drugs Liable to Produce Addiction of the World Health Organization that there should be intensification of medical research on drug addiction (JAMA 1950). The editor also concluded that

> while such research is needed and should provide much helpful information, the medical profession already has sufficient information to permit awareness of some of the pressing phases of drug addiction. By being alert itself, the profession can stimulate others to lend their aid in the prevention and correction of this vicious health problem. This is a field in which the medical profession can assume forceful leadership and at the same time demonstrate the effectiveness with which local problems can be solved by local groups.

Interestingly, little mention was made of clinical problems such as hepatitis.

Within a few years, however, reports began to emerge of hepatitis cases. Alter and colleagues, in an important paper in 1958, drew attention to the possible complications of using and sharing injecting equipment and referred to and recorded some of the conditions that have been associated with injecting, dating back in some cases many years. The paper was principally about hepatitis (then known as serum hepatitis and possibly including hepatitis B and hepatitis C). Evidence was emerging of a medical condition associated with injecting opiates. An outbreak of hepatitis was reported in New York (Cardon 1952).

> The marked increase in drug addiction among adolescents has been amply documented as has the transmission of malaria, tetanus, acute endocarditis and septicaemia among drug addicts. To our knowledge the first report in the American literature of viral hepatitis in drug addicts was that by Steigmann and his co-workers in 1950. They reported a group of 23 addicts with homologous serum hepatitis that they thought was spread by infected needles and syringes. Appelbaum and Kalkstein described a group of addicts with hepatitis, several of whom had a needle-sharing associate with a history of jaundice. The increased prevalence of viral hepatitis at Bellevue Hospital was thought to be associated with the increase in the intravenous use of narcotics, particularly in the younger age groups.
>
> (Levine 1960, Alter and Michael 1958, Steigmann et al. 1950, Alepbaum et al. 1951)

In these early descriptions, mortality varied, some reporting transitory jaundice while others recorded considerable mortality. Predating the availability of tests for hepatitis B and C, it was not at all clear that there might be more than one virus active in these communities. These clusters and local outbreaks of infection may have had different virological characteristics accounting for the variability in severity of the outcomes. Similar disasters were to be later described in outbreaks in haemodialysis units where mortality was high. The higher morbidity and mortality might have been due to more virulent strains of one or more viruses, a combined infection of two or more variants, hepatitis B with associated delta factor (hepatitis D). The mortality from hepatitis B is generally low as in New York (Friedman 1966) but outbreaks with high mortality were described in Manchester and in Edinburgh in 1969 where contaminated blood or inadequate control led to cases in the haemodialysis units. Hepatitis B was detected in blood donations when testing became avaiable (Hopkins 1977) In the Edinburgh case, various hypotheses were explored to explain the virulence of the outbreak, including a specially virulent strain of the virus and, more plausibly, the additive or synergistic action of two viruses. The second virus was described at the time using the current term at that time, non A non B (NANB). This virus was later identified as hepatitis C.

> Clinical aspects of illness in the outbreak. The clinical features, in general, resembled those of other outbreaks of viral hepatitis except for the high mortality. There were seven deaths (24%) directly related to HBV infection in 29 episodes of hepatitis in the renal patients and four deaths (31%) in the 13 cases that occurred in staff members. There were two cases of hepatitis in 123 home contacts of dialysis patients (neither was fatal), and there were no cases among home contacts of staff.
>
> (Bone et al. 1971, Marmion et al. 1982, Burrell et al. 1977)

> Studies of posttransfusion hepatitis have identified sequential dual infections with HBV and non-A, non-B hepatitis virus, but disease has not been any more severe as a result (J. W. Mosley, personal communication) (Marmion 1982)

Understanding these underlying factors was only possible as a better knowledge of the nature of the viruses involved emerged, and as the distinction was made between virus strains and testing became more widely available, the natural history of hepatitis caused by infections became clearer. Coinciding with the rapid increase in drug use from 1970 to the present time, outbreaks of hepatitis B and, more recently, the possibility of testing for hepatitis C, the drive to vaccinate against the former and treat cases of the latter came to dominate drug policy in this area.

The early descriptions of cases of hepatitis in UK drug users were, by the late 1970s, studied in more detail, although it was not until 1989 when non A non B was identified as hepatitis C, and a separate test showed that a dual epidemic was present in most of these cases. Testing across Europe coincided with the rapid increase in drug injecting in many centres raised alarm bells, although the importance of the phenomenon failed to adequately recognise that there was a second virus, that of HIV, which was already circulating in these populations. Testing for HIV became available in 1985 with a clinical, social and political revolution, described in Chapter 3. By 1990, when widespread testing for hepatitis C, the third virus in this syndemic, was available, the extent of this additional problem became clear (van Asten et al. 2004).

The Edinburgh experience of hepatitis B in a drug-using population in the early 1980s was a good case study of how infection can become epidemic when the conditions for transmission are all present. The sudden increase in availability and street marketing of a heroin supply of unusually high purity led to a local population beginning to inject. These young people had no previous experience of drug use and were therefore extremely vulnerable and lacking in any immunity from prior exposure to hepatitis or active immunisation which wasn't then in the childhood immunisation programme. Combined with this vulnerability, there was a lack of support services, no needle or syringe equipment provision and a rudimentary opiate treatment programme (Robertson 1985). Injecting equipment was shared widely, in groups and from suppliers who "rented" used equipment. A commercial outlet run by a single-handed retailer of medical equipment recognised the requests for needles and syringes as coming from people using illegal drugs and after careful consideration agreed to sell sterile sets of syringes and needles. He was unfortunately forced out of business through an unfortunate combination of pressure from police and deterioration in other customers. Subsequently "shooting gallery" style sharing became more common and the incidence of hepatitis B and clinical cases of jaundice and associated symptoms became common. Laboratory tests identified these cases as acute hepatitis and the serum stored in the virus laboratory later showed that at the time of the hepatitis B epidemic hepatitis C and HIV were being transmitted as well (Robertson et al. 1985, 1986).

This combination of virus transmission was similar to events in other US and European cities. An epidemic of HIV transmission was noted in New York associated with similar conditions among the prohibited and poorly supported heroin injecting community in poorer areas of the city (Schrager et al. 1991). Over the next few years, conditions in many cities in Europe and later Eastern countries identified the rapid spread of these blood-borne viruses. An almost identical epidemic to that in Edinburgh of heroin use was challenging health officials in Dublin and Milan and later in Glasgow (O'Kelly 2012, Lazzarin 1985, Gruer 1991). Amsterdam was in the slightly unusual situation of having identified and made some response to her heroin injecting of recent years and had led the response in Europe through community and drug-using agencies to scale up the opiate treatment programmes and availability of injecting equipment (van Santen et al. 2021, Van Ameijden 1993).

More recently, harm reduction measures have not been shown to completely eliminate the risk of blood-borne virus transmission. In these articles, the risk of assuming adequate provision of equipment is reducing sharing depends on a stable and accessible system of delivery. Scaling up of these vital services is required (McAuley et al. 2019, Larney et al. 2017).

Interestingly, and perhaps not surprisingly, the novelty and alarming threat of the HIV/AIDS epidemic eclipsed the hepatitis B epidemic. By the time testing for hepatitis C became possible and the enormous caseload was revealed, the initial panic about AIDS had somewhat subsided, and attention could quickly be attended to adjusting services to cope with another clinical problem.

As the awareness of viral infection in people who inject drugs became more common, most western countries introduced guidelines for vaccination for hepatitis B and, of course, early treatment for hepatitis C. Early interventions with the hepatitis B vaccine explored the best approach to ensuring compliance with vaccine schedules but found cooperation to be good in many settings, with flexibility by services already delivering care being essential. Limitations were initially in treatment services rather than in an unwilling population of people at risk (Budd et al. 2004). Packages of care for people using drugs by injection (intravenous or intramuscular) include the risk of other problems such as HIV, overdose and sepsis. Increasingly, the public health preventive measures include discussions about safer injecting facilities, decriminalisation and more aggressive outreach and inclusion programmes. In the UK and worldwide vaccination programmes are embedded in the national guidelines for the management of people who use drugs (Clinical Guidelines Departments of Health 2017, World Health Organisation 2022).

Injection drug use remains the most common risk factor for acquiring hepatitis C in Europe and North America. In the year 2021, one study in the USA reported that 57% of cases reported drug use as their main risk factor for hepatitis C infection (CDC 2023). Among those who inject drugs, this study found that between 20% and 30% become infected with hepatitis C within the first two years of injecting (Pouget et al. 2012).

The number of people infected decreased between 1992 and 2002, resulting from the increased availability of injecting equipment following the HIV epidemic, but increased again in the years of the ongoing opioid epidemic.

The Infected Blood Inquiry

The plan to have an inquiry in the UK into the consequences of infections caused by blood transfusions and contaminated products like Factor 8 were announced in the British Parliament in July 2017 and began in 2018. It spent a long time gathering evidence and taking evidence and eventually reported in May 2024. Changes in health care had by this time changed and modernised but for those infected, many of whom had died by the time of the report, the legacy of the failure to prevent these problems still resonates. The report found that since the 1970s 30,000 people had been infected with hepatitis B or hepatitis C and, in the case of infected Factor 8, patients with haemophilia.

The Inquiry found that there had been failures in the National Health Service in several respects. As well as failure to explore ways to inactivate viral infection in Factor 8 concentrates (which were derived from several thousand blood donations), there had been a failure to select and screen donors who might present increased risk. The Inquiry found that clinicians had not recognised or accounted for the increased risk to patients, and there was some denial about the dangers presented.

There was a failure to recognise early enough the risk of HIV in imported products from the United States and Austria and to become self-sufficient in the United Kingdom. Specifically, the Inquiry found that clinicians had placed children at risk of infection by injecting concentrates derived from multiple donations.

Under the heading "Collection of blood from prisons", the Inquiry concluded that mistakes were made and early recognition was flawed, and that people who had used drugs were included in the collection of donations.

> "Both the DHSS and the SHHD knew from the early 1970s that the collection of blood from prisons and similar institutions led to an increased risk of transmission of Hepatitis B. Despite this indication that prison donation might not be safe, blood collection from prisons was a common practice in the UK throughout the 1970s and early 1980s. The Report found that in May 1975 a "Dear Doctor" letter from the CMO, Sir Henry Yellowlees, advised that collections could continue, despite the higher risk of Hepatitis B. This letter, which relied on the fact that there were other high risk groups such as drug users as a reason to continue to collect from prisons, contained deeply flawed logic and effectively endorsed and encouraged this practice. The hands off approach of the DHSS and SHHD, leaving blood safety entirely to the judgement of local Regional Transfusion Directors, was wholly unacceptable. It should have been taken seriously by government and was not. It was also wrong not to bring the issue of prison donation to the attention of ministers. It was not raised with a Scottish minister until May 1983; it was never raised with ministers in the DHSS".

The risk of AIDS transmission through blood or donations and blood products was known as early as the middle of 1982, but information was not distributed to local blood transfusion services until September 1983 and arrangements were allowed by the Department of Health to be at the discretion of regional services. At that time, donors of blood were requested to not give blood rather than being instructed that they must not. In relation to people who had or did inject drugs, the 1984 advice was advisory, and it wasn't until 1985 that the wording of the advice was strengthened and even then, it referred to people who inject drugs rather than including those who had injected in the past but no longer did so. The Inquiry noted that the UK Expert Advisory Committee on AIDS was not established until 1984 and at that time, the importance of injecting users was not recognised as the most important issue causing a risk to the blood supply but also the non-drug-using heterosexual community.

A compensation scheme was later announced to recognise the problems arising from the transmission of viruses through transfusion or treatment, including those that had developed complications such as liver cancer or cirrhosis and neurological or mental health problems. The British Government has been criticised for the slow response to the infections caused by transfusion and treatment. No one has been prosecuted, unlike cases in France and the USA where high-profile cases resulted in the conviction of a Minister and the acquitting of two others on a charge of manslaughter. Cases in other countries have been brought against pharmaceutical companies and distributors of blood products, and governments in the USA, Japan and some European countries awarded compensation for people infected with HIV as early as the mid-1990s.

Conclusion

As with other problems for people who inject drugs, the risk of hepatitis, either viral or toxin and alcohol-related, is associated with inequalities, race and the social and commercial determinants of health (Friel et al. et al2023). Risk of infection increases when exposure to infected equipment is increased in the absence of a sterile supply of needles and syringes and an environment where adequate hygiene exists (Des Jarlais and Friedman 1987). Preventing transmission of hepatitis viruses is clear when a range of interventions are present. There is now good evidence for the effectiveness of opiate agonist treatment and needle and syringe programmes, alone and in combination, in reducing injecting risk behaviour and hepatitis C virus and HIV transmission (Palmateer et al2022). Programmes like these are far from universal and are at the mercy of political approval and resource allocation. The absence of epidemic hepatitis B transmission in some areas where vaccination programmes have reduced the incidence of this disease should not be room for complacency, as vaccination uptake depends on a combination of factors including the perception of risk in communities. Vaccination campaigns in custodial settings has been associted with reduction in hepatitis B among people who inject drugs (Palmateer 2018). Stigma at all levels in drug use and lack of education remain a constraint on providing a hepatitis-free situation.

References

Aguilera A, Trastoy R, Barreiro P, Costa JJ, de Mendoza C, Peña JM, Soriano V. Decline and changing profile of hepatitis delta among injection drug users in Spain. *Antivir Ther.* 2018;23(1):87–90. https://doi.org/10.3851/IMP3161.

Alter AA, Michael M Jr. Serum hepatitis in a group of drug addicts. *N Engl J Med.* 1958 Aug 21;259(8):387–9. https://doi.org/10.1056/NEJM195808212590807.

Appelbaum E, Kalkstein M. Artificial transmission of viral hepatitis among intravenous diacetylmorphine addicts. *JAMA.* 1951;147:222–4.

Asselah T, Rizzetto M. Hepatitis D Virus Infection. *N Engl J Med.* 2023 Jul 6;389(1):58–70. https://doi.org/10.1056/NEJMra2212151. Erratum in: *N Engl J Med.* 2023 Oct 12;389(15):1444. https://doi.org/10.1056/NEJMx230006.

Bewley TH, Ben-Arie O, James IP. Morbidity and mortality from heroin dependence. 1. Survey of heroin addicts known to home office. *Br Med J.* 1968 Mar 23;1(5594):725–6. https://doi.org/10.1136/bmj.1.5594.725.

Blumberg BS, Alter HJ, Visnich S. A "new" antigen in leukemia sera. JAMA. 1965 Feb 15;191:541–6. https://doi.org/10.1001/jama.1965.03080070025007.

Bone JM, Tonkin RW, Davison AM, Marmion BP, Robson JS. Outbreak of dialysis-associated hepatitis in Edinburgh, 1969–1970. *Proc Eur Dial Transplant Assoc.* 1971;8:189–97.

Budd J, Robertson R, Elton R. Hepatitis B vaccination and injecting drug users. *Br J Gen Pract.* 2004 Jun;54(503):444–7.

Burrell CJ, Tonkin RW, Proudfoot E, Leadbetter G, Cowan P, Lockerbie L, Gore S, Lutz W, Marmion BP. Prevalence of antibody to hepatitits B surface antigen among staff in an Edinburgh hospital. *J Hyg (Lond).* 1977 Feb;78(1):57–68. https://doi.org/10.1017/s0022172400055935.

Cardon PV, Beck EM. The recent occurrence of hepatitis among drug addicts of New York City. *N Y State J Med.* 1952 Apr 15;52(8):1037 8.

CDC, Centers for Disease Control and Prevention. Hepatitis C Surveillance 2021. Published August 2023.

Clinical Guidelines on Drug Misuse and Dependence Update 2017 Independent Expert Working Group. *Drug Misuse and Dependence: UK Guidelines on Clinical Management.* Department of Health, London, 2017

Cochrane A, Searle B, Hardie A, et al. A genetic analysis of hepatitis C virus transmission between injection drug users. *J Infect Dis.* 2002 Nov 1;186(9):1212–21. https://doi.org/10.1086/344314.

Cooke GS, Nayagam S. Liver disease: at the heart of public health challenges for Europe in the 21st century. *Lancet.* 2022 Jan 1;399(10319):9–10. https://doi.org/10.1016/S0140-6736(21)02728-8.

Des Jarlais DC, Friedman SR. HIV infection among intravenous drug users: epidemiology and risk reduction. *AIDS.* 1987 Jul;1(2):67–76.

Drucker E, Alcabes PG, Marx PA. The injection century: massive unsterile injections and the emergence of human pathogens. *Lancet.* 2001 Dec 8;358(9297):1989–92. https://doi.org/10.1016/S0140-6736(01)06967-7. PMID: 11747942.

European Dialysis and Trans plant Association. Vol. 8. Pitman Medical, London, 1971, pp. 189–97.

EUDA 2024. European Monitoring Centre for Drugs and Drug Addiction. *European Drug Report 2024: Trends and Developments*, 2024. https://www.emcdda.europa.eu/publications/european-drug-report/2024_en.

Friedman EA, Thomson GE. Hepatitis complicating chronic haemodialysis. *Lancet.* 1966 Sep 24;2(7465):675–8. https://doi.org/10.1016/s0140-6736(66)92833-9.

Friel S, Collin J, Daube M, et al. Commercial determinants of health: future directions. *Lancet.* 2023 Apr 8;401(10383):1229–40. https://doi.org/10.1016/S0140-6736(23)00011-9.

Gamkrelidze I, Pawlotsky JM, Lazarus JV, et al. Progress towards hepatitis C virus elimination in high-income countries: an updated analysis. *Liver Int.* 2021 Mar;41(3):456–63. https://doi.org/10.1111/liv.14779.

Gisselquist, D. (2008) Points to consider: Responses to HIV/AIDS in Africa, Asia, and the Caribbean. London: Adonis & Abbey Publishers.

Gruer LD, Peedle M, Carrington D, Clements GB, Follett EA. Distribution of HIV and acute hepatitis B infection among drug injectors in Glasgow. *Int J STD AIDS.* 1991 Sep-Oct;2(5):356–8. https://doi.org/10.1177/095646249100200509.

Haukoos J, Rothman RE, Galbraith JW, et al. Hepatitis C screening in emergency departments: the DETECT Hep C randomized clinical trial. *JAMA.* Published online July 09, 2025. https://doi.org/10.1001/jama.2025.10563.

Hepatitis and renal dialysis. *Br Med J.* 1965 Nov 20;2(5472):1199–200.

Hopkins R. *Hepatitis B Antigen and Blood Transfusion.* Doctoral [Ph.D.] dissertation. University of Edinburgh, Edinburgh, Scotland, 1977.

Houghton M. Discovery of the hepatitis C virus. *Liver Int.* 2009 Jan;29 Suppl 1:82–8. https://doi.org/10.1111/j.1478-3231.2008.01925.x.

Hutchinson SJ, Bird SM, Goldberg DJ. Modeling the current and future disease burden of hepatitis C among injection drug users in Scotland. *Hepatology.* 2005 Sep;42(3):711–23. https://doi.org/10.1002/hep.20836.

Hutin YJ, Sabin KM, Hutwager LC, et al. Multiple modes of hepatitis A virus transmission among methamphetamine users. *Am J Epidemiol* 200;152:186–92.

JAMA.(editorial) DRUG ADDICTION (editorial). 1950;143(11):973–4. https://doi.org/10.1001/jama.1950.02910460031013

Larney S, Peacock A, Leung J, et al. Global, regional, and country-level coverage of interventions to prevent and manage HIV and hepatitis C among people who inject drugs: a systematic review. *Lancet Glob Health.* 2017 Dec;5(12):e1208–e1220. https://doi.org/10.1016/S2214-109X(17)30373-X.

Levine RA, Payne MA. Homologous serum hepatitis in youthful heroin users. *Ann Intern Med.* 1960 Jul;53:164–78. https://doi.org/10.7326/0003-4819-53-1-164.

Magiorkinis G, Magiorkinis E, Paraskevis D, Ho SY, Shapiro B, Pybus OG, Allain JP, Hatzakis A. The global spread of hepatitis C virus 1a and 1b: a phylodynamic and phylogeographic analysis. PLoS Med. 2009 Dec;6(12):e1000198. https://doi.org/10.1371/journal.pmed.1000198.

Makino S, Chang MF, Shieh CK, Kamahora T, Vannier DM, Govindarajan S, Lai MM. Molecular cloning and sequencing of a human hepatitis delta (delta) virus RNA. Nature. 1987 Sep 24–30;329(6137):343–6. https://doi.org/10.1038/329343a0.

Marmion BP, Burrell CJ, Tonkin RW, Dickson J. Dialysis-associated hepatitis in Edinburgh; 1969–1978. Rev Infect Dis. 1982 May-Jun;4(3):619–37. https://doi.org/10.1093/clinids/4.3.619.

McAuley A, Palmateer NE, Goldberg DJ, et al. Re-emergence of HIV related to injecting drug use despite a comprehensive harm reduction environment: a cross-sectional analysis. *Lancet HIV.* 2019;6:e315–24.

McDonald, S, Palmateer, N, McAuley, A, Gunson, RN, Barclay, S, Dillon, JF, Hickman, M, Hutchinson, S Estimating incidence rates of primary infection and reinfection with hepatitis C virus among people who inject drugs in Scotland: a model-based analysis of repeated cross sectional survey data. *Lancet Regional Health - Europe.* 2025.

Mitchell H, Costella A , Clancy I, et al. *Hepatitis C in England 2024: Working to Eliminate Hepatitis C as a Public Health Problem. Data to End of 2023.* UKHSA, London, January 2025.

Negro F, Lok AS. Hepatitis D: a review. *JAMA.* 2023;330(24):2376–87. https://doi.org/10.1001/jama.2023.23242

Nelson PK, Mathers BM, Cowie B, Hagan H, Des Jarlais D, Horyniak D, Degenhardt L. Global epidemiology of hepatitis B and hepatitis C in people who inject drugs: results of systematic reviews. *Lancet.* 2011 Aug 13;378(9791):571–83. https://doi.org/10.1016/S0140-6736(11)61097-0.

O'Donovan D, Cooke RPD, Joce R, et al. An outbreak of hepatitis A among injecting drug users. *Epidemiol Infect.* 2001;127:469–73.

Palmateer NE, Goldberg DJ, Munro A, et al. Association between universal hepatitis B prison vaccination, vaccine uptake and hepatitis B infection among people who inject drugs. *Addiction.* 2018;113(1):80–90

Palmateer N, Hamill V, Bergenstrom A, et al. Interventions to prevent HIV and Hepatitis C among people who inject drugs: Latest evidence of effectiveness from a systematic review (2011 to 2020). *Int J Drug Policy.* 2022 Nov;109:103872. https://doi.org/10.1016/j.drugpo.2022.103872.

Pouget ER, Hagan H, Des Jarlais DC. Meta-analysis of hepatitis C seroconversion in relation to shared syringes and drug preparation equipment. *Addiction.* 2012 Jun;107(6):1057–65. https://doi.org/10.1111/j.1360-0443.2011.03765.x.

Public Health Scotland, Glasgow Caledonian University and the West of Scotland Specialist Virology Centre. *The Needle Exchange Surveillance Initiative (NESI): Prevalence of Blood-Borne Viruses and Injecting Risk Behaviours Among People Who Inject Drugs Attending Injecting Equipment Provision Services in Scotland, 2008 to 2020.* Public Health Scotland, Glasgow, March 2022.

Pybus OG, Cochrane A, Holmes EC, Simmonds P. The hepatitis C virus epidemic among injecting drug users. *Infect Genet Evolut,* 2005;5(2):131–9. https://doi.org/10.1016/j.meegid.2004.08.001.

Pybus OG, Markov PV, Wu A, Tatem AJ. Investigating the endemic transmission of the hepatitis C virus. *Int J Parasitol.* 2007;37(8–9):839–49. https://doi.org/10.1016/j.ijpara.2007.04.009.

Raimondo G, Smedile A, Gallo L, Balbo A, Ponzetto A, Rizzetto M. Multicentre study of prevalence of HBV-associated delta infection and liver disease in drug-addicts. *Lancet*. 1982 Jan 30;1(8266):249–51. https://doi.org/10.1016/s0140-6736(82)90976-x.

Robertson JR. Drug users in contact with general practice. *Br Med J* (Clin Res Ed). 1985 Jan 5;290(6461):34–5. https://doi.org/10.1136/bmj.290.6461.34.

Robertson JR, Bucknall AB, Welsby PD, Roberts JJ, Inglis JM, Peutherer JF, Brettle RP. Epidemic of AIDS related virus (HTLV-III/LAV) infection among intravenous drug abusers. *Br Med J* (Clin Res Ed). 1986 Feb 22;292(6519):527–9. https://doi.org/10.1136/bmj.292.6519.527.

Roy K, Howie H, Sweeney C, et al. Hepatitis A virus and injecting drug misuse in Aberdeen, Scotland: a case-control study. *J Viral Hepat.* 2004;11:277–82.

Robson P. *Heroin and the Opioids, Historical Background. Forbidden Drugs* 2nd ed. Oxford University Press, Oxford 1999.

Rizzetto M, Smedile A, Ciancio A. Hepatitis D. In: Richman DD, Whitley RJ, Hayden FG, eds. *Clinical Virology*. 4th ed. ASM Press, Washington, DC, 2017, pp. 1409–23.

Rizzetto M, Hamid S, Negro F. The changing context of hepatitis D. *J Hepatol* 2021;74:1200–11.

Schrager L, Friedland G, Feiner C, Kahl P. Demographic characteristics, drug use, and sexual behavior of i.v. drug user with AIDS in Bronx, New York. *Public Health Rep.* 1991 Jan-Feb;106(1):78–84.

Smith DB, Pathirana S, Davidson F, Lawlor E, Power J, Yap PL, Simmonds P. The origin of hepatitis C virus genotypes. J Gen Virol. 1997 Feb;78 (Pt 2):321–8. https://doi.org/10.1099/0022-1317-78-2-321.

Steigmann, F., Hyman, S., and Goldbloom, R. Infectious hepatitis (homologous serum type) in drug addicts. *Gastroenterology* 15:642646,1950.

Stroffolini T, D'Egidio PF, Aceti A, Filippini P, Puoti M, Leonardi C, Almasio PL; DAVIS Drug Addicted, HCV Prevalence in Italy an Epidemiological, Observational, Cross-Sectional, Multicenter Study Participating Centers. Hepatitis C virus infection among drug addicts in Italy. *J Med Virol.* 2012 Oct;84(10):1608–12. https://doi.org/10.1002/jmv.23370.

Syed NA, Hearing SD, Shaw IS, et al. Outbreak of hepatitis A in the injecting drug user and homeless populations in Bristol: control by a targeted vaccination programme and possible parenteral transmission. *Eur J Gastroenterol Hepatol.* 2003;15:901–6.

UK immunisation schedule. (2022). In M. Ramsay (Ed.), *Immunisation against infectious disease.* https://assets.publishing.service.gov.uk/media/622faef9d3bf7f5a83369a4b/Greenbook-chapter-11-11Mar22.pdf

UKHSA. *UAM Survey of HIV and Viral Hepatitis Among People Who Inject Drugs (PWID), Data to End of 2022.* UK Health Security Agency, London, January 2024.

Van Ameijden EJ, Van den Hoek JA, Mientjes GH, Coutinho RA. A longitudinal study on the incidence and transmission patterns of HIV, HBV and HCV infection among drug users in Amsterdam. *Eur J Epidemiol.* 1993 May;9(3):255–62. https://doi.org/10.1007/BF00146260.

van Asten L, Verhaest L, Lamzira S, et al. The spread of Hepatitis C virus among European injecting drug users infected with HIV: a phylogenic analysis. *J Infecti Dis.* 2004;189:292–302.

van Santen DK, Coutinho RA, van den Hoek A, et al. Lessons learned from the Amsterdam Cohort Studies among people who use drugs: a historical perspective. *Harm Reduct J* 2021;18:2. https://doi.org/10.1186/s12954-020-00444-6.

Ventura-Cots M, Bataller R, Lazarus JV, Benach J, Pericàs JM. Applying an equity lens to liver health and research in Europe. *J Hepatol.* 2022 Dec;77(6):1699–710. https://doi.org/10.1016/j.jhep.2022.07.021.

World Drugs Report 2024. WDR24_Key_findings_and_conclusions.pdf.

World Health Organisation. 2024. https://www.who.int/health-topics/hepatitis.

World Health Organization. *WHO Consolidated Guidelines on HIV, Viral Hepatitis and STI Prevention, Diagnosis, Treatment and Care for Key Populations*. World Health Organization, Geneva, 2022.

Yakovleva A, Kovalenko G, Redlinger M, et al. Hepatitis C virus in people with experience of injection drug use following their displacement to Southern Ukraine before 2020. *BMC Infect Dis*. 2023;23(1):n.p.

3 Human Immunodeficiency Virus – Acquired Immune Deficiency Syndrome

Background

The astonishing figures of the HIV pandemic are updated regularly by the United Nations Programme on AIDS (UNAIDS), which is based in Geneva, and the World Health Organization. The worldwide epidemic affects most countries, and within countries, different populations are at risk (Piot 2001). Of all risk activities, injecting drugs is among the greatest; although for HIV to be transmitted, injecting conditions must include sharing with a partner who has already been infected. Prevention, therefore, is deceptively possible. As ever with drug use, injecting or other modes of use, the illegality and consequently the cryptic nature of the activity greatly add to the risk of unwise or reckless use.

Since the beginning of the epidemic, 91.4 million [range 73.4–116.4 million] people have been infected with the HIV virus and about 44.1 million [range 37.6–53.4 million] people have died from HIV-related causes

A press release from the UNAIDS organisation in September 2024 pointed out the advances made in the last twenty years (UNAIDS September 2024).

> The extraordinary advances made in the global HIV response are a success story of multilateralism. At the end of 2023, 30.7 million people out of a total of 39.9 million people living with HIV worldwide were on life-saving treatment – four times higher than the 7.7 million who were on treatment in 2010. Since 2010, AIDS-related deaths have been halved and new HIV infections among children have been reduced by 62%
>
> (UNAIDS. Leaders pledge bold action to end AIDS by 2030)

Globally, 40.8 million [37.0–45.6 million] people were living with HIV at the end of 2024. An estimated 0.7% [range 0.6–0.8%] of adults aged 15–49 years worldwide are living with HIV, although the burden of the epidemic continues to vary considerably between countries and regions.

The WHO African Region remains most severely affected, with nearly 1 in every 30 adults (3.1%) living with HIV and accounting for more than two-thirds of the people living with HIV worldwide.

DOI: 10.4324/9781003611097-3

In 2024, 1.3 million people were newly infected with HIV (estimates range from 1.1 million to 1.7 million) and 40.8 million (range 37–45.6 million) people were living with HIV in 2024. In the same year, 630,000 people died of AIDS-related illnesses.

Despite these alarming statistics, the United Nations has announced a target of 2030 to eliminate new cases of transmission of the virus. This ambitious proposal was included in a report released in July 2024 (AIDS at a crossroads UNAIDS).

However the report further raises concerns about the direction of travel towards eliminating new cases;

> The expansion of people accessing treatment is a landmark public health achievement that has seen AIDS-related deaths halved since 2010—from 1.3 million to 630 000 in 2023. However, the world is off track to meet the 2025 target of reducing AIDS-related deaths to below 250 000. Although tremendous progress has been made in preventing new HIV infections which have fallen by 39% since 2010 globally, and by 59% in eastern and southern Africa, the report shows that new HIV infections are rising in three regions, the Middle East and North Africa, Eastern Europe and central Asia and Latin America, and gaps and inequalities persist.

The report makes the important observation in relation to people who inject drugs. This risk group is clearly becoming an increasing focus of concern.

> People who inject drugs are disproportionally affected by HIV....In 2022, the relative risk of acquiring HIV was 14 times higher for people who inject drugs than for people in the overall adult population....Since 2019, among the 35 countries that reported the number of needles and syringes distributed per person who injects drugs per year by needle–syringe programmes, only three countries reported achieving the recommended more than 200 needles and syringes distributed per person who injects drugs per year.
>
> (UNAIDS 2024 2024 global AIDS report – The Urgency of Now: AIDS at a Crossroads)

Prevention initiatives including a longer acting pre-exposure treatment (PrEP) formulation give further optimism for eradicating HIV. PrEP is a primary prevention medication taken on a regular basis to prevent infection with HIV. There is considerable evidence that treatment in this way has decreased the risk of infection among men who have sex with men and more recently among people who inject drugs. Less information about its use among heterosexuals is available, and compliance among people who inject drugs has additional challenges (Murchu et al. 2022).

A long acting antiviral injection which can be administered every 2 months, and possibly up to once a year is licensed in the USA and the United Kingdom. The hope is that this will help to meet the ambition of ending new cases and HIV infection by the target date for the United Nations of 2030.

HIV/AIDS epidemic

The unveiling of the HIV epidemic did not happen quickly. From the early descriptions based on epidemiological tracking of a new unknown infectious agent, the world of science and medicine turned its huge resources to identifying the agent causing a "modern plague" and to trying to understand its mode of actions, transmissibility and pattern of pathologies in humans. As usual, the focus of research was based on what was already known about existing and novel viruses. The earlier discoveries of Marburg virus, after an outbreak in a laboratory in Germany in 1967, and of Ebola virus in Sudan and Zaire in 1976 alerted everyone to the emergence of modern virus infections in Africa. The rare outbreaks of haemorrhagic fever illnesses such as Marburg have now been reported in several sub-Saharan countries. The worst outbreak of Ebola in the 2014–2016 episode occurred in Guinea, then moved across land borders to Sierra Leone and Liberia. These viruses, which were new in humans, reignited infectious diseases as a clinical speciality which had been in decline since the apparent triumph of antibiotics over tuberculosis and bacterial infections. Mosquito-transmitted infections such as yellow fever had historically caused devastation but were controlled by vaccination, and efforts to control malaria were concentrating on anti-malarial drugs and the vision of a vaccine.

In the early days of HIV, there were outbreaks often identified and categorised by risk group. The sexually transmitted outbreaks in gay men in the USA and the heterosexually transmitted epidemic in sub-Saharan Africa, the blood transmitted outbreak in the recipients of blood donations and medical products, such as Factor 8, for people with haemophilia and the other blood-borne virus transmission risk group of injecting drug users. Cases of AIDS in other risk groups identified by ethnic origin, such as Haitian immigrants to the USA, were quickly reassigned to a more plausible risk activity. The super-infectivity of the haemorrhagic fevers appeared to not apply to HIV as simple observation of populations presenting didn't support this, but exactly how HIV was transmitted and who might be at risk was still unknown in the early 1980s.

Alarm bells were ringing in communities and medical circles. How infectious was HIV? Was it transmitted by close household or workplace contact in the absence of sexual contact? Was it transmitted by skin contact with body fluids? What was the incubation period and was everyone infected likely to get the full impact of the immune system destruction leading to uncontrollable infection (in hepatitis B studies it was clear that spontaneous recovery from infection was common)? Equally important, where had it come from and why now?

Conspiratory theories encouraged by prejudicial views of men who have sex with men, people who inject drugs and ethnic minorities and speculation about possible origins suggested an organised biological attack on these groups. Speculation about the origins was varied. The possibility that transmission of an immunodeficiency virus known to exist in a Simian population (SIV) during polio vaccine development in Kinshasa in the 1950s gained some credibility (Reinhardt and Roberts 1997, Hooper 2000). Kinshasa was the pre-colonial name of a town called Leopoldville (after King Leopold) when it was in the Belgian Congo.

After independence in 1960 it became the Democratic Republic of Congo. This transmission theory has, however, largely been discounted by genetic experts as the single origin of HIV in humans (Dickson 2000, Weiss 2001). The balance of the case against the introduction of SIV by this means seems to be that the polio vaccine was prepared from cells from a Macaque monkey which does not harbour a prototype virus and not chimpanzee tissue which, potentially, does.

The reuse of disposable injecting equipment in developing countries provides a different theory about the introduction of a primate virus into humans through serial passage of infected material (Drucker et al. 1991) In their article, they draw attention to the policy of the WHO which, until recently, allowed the reuse of injecting equipment up to 200 times in vaccination programmes provided "adequate" sterilisation procedures had been applied (WHO 1999). This policy and the widespread knowledge that scarce injecting equipment is reused in areas which are critically under-resourced for medical support lend a plausible explanation of the prevalence of HIV in some countries.

The use and ownership of injecting equipment in some countries such as Uganda became common as government control declined and private use by untrained medical practitioners raised concerns about the reuse of unsterile equipment (Birungi and Whyte 1994). In retrospect the massive spread of HIV/AIDS in that country must have been partially connected. Combined with the availability of non-prescribed antibiotics in many countries worldwide, including injectables, the risk of viral transmission is increased. In one study, 35 community surveys from five continents showed that non-prescription use occurred worldwide and accounted for 19–100% of antimicrobial use outside of northern Europe and North America (Morgan et al. 2011).

Further scientific evidence of the origins of HIV in human populations comes from genetic analysis of samples of immunodeficient people. Marx and colleagues concluded that:

> "We examined the rapid growth of unsterile injections in Africa beginning in the 1950s as a biologically plausible event capable of greatly increasing serial human passage of SIV and generating HIV by a series of multiple genetic transitions. We conclude that increased unsterile injecting in Africa during the period 1950–1970 provided the agent for SIV human infections to emerge as epidemic HIV in the modern era."
>
> (Marx et al. 2001)

In their analysis of epidemics of the state of transmission of haemorrhagic fevers by 2010, Allaranga and colleagues found that "*26 haemorrhagic epidemic outbreaks have been registered in 12 countries: 18 caused by the Ebola virus and eight by the Marburg virus. About 2551 cases have been reported, among which 268 were health workers (9.3%)*" (Allaranga et al. 2010).

The adoption of accounts of virus infections such as Ebola and HIV has been the source of many theories and incorporated into belief systems and cultural requirements. For some, the appropriation of plagues and epidemics into literature and media allows them to become analysed and characterised as "urban legends" (Weldon 2001). In historical terms, the unveiling of the nature and epidemiological characteristics of HIV emerged rapidly during the 1980s and 1990s, but translating evidence-based science into public health policy and, most importantly, into health care delivery is not always seamless and practical.

HBV/HIV coinfection

About 1% of persons living with HBV infection (2.7 million people) are also infected with HIV. Conversely, the global prevalence of HBV infection in HIV-infected persons is 7.4%. Since 2015, WHO has recommended treatment for everyone diagnosed with HIV infection, regardless of the stage of disease. Tenofovir, which is included in the treatment combinations recommended as first-line therapy for HIV infection, is also active against HBV (WHO).

The relative risk of acquiring HIV is 14 times higher for those who inject drugs than in the wider population globally. About one in eight people who inject drugs (an estimated 1.6 million) were living with HIV in 2022. The highest proportions of PWID who live with HIV continue to be reported in South-West Asia (29.4%), Eastern Europe (25.6%) and Southern Africa (22.3%), with rates twice as high as the global average (11.6%) (World Drugs Report 2024).

The Scottish experience of HIV/AIDS in context with what happened elsewhere

HIV was unknown in 1980 when the Edinburgh wave of heroin injecting erupted in Edinburgh and Dundee and Glasgow. Early warnings of the medical problems were of injection site problems, septic infections in skin and tissues, sudden overdose deaths, and initially the most worrying, for reasons in the previous chapter on hepatitis, blood-borne infections. Public Health officials were alerted to the hepatitis epidemic, and the local virology laboratory gathered data and stored samples for future reference. As in earlier studies predating HIV, hepatitis B infection was a marker of injecting drug use with shared equipment. Sadly, earlier studies came at a time when hepatitis B vaccination was not available, and the importance of hepatitis and the longer-term risk of cirrhosis and hepatocellular carcinoma was emerging but less well understood (Bewley et al. 1968, Sullman and Zuckerman 1971). By the early 1980s, hepatitis B should have been a warning sign of the risk of infectious diseases spread by injecting with shared equipment.

It is of importance that the Edinburgh and East of Scotland increase in heroin use was characterised by injecting as the principal, and sometimes the only, mode of administration at a time when much of heroin use in the rest of the United Kingdom was by inhalation. Subsequent studies confirmed that in other regions smoking and "chasing" by inhalation of heated heroin was and remained the preferred initiation into heroin use (Strang et al. 1992). During the initial wave of heroin injecting in Edinburgh from 1979 until 1982, the combination of high purity heroin and injecting accounted for many sudden deaths from overdose. The source of the Edinburgh

AIDS virus remains unclear although genetic typing of the virus circulating in Edinburgh and the East of Scotland suggests that it originated from a northern European transmission event and personal testimony of people using injection drugs supported a link with Amsterdam. Speculation about an American drug injector as a source of HIV infection or altrnatively the possibility of infection being acquired when Scottish fans travelled to Spain for the 1982 football World Cup were less credible. Individuals who had travelled, and injected heroin, in Kenya and West Africa similarly failed to gain any scientific support.

This headline from the local Edinburgh newspaper encapsulated the enormity of the introduction of the HIV infection agent.

> Some time within the last two years a person visited Edinburgh and left the City with a sinister legacy. Who it was and where they came from will never be known. Except that it was a drug addict, carrying the AIDS virus, who shared a needle with one or other of the local addicts and, as a result, launched Edinburgh on its trail of notoriety as the second-highest centre of AIDS virus-infected drug addicts in the World.
>
> (Evening News, 10 January, 1986)

Policy on supplying sterile equipment remained controversial until the publication of a report from a national (Scottish) committee which unreservedly demanded action including the supply of clean injecting equipment. The group suggested the supply of needles and syringes to prevent the practice of sharing injecting equipment and the scaling up of methadone treatment (Scottish Home and Health Department 1986, Brettle 1996).

A further report expanded recommendations in recognition of the potential needs of the female population of people at risk, already infected with HIV or contemplating or currently being pregnant. The report recognised the need for research

A CITY WAITS

AIDS

- A special Cabinet Committee set up by the Prime Minister to combat AIDS will almost certainly decide next week on a deal for free needles. Experts believe this is overdue.
- DRUG addicts will either be given clean needles free or on an exchange basis.
- IN Edinburgh, because of a shortage of needles, drug addicts have formed 'shooting galleries' to use the one and only syringe amongst a group of a dozen or more.
- THE disease has run rampant because of contaminated needles and next year, experts predict, 100 young Scots will die a certain death from AIDS.
- TODAY we look at the plight of Edinburgh's addicts.

SCOTLAND'S capital is facing an epidemic on a scale larger by far than any other British city.

And those in the front line, trying to fend off the contagion, believe one of the direct causes was a shortage of hypodermic syringes in Edinburgh's drug sub-culture.

Dr Roy Robertson, a GP in Edinburgh's Pilton and Muirhouse areas—where drug abuse is endemic—said:

"AIDS spread through Edinburgh at a quicker rate than it did in New York.

VIRUS

"Needles were in short supply from 1982 onwards for a variety of reasons.

"One of them was a decision not to allow addicts to be supplied them in the hope that this would control addiction.

"Another was intense police activity against dealers and users. Acting with the best of intentions they seized syringes during raids and took them away for evidence."

In other areas of Britain addicts can get supplies of purer heroin, which they can sniff or smoke rather than take intravenously.

For some odd reason, heroin available in Edinburgh was usually so impure that addicts were forced to inject it.

Free needles could halt the epidemic

By ARNOT McWHINNIE

In Glasgow however—it has about 5,000 heroin addicts compared to Edinburgh's 2000—the AIDS epidemic was not so calamitous.

There are, currently, 154 identified AIDS virus carriers in Glasgow, compared to about 1700 in Edinburgh.

No-one is complacent, however, and Liberal MP Archy Kirkwood believes that Glasgow is standing on the verge of an AIDS disaster.

Edinburgh junkies infected by the disease are travelling to the west to buy supplies.

Dr Robertson, serving on the Scottish Advisory Committee on the AIDS Virus, said:

"We have got to supply these addicts with clean, sterilised needles as soon as possible, in a bid to halt the epidemic.

"Those against this idea say it encourages drug abuse.

"The dangers of drug abuse addiction are considerably less than AIDS, and, as far as treatment and prevention is concerned, I believe AIDS has to be given priority."

Scots Secretary Malcolm Rifkind, and former Scots Health Minister [illegible] both against dishing out needles.

Mr MacKay is on record as having criticised the suggestion.

It would be wrong, according to him, for the Government to encourage the illegal consumption of drugs and for doctors to hand out needles.

There was a similar controversy in Amsterdam in 1984, when the health authorities started a "needle exchange scheme." Junkies got new needles for old.

DEATH

Critics promised a rise in drug addiction. There was none and, currently, about 100,000 needles are being distributed every year.

Scotland—and Edinburgh in particular—is in the front line of an epidemic disease which doctors are already likening to the Great Plague.

Studies have shown intravenous drug users catch the AIDS virus.

Not everyone who is a carrier goes on to develop the full blown disease, with no cure and an inevitable death.

But each carrier has a 30 per cent chance of getting it.

It is even affecting babies—26 have been born in Scotland to AIDS infected mothers—six in Tayside and 20 in Lothian.

The mothers of most were drug addicts who used dirty needles.

Between half and a third of these innocent young babies will go on to develop AIDS—and die.

That's why doctors like Roy Robertson believe that needles should be given to addicts urgently.

"I am not asking for them to be dished out by the bucketload, but surely doctors should be able to give them to anyone in danger of catching this

DRIVE YOUR HEATER IN FOR £15 PART EXCHANGE

Figure 3.1 The supply of injecting equipment was still controversial.

and to establish a clinical centre of treatment in the City Hospital. The expectation that palliative care facilities might also be urgently required set up a train of planning for an AIDS hospice (Scottish Home and Health Department, Report of the National Working Party on Health Service Implications of HIV Infection 1987). Almost as quickly as HIV spread among drug users in Edinburgh, the transmission pattern changed, and few new cases were recorded. Speculation and explanation about this pattern include the behaviour change in reducing sharing after the introduction of needle and syringe supplies and a plateau effect of an epidemic when all those at risk in the community are already infected or are immune by virtue of safer behaviour characteristics. The possibility that the self-termination of the epidemic was caused by the virus changing remains unproven (Burns et al. 1996). The follow-up research suggested that a change in the behaviour of people injecting in Edinburgh undoubtedly took place in the aftermath of the HIV epidemic (Peters et al. 1994).

Pathologists working in the city mortuary invariably chose to identify death from drugs as related to overdose but with little additional detail from post-mortem examination. Concerns were uncoordinated in other specialist services and police reactions to the supply of the heroin problem were limited due to a lack of resources allocated to the "drug problem". Control over the supply of injecting equipment was increased with a single commercial source closing at the height of the blood-borne virus epidemic (Robertson 1996).

In the early 1980s prior to the discovery of HIV in this population police officers from the Home Office UK Inspectorate, located in the Leeds office in the North of England, made occasional visits largely to monitor prescribing of "Controlled Drugs" such as diamorphine, cocaine and methadone. Concerns about the rapidly increasing numbers of people referred to and recorded on the UK Government's Addicts Index were viewed through a criminal justice lens and reactions were to tighten control. This was limited to an extent due to the poor allocation of resources in local police forces to monitor, detect and enforce the law, but the severity of sentencing policy in the courts reflected a punitive attitude.

Treatment of the effects of drug injecting was limited to management of symptoms, nursing care of wounds, skin lesions and injection sites, and antibiotics where necessary for sepsis. The symptoms of most cases of hepatitis resolved spontaneously, with a small number showing persistent and possibly ongoing disease progression when blood testing was available.

Treatment for opiate dependency was in crisis and, as in other centres, public health policy depended on local infrastructure, including law enforcement policy and practice, the law and the legal system prevalent at the time and the capacity of the health care system to adjust quickly to a new threat, in this case a threat surrounded in controversy. Described in an important PhD thesis examining the epidemic in Edinburgh, the postgraduate student examines the conditions and responses between 1982 and 1994 (Coyle 2008). In her thesis, she outlines the disagreement and controversy among the medical profession about participation in supplying needles and syringes and the restrictive rules employed by local health authorities. At the start, needles and syringes were to be limited to three sets and, although not mandatory, should be exchanged rather than given alone. Reluctance was shared by Ministers, and disagreement between Scottish and English health departments caused confusion. The Westminster Advisory Council initially advised against the supply of injecting equipment as it might encourage illegal drug injecting.

> On 9 April 1987, almost two years after the first study showed a high incidence of HIV amongst Edinburgh drug misusers, and amid much publicity and great reluctance on many fronts, the LHB *(Lothian Health Board)* needle exchange scheme opened its doors. Edinburgh was the first of the three schemes in Scotland to open. Dundee followed shortly after Edinburgh, but Glasgow took much longer due to local opposition, which resulted in a change of location. It was considered essential by the SHHD *(Scottish Government) to* set up a scheme in Glasgow despite the incidence of HIV infection amongst drug misusers being much lower compared with Edinburgh and Dundee. However, it was believed that Glasgow would serve to enable comparisons to be drawn between areas of low and high incidence of infection.
>
> (Coyle 2008)

Similar initial restrictions applied to the prescription of methadone, which was ironically, and to the dismay of the infectious diseases consultant leading the clinic, restricted by the local health authority to HIV-positive patients only.

AIDS was spreading in the USA. The early spread from the African continent to the USA seems to have come via Haiti and to have entered the east coast of the USA circulating cryptically in the United States for approximately 12 years before the recognition of AIDS in 1981 (Gilbert et al. 2007). The place of injecting drug use in the spread of HIV became increasingly significant once the virus enetered this population as sharing of injecting equipment was a perfect route of transmission among closely connected drug using communities.

Early warnings of the role that injecting drug use might play in the emerging AIDS epidemic were clear to some and alarm bells should have been louder in recognising the risk to the wider non-drug-using heterosexual population and the position of injecting drug use as a vector for this and other infectious diseases (Ron and Rogers 1989, Des Jarlais and Friedman 1987, Des Jarlais et al. 1996). Among people who inject drugs, an epidemic was being witnessed by dedicated hospital staff in New York and California. By 1984, the wards were filled with men and women dying of a mysterious wasting syndrome which was already prevalent in the gay communities in San Francisco, Florida and New York. The drug users were a different population. In the wards of the Montefiore Medical Centre at the Albert Einstein College of Medicine in the North Bronx, there were increasing numbers of young people with the characteristic signs and symptoms of AIDS. Opportunistic infections resulting from the failure of their immune system, diseases such as tuberculosis, cryptosporidium and sepsis, were complicated by addiction problems, poverty and mental health issues. The challenges for the health care system were enormous, and the risks and threats of contamination were unknown. Until 1985, no virus had been identified, and the nature of the presumed agent was unclear.

Critically important for understanding the illness and its transmission was the missing evidence of the period which occurred between transmission to an individual and the onset of symptoms. Previous experience of the incubation period of other viruses was assumed to be an indicator that the wasting and collapse of the immune system would take place a few months or slightly longer after infection. In fact, the time between entry of the HIV infection into the system and the onset of sufficient immune destruction is known now to be much longer. Infection may not be apparent for many years after the virus establishes itself in the body. This means that by the time symptoms emerge, the person may have been infected, and infectious, for years. Clearly this knowledge alters the understanding of how the virus can spread through susceptible communities for years before noticed.

The virus was isolated by scientists in the USA and in the Pasteur Institute in Paris at the same time between 1983 and 1984 and was initially called, by its US scientist Robert Gallo, HTLV3 (as it is similar to other already known Human T-lymphotropic viruses) and, by Luc Montagnier in Paris, LAV (Lymphadenopathy associated virus). The virus was later renamed HIV (Human Immunodeficiency Virus).

A laboratory test became available in 1985. This was a turning point in understanding and managing the AIDS epidemic. For the first time, it was possible to identify cases early, before the onset of symptoms. It was also possible to begin to understand the passage of the virus between individuals and in communities. New populations of infected people who had still not developed AIDS were identified. It was also possible to identify who was not infected, and groundbreaking research showed that transmission after contact with infected people was unlikely unless there had been significant exchange of body fluids. This included sexual intercourse, transmission during birth, injecting drug use with shared equipment, transfusion of contaminated blood products or, the less likely, penetrating wounds with a contaminated needle or sharp instrument. For people in the AIDS wards of hospitals in the USA research showing lack of transmission among household contacts was a relief (Friedland et al. 1986). This paper by Gerald Friedland and colleagues studied household contacts of index cases with HIV an HIV positive test who had lived in the same household for at least 3 months. Of the 101 non-sexual contacts, only one was HIV positive, a five-year-old child. This child was considered to have contracted the infection perinatally.

Extract from a physician's diary 1986

> I was sitting in a bar in Manhattan with Andrew Moss, an internationally renowned epidemiologist from San Francisco, talking about the spectre of a heterosexual epidemic and wondering if we were the only people in the Western World that understood the gravity of what we had discovered in the drug using population. We were aware that politicians and public health officials in western countries were focused on the MSM community and the disastrous mortality in that group. Energised by activists and articulate lobbying groups there was no doubt where the drive for change was coming from.

> People who inject drugs, and, perhaps more importantly, their heterosexual partners represented an entry for AIDS into the general population. This group was without a vocal leader and were excluded from most opportunities to influence change. The prospect of an epidemic on the scale emerging in African countries seemed to us something we had to do something about. Official estimates are only just realising the enormity of the pandemic.

The newspaper cutting, below, draws attention to the emerging realisation that early numbers of worldwide prevalence of AIDS were wildly underestimates of the possible caseload. Even the speculation in this report were totally ignorant of the real situation which was of several hundred thousand in the USA and many more in Africa.

Belief in the relative safety of those outside "risk groups" took time to become embedded. Organisations quite rightly looked at procedures and safety measures to minimise any potential body fluid or blood exposure. Among social, police and other public services, anxiety about possible contamination and transmission of HIV infection was everywhere. New measures and guidelines emerged to address real and imagined concerns; some organisations debated the introduction of disposable drinking vessels, including the Communion Cup. All began to recognise a new era in hygiene and responsible health protection.

The media in print and screen adopted varying approaches. Speculation about the scale of the epidemic and ways to prevent further transmission gave rise to alarming headlines warning of further things to come.

Others reported the actions of Government.

The education message was important for other headline writers trying, at times desperately, to introduce an important reassurance to the readers that there were ways to avoid infection.

100,000 may have AIDS

PARIS, Monday. – AIDS, the disease once thought mostly to afflict homosexual men and drug addicts, is crossing all geographical and sociological barriers and may have infected as many as 100,000 people around the world, the head of the World Health Organisation said today.

Dr Hafdan Mahler told an international gathering of 2,500 AIDS specialists here that official figures accounting for less than 30,000 AIDS cases worldwide were a "gross underestimation."

"Extrapolating from studies, ... a generous global estimate of the number of AIDS cases would probably not exceed 100,000," he said at the start of the three-day conference.

Speakers of the opening session expressed cautious optimism that a vaccine could be produced, though it might not be available for general use for some time.

The conference chairman Prof Jean-Claude Gluckman, said researchers agreed that genetic engineering would lead to a vaccine "in the long run" and that "first trials have been encouraging."

Prof Luc Montagnier, whose French team discovered the AIDS virus, said it should be known by the end of this year if a vaccine could protect chimpanzees. "But I think it will be a long time before it is in general use in man," he added.

Washington: Employers who believe they are taking action to prevent the spread of AIDS may discriminate against people afflicted with the disease, the Justice Department said today.

The office of legal counsel in the federal Government's legal branch ruled that the nation's civil rights laws provide some protection to victims of the virus.

According to the ruling if a person was dismissed from a job or excluded from a federal programme solely because he suffered from the effects of AIDS, his dismissal would be illegal if he is otherwise qualified for the position.

However, if the person was excluded because of concern by the employer that he would spread the disease, the dismissal generally would be legal unless the fear of spreading it was merely "a pretext for discrimination."

A spokesman for the American Civil Liberties Union said his organisation was "very disturbed that the Justice Department has taken the position that AIDS victims can be fired, and that they're essentially not protected by the civil rights laws." – Reuter and AP.

Scotsman 24·6·86

Figure 3.2 The estimates at the second international AIDS conference in Paris were still a wild underestimate of the size of the pandemic.

These and other media communications were transmitting a message of some hysteria and panic based on inadequate information but also prejudice and hyperbole.

Anxiety verging on panic was prevalent elsewhere. Typified by the celebrated "Florida dentist case", the public and medical establishment were concerned about the transmission of HIV infection by routes other than the clearly defined areas of sexual transmission and blood-to-blood contact through transfusion or injection of contaminated products. The case of the dentist in a small town in Florida alleged that he had transmitted HIV to patients by contaminated equipment and procedures. Initially, the Centre for Disease Control suggested that this was the case, but controversy remained, and further evidence made the mode of transmission unclear (Barr 1990).

What was clear was the need to overhaul, inspect and regulate medical and surgical procedures and to provide a new level of evidence to support acceptable standards.

An extract from a clinician's diary

My experience and interest in people who use drugs began as a postgraduate in Edinburgh hospitals where occasionally young people with addiction to heroin were in the wards with other issues such as hepatitis B (hepatitis C was unknown at that time). These cases were unusual outside the psychiatry department which was established as in 1968 under the new designated Drug Dependency Unit for South East Scotland. Even then numbers were small, and a research worker called Moya Woodside reported on the first 3 years of the unit in 1973. Her paper was entitled the "The First 100 referrals to a Scottish Drug Treatment centre.

In another report from a Scottish hospital, between 1949 and 1960 there were 120 admissions to hospital with addiction problems (a mixture of heroin,

AIDS

HOW MANY PEOPLE WILL GET IT FOR CHRISTMAS?

[redacted]

Deadly warning . . . one of the posters

£20m war on AIDS

THE government yesterday stepped up the fight against AIDS into a £20 million crusade.

Health Secretary Norman Fowler announced that a special health education authority will be set up in April next year to co-ordinate a nationwide campaign against the disease.

And he revealed during a special Commons debate that £20 million will be available for a public information campaign — four times the original suggested figure.

The advertising campaign will spell out in explicit language the threat posed by AIDS, which has already killed 284 people in Britain.

The 12-month campaign starts in newspapers on Sunday and will be stepped up over Christmas.

There will also be posters in 1500 sites around the country, a youth campaign using magazines, radio and cinema and a New Year leaflet drop to 23 million households accompanied by TV and radio advertising.

FOWLER'S CRUSADE: SEE PAGES 4 AND 5

Figure 3.3 The advertising campaign was brutally direct.

Daily Record – Thursday 4 December 1986 – Page 34.Reproduced with permission Reach plc.

THE INDEP

No 41 SATURDAY 22 NOVEMB

Rock star, DJ and blunt language will launch government campaign to change sexual habits

£20m bid to halt spread of Aids disease

Figure 3.4 Identifying those affected and range of interventions.

Independent newspaper front page Saturday 22nd November 1986.Reproduced with permission Independent Digital News & Media Ltd.

barbiturates, and amphetamines). Sixty-five of these cases were doctors or nurses.

But during an explosive period of heroin availability beginning in 1979 or 1980 something new and incredible happened. For the first time heroin became available in a purity previously unknown (colleagues at the time reported from New York a purity of 5–10% whereas we were finding 50% plus). This was circulating in communities in Scotland know to have a high level of inequalities.

At the same time social unrest was being reported in English cities. Lord Scarman's report linked some of this to racial tensions but also noted the poor state of inner cities as a contributory factor (Scarman Report 1981).

THE TIM

No 62,622 SATURDAY NOVEMBER 22 1986

Fowler's £20m shock package in war on Aids

Figure 3.5 Government in the UK was finally responding after a visit by the Health Minister to San Francisco.

Permission from News UK / News Licensing.

SCOTTISH DAILY EXPRESS

Wednesday May 7 1986 • 20p

THE VOICE OF SCOTLAND

Doctors warn : Stay faithful and live

NEW AIDS NIGHTMARE

Epidemic fear for thousands

Figure 3.6 Headline suggests that sex outside a single relationship is dangerous.

Permission from News UK / News Licensing.

In my practice in North West Edinburgh, we were having daily encounters with people injecting heroin and using this is a way likely to cause harm from infection, sudden death and hostile encounters with a poorly prepared criminal justice system. Needles and syringes were confiscated by the police and a local supplier who bravely supplied clean equipment was closed down. People using heroin were young, many having left local schools the year before and had little or no knowledge of the dangers of injecting heroin. Our patients were injecting three times more often and sharing with twice as many people as their counterparts in Glasgow. Between 1982 and 1986 syringes contaminated with heroin were being used as evidence of possession of a Class A drug and dealers began to insist that they were used on the premises. Treatment services were likewise unprepared and local and voluntary groups became activists advocating for their miserable clients.

Conditions couldn't have been contrived in a more efficient way for the spread of a blood-borne virus such as HIV and it was clear that the health and social care systems as well as the criminal justice sector were struggling in unfamiliar territory.

Notes from another Edinburgh doctor practising in the community at the time

As things unfolded there was a timeline with key events and dates which seem, to me, to illustrate the story of drugs and AIDS in Edinburgh during the period we are talking about. The realisation in 1980 – 1982 that we had an "epidemic" of heroin availability and drug injecting in groups sharing needles and syringes.

- *The availability and subsequent testing in 1985 for HTLV3 (HIV) of stored blood samples originally taken to look for hepatitis B infection.*

- *The organisation of Ward 7a, Milestone House and community care, the Church, voluntary groups, social work etc. The cavalry hadn't exactly arrived, but groups of dedicated people were inventing systems to manage a vulnerable and traumatised caseload.*
- *Groundbreaking research into heterosexual transmission of HIV which showed a very small transmission rate in our population. This was in collaboration with the Middlesex hospital and the European Research group (the resulting paper was published in the* New England Journal of Medicine *in 1984).*
- *The launch of an effective antiviral chemotherapy in 1995, Sadly too late for many of our patients.*

I was the community medicine doctor responsible for controlling infectious diseases were desperate to ensure that sufficient supplies of clean needles could be available. We were in uncharted territory. Needles and syringes were not allowed on prescription or by supply from doctors, methadone was recommended but in short-term reducing doses only. Until the mid-1980s, when the HIV test became available, sexual transmission was not a priority. Confrontation with the police and social services was common and specialist services increasingly limited as the Drug Dependency Unit closed its engagement with heroin users in 1984 and, until a new unit opened in the infectious diseases ward, for people who were using drugs admission to hospital was not possible.

Another GP diary entry, 1986

> Managing young people in the Practice with a lethal illness was a new experience and a considerable challenge. Managing our caseload of 300 known heroin users (there were undoubtedly many more) was difficult and looking back at case notes we were struggling with guidelines which were designated for the 1960s and a stigma and prejudice that was institutionalised from Government down to local services. Overdose deaths were common, multiple members in families were taking drugs, parents were distressed, and children were at risk. Support came from Ray's unit, Scottish Aids Monitor, Milestone House and local groups such as the North Edinburgh Drug Advice Centre and, together, we did our best to help to help individuals and families struggling in a World changing by the day. An extraordinary set of experiences of talking to politicians, researchers from TV and media companies and collaborations with research groups around the world emerged.

Other personal testimonies of the early days of the AIDS epidemic in the United States are many, but one evocative account of the early unfolding alarm and panic that spread as cases emerged in units outside the bigger cities is included in the extraordinary book by a physician working in Johnson City, Tennessee. The first case experience in the intensive care unit was a young man returning to his home county after living in New York. The harrowing account of the final illness and death from pneumocystis pneumonia describes the combination of alarm, outrage, prejudicial attitudes again homosexuality and the complete ignorance of the nature of the virus. The panic and confusion are vividly described as each member of the clinical team who participated in a cardiac arrest resuscitation attempt considered his or her exposure to blood, sweat and other body fluids of the dying man during attempts to resuscitate. The account of these events was published in his book "My Own Country" in 1994, by which time infectivity was more clearly defined and risks better understood, but the stigma and prejudice associated with AIDS and its links with homosexuality and drug use still resonated.

The experience in the main centres of the AIDS epidemic, New York, Florida and California, inevitably spread around the country. Personal accounts of a more secret and insidious spread of the virus far from the protests and energy of the activists and outspoken public health officials emerged. By 1988, seven years into the epidemic and with no active treatment, accounts from Johnson City in Tennessee described an evolving caseload without the support or resources of the major centres.

> I had assumed that the customs and conventions of monolithic institutions like the NIH, FDA and CDC were carved in stone, handed down from God not amenable to change. But gay men in the form of ACT UP had done what cancer patients, diabetes, lung disease patients, heart disease patients had never done: they questioned authority and brought about change.
>
> But in our town, we simply watched the television spectacle of mass arrests, heard the fiery speeches, saw the five second newsflash of a bridge being blocked by activists. My patients were, by contrast, were in hiding. They were not included in a public demonstration of any sort, scared least the tragedy of their HIV infection be compounded by their neighbours'' knowledge of it
>
> (Abraham Veghese. My Own Country, a doctor's story).

Insights into the passage of HIV in human populations allowed researchers to look around the world at the state of the pandemic. Attention turned to Africa where the disease was already widespread in the heterosexual population. The realisation emerged that the global pandemic was considerably greater in the heterosexual population and those born to infected mothers. Testing revealed a massive and alarming prevalence in several sub-Saharan countries, enough to not only impact lives but economies and whole populations. Over the years following the introduction of the test, the impact of the worldwide pandemic unfolded and for people who use drugs by injection, their place as a pool of infection and an introduction into the wider heterosexual population became an imperative for governments.

Testing was not always available in poorer countries at the onset of availability, and regrettably, the confusion and misinformation about AIDS as a disorder inhibited logical public health interventions and prevention programmes. Mixed in with this was the residual anxiety about casual spread, which, along with prejudice against minority groups, generated hostility and anxiety. In most countries, a proliferation of guidance led to widespread access to testing for those at risk or concerned. Cultural, traditional and political orders were challenged, and adjustments were piecemeal and gradual. Examples of setbacks included the outright denial of Thabo Mbeki, who served as president of South Africa from 1999 to 2008. He delayed the implementation of antiretroviral therapy until late 2003, suggesting that AIDS might be caused by poverty and that there needed to be investigation into alternative causes of the disease. Research has suggested that these delays caused hundreds of thousands of preventable deaths (Chigwedere et al. 2008).

In Scotland, the first sign that HIV had arrived in the drug-using population came when the first test for the HTLV-3 virus was carried out on people attending the accident and emergency department in Edinburgh Royal Infirmary. The results were published in the *Lancet* journal (Peutherer et al. 1985) and subsequently elaborated on in a study of a cohort of injecting drug users attending a general practice in North West Edinburgh (Robertson et al. 1986). Testing followed in other groups to try to assess the potential spread into the heterosexual population (Scott et al. 1997) and research in collaboration with other UK centres followed a cohort of people who had acquired infection from injecting heroin to see if their non-drug-using heterosexual partners had become infected; mostly they had not. This was an important finding and, added to the finding of Friedland and colleagues in New York in household contacts, gave some comfort. Anxiety remained in the press and medical extablishment of the possible extension of spread to children and neighbouring centres of drug using popuations. (Ronald et al. 1993, Downs and De Vincenzi 1996).

Since the 1980s, the number of reports of cases of HIV has changed, and numbers have declined, as reported by *Public Health Scotland.*

- In 2023, a total of 385 reports of HIV diagnoses were recorded in Scotland. This includes 126 first-time diagnoses. Since 2017, the annual number of first-ever diagnoses recorded has nearly halved, decreasing from 226 to 126.
- For the second successive year, the majority of new reports (67%, 259/385) were previously known diagnoses, largely due to a continued increase in infections acquired through heterosexual sexual intercourse and diagnosed outwith Scotland.
- Recently acquired HIV infections (within the previous 3–4 months) continue to decline.
- At 31 December 2023, an estimated 6,761 people were living with HIV in Scotland. Of the 6,288 (93%) diagnosed, 78% (4,926/6,288) received Anti Retroviral Treatment between 1 July 2022 and 31 December 2023, and 97% (4,795/4,926) had a suppressed viral load By 2025 the transmission categories had changed and the majority of cases were among heterosexual people who had acquired the infection outside Scotland.

THE SHOCKING FACTS ABOUT DRUGS

BRITAIN'S 'HABIT' NOW AT £400m A YEAR

Community

Children in AIDS nightmare

By MARGARET HARKER

Early cure unlikely

Figure 3.7 For the first time in the UK, children were infected with HIV.

Edinburgh Evening News 3rd September 1985.Copyright of The Scotsman and used with their kind permission.

HIV remains a risk for people who inject drugs

The recurrence of HIV among drug injectors in Scotland came as a surprise in Glasgow in 2015, although, in retrospect, it may have been predicted, among the homeless and disenfranchised population in the city centre. The research team that investigated the reasons behind the outbreak concluded that,

> Despite high coverage of harm reduction interventions, Glasgow has experienced a rapid rise in prevalence of HIV among its PWID population, associated with homelessness, incarceration, and a major shift to injection of cocaine. Robust surveillance through regular HIV testing of high-risk

SCOTLAND'S NEWSPAPER

CITY EDITION

GLASGOW HERALD

LANGS SUPREME SCOTCH WHISKY

204th year—No. 258

SATURDAY, NOVEMBER 22, 1986

Twenty Five Pence

Lander Alarms 041-429 5711

THINK WHAT YOU COULD BE MISSIN

Aids explosion forecast in Glasgow

By STUART TROTTER Political Correspondent

Editorial Comment: Page 6

Figure 3.8 There were understandable fears that the people who inject drugs in Glasgow would be the next high-risk group for contracting HIV.

With permission from the Glasgow Herald (now the Herald).

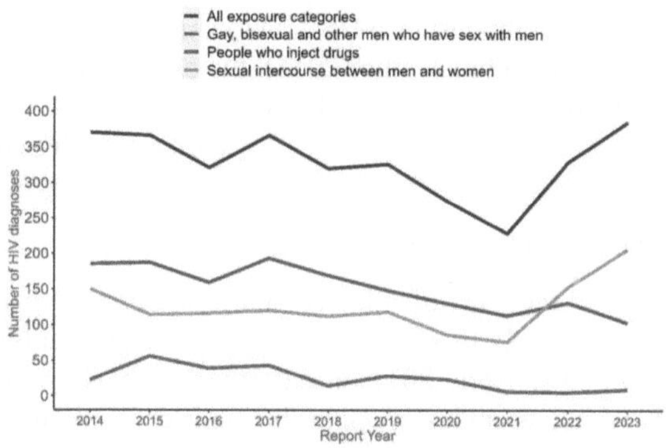

Figure 3.9 The majority of new cases reported in Scotland are now in people who have acquired the infection outside Scotland by heterosexual transmission.

Source: Public Health Scotland (HIV in Scotland Update to 31 December 2023, revised 14 January 2025).

populations is crucial to ensure outbreaks are detected and rapid responses are informed by the best available evidence.

(McAuley et al. 2019)

Among the other causal factors identified, the rise in cocaine injecting is interesting as this had been less of a problem in previous virus infection incidents, which were at a time when the predominant drug of injection was heroin. It is interesting that studies from the US HIV epidemic of the early 1980s clearly identified cocaine injecting as an aggravating factor in transmission due to the frequency of injections with this drug (Anthony et al. 1991, Chaisson et al. 1989). More recently similar episodes have indicated cocaine, with or without heroin, is responsible for HIV transmission in people who inject drugs (Arendt et al. 2019).

These studies underscore the importance of targeted harm reduction strategies, including needle and syringe exchange programmes, supervised consumption facilities and comprehensive HIV testing and treatment services, to mitigate the risk of HIV transmission among people who inject drugs. In other communities the riks of stigma, racial prjudice and incarceration decrease uptake in testing people who use drugs for HIV. (Wise 2023).

The recent Glasgow outbreak is by no means over despite intensive interventions to reduce injecting and sharing of equipment. These measures include the opening of a Heroin Assisted Treatment Clinic and a Safe injecting facility in the city centre. Surveillance in the 2022 study shows that

More than half of participants in 2019–20 who were found to have chronic HCV or HIV (based on their anonymous dried blood spot test) reported that they were unaware of their infection. Seventy-three cases of HIV were detected in 2019–20, equating to a national prevalence of 3.1%. Most of these cases were interviewed at sites in NHS Greater Glasgow and Clyde

> (GGC) (n=49) and neighbouring NHS Lanarkshire (n=16). In NHS GGC (the setting of an HIV outbreak since 2015), the prevalence of HIV has stabilised at 4.8% in both the 2017–18 and 2019–20 surveys.
>
> (Public Health Scotland 2022)

HIV/AIDS in the USA and Europe

During the discovery of the HIV infection epidemic among young drug injectors in Edinburgh and Dundee, early reports of almost identical problems were emerging in Dublin (O'Kelly and O'Kelly 2012) and northern Italy (Lazzarin et al. 1985). Amsterdam, a city with a recent history of problematic drug use, which was an early adopter of harm reduction measures such as easy access to injecting equipment and opiate agonist treatment, recorded a rise in the number of cases over the early years of the 1980s, but significantly not the rapid increase seen in these other centres (van Santen et al. 2021).

In the USA, problems emerged early among injecting drug users in California and New York City, where an existing population of people using injecting heroin had been increasing over the previous decade. In his epic journalistic account of the spread of HIV in the gay communities of San Francisco, New York and the Florida Keys, Randy Shilts traces the unfolding of a "gay plague" of infection killing tens of thousands of people, mainly men (Bois 1981). He recognises injecting drug use as a coexisting risk group and the threat they pose to the heterosexual population (Shilts 1987). AIDS arrived as a catastrophic wave of cachectic and terminally-ill people at a time before the test for HTLV3 (HIV) was available. Prior to 1985, when the antibody test became available, this clinical caseload was managed by physicians in state-run hospitals and largely treated people for the complications of a collapsed immune system, with the expectation that they had little time to live. The experience in these wards, at a time of little knowledge of the cause and infectivity of the unknown virus, was difficult and at times frightening for clinical staff and terrifying for a caseload with little resources. The household contact study was an important source of some encouragement that medical staff were only at risk if suffering from a penetrating injury involving infected human body fluid (Friedland et al. 1986). Peter Selwyn, one of the young physicians at the time, has an extensive canon of publications resulting from his experience in the Bronx as a clinician treating people who had become ill with the virus infections because of transmission during injecting drugs. He has spent most of his career at Montefiore and Einstein medical centre, where he became professor of family and social medicine, of epidemiology and population health, of medicine and of psychiatry and behavioural sciences. He is chair of family and social medicine and director of the palliative care programme at Montefiore.

When asked more recently about the way AIDS in people who use drugs was unfolding and what the key challenges in HIV/AIDS today were, Professor Selwyn commented that "access to care, especially internationally. And while people with HIV are living longer, they are experiencing a whole range of early chronic illnesses: heart disease, diabetes, lung disease—and on and on. This is the second wave of HIV" (Selwyn 1998).

HIV/AIDS elsewhere around the world

It is an often overlooked fact that in 2024, 30% of the global HIV epidemic outside sub-Saharan Africa is among injecting drug users. This has caused alarm among United Nations agencies. Nearly 10% of global HIV infections are due to unsafe injecting drug use. The difficulties faced by people who use drugs in many countries have given rise to human rights initiatives and increasing grassroots organisations representing a population with multiple social, mental health and suffering from stigma and prejudice issues (UNAIDS 2024).

The importance of injecting drug use as a major factor in the spread of HIV took some time to be recognised but now people who inject drugs are responsible for the majority of incident infections in the USA and Europe. In other countries, there is a rapid growth in injecting drug use, a consequence of which is sporadic outbreaks of HIV transmission and a rising prevalence (Mann and Tarantola 1996, Stimson 1993).

In response to increasing concerns about the rising numbers of people who use drugs in countries such as India, Pakistan, Iran and many other countries, UNAIDS has issued a "Call for urgent action to improve coverage of HIV services for injecting drug users". This urgent alert follows from a review of the scale of HIV prevention services across the world and the belief that prevention is possible if opiate treatment services, provision of injecting equipment and investment in support for men and women who use injection drugs or are in sexual relationships with someone who does. Services, in the words of UNAIDS, should allow "access to services for all drug users.UNAIDS believes that drug users can be protected from becoming infected with HIV if comprehensive, evidence-informed and human-rights-based interventions are made accessible to all drug users". The needs of marginalised groups and women should be considered in routine service provision (Giang 2023, Ibitoye 2024). A rapid response in the event of outbreaks of injection related virus transmission requires a public health awarenes with the ability to respond quickly and decisively to a crisis (Palayew 2024).

While harm minimisation has become mainstream in many European and North American administrations, there are still a range of political, cultural and economic barriers to instituting even basic services in many countries. Institutional stigma pervades governments and the electorate in democratic countries, and examples of harsh penalties for drug possession – and even, in a few countries, the death penalty for trafficking – still exist. In a larger number of countries, including some Western democracies, the provision of injecting equipment and specific substance dependency treatments remains controversial.

The damaging impact of US cuts in aid, particularly in Africa, has threatened treatment and prevention services, and reports in the Lancet outline the scale of this disaster for the continent.

> The sudden cessation of PEPFAR funding by the US government will likely result in tens of thousands of HIV deaths and new infections. Conclusions from one study are grim; "USAID funding has significantly contributed to the reduction in adult and child mortality across low-income and middle-income countries over the past two decades. Our estimates show that, unless the abrupt funding cuts announced and implemented in the first half of 2025 are reversed, a staggering number of avoidable deaths could occur by 2030."
>
> (Calvacanti 2025).
>
> These losses of life and health should compel the United States government to rapidly and fully re-instate one of the most successful health programs in history.
>
> (Hontelez et al. 2025)

Conclusion

Much has been learned since the first description of a cluster of cases of AIDS in the USA in 1981. The unfolding pandemic in the few years following that gradually exposed national disasters in Africa, Europe and North America. Epidemics in different countries and populations had similar clinical outcomes but individual characteristics and widely varying responses. Prejudice, denial and fear translated into poor policy and unnecessary suffering. Lessons had to be learned and relearned as new populations turned out to have HIV present. Drug users continue to be low down on priority agendas in many, if not most, countries and examples of open hostility and persecution are not unusual in varying degrees. In the year 2024, as reported by UNAIDS, the position of drug injectors as 10% of new HIV infections causes considerable cause for concern. This global figure for HIV infections are due to unsafe injecting drug use. The availability of proven prevention measures such as needle and syringe and opiate agonist treatment programmes is far from universal and depends on political insight and public awareness. Media campaigns have an important role to in encouraging engagement with services such as opiate agonist treatment and blood-borne virus testing (Ross 1993).

The need for education and public health is present in many if not most countries, and the critical role of a functional community-based public health care system is often overlooked in favour of temporarily funded projects established to manage crises. It is often said that it takes a crisis to make change, but once the crisis passes, lessons in prevention require constant vigilance and maintenance of prevention measures. Fortunately the expeience of prevention services in New York during the COVID-19 pandemic demonstarted some resilience in services designed to prevent virus transmission (Des Jarlais 2023)

Success stories are however not absent. The discovery of the virus by labs in the USA and France and the nature of HIV infection, its infectivity and the limits of contagion have largely allowed for informed education and public health responses. The testing of Zidovudine as a treatment and the discovery of the Highly Active

Antiretroviral Therapy in 1996 transformed the treatment and changed AIDS from an inevitably fatal disease to one with a treatment which didn't cure but did suspend the progression of the disease.

It is not too much of an exaggeration to say that the AIDS pandemic had a seismic effect onthe management of patients and the delivery of health care. Confidentiality, stigma, consentto use information, septic techniques, data keeping and sharing were all scrutinised in a new paradigm and changed forever. Activists in the HIV communities were responsible for arevolution in all these areas and more. Recognition of gay rights and a humanitarian approach to vulnerable and stigmatised groups demanded reassessment of attitudes and responsibilities from Government and Local Authorities to grassroots delivery of services.

The world had changed.

References

Allaranga Y, Kone ML, Formenty P, Libama F, Boumandouki P, Woodfill CJ, Sow I, Duale S, Alemu W, Yada A. Lessons learned during active epidemiological surveillance of Ebola and Marburg viral hemorrhagic fever epidemics in Africa. *East Afr J Public Health.* 2010 Mar;7(1):30–6.

Anthony JC, Vlahov D, Nelson KE, Cohn S, Astemborski J, Solomon L. New evidence on intravenous cocaine use and the risk of infection with human immunodeficiency virus type 1. *Am J Epidemiol.* 1991 Nov 15;134(10):1175–89. https://doi.org/10.1093/oxfordjournals.aje.a116021.

Arendt V, Guillorit L, Origer A, Sauvageot N, Vaillant M, Fischer A, Goedertz H, François JH, Alexiev I, Staub T, Seguin-Devaux C. Injection of cocaine is associated with a recent HIV outbreak in people who inject drugs in Luxembourg. *PLoS One.* 2019 May 16;14(5):e0215570. https://doi.org/10.1371/journal.pone.0215570.

Barr S. The 1990 Florida dental investigation: is the case really closed? *Ann Intern Med.* 1996 Jan 15;124(2):250–4. https://doi.org/10.7326/0003-4819-124-2-199601150-00009.

Bewley TH, Ben-Arie O, Marks V. Morbidity and mortality from heroin dependence. 3. Relation of hepatitis to self-injection techniques. *Br Med J.* 1968 Mar 23;1(5594):730–2. https://doi.org/10.1136/bmj.1.5594.730.

Birungi H, Whyte SR. Injections in Uganda -- cause for concern. *Essent Drugs Monit.* 1994;(18):11–2. PMID: 12288385.

Bois RMD, Branthwaite MA, Mikhail JR, Batten JC. 1981. Primary pneumocystis carinii and cytomegalovirus infections. *Lancet.* 1981;318. https://doi.org/10.1016/S0140-6736(81)91353-2help_outline

Brettle RP. Clinical features of drug use and drug use related HIV. *Int J STD AIDS.* 1996 May Jun;7(3):151–65. https://doi.org/10.1258/0956462961917483.

Brown AJL, Lobidel D, Wade CM, et al. The molecular epidemiology of human immunodeficiency virus type 1 in six cities in Britain and Ireland. *Virology* 1997;235:166–77. https://doi.org/10.1006/viro.1997.8656.

Burns SM, Brettle RP, Gore SM, Peutherer JF, Robertson JR. The epidemiology of HIV infection in Edinburgh related to the injecting of drugs: an historical perspective and new insight regarding the past incidence of HIV infection derived from retrospective HIV antibody testing of stored samples of serum. *J Infect.* 1996 Jan;32(1):53–62. https://doi.org/10.1016/s0163-4453(96)80010-7.

Cavalcanti DM, de Oliveira Ferreira de Sales L, da Silva AF, et al. Evaluating the impact of two decades of USAID interventions and projecting the effects of defunding on mortality up to 2030: a retrospective impact evaluation and forecasting analysis. *Lancet.* 2025;406(10500):283-294. https://doi.org/10.1016/S0140-6736(25)01186-9

Chaisson RE, Bacchetti P, Osmond D, Brodie B, Sande MA, Moss AR. Cocaine use and HIV infection in intravenous drug users in San Francisco. *JAMA*. 1989 Jan 27;261(4):561–5.

Chigwedere P, Seage, G R, Gruskin, S JD, Lee, T-H, Essex, M. Estimating the Lost Benefits of Antiretroviral Drug Use in South Africa. *JAIDS*. 2008;49(4):410–5. https://doi.org/10.1097/QAI.0b013e31818a6cd5.

Coyle H. 2008. *A Tale of One City: A History of HIV/AIDS Policy-Making in Edinburgh, 1982–1994*. PhD thesis, University of Edinburgh.

Des Jarlais DC, Friedman SR. HIV infection among intravenous drug users: epidemiology and risk reduction. *AIDS*. 1987 Jul;1(2):67–76.

Des Jarlais DC, Stimson GV, Hagan H, Perlman D, Choopanya K, Bastos FI, Friedman SR. Emerging infectious diseases and the injection of illicit psychoactive drugs. *Curr Issues Public Health* 1996;2:102–37.

Des Jarlais DC, Weng CA, Feelemyer J, McKnight C. COVID-19 vaccination and HIV transmission among persons who inject drugs during the first two years of the COVID-19 pandemic in New York City. *Harm Reduct J*. 2023 May 3;20(1):63. https://doi.org/10.1186/s12954-023-00791-0.

Dickson D. Tests fail to support claims for origin of AIDS in polio vaccine. *Nature*. 2000 Sep 14;407(6801):117. https://doi.org/10.1038/35025249.

Downs AM, De Vincenzi I. Probability of heterosexual transmission of HIV: relationship to the number of unprotected sexual contacts. European Study Group in Heterosexual Transmission of HIV. *J Acquir Immune Defic Syndr Hum Retrovirol*. 1996 Apr 1;11(4):388–95. https://doi.org/10.1097/00042560-199604010-00010.

Drucker E, Alcabes PG, Marx PA. The injection century: massive unsterile injections and the emergence of human pathogens. *Lancet*. 2001 Dec 8;358(9297):1989–92. https://doi.org/10.1016/S0140-6736(01)06967-7.

Friedland GH, Saltzman BR, Rogers MF, Kahl PA, Lesser ML, Mayers MM, Klein RS. Lack of transmission of HTLV-III/LAV infection to household contacts of patients with AIDS or AIDS-related complex with oral candidiasis. *N Engl J Med*. 1986 Feb 6;314(6):344–9. https://doi.org/10.1056/NEJM198602063140604.

Giang HT, Duc NQ, Khue PM, et al. Gender Differences in HIV, HCV risk and Prevention Needs Among People who Inject drug in Vietnam. AIDS Behav. 2023 Jun;27(6):1989–97. https://doi.org/10.1007/s10461-022-03932-x.

Gilbert MT, Rambaut A, Wlasiuk G, Spira TJ, Pitchenik AE, Worobey M. The emergence of HIV/AIDS in the Americas and beyond. *Proc Natl Acad Sci U S A*. 2007;104(47):18566–70. https://doi.org/10.1073/pnas.0705329104.

Hontelez JAC, Goymann H, Berhane Y, et al. The impact of the PEPFAR funding freeze on HIV deaths and infections: a mathematical modelling study of seven countries in sub-Saharan Africa. *EClinicalMedicine*. 2025 Apr 25;83:103233. https://doi.org/10.1016/j.eclinm.2025.103233.

Hooper E. *The River: A Journey to the Source of HIV and AIDS*. Back Bay Books, New York, 2000.

Ibitoye M, Bennett AS, Des Jarlais DC, Bugaighis M, Chernick LS, Aronson ID. I didn't know what they're gonna do to me: so that's why i said no: why youth decline HIV testing in emergency departments. *Behav Med*. 2024 Jan-Mar;50(1):47–54. https://doi.org/10.1080/08964289.2022.2100864.

Lazzarin A, Galli M, Geroldi D, Zanetti A, Crocchiolo P, Aiuti F, Moroni M. Epidemic of LAV/HTLV III infection in drug addicts in Milan: serological survey and clinical follow-up. *Infection* 1985;13(5):216–8. https://doi.org/10.1007/BF01667214.

McAuley A, Palmateer NE, Goldberg DJ, Trayner KMA, Shepherd SJ, Gunson RN, Metcalfe R, Milosevic C, Taylor A, Munro A, Hutchinson SJ. Re-emergence of HIV related to injecting drug use despite a comprehensive harm reduction environment: a cross-sectional analysis. *Lancet HIV*. 2019 May;6(5):e315–24. https://doi.org/10.1016/S2352-3018(19)30036-0.

Mann JM, Tarantola D. eds. *AIDS in the World II: Global Dimensions, Social Roots, and Responses*. Oxford University Press, Oxford, 1996.

Marx PA, Alcabes PG, Drucker E. Serial human passage of simian immunodeficiency virus by unsterile injections and the emergence of epidemic human immunodeficiency virus in Africa. *Philos Trans R Soc Lond B Biol Sci.* 2001 Jun 29;356(1410):911–20. https://doi.org/10.1098/rstb.2001.0867.

Morgan DJ, Okeke IN, Laxminarayan R, Perencevich EN, Weisenberg S. Non-prescription antimicrobial use worldwide: a systematic review. *Lancet Infect Dis.* 2011 Sep;11(9):692–701. https://doi.org/10.1016/S1473-3099(11)70054-8.

Murchu E, Marshall L, Teljeur C, et al. Oral pre-exposure prophylaxis (PrEP) to prevent HIV: a systematic review and meta-analysis of clinical effectiveness, safety, adherence and risk compensation in all populations. *BMJ Open.* 2022;12(5):e048478. https://doi.org/10.1136/bmjopen-2020-048478.

O'Kelly FD, O'Kelly CM. The natural history of injecting drug use: a 25-year longitudinal study of a cohort of injecting drug users in inner city Dublin. *Ir J Med Sci.* 2012 Dec;181(4):541–8. https://doi.org/10.1007/s11845-012-0814-9.

Palayew A, Knudtson K, Purchase S, Clark S, Possehl L, Healy E, Deutsch S, McKnight CA, Des Jarlais D, Glick SN. HIV risk and prevention among clients of a delivery-based harm reduction service during an HIV outbreak among people who use drugs in northern rural Minnesota, USA. *Harm Reduct J.* 2023 Aug 2;20(1):102. https://doi.org/10.1186/s12954-023-00839-1.

Peters AD, Reid MM, Griffin SG. Edinburgh drug users: are they injecting and sharing less? *AIDS.* 1994 Apr;8(4):521–8.

Peutherer JF, Edmond E, Simmonds P, Dickson JD, Bath GE. HTLV-III antibody in Edinburgh drug addicts. *Lancet.* 1985 Nov 16;2(8464):1129–30. https://doi.org/10.1016/s0140-6736(85)90721-4.

Piot P, Bartos M, Ghys PD, Walker N, Schwartländer B. The global impact of HIV/AIDS. *Nature.* 2001;410:968–73. https://doi.org/10.1038/35073639.

Public Health Scotland, Glasgow Caledonian University and the West of Scotland Specialist Virology Centre. *The Needle Exchange Surveillance Initiative (NESI): Prevalence of Blood-Borne Viruses and Injecting Risk Behaviours Among People Who Inject Drugs Attending Injecting Equipment Provision Services in Scotland, 2008 to 2020.* Public Health Scotland, Glasgow, March 2022.

Public Health Scotland. HIV in Scotland: update to 31 December 2023 - HIV in Scotland - Publications - Public Health Scotland, 2025.

Reinhardt V, Roberts A. The African polio vaccine-acquired immune deficiency syndrome connection. *Med Hypotheses.* 1997 May;48(5):367–74. https://doi.org/10.1016/s0306-9877(97)90030-x.

Robertson JR, Bucknall AB, Welsby PD, Roberts JJ, Inglis JM, Peutherer JF, Brettle RP. Epidemic of AIDS related virus (HTLV-III/LAV) infection among intravenous drug abusers. *Br Med J (Clin Res Ed).* 1986 Feb 22;292(6519):527–9. https://doi.org/10.1136/bmj.292.6519.527.

Ron A, Rogers DE. AIDS in New York City: the role of intravenous drug users. *Bull N Y Acad Med.* 1989 Sep;65(7):787–800.

Ronald PJ, Robertson JR, Wyld R, Weightman R. Heterosexual transmission of HIV in injecting drug users. *BMJ.* 1993 Nov 6;307(6913):1184–5. https://doi.org/10.1136/bmj.307.6913.1184.

Ross JD, Scott GR. The Association between HIV media campaigns and number of patients coming forward for HIV antibody testing. *Genitourin Med* 1993;63:193–5.

Scarman, L. (1981) The Brixton Disorders 10–12 April 1981: Report of an Inquiry by the Rt Hon Lord Scarman OBE. London: HMSO.

Scott G, Goldberg D, Weir M, Cameron S, Peutherer J, Carrington D, Follett E, Leadbetter G, Scoular A. Prevalence of HIV-1 infection among heterosexual men and women attending genitourinary clinics in Scotland: unlinked anonymous testing. *BMJ.* 1997 Nov 15;315(7118):1281–2. https://doi.org/10.1136/bmj.315.7118.1281.

Scottish Home and Health Department. HIV In Scotland - Report of the Scottish Committee on HIV Infection and Intravenous Drug Misuse (Edinburgh, September 1986).

Scottish Home and Health Department, Report of the National Working Party on Health Service Implications of HIV Infection (Edinburgh, May 1987).

Selwyn PA. *Surviving the Fall: The Personal Journey of an AIDS Doctor.* Yale University Press, New Haven, 1998.

Shilts, R. *And the Band Played On.* Penguin Books, London, 1987.

Strang J, Griffiths P, Powis B, Gossop M. First use of heroin: changes in route of administration over time. *BMJ.* 1992 May 9;304(6836):1222–3. https://doi.org/10.1136/bmj.304.6836.1222.

Stimson GV. The global diffusion of injecting drug use: implications for human immunodeficiency virus infection. *Bull Narc.* 1993;45(1):3–17.

Sullman SF, Zuckerman AJ. Viral hepatitis in drug addicts. *Postgrad Med J.* 1971 Jul;47(549):473–5. https://doi.org/10.1136/pgmj.47.549.473.

UNAIDS 2024 2024 global AIDS report — The Urgency of Now: AIDS at a Crossroads.

UNAIDS September 2024. available at, Leaders pledge bold action to end AIDS by 2030 | UNAIDS.accessed 25/02/26

van Santen DK, Coutinho RA, van den Hoek A, van Brussel G, Buster M, Prins M. Lessons learned from the Amsterdam cohort studies among people who use drugs: a historical perspective. *Harm Red J.* 2021;18(1):2. https://doi.org/10.1186/s12954-020-00444-6.

Verghese A. *My Own Country. A Doctor's Story.* Vintage Books, Random House, New York, 1994.

Weiss RA. Polio vaccines exonerated. *Nature.* 2001 Apr 26;410(6832):1035–6. https://doi.org/10.1038/35074222.

Weldon RA. An "Urban legend" of global proportion: an analysis of nonfiction accounts of the Ebola virus. *J Health Commun.* 2001 Jul-Sep;6(3):281–94. https://doi.org/10.1080/108107301752384451.

World Drugs Report 2024. Available at; WDR24_Key_findings_and_conclusions.pdf.

WHO 1999. *Product Information Sheets: Global Program for Vaccine and Immunization: Expanded Program on Immunization.* WHO, Geneva, 1999.

Wise A, Kianian B, Chang HH, L, et al. 2023. Socioeconomic and racial/ethnic spatial polarization and incarceration among people who inject drugs in 19 US metropolitan areas, 2015. *SSM Popul Health.* 2023 Aug 10; 23:101486. https://doi.org/10.1016/j.ssmph.2023.101486.

4 Drug-related deaths and injecting drug use

Background

Drug deaths are one of the important issues of the present time in the world of substance use and drug dependence policy and practice. The political establishment, the social policy and health care services are all acutely aware of the unacceptable morbidity and mortality related to substances.

The risks associated with drug-related deaths are multifactorial, inter-related and cumulative over time. Increased mortality is associated with a wide range of health, social, structural, behavioural and situational factors, such as blood-borne virus infections, injecting and polydrug use, physical and mental health comorbidities, early life adversity and homelessness. Other factors have an impact on increasing the risk of death, Opioid Agonist Therapy (OAT) induction and cessation periods following detoxification, residential rehabilitation and prison and child removal and child protection services involvement (Mathers et al. 2008; Tweed et al. 2022).

Drug deaths mirror the waves of drug use over the last 50 years described by the Centre for Disease Control (CDC) in the USA as occurring in three distinct waves. Similar waves have been identified in Western Europe, Australia and New Zealand. Asian countries and Africa have their own episodes.

The first wave described by CDC began with increased prescribing of opioids in the 1990s. Overdose deaths involving prescription opiates (natural and semi-synthetic opioids and methadone) increased starting around 1999. This has declined in recent years. The second wave began in 2010, with rapid increases in overdose deaths involving heroin. However, in recent years, heroin overdose deaths have been declining. The third wave began in 2013, with substantial increases in overdose deaths involving synthetic opioids, particularly those involving illegally made fentanyl and fentanyl analogues which have saturated the illegal drug supply. They are often found in powder form or pressed into counterfeit pills and can be mixed into other drugs. More recently, non-opioid sedatives, such as xylazine, have been found mixed into these analogues. In the current landscape, many opioid overdose deaths also involved other drugs (CDC 2024).

The incredible episodes in North America of the prescription drugs prescribing tragedy and the more recent emergence of the replacement of heroin with the stronger synthetic fentanyl and its derivatives and the benzimidazole opioids

DOI: 10.4324/9781003611097-4

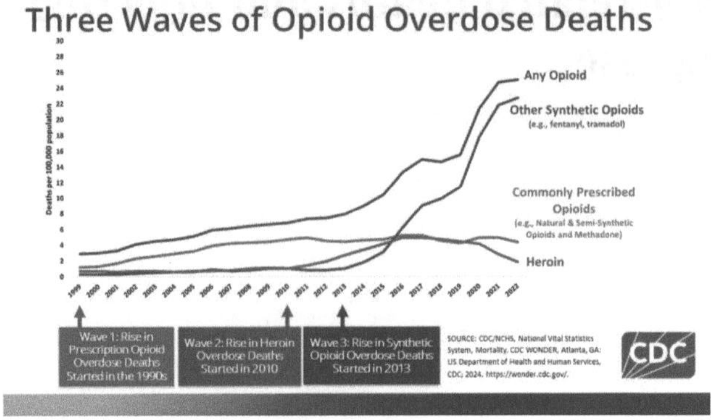

Figure 4.1 The rise in opioid overdose deaths is shown in three waves, with a slight decrease from 2022 to 2023.

(nitazines) have ushered in a new era of death in unprecidented numbers. Since 2000, almost 0.5 million Americans have died from drug overdoses. This modern plague has been largely driven by opioid addiction and has ushered in a new approach to control based on public health. Expanding education and treatment opportunities (Burke 2016 Salekešin 2024).

A fourth wave of overdose deaths in the USA indicates the fluctuant nature of drug use as supply evolves into the era of synthetic substances. The fourth wave is characterised by illicit opiates such as fentanyl and stimulants, mostly methylamphetamine, in the USA and Canada (Friedman and Shover 2023). Looking further back to the 1970s in the USA, an "exponential curve" of deaths is attributed to successive waves of substances such as primarily prescription opioids, heroin, methadone, synthetic opioids, cocaine, and methamphetamine occurring in different localities in various populations (Jalal et al. 2018, CDC 2018).

Common prescription opiates include hydrocodone (trade names such as Vicodin, Norco), oxycodone (trade names such as OxyContin, Percocet) and morphine (trade names such as MS Contin, Kadian).

Reports from the World and European Drugs reports highlight the changing landscape and the complexity of tracking the ever-changing marketplace of illegal substances (EMCDDA 2024, UNODC 2024).

This changing environment of toxic substances has special relevance for people who inject drugs, as super strength synthetic opiates can quickly cause respiratory depression, and when used in combination with benzodiazepine, alcohol and other sedating substances, can quickly cause death.

Drug-related deaths in Scotland

There were 1,172 drug-related deaths in Scotland in 2023 (in 2020 they overtook alcohol deaths when the total reached 1,339).

Key points from the report of the National Records for Scotland (released September 2025):

- In 2024, there were 1,017 drug misuse deaths registered in Scotland, a decrease of 13% (155 deaths) compared with 2023 when there were 1,172 deaths.
- Drug misuse deaths increased over the last two decades to their peak in 2020 (1339). They have generally decreased since then, with the exception of a 12% increase in 2023. The latest figure is the lowest number registered in any year since 2017.
- After adjusting for age, there were 19.1 drug misuse deaths per 100,000 people in 2024. This is 3.6 times as high as when the series began in 2000.
- In 2024, males were more than twice as likely to have a drug misuse death as females. Both male and female deaths decreased in the past year.
- The age profile of drug misuse deaths has become older over time. The average age of drug misuse deaths has increased from 32 years in 2000 to 45 years in 2024.
- In 2024, people in the most deprived areas of Scotland were 12 times as likely to have a drug misuse death compared to people in the least deprived areas. In contrast, for all causes of death, people in the most deprived areas are around twice as likely to die as those in the least deprived areas.
- After adjusting for age, Glasgow City, Dundee City and Inverclyde had the highest rates of drug misuse deaths in the period 2020–2024.
- The most common drugs implicated in drug misuse deaths in 2024 were opiates/opioids (80% of deaths), benzodiazepines (56%) and cocaine (47%).
- The number of drug misuse deaths which implicated opiates/opioids and benzodiazepines fell in 2024. The number which implicated cocaine remained the highest in the series (479 deaths in both 2023 and 2024).
- The majority (91%) of drug misuse deaths were classified as accidental poisonings, with 6% classed as intentional self-poisonings.

Source: National Records of Scotland (2025)

Of interest, drug-related deaths remained stable in Scotland during the Covid-19 pandemic despite rising rates of DRDs worldwide (Glancy et al. 2025).

Alcohol-specific deaths in Scotland 2023

Main findings

- There were 1,277 alcohol-specific deaths registered in Scotland in 2023, an increase of one death from 2022. This is the highest number of alcohol-specific deaths registered in a year since 2008.

- The rate of mortality for alcohol-specific deaths was 22.7 deaths per 100,000 people in 2023. This measure takes into account the size and age structure of the population.
- Male deaths continue to account for around two-thirds of alcohol-specific deaths. Over the last year, male alcohol-specific deaths increased by 25, while female deaths decreased by 24.
- The age profile of alcohol-specific deaths has become older over time, with the average age at death increasing from 56 to 60 in the last decade. In 2023, the alcohol-specific mortality rates for those aged 65 to 74, and 75+ were at their highest since the series began in 1994.
- After adjusting for age, the alcohol-specific mortality rate was higher than the Scottish average in the council areas of Inverclyde, Glasgow City, North Lanarkshire and Dundee City.
- After adjusting for age, the alcohol-specific mortality rate was higher than the Scottish average in the council areas of Inverclyde, Glasgow City, North Lanarkshire and Dundee City.
- Alcohol-specific deaths were 4.5 times as high in the most deprived areas of Scotland compared to the least deprived areas in 2023. This compares to a ratio of 1.8 times for all causes of death. This ratio has decreased over time.

Scotland continued to have the highest alcohol-specific death rate of the UK constituent countries in 2022 (the latest year for which comparable data exists). Data for the rest of the United Kingdom is yet to be released for 2023. The difference between Scotland and the other UK countries has narrowed over the last two decades. In 2001, the alcohol-specific mortality rate for Scotland was between 2.1 and 2.9 times as high as other UK countries. The rate for Scotland was between 1.2 and 1.6 times as high in 2022.

Source: National Records of Scotland (2025)

Causes of death

Although the principal cause of death in people using drugs, especially opiates, is what is described in official datasets as drug toxicity or intoxication. As the cohorts from the 1980s age, there are other causes increasingly recorded, including non-communicable diseases such as suicide, obstructive airways diseases, liver cirrhosis and cancer (Lewer et al. 2022). Ageing cohorts of people who have used substances have legacy illness from past injecting and multimorbidity related to premature ageing and tobacco and alcohol use. Accidents, trauma and homicide maybe higher in the drug using population (personal communiaction Prof Bouhaidar, Edinburgh University). Comorbidity with hepatitis C is a clearly defined cause of morbidity emerging since the introduction of virological testing for this virus (McDonald et al. 2021).

Although it may notseem obvious to the non-specialist, attributing a cause of death is not always simple. This can be for a number of reasons: decomposition of the body in cases where the person was not found for some time, the absence of a clear history of drug taking or other candidate risk factors, or multiple injuries, novel drugs and post mortem redistribution. In cases of toxicity or intoxication, there is sometimes a single drug involved progressive respiratory suppression leading to respiratory arrest and death. This is most common in toxicity due to an opiate such as heroin, methadone, fentanyl or another drug that acts to suppress the respiratory centre in the brain. Stimulants such as methyamphetamine and cocaine usually affect the heart or brain causing cardiac arrhythmia and cardiac arrest or cerebrovascular accident. Increasingly, however, the pathologist and toxicologist identify multiple drugs when post-mortem examination and laboratory testing are performed. Formal certification maybe made by the coroner (Procurator Fiscal in Scotland) or the courts when an inquirey is ordered. Post mortem findings may allow a clear causal compound when a significantly toxic level is recorded, but frequently multiple toxicities are competing to account for the death. Most toxicology results from fatal cases show significant levels of all the compounds detected which in combination lead to toxic levels. Single drugs implicated are increasingly an unusual finding. Obviously, where a single drug is detected at post-mortem, then the cause of death can be attributed to this drug. Where multiple toxic levels are found, a judgement can be made based on the relative toxicity of all drugs present that can be implicated in diagnosing causation. Causation given to cocaine is sometimes given by excluding other drugs, diseases, trauma or other causes of death and suggested that a cardiac arrhythmia is the fatal event.

Recently, investigations into drug-related toxicity are based on historically missed drugs. In the past, suites of laboratory detection kits have included the commonly used drugs in the locality, but more recently, as more drugs are in use and detection capability is increased, analyses on stored samples can improve the record and identify previously unseen trends.

Several commonly used drugs are likely to cause respiratory depression when present in sufficient quantity or in combination. The opiates, either singly or in combination, account for frequent explanation, but combined with other depressants such as benzodiazepines, and non-opiate pain killers or stimulants such as cocaine and methylamphetamine, this allows for the need to consider a more detailed interpretation of toxicology results and reports of pre-mortem clinical features. Newer drugs and synthetic compounds are now complicating diagnostic clarity in deaths caused by drugs. The role of some of these newer drugs may be transitory in different localities, and their impact in different subsets of the substance-using populations is less well understood. Atypical benzodiazepines and gabapentinoids have recently been included in the several drugs leading to death in some populations, notably in older members of a cohort reported in 2023, with adverse effects seen more in older women (Ciesluk et el. 2024). The changing role of benzodiazepines further exemplifies the relationship between the availability and supply of illegally sourced and manufactured drugs, prescription practices and policy and causation of drug-related death (McAuley et el. 2022). In reported data from the National Records for Scotland in 2013, for example, methadone was not prescribed at the time of death in 41% of cases where it was implicated as a cause of death, suggesting that prescription drugs may be used by individuals other than the one in treatment (Bird 2024).

Bird identifies clearly the difference between the coronial system in England and Wales and the Scottish Procurator Fiscal system, which provided additional data.

> In England and Wales, the Office of National Stistics (ONS) does not have access to post-mortem reports or toxicology results. Hence, ONS's subclassification of drug poisoning deaths depends on the information provided by the coroner on the death certificate. Coroners may list only some (or none) of the substances involved or provide only a general category of substance, such as prescribed medication or painkillers. For example, in 2021 when 4859 drug poisoning deaths were registered, 1219 had no information available to ONS on the drug(s) involved. Of the 3640 drug poisoning deaths with drug information available from coroners, ONS could identify 3060 (84.1%) as drug misuse deaths (DMDs). Hence, tables for England and Wales refer to DMDs with at least 1 opiate mentioned on the death certificate as drug misuse deaths due to opiates (DMD-Os) and their counterpart as non DMD-Os.
>
> By contrast, NRS receives more complete information on the substances involved in DRDs from Procurators Fiscal: if the death involved drugs or the person was a drug user, the pathologist sends a form to NRS. This form tells NRS which substances were found in the body and which of them contributed to the death.

At post-mortem there may be an obvious cause of death with pathological findings supporting respiratory depression or cardiac arrest. There may be trauma or injury to account for the death. There may evidence supporting past drug use, findings such as track marks, nasal erosion, chronic inguinal injection sinuses, liver damage or organ damage which could be attributed to recent or past drugs use.

The clinical history may well inform a diagnosis of drug-related cause, HIV, hepatitis or other infections and allow appropriate biological investigation. Information about prescribed drugs and self-medication substances is important as is a recent or past history of previous overdoses accidential or intentional, illnesses and treatments. Information about the circumstances of death, the presence of injecting paraphernalia, pills and substances. Information about the recent mental state of the dead person may suggest suicidal intentions or increased reckless behaviour.

Toxicological analysis is usually required in sudden, unexplained or drug-related deaths. Blood, urine, hair, vitreous humour or tissue analysis may reveal one or several substances and can inform the diagnosis when levels are significantly toxic or likely to be cumulative in effect on the respiratory centre.

In some cases, the cause of death is less clear. When decomposition has taken place when the person was undiscovered for a prolonged period after death, toxicology and post-mortem findings may be obscure. The absence of macro or microscopic findings may not allow a clear result in terms of a suitable diagnosis to enter onto certification of death. In other cases, a judgement is made as to the most like causal factor. When, for example, multiple drugs are found at toxicology there may be one that has a higher level than others and can be assumed to have caused the fatal episode. If this is an opiate it is more likely that attribution will be implied. In many, if not most, fatal drug-related cases, there are several drugs present in the toxicology samples and the combined effects of more than one respiratory depressant is concluded to be the fatal factor. In cases when drugs such as benzodiazepines and cocaine there is little in the way of clinical findings at autopsy and unless there are other factors a cardiac arrhythmia might be suggested. Cardiac arrhythmia is a plausible diagnosis when no other cause of death can be identified as it leaves no trace unless it was witnessed and observed on cardiography recording at time of death. The importance of other information is clear in cases like this. If an eyewitness can describe the individual suffering sudden loss of consciousness, in the absence of any other cause for sedation, a complaint of chest pain or difficulty breathing then this might suggest a catastrophic cardiac cause for the death. This diagnosis, of exclusion, is especially likely in the case of stimulant drugs such as cocaine or methylamphetamine. Chronic cocaine use is however sometimes responsible for atheroma in coronary arteries, and the fatal event is a cardiac infarction (sudden death due to cardiac arrest). Pathological findings may be minimal in these cases, and as described above, the cause of death is a clinical judgement based on a combination of circumstance and knowledge of the events and behaviours present at the time of death.

The use of post-mortem computerised, or MRI scanning is likely to increase in the future to facilitate non-invasive autopsy procedures (Leith 2007, Poulsen and Simonsen 2007).

The numbers of drug related daeths reported are an underestimate of the real totals

In Scotland, the definition of drug-related death is outlined in the National Records of Scotland report, which draws attention to the evolution of the recording process since the ACMD wrote a report called Reducing Drug Related Deaths (Advisory Council on the Misuse of Drugs 2000). One of the recommendations was to establish a standardised reporting system of drug-related deaths (Larney et al. 2017). The predecessor of National Records of Scotland (General Register Office for Scotland-GROS) was part of this working group, which agreed on a standard definition for drug misuse deaths. This definition is used by the Office of National Statistics (ONS) and the Northern Ireland Statistics and Research Agency (NISRA) to produce drug misuse death figures for England, Wales and Northern Ireland. It is also used as the baseline definition for the UK Drugs Strategy.

The definition is not entirely simple. Drug misuse deaths are defined using ICD 10 codes including 'mental and behavioural disorders due to psychoactive substance use' with a list of controlled drugs relating to these codes implicated in individual cases at post-mortem toxicology. Also included are deaths which are coded where a drug listed under the Misuse of Drugs Act (1971) is known to be present in the body at the time of death.

It is noted in the European Report that the term "drug-induced death" is intended to capture those deaths that are directly attributable to the consumption of drugs. These are therefore principally drug overdose deaths. It is further noted, by the NRS, that these estimates of drug-induced deaths only represent part of the overall mortality associated with drug use, as the figures do not include mortality from other causes such as from motor vehicle and other accidents, violence, suicides by means other than drug poisoning, or chronic disease such as blood-borne bacterial or viral infections where drug use may have played a role. A need exists therefore, through cohort studies and other approaches, to extend our understanding in these other important areas of drug-related mortality to avoid underestimating the scale and scope of the challenge we face. In a critically important series of papers, Larney and colleagues report on a total of 19 cohorts which they included in the analysis of the distribution of causes of drug-related death, mostly originating from Western Europe. Poisoning and substance-related deaths were the most common cause, accounting for 31.5% of deaths. Non-communicable diseases accounted for 24.1% of deaths. Infectious diseases accounted for 19.7% of deaths and trauma for 18.1%. In 6.5% the cause of death was unknown (Degenhardt et al. 2011, Degenhardt 2014, Larney et al. 2015, 2020).

The proportion of deaths that are directly attributed to the practice of injecting is not recorded in any international study. It is difficult to separate injection of a fatal drug from ingestion in the process of recording causes of death as causality is not directly related to the mode of use so much as the drug toxicity. Other diagnoses entered on the death certificate of fatal cases similarly attribute causality to the mechanism, hanging, trauma, infection, cancer, etc. rather than the mode of administration. There can be no doubt, however, that injecting carries a greater risk of mortality than other routes of administration and must be regarded as a singularly important risk factor. Interventions to reduce the toll of mortality, whether it be from acute overdose after injecting a lethal dose or the longer-term impact of introducing a virus infection such as the Human Immunodeficiency or hepatitis viruses, must consider measures to discourage injecting.

It is clear therefore that the statistics which only include overdose deaths are an underestimate of the true burden of mortality. The non-fatal physical and mental health morbid conditions accounting for disability are quantified to some degree in national figures of disability and years of disability.

The cumulative total of deaths due to immediate, short-term and long-term effects of drug misuse must include the attrition over years due to many factors where there are periodic episodes of damage caused by infections such as hepatitis B and C and HIV. Less common are clusters of infections due to contaminated batches of drugs such as the fatal outcomes from spore-forming bacilli contamination cluster

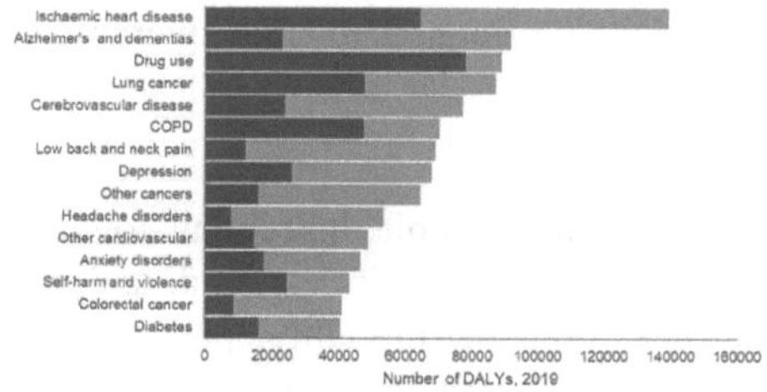

Figure 4.2 Leading 15 causes of population health loss and extent of health loss inequalities. Areas coloured red show the size of the burden that is attributable to deprivation.

Appendix 1: The Health of our Nation – Realistic Medicine – Doing the right thing: Chief Medical Officer annual report 2022 to 2023 – gov.scot.

incidents (Palmateer et al. 2013, Dunleavy et al. 2018). Individual cases of suicides connected to drugs, endocarditis, vasculopathies, stroke and embolic fatalities are reported in cohort series and national data gathering exercises (Robertson et al. 2021, Fraser et al. 2024). Several studies have suggested that treatment is helpful in reducing harms such as suicide in people who use drugs and note that suicide is more common in men, but other self-inflicted harms are more common in women. Rather than having a single cause, they are a complex interplay of social, environmental and personal issues throughout a life course (Knipe et al. 2022).

The Scottish Burden of Disease study acknowledges the high cost of drug misuse when itcomes to morbidity (ScotPHO 2017).

> The illicit use of drugs and particularly opiates, benzodiazepines and psychostimulants, causes significant problems within Scotland as it does in other parts of the UK and Europe. Some of these problems are primarily social in nature, involving, for example, increases in acquisitive crime, prostitution, unemployment, family breakdown and homelessness. Others are more clearly associated with health problems, for example, the transmission of communicable diseases (HIV, hepatitis), injecting-related injuries and increased demands upon health care services.

Explaining excess mortality

For many years, the health problems in Scotland have been the source of public health and political concern. This is especially true of Glasgow and the post-industrial areas in the west of the country. In an important report in 2016 entitled 'History, politics and vulnerability: explaining excess mortality in Scotland and Glasgow', several causes were identified, including vulnerability to high levels of deprivation (specifically overcrowding) over a long period of time; urban planning decisions in the post-war decades (e.g. the creation of larger, relatively poor-quality, peripheral housing estates); UK Government Scottish Office regional economic policies in the

1950s–1970s; local government responses to UK Government policy in the 1980s (Walsh 2017).

Quote from Public Health Scotland:

> The scale of this excess is considerable. It accounts for approximately 5,000 extra, "unexplained", deaths per year in Scotland, and makes a substantial contribution to the other principal mortality 'phenomena' associated with Scotland in recent times: the lowest, and most slowly improving, life expectancy in Western Europe; the widest mortality inequalities in Western Europe; and the persistently high rates of mortality among those of younger working ages. After adjustment for differences in deprivation, premature mortality (<65 years) in Scotland is 20% higher than in England & Wales (10% higher for deaths at all ages); similarly, the excess for Glasgow compared with Liverpool, Manchester and Belfast was shown (in research published in 2010 and 2012 respectively) to be approximately 30% for premature mortality, and around 15% for deaths at all ages. Updated analyses of deprivation and mortality in Glasgow, Liverpool and Manchester published in 2021 showed that high levels of excess mortality persist although the excess for female premature mortality had reduced, in large part because of worsening death rates in the English cities (likely related to the impact of UK Government austerity measures).
>
> (CMO 2023)

McCartney and others have attributed UK Government's, past and present, policies as having an increasing effect on growing inequalities and subsequent morbidity. This is especially damaging in alcohol and drug use sector and may account for the variation in numbers of substance related deaths between Scotland and England. This has implications for policy both in the need to invest in treatment services and potential revisions in the criminal justice system (Parkinson et al. 2018, McCartney et al. 2012, 2016, van Amsterdam et al. 2021, ScotPHO 2023, Schofield 2016, Scott-Samuel 2014, Walsh 2017).

Scotland's "problem" may have been underestimated or misunderstood by politicians and clinicians who devolve responsibility without properly resourcing frontline services. Inequalities and deprivation have only recently achieved significant political urgency, but drug and alcohol treatment services remain relatively low down the priority agenda in health and social care sectors.

The Scottish problem of drug and alcohol use may therefore have several contributing factors, but comparison with other similarly sized countries in Europe, such as France, still makes difficult reading. France has a similar sized population to the United Kingdom but considerably smaller numbers of drug-related deaths. This may be related to many factors, not least the variation in reporting figures. The last official figure available for drug-related deaths in France in one year is 628, but this was reported in 2023 and more recent figures are not available (EUDA 2025). There is clearly a striking difference in the number of deaths attributed to drugs, and various observations have been cited to explain this variation. The EUDA is prepared to recognise that different countries have different definitions of what constitutes death by drugs, and this systems variation might include definition, availability of a forensic science service that represents all parts of each country, reporting and legal infrastructure and analytical capacity to assemble and report national results. There are also factors that may not be immediately apparent and which contribute to a larger or smaller number of at-risk cases. The number of people using drugs in a fashion likely to increase the risk of death might include historic deindustrialisation and inequalities, variation in choices and availability of drugs (less opiates in France than Scotland and more cocaine and stimulants), and a less punitive and more universal public health approach to the care of people who use drugs. One striking difference is the widespread use of prescribed buprenorphine, which, in France, is prescribed in general practice in preference to methadone.

Evidence gaps

Understanding causes of death among people who use drugs is not a single issue. Sudden loss of consciousness from a toxic dose of an opiate can give rise to an uncomplicated diagnosis of respiratory depression causing asphyxiation and death. In such cases, the diagnosis is supported by a history of administration of an oral or injection of an opiate and confirmed by the absence of other causes of death during a post-mortem examination and a forensic post-mortem sample of blood or other body fluid confirming a lethal level of drug. Conclusions become a bit more complicated when the drug level is low or when, not infrequently, there are multiple drugs present. Attributing death to one drug may then be complicated, and certification may consider the cumulative effect of two or more respiratory depressants, including sometimes alcohol. Sudden death in the case of cocaine excess is more difficult to diagnose in the absence of a clear history as pathological findings are less specific. Death in this case may be due to cardiac arrhythmia which at post-mortem has no macroscopic or histological sign. Confirmation depends on the support of toxicological findings of the drugs in body fluid.

Nationally reported statistics on deaths due to overdose are compiled differently by different authorities and depend upon systems for identifying cases, analysing capacity for forensic samples and categorisation and analysis of resulting data. Systematic weaknesses are present at all levels, and changing patterns of substance use demand revision of data analysis. Attributing death to a single drug, ignoring the contribution made by that substance in the case of a multiple drug overdose, will give rise to an underestimate of the numbers of people dying from that drug. The England and Wales system, for example, records deaths from opiates but currently fails to include opiates in the total when multiple drugs are detected after death. This gives rise to an estimated 365 underestimate of opiate-related deaths in 2023 (1264 deaths identified by the Office of National Statistics compared to 1980 when cases where polydrug overdose included opiates) (Chen et al. 2025). This correlates with the increase in cases reported where several drugs are present. In the year 2011, the average number of drugs found at forensic analysis was four compared to six the following year. This trend in multiple drugs present at post-mortem analysis is seen elsewhere.

Compiling accurate and inclusive datasets for mortality related to substance use must form a cornerstone for understanding which substances are implicated and how many cases there are and whether or not numbers are increasing. Underestimates and inaccurate data will be, and are, leading to failure to invest in prevention and treatment services (Black 2021).

Prevention

Since the rapid increase in drug-related deaths became an international phenomenon, efforts have been made at political, clinical and academic levels to describe and evaluate interventions to prevent overdose.

The most obvious starting points are basic education of the risks associated with drug taking and the upscaling of treatments and programmes which deliver opiate agonist treatments, needle and syringe provision, naloxone supplies, counselling and support and mental health supervision and diagnosis.

As substance use becomes a mainstream academic and clinical priority, more evidence for the benefits of medical treatments emerges, but energising a wide spectrum of changes takes time and commitment. Demands for support for residential rehabilitation compete with investment in statutory and non-statutory services involved with the delivery of an increasing number of services. Our target populations also increase as the range of substances in common use increases and the modalities of defined dependency conditions increase. Lobbying for support for preventing deaths from opiates and other respiratory depressants is closely aligned with concerns about dependency on non-drug use behaviours such as eating disorders, gambling and extreme exercise, all of which have serious and sometimes fatal consequences.

Practical developments to prevent death include the widespread availability of opiate antagonists such as naloxone and its provision to super high-risk groups such as people released from custody. Improvements in delivery systems for opiate treatments such as long-acting injections of buprenorphine are likely to have an impact on drug deaths, as is the provision and awareness of naloxone injection or inhalations in domestic and institutional situations. A “realistic review” of evidence to implement naloxone-based interventions to prevent deaths found that context was important. Peer support and sensitivity to the situation that at-risk people find themselves in are likely to be necessary to deliver this intervention successfully (Miller et al. 2022). The use of naloxone in hospital emergency departments and by paramedics on the scene of a casualty is not new, but the prospect of bystanders and first responders such as prison officers and police using naloxone is emerging, and evidence of lives saved is being recorded (Rando et al. 2015). The clear relationship between release from hospital after an admission for a drug-related overdose and a heightened risk of subsequent death from overdose makes it essential that naloxone training and supply of appropriate kit be provided on discharge (Merrall et al. 2013).

Mechanical and electronic devices that might detect the presence of clinical states indicating apnoea and asphyxia are developing in various trials. Examples of these are devices attached to the chest that detect failure in respiratory effort lasting 30 seconds or more. In this project, the level of signal energy (the amount that the chest is moving) below which an alarm will be generated has been determined from clinical studies on patients experiencing central apnoea. Where the signal energy falls below a preset level, for a preset duration, the device will alarm. This can be both a local audible alarm as well as alerting a third-party responder or emergency medical services (Adam et al. 2025). Limitation to these interventions include compliance of the at-risk population, absence of domestic support to respond to an alarm call from the device, and the capacity of emergency services to respond on time to prevent a fatal outcome.

Learning from experience forms a useful avenue to prevent avoidable deaths. Multidisciplinary team (MDT) conferences and discussions are likely to identify failings in services, missed opportunities and ideas for future prevention initiatives. Formalised groups exist in many areas and specialities in clinical practice which examine events such as unexpected deaths or even those who have been in care. Forums like these are designed to determine what might have been managed better, what signs might have been present and were ignored or, in the case of unexpected death, missed completely. Meetings might include clinicians involved with a fatal case including doctors, nursing staff and third sector workers and others contributing to the case process such as pharmacists and laboratory workers. The input from the pathologist performing a post-mortem examination and forensic scientists responsible for blood and body fluid analysis, are likely to offer insights into the ongoing or sudden morbid processes present. Extending the MDT to other case workers and even family can help to derive useful conclusions about future case management in a world now expecting the management of drug dependency to be the responsibility of multiple team members.

Sharing information in this way helps to define territories which individual sectors can take responsibility for and what can or should be shared. Joint working depends on good communication, and failures sometimes arise from a lack of coordination and integration of services. Importantly, a collation of case information can often reassure staff and family that, in the face of a painful and sometimes tragic event, something can be learned to prevent future deaths. Also important is consolidating the efforts of a team and giving mutual support.

Inevitably the work of a multidisciplinary team might work most effectively before a death happens. Limited resources and planning without integrating specialities and associated workers often conspire to overlapping working with cases or, worse, gaps in service provision. As with MDT work in complex cases in hospital medicine, specialities community MDT work should be undertaken for longstanding, acute crisis or other difficult or unusual cases. Where a toxic level or combination of drugs is being used or comorbidity increases the risk of death, a meeting of key workers might be convened to assess the risk and to take joint responsibility for planning. Better outcomes depend on better coordination and communication.

Models of care

The development of a system of cooperation of parts of the health and social care system for people who inject drugs (PWID) developed in the 1980s and beyond in the wake of the rising numbers of people injecting heroin, the increase in deaths and the recognition of the complexity of responses required. Early notions that short-term interventions might effect sustained abstinence moved towards sustained intervention and longer term support models with all their limitations (Healy 2024). The investment of time, energy and expertise required for a larger number of individuals allowed the development of a "shared care" system. Although the notion of separate services sharing the care of a complex case was not new, there were already well-established patterns of engagement of a primary or community care worker calling upon specialist colleges and using resources of hospitals, laboratories and a team approach to chronic disease conditions. It wasn't hard to conceptualise the strategy of generalists managing the identification, early diagnosis and continuity of a person with substance use issues and the collaboration with specialists to confirm or define the more complex cases and systems of inpatient or residential care as required. National guidelines outlined in a more expansive format the inclusion of a wider range of participants including housing, social care, third sector and lived experience input with statutory services (Clinical Guidelines on Drug Misuse and Dependence Update 2017). The understanding of substance use as a complex interdisciplinary condition requiring a shared care model rapidly took over from a condition that could be managed by a single practitioner over a long period of time. Problems remain in the delivery of systems like this. Different geographical areas have varying component parts making universally similar systems unlikely. As shared care developed, different models emerged based on requirements such as HIV, hepatitis and drug injecting populations requiring immediate interventions to prevent viral contamination, hospital liaison for people presenting to accident departments and the longer-term measured needs of those seeking psychological and residential care (Gruer et al. 1993, Greenwood 1996, Gerada and Tighe 1999). As models developed, the key elements of engagement of service users with appropriate parts of the caring systems have been identified as matching the needs of the user and collaboration between service providers and effective service delivery (Pomey et al. 2015, Bombard 2020).

A shared care model can, therefore, mean different things to different people depending upon the nature and local requirements, the infrastructure system in place and funding arrangements. Key elements described by Thom and colleagues include primary care providers such as general practitioners, nurses and community mental health workers collaborating with "link workers" who provide a triaging gateway to a range of services, community pharmacists, health visitors, social care services and third sector substance use agencies (Thom 2025). These community resources have close and regular referral systems to specialist psychiatric inpatient and outpatient services and the whole range of clinical practitioners in hospital-based practices. The multidisciplinary team meeting provides an additional and critically important element. Inclusion in case discussions can include the core workers with occasional additional colleagues such as forensic and clinical toxicologists, laboratory specialists and pathologists depending upon the case under review.

Conclusion

Drug-related deaths have become so commonplace that there is a danger of familiarity fatigue among the public and professionals. Increasing numbers are the result of more substance use and ageing cohorts since the rise in the number of people injecting drugs worldwide in the last few decades. New drugs, new populations using drugs and increased supply through international trafficking and national marketing of pharmaceutically prepared substances have all contributed to the death rate increase.

Despite awareness, the total recorded impact is likely to be an underestimate of the true numbers, as agencies gathering and reporting data fail to include secondary causes and delayed deaths. There are examples of good practice in provison of multiagency cooperation and care for the needs of multimorbid people who are affected by drugs but comprehensive services are not available everywhere and substance use, particulaly injecting, retains a high risk of direct or indirect mortality (van Santen 2021).

Prevention includes political initiatives, improved services for people who use drugs, education and research. The increased awareness of the failure to reduce drug deaths by punitive measures and restricting access to injecting equipment has allowed the development of a more humane approach to people who use drugs and, with it, the provision of more appropriate and targeted services.

References

Adam A, et al. Systematic Literature Review: Diagnostic Definitions of Overdose and (Opioid-Induced) Respiratory Depression Relevant to Remote Monitoring via Accelerometry, 2025. [Manuscript in preparation]

Advisory Council on the Misuse of Drugs (2000) Reducing Drug Related Deaths: A Report by the Advisory Council on the Misuse of Drugs. London: The Stationery Office.

Bird SM. Opioid-related deaths and their counterpart by occurrence era, age group and coimplicated drugs: Scotland vs. England and Wales. *Br J Clin Pharmacol.* 2024 Apr;90(4):996–1015. https://doi.org/10.1111/bcp.15976.

Black DC. Review of drugs part two: prevention, treatment and recovery: annexes. UK: Report for the Department of Health and Social Care. 2021 Jul.

Bombard Y., Baker G.R., Orlando E. *et al.* (2018). Engaging patients to improve quality of care: a systematic review. *Implement Sci.* 2018;13(1):98. https://doi.org/10.1186/s13012-018-0784-z.

Burke DS. Forecasting the opioid epidemic. *Science.* 2016 Nov 4;354(6312):529. https://doi.org/10.1126/science.aal2943.

Chen S, Mais D, Copeland CS. Comparison of Office for National Statistics (ONS) and National Programme on Substance Use Mortality (NPSUM) data suggests that opioid-related deaths in England & Wales have been systematically underestimated. *Int J Drug Policy.* 2025 Aug 30;145:104976. https://doi.org/10.1016/j.drugpo.2025.104976.

Ciesluk B, Inglis DG, Parke A, Troup LJ. Systematic review: the relationship between gabapentinoids, etizolam, and drug related deaths in Scotland. *PLoS One*. 2024 Oct 9;19(10):e0310655. https://doi.org/10.1371/journal.pone.0310655.

Clinical Guidelines on Drug Misuse and Dependence Update 2017 Independent Expert Working Group (2017) *Drug Misuse and Dependence: UK Guidelines on Clinical Management*. Department of Health, London.

CDC 2024. Understanding the Opioid Overdose Epidemic | Overdose Prevention | CDC accessed on 25/5/2025

CDC 2018. Center for Disease Control and Prevention; Atlanta, GA, U.S. drug overdose deaths continue to rise; increase fueled by synthetic opioids. (https://www.cdc.gov/media/releases/2018/p0329-drug-overdose-deaths.html).

CMO 2023 Realistic Medicine - Doing the right thing: Chief Medical Officer annual report 2022 to 2023 - gov.scot

Degenhardt L.,Larney S.,Randall D.,Burns L., Hall W. Causes of death in a cohort treated for opioid dependence between 1985 and 2005. *Addiction.* 2014;1091:90–9.

Degenhardt L, Bucello C, Mathers B, et al.

Dunleavy K, Munro A, Roy K, Hutchinson S, Palmateer N, Knox T, Goldberg D, Hope V, Campbell J, Hamilton E, Liddell D, Penrice G, Taylor A. Spore forming bacteria infections and people who inject drugs: Implications for harm reduction. *Int J Drug Policy*. 2018 Mar;53:45–54. https://doi.org/10.1016/j.drugpo.2017.12.001.

EMCDDA. European Monitoring Centre for Drugs and Drug Addiction (2024), *European Drug Report 2024: Trends and Developments.* https://www.emcdda.europa.eu/publications/european-drug-report/2024_en.

EUDA 2025. European Drug Report 2025: Trends and Developments | www.euda.europa .eu.

Fraser R, Yeung A, Glancy M, Hickman M, Jones HE, Priyadarshi S, et al. Suicide in people prescribed opioid-agonist therapy in Scotland, United Kingdom, 2011–2020: a national retrospective cohort study. *Addiction.* 2024. https://doi.org/10.1111/add.16680.

Friedman J, Shover CL. Charting the fourth wave: geographic, temporal, race/ethnicity and demographic trends in polysubstance fentanyl overdose deaths in the United States, 2010–2021. *Addiction.* 2023 Dec;118(12):2477–85. https://doi.org/10.1111/add.16318.

Glancy M, McAuley A, Palmateer N, Trayner K, Yeung A, Barnsdale L, Priyadarshi S, Horsburgh K, Hickman M, Hutchinson S. Risk of drug-related mortality among people receiving opioid-agonist treatment during the COVID-19 pandemic in Scotland. *Int J Drug Policy*. 2025 Jul 5;143:104912. https://doi.org/10.1016/j.drugpo.2025.104912.

Gerada C. and Tighe J. A review of shared care protocols for the treatment of problem drug use in England, Scotland and Wales. *Br J Gen Pract.* 1999;49:125–6.

Greenwood J. Six years' experience of sharing the care of Edinburgh's drug users. *Psych Bulletin.* 1996;20:8–11.

Gruer L, Cameron J, Elliott L. Building a city wide service for exchanging needles and syringes. *BMJ.* 1993 May 22;306(6889):1394–7. https://doi.org/10.1136/bmj.306.6889.1394.

Healy E, Means AR, Knudtson K, Frank N, Juarez A, Prohaska S, McKnight C, Des Jarlais D, Asher A, Glick SN. Facilitators and barriers to monitoring and evaluation at syringe service programs. *Harm Reduct J.* 2024 Aug 28;21(1):157. https://doi.org/10.1186/s12954-024-01073-z.

Jalal H, Buchanich JM, Roberts MS, Balmert LC, Zhang K, Burke DS. Changing dynamics of the drug overdose epidemic in the United States from 1979 through 2016. *Science.* 2018 Sep 21;361(6408):eaau1184. https://doi.org/10.1126/science.aau1184.

Knipe D, Padmanathan P, Newton-Howes G, Chan LF, Kapur N. Suicide and self-harm. *Lancet*. 2022 May 14;399(10338):1903–16. https://doi.org/10.1016/S0140-6736(22)00173-8.

Lancet Public Health. 2022 Feb;7(2):e126–e135. https://doi.org/10.1016/S2468-2667(21)00254-1.

Larney S, Peacock A, Mathers BM, Hickman M, Degenhardt L. A systematic review of injecting-related injury and disease among people who inject drugs. *Drug Alcohol Depend.* 2017 Feb 1;171:39–49. https://doi.org/10.1016/j.drugalcdep.2016.11.029.

Larney S, Bohnert AS, Ganoczy D, Ilgen MA, Hickman M, Blow FC, Degenhardt L. Mortality among older adults with opioid use disorders in the Veteran's Health Administration, 2000–2011. *Drug Alcohol Depend.* 2015 Feb 1;147:32–7. https://doi.org/10.1016/j.drugalcdep.2014.12.019.

Larney S, Tran LT, Leung J, Santo T Jr, Santomauro D, Hickman M, Peacock A, Stockings E, Degenhardt L. All-Cause and cause-specific mortality among people using extramedical opioids: a systematic review and meta-analysis. *JAMA Psych.* 2020 May 1;77(5):493–502. https://doi.org/10.1001/jamapsychiatry.2019.4170.

Leth PM. The use of CT scanning in forensic autopsy. *Forens Sci Med Pathol* 2007;3:65–9. https://doi.org/10.1385/FSMP:3:1:65.

Lewer D, Brothers TD, Van Hest N, Hickman M, Holland A, Padmanathan P, Zaninotto P. Causes of death among people who used illicit opioids in England, 2001–18: a matched cohort study. Lancet Public Health. 2022;7(2):e126–35.

McAuley A, Matheson C, Robertson JR. From the clinic to the street: the changing role of benzodiazepines in the Scottish overdose epidemic. *Int J Drug Policy.* 2022 Feb;100:103512. https://doi.org/10.1016/j.drugpo.2021.103512.

McCartney G, Bouttell J, Craig N et al. Explaining trends in alcohol-related harms in Scotland, 1991–2011 (I): the role of incomes, effects of socio-economic and political adversity and demographic change. *Public Health.* 2016;132:13–23.

McCartney G, Collins C, Walsh D, Batty GD. Why the Scots die younger: synthesizing the evidence. *Public Health.* 2012 Jun;126(6):459–70. https://doi.org/10.1016/j.puhe.2012.03.007.

McDonald SA, McAuley A, Hickman M, Bird SM, Weir A, Templeton K, Gunson R, Hutchinson SJ. Increasing drug-related mortality rates over the last decade in Scotland are not just due to an ageing cohort: a retrospective longitudinal cohort study. *Int J Drug Policy.* 2021 Oct;96:103286. https://doi.org/10.1016/j.drugpo.2021.103286.

Mathers BM, Degenhardt L, Phillips B, et al., 2008. Global epidemiology of injecting drug use and HIV among people who inject drugs: a systematic review. *Lancet.* 2008;372:1733–45. https://doi.org/10.1016/S0140-6736(08)61311-2.

Merrall EL, Bird SM, Hutchinson SJ. A record-linkage study of drug-related death and suicide after hospital discharge among drug-treatment clients in Scotland, 1996–2006. *Addiction.* 2013 Feb;108(2):377–84. https://doi.org/10.1111/j.1360-0443.2012.04066.x.

Miller NM, Waterhouse-Bradley B, Campbell C, et al. How do naloxone-based interventions work to reduce overdose deaths: a realist review. *Harm Reduct J.* 2022;19:. https://doi.org/10.1186/s12954-022-00599-4.

National Records of Scotland. *Drug-Related Deaths in Scotland, 2024.* National Records of Scotland, Edinburgh, 2025.

Parkinson J, Minton J, Lewsey J, Bouttell J, McCartney G. Drug-related deaths in Scotland 1979–2013: evidence of a vulnerable cohort of young men living in deprived areas. *BMC Public Health.* 2018 Mar 27;18(1):357. https://doi.org/10.1186/s12889-018-5267-2.

Palmateer NE, Hope VD, Roy K, et al. Infections with spore-forming bacteria in persons who inject drugs, 2000–2009. *Emerg Infect Dis.* 2013 Jan;19(1):29–34. https://doi.org/10.3201/eid1901.120044.

Pomey M-P, Ghadiri DP, Karazivan P, et al. Patients as partners: a qualitative study of patients' engagement in their health care. *PLoS One.* 2015;10(4):e0122499. https://doi.org/10.1371/journal.pone.0122499.

Poulsen K, Simonsen J. Computed tomography as routine in connection with medico-legal autopsies. *Forensic Sci Int.* 2007 Sep 13;171(2–3):190–7. https://doi.org/10.1016/j.forsciint.2006.05.041.

Rando J, Broering D, Olson JE, Marco C, Evans SB. Intranasal naloxone administration by police first responders is associated with decreased opioid overdose deaths. *Am J Emerg Med.* 2015;33(9):1201–4.

Robertson R, Broers B, Harris M. Injecting drug use, the skin and vasculature. *Addiction.* 2021 Jul;116(7):1914–24. https://doi.org/10.1111/add.15283.

Salekešin M, Vorobjov S, Des Jarlais D, Uusküla A. Mortality among people who inject drugs - the interwoven roles of fentanyl and HIV: a community-based cohort study. *Eur J Public Health.* 2024 Apr 3;34(2):329–34. https://doi.org/10.1093/eurpub/ckad204.

ScotPHO 2023 Excess Mortality in Scotland and Glasgow - ScotPHO accessed 25/02/2026

Schofield L, Walsh D, Munoz-Arroyo R, et al. Dying younger in Scotland: trends in mortality and deprivation relative to England and Wales, 1981–2011. *Health Place.* 2016;40:106–15. https://doi.org/10.1016/j.healthplace.2016.05.007.

Scott-Samuel A, Bambra C, Collins C, Hunter DJ, McCartney G, Smith K. The impact of thatcherism on health and well-being in Britain. *Int Health Serv.* 2014;44:53–71. https://doi.org/10.2190/HS.44.1.d

Thom, B. 2025. Preventing drug-related deaths in Scotland: Perceptions and experiences of a 'shared care' model of service delivery. In press.

Tweed EJ, Leyland AH, Morrison D, Katikireddi SV. Premature mortality in people affected by co-occurring homelessness, justice involvement, opioid dependence, and psychosis: a retrospective cohort study using linked administrative data. *Lancet Public Health.* 2022;7:e733–e743. https://doi.org/10.1016/S2468-2667(22)00159-1.

UNODC. World Drugs Report 2024 WDR24_Key_findings_and_conclusions.pdf.

van Amsterdam J, van den Brink W, Pierce M. Explaining the Differences in Opioid Overdose Deaths between Scotland and England/Wales: Implications for European Opioid Policies. Eur Addict Res. 2021;27(6):399–412. https://doi.org/10.1159/000516165..

van Santen DK, Coutinho RA, van den Hoek A, van Brussel G, Buster M, Prins M. Lessons learned from the Amsterdam Cohort Studies among people who use drugs: a historical perspective. *Harm Red J.* 2021;18:2. https://doi.org/10.1186/s12954-020-00444-6.

Walsh D, McCartney G, Collins C, Taulbut M, Batty GD. History, politics and vulnerability: explaining excess mortality in Scotland and Glasgow. *Public Health.* 2017;151:1–12.

5 Physical impact of injecting drug use beyond infectious diseases

Background

Adverse consequences of drugs are visible everywhere in public life, political discourse and personal situations affecting increasing numbers of individuals and families. In hospital departments and the wider medical arena, there is hardly a speciality or department that doesn't see problematic manifestations of psychoactive drug use. There are many examples of drug-related conditions affecting most parts of the body, and consequently, most departments in general hospitals have people with drug-connected harmful conditions. The well-publicised appalling death rate from drug use in Scotland and other countries is the most visible harm caused by drugs, but the impact on the lives of individuals and families extends much wider (Scottish Burden of Disease Study 2019, Nutt et al. 2010).

The damage caused by injecting drugs is enormous and can affect all systems and structures in the body. The mechanism by which drugs enter the brain, causing the psychoactive effect, through injecting, inhalation and ingestion (swallowing) is important in understanding the consequences for experiencing the benefits and the risks of substances. The very nature of injecting into a vein or, less frequently, beneath the skin or into muscle bypasses the essential protection of the skin and allows access to soft tissue or the venous system and therefore directly to the heart from where it travels through the arterial system to the brain. Inhalation into the lungs or nasopharynx gives rapid access through the nasal mucosa or lung alveoli into the pulmonary arterial system and to the brain. Both intravenous and inhalation routes provide entry to the brain within seconds. Ingestion into the gastrointestinal tract also allows access to the bloodstream but at a slower pace and with a degree of filtration as drugs pass through the liver and can be degraded in the liver, a process known as "first pass".

As well as allowing the rapid onset of effect, injecting has additional important hazards, adding to the toxicity of any substance entering the body in several ways. It adds an immediate concentrated bolus of the substance which increases the impact and positive or negative effects. In addition, injecting introduces toxins, poisons or infective agents directly into the bloodstream with no protection from the immune system or the particle size filtration system and the metabolic degradation effected by the intestinal mucosa and liver. The blood circulation reaches every part of the body and therefore it is not surprising that problems can arise anywhere, in

DOI: 10.4324/9781003611097-5

skin, in organs and in the vascular system itself. Importantly, injecting a substance into the circulatory system allows access of toxins, poisons or infective agents into any of the vital organs of the body. It causes potential collateral damage to the cardiovascular system with potential to cause short-term acute vascular obstruction or longer-term harms to the circulation in a local or remote part of the body. As venous blood travels to the right side of the heart and then to the lungs for reoxygenation, any contaminations can lodge in the lung with consequent cumulative damage to the lungs. Entering the heart, infective agents can lodge on heart valves where turbulence of blood flow occurs. Infection encounters the tricuspid valve first as it enters the right side of the heart on its way to the lung for reoxygenation, making this valve the most common site of endocarditis (infection of a heart valve).

The nature of the drug injected and the variations in purity and content vary widely in localities and across countries. Types of heroin differ in their solubility and suitability for injection. In recent decades, powdered heroin coming from South East Asia is the most common type of opiate in Europe. Black tar, a resinous poor-quality heroin from South America and Mexico, is more common in the west of the USA and Colombian powder heroin in the east (Summers et al. 2017, Mars

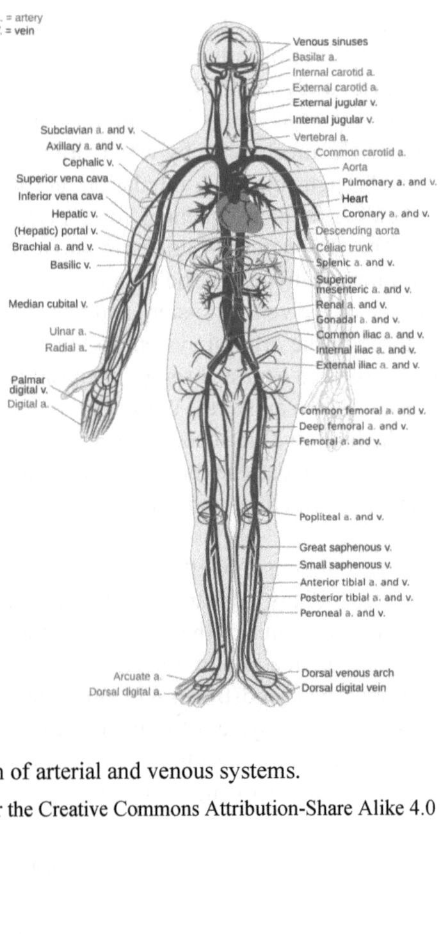

Figure 5.1 Circulation of arterial and venous systems.

et al. 2016). Chinese white heroin was, until recently, the most common variety in Australia. These differences in materials have implications for their impact on injection sites and vessel damage (Mars et al. 2018).

One study suggested that damage to the skin and vasculature was among the most important consequences of injecting drug use.

> Once the skin has been damaged or breached problems can arise at the site of injection, in and beneath the skin, in the blood vessel that has been penetrated, in the subcutaneous fascia and muscle tissue and at remote sites in distant organs in the body. Blood vessels form part of the structure of all tissues and organs in the body and are, therefore, the entry point for contaminated products or foreign bodies to be introduced into organs such as the lungs, kidneys, the heart, brain or liver but also into muscle and bone tissue. Many subsequent problems are because of bacterial, viral or fungal infections but drug toxicity, irritants and contaminants can also cause aseptic damage to all these organs and structures. Repeated trauma to vessels gives rise to superficial or deep damage.
>
> (Robertson et al. 2021)

Educational programmes on wound care, injection site hygiene, equipment provision and early interventions for infections and sepsis are all likely to prevent tissue and vascular damage (Phillips et al. 2013). Initiatives to include marginalised people in treatment and those using in constrained or outdoor situations include outreach and peer support programmes and even supervison of injection technique (Ng et al. 2017).

In their article "The Heroin Epidemic in America: A Surgeon's Perspective", Bauman and colleagues from several US states draw attention to the many surgical interventions required as a result of injecting drug use (Bauman et al. 2019).

> In 2011, intravenous drug use-related infections resulted in 1.25 million visits to U.S. emergency departments, a 100% increase from 2004. The market dominance of black tar heroin, the popularity of skin-popping, and the combination of heroin with other illicit drugs have resulted in the dramatic emergence of Clostridium and other bacterial infections among heroin abusers. Abscesses, septic thrombophlebitis, and necrotizing soft tissue infections are some of the various surgical diseases related to heroin injection and are increasingly common.

Although complications of injecting connect systems in the body and depend upon the substance injected, the dose and the contaminants, the impact might be divided into direct traumatic problems, damage remote from the injection site, toxic damage including overdose, access to organs, infective agents and rare and unusual events.

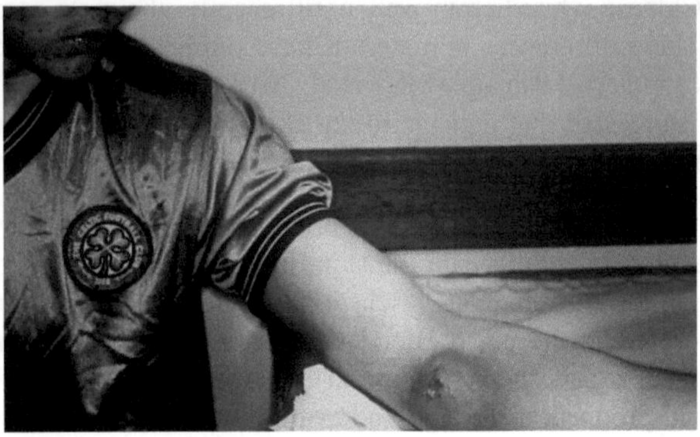

Figure 5.2 Soft tissue skin infection in an inexperienced injector.

From author's own collection.

Toxicity and end organ damage

Drugs vary in their toxicity to tissues and organs. Ethyl alcohol, consumed in marketed products, is, at first sight, a drug that is toxic when consumed in excess, but otherwise benign. This illusion of safety is not represented in the facts listing harms caused by alcohol. It is extraordinary how much damage alcohol causes to many parts of the body. Liver damage is well known, progressive damage starting with fatty liver and progressing to fibrotic changes, cirrhosis and a particularly virulent form of neoplasia known as hepatocellular cancer. In addition to this is the toxicity of alcohol to brain tissue, causing various forms of cognitive loss and dementia. A long list of other specific types of organ damage occurs with excess alcohol use, including cardiomyopathies, heart failure, vitamin B1 deficiency causing a Beriberi syndrome, peripheral vascular damage and hypertension. Less commonly considered but equally important as causes of death are the increased risks caused by alcohol of a variety of cancers affecting the mouth, pharynx, larynx, large bowel, liver, breast and probably also the pancreas (World Health Organization 2023).

Compared to this, many drugs thought to be inherently toxic have less of a direct effect on the tissue of most organs. Paradoxically, drugs classified under the controlled drugs legislation have less direct toxicity to tissues. Despite the ABC classification in the UK Misuse of Drugs Act into those with more or less damaging effects, these substances have considerably less direct trauma to tissues in the body. Leaving aside for a while the addiction/dependency issue and the harms caused by the illegal status of controlled drugs, and all that implies in psychological, financial and social harms, many controlled drugs seem considerably less harmful. The major harm from most drugs, as with alcohol, comes from overdosage and acute exacerbation of the accumulated primary side effect. In the case of many, this is respiratory depression leading to coma and death. Rather than toxic effect on tissues the main hazards of drug use are, toxicity caused by overdoses and the harmful effects of injecting.

The individual and public health burdens of opiate use disorder (OUD) are immense; 26.8 million people were estimated to be living with OUD globally in 2016, with more than 100,000 opioid overdose deaths annually. The total number of deaths in the USA in 2017 was 47,000 rising to 110,037 in 2023 before falling considerably to an estimated total of 80,391 n 2024 (Strang et al. 2020 CDC 2026). Most of these deaths are caused by overdose or indirect effects of using the drug such as infection introduced by injecting rather than direct organ damage. The opioid overdose epidemic in the USA has been attributed to various waves of synthetic opiates, illicit heroin and fentanyl (Jones et al. 2020). Specific organic syndromes attributable to opiates include gastrointestinal upset, gastritis, malabsorption and constipation, but increased organ failure or cancer-related conditions are rare.

Direct trauma to blood vessels and ischaemic limbs

The medical literature is full of reports of soft tissue and injection site problems. Infected or damaged veins and the surrounding tissues are probably the most frequent cause of attendance at emergency departments or community health clinic venues (Lewer et al. 2017, Larney et al. 2017, Murphy et al. 2001). The most favoured site of injecting is the upper limb, most frequently the veins of the cubital fossa in the non-dominant arm This site, particularly in young people early in their injecting career, is prominent and accessible, and most of the time covered by clothing, making it less visible. Veins in the body are less exact in their anatomy than arteries, and in peripheral sites, can be wider or narrower from person to person. Some people can spend many years accessing the venous system in the same site, whereas others, through luck or unfortunate damage and repeated trauma, have to move from site to site as time goes on. Some substances and preparations are more irritant than others, and injecting equipment and tissue infection can lead to thrombosis and eventual loss of patency of the vein. Alternative injection sites are many, and progression can occur from the more accessible veins in the upper limb and hands to lower limbs and feet. Puffy hand syndrome is not uncommon after longstanding injecting in the dorsal surface veins in the hand (Andresz et al. 2006). Common in experienced users of injection drugs is the femoral vein, sited in the inguinal or groin area close to the femoral artery and nerve, which supply the lower limb (Maliphant et al. 2005). This is a large vein draining into the iliac vessel and the inferior vena cava. It is, however, less accessible, not being visible on the surface of the skin and identified by its proximity to the pulsing of the femoral artery. A longer needle may be required. Trauma to this vein can result in a pseudoaneurysm or collateral damage to the artery compromising circulation to the leg. Rarely pseudoaneurysm can occur in the upper limb (Siu et al. 2005). The disaster of injecting into the artery rather than the vein can lead to ischaemia and even surgical amputation of the limb.

The use of other veins is either because of loss of function of the more obvious vessels or a desire to conceal injection sites (Karimi et al. 2014). Injecting is not uncommon in jugular veins or even into small surface veins in the breast, abdomen or scalp.

Robertson R, Broers B, Harris M. Injecting drug use, the skin and vasculature. *Addiction.* 2021;116(7):1914–24. https://doi.org/10.1111/add.15283

Damage is most commonly to veins or the surrounding areas when injected substances leak into surrounding tissues such as skin or muscle. Injection into muscle or subcutaneous tissue is common and seen by some to be less risky and often used when venous access is impaired through prolonged use. Swelling, local abscesses and muscle damage causing fibrosis are reported. The veins most commonly used to access the circulation are the relatively small veins in the arms or, when these become fibrosed and occluded, the legs. The femoral vein in the groin is a larger vessel which proximity to the femoral nerve and artery adds an additional hazard such as intra-arterial injection (Coughlin and Mavor 2006). Injecting or hitting the femoral nerve with a needle will cause acute pain. Arterial spasm and stroke because of stimulants may occur because of haemorrhage or thrombosis or vasospasm. The drug type may be important in causation, cerebral haemorrhage being more commonly associated with methamphetamine and cocaine and stroke caused by vasospasm with ecstasy (Lappin et al. 2017, Huang et al. 2016, Darke and Rose 2000, Sordo et al. 2014, Reneman et al. 2000).

Amputation of lower limbs is regrettably not uncommon among those who have ischaemia or infection introduced by injecting into a femoral vein. The role of the vascular surgeon is crucial when an infected femoral pseudoaneurysm resulting from the femoral vein or inadvertently the artery is involved. This lesion should be suspected in any injecting drug addict with an appropriately sited swelling in the femoral area associated with pain and fever (Woodburn and Murie 1996, Coughlin and Mavor 2006, Tsao et al. 2002).

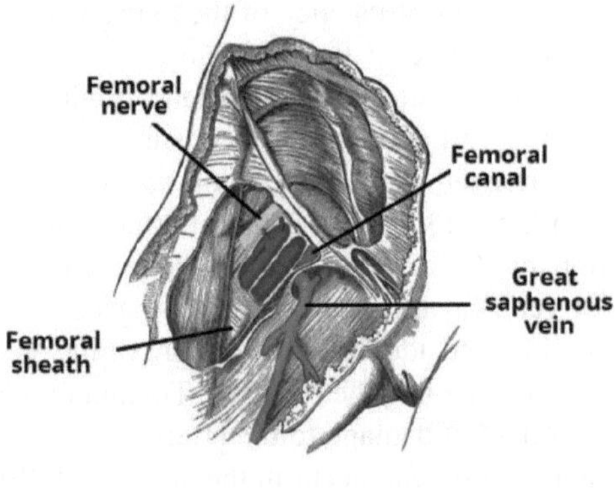

Figure 5.3 The femoral artery, vein and nerve are closely related in the upper part of the thighs.

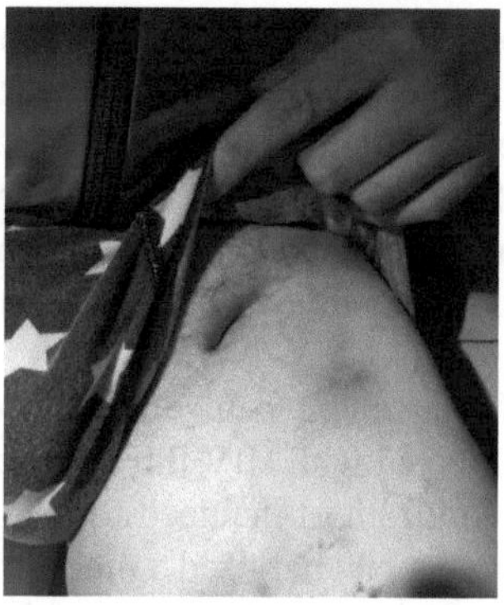

Figures 5.4 Longstanding injectors often resort to deep vein injections forming a sinus. From author's own collection.

Other organs are infected or damaged by intravenous injection of toxic or infected material. Embolization from infected valvular vegetations may cause cerebral infarction, intracranial hemorrhage, and the formation of brain abscess. Focal intracranial infections such as brain abscess and spinal epidural abscess occur occasionally and a high level of suspicion is required to interpret unusual symptoms in persons who have injected (Tunklel 2002).

Pregnancy and injecting drug use

Recent history resonates with the change HIV/AIDS has had on social structures and health care. Policy, politics and public opinion were shocked into a new arena of attitudes to minority groups, understanding of, previously, marginalised behaviours. Even a few decades since the explosive introduction of the virus, it

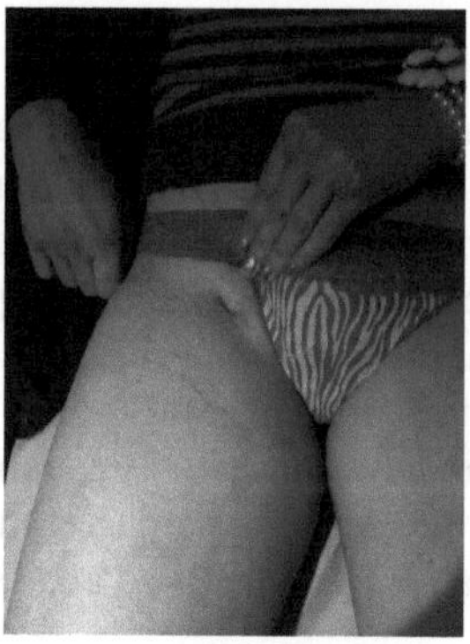

Figure 5.5 Longstanding injectors often resort to deep vein injections forming a sinus. From author's own collection.

is easy to forget the profound influence the AIDS pandemic had on health. For the medical profession, a whole new era of cooperation emerged with patients' management of risks and expectations for control and ownership, of information, data and personal details. Suddenly blood was a material that had to be handled as potentially infectious, blood transfusions became something to be considered carefully rather than as a routine and testing for HIV and other viruses became an integral part of assessment.

One of the many areas of change was in maternity and childcare, and the cohort of women injecting drugs or infected with HIV through sexual contact with someone who used drugs was at the forefront of the need for change. The epidemic of HIV among men who have sex with men energised a modernisation of attitudes but also a revolution in sharing personal data and decision making in treatment. People who inject drugs became, for the first time, a group that had to be considered seriously and even listened to by anyone interested in the health of the nation. The risk of women and babies being infected added to the tsunami of change in health, social care, the justice system and business.

Maternity care, always a critical part of health care, was changing and continues to adjust to the needs and demands of the new standards required by infection control and a new range of choices by a constituency more engaged with the process and much more knowledgeable and in control of decisions. Accommodating change has been a challenge for maternity services in the National Health Service. Figures for maternal deaths and problematic delivery outcomes have remained stubbornly high. In the National Confidential Enquiry into Maternal Deaths and Morbidity 2021–2023, substance use was mentioned 132 times throughout the text and lessons learned were applicable to clinicians, pathologists and maternity care planners (Felker 2025). Among other conclusions, the national survey recorded

> In 2021–23, 67 women died in relation to substance use in the UK and Ireland during pregnancy or up to one year after pregnancy, a maternal mortality rate of 3.09 per 100,000 maternities (95% CI 2.39-3.92). This is not statistically significantly different from rates of deaths associated with substance use in 2017–19 or 2020.

Substance use and inadequate utilisation of antenatal care services are both independently associated with increased risk of maternal death in the United Kingdom and a national study identified six risk factors associated with maternal death from direct pregnancy complications: inadequate use of antenatal care services, substance misuse, medical comorbidities, hypertensive disorders of pregnancy, previous pregnancy problems and Indian ethnicity (Nair et al. 2015). Children born to mothers who have injected drugs remain at risk of infection with blood borne viruses but also the collateral damage caused by the neglect and other health problems of a marginalized group (Bond and Buckley 2024, Canfield et al. 2017).

The UK Government report, Hidden Harm, estimated that there were between 200,000 and 300,000 children in England and Wales where one or both parents have a serious drug problem, representing 2–3% of children under 16 years. Only 37% of fathers and 64% of mothers were still living with their children (ACMD 2003). The more serious the drug problem, the less likely was the child to be living with the parent, and often, the child was living with other relatives. One study estimated there are between 41,000 and 59,000 children in Scotland with a problem drug-using parent. This represents about 4–6% of all children under 16 (Manning 2009). Existing estimates of numbers of children of problem drug users vary from 250,000 to 350,000 and a greater number of children of problem alcohol users (ACMD 2003).

Problems arise, however, in estimating numbers of mothers and children affected by drugs. Defining drug use and differentiating "serious drug use" and distinguishing between cannabis use and other recreational drugs, as well as cocaine and opiates, presents challenges. Few studies look at the smaller numbers of people having children who inject drugs rather than take drugs orally. Most studies are from household questionnaires or other self-reported data and fail to record a more detailed account of the drugs involved or the extent and damage caused. In at least one study of maternal HIV infection, there was no adverse effect on growth in uninfected infants, and the effect of drug use during pregnancy is limited to a small decrease in size at 3 years (Ross et al. 1995). Various surveys, including the British Crime Survey and the Scottish Crime Studies, reported in the year 2000 that around 335,000 children lived with a drug-dependent user, 72,000 with an injecting drug user, 72,000 with a drug user in treatment and 108,000 with an adult who had overdosed. The Scottish Crime Survey recorded that around 12,000 children had witnessed force being used against an adult in the household by their partner while drinking alcohol and almost 6,000 children while using drugs (Best et al. 2009). Other sties suggest that early interventions can improve outcomes and that, with support, drug-using parents can reduce drug use and achieve better family management. It is also noted that children have rarely been directly the focus of intervention (Barnard and McKeganey 2004).

While harm from parental injecting substance use is not inevitable, the number of children living with substance-misusing parents exceeds earlier estimates. Widespread patterns of binge drinking and recreational drug use may expose children to suboptimal care and substance-using role models.

Multimorbid condition contributing to illness and premature death

The comorbid issue of smoking is responsible for a considerable additional set of health problems. The societal and economic costs are also huge. In the USA, an estimated $300 billion dollars in the case of tobacco alone. These costs are largely deferred to other sectors like healthcare (Gilmore et al. 2023, CDC 2021). As outlined in Chapter 13, the international pandemic of smoking-related disorders spans the 20th century and shows signs of continuing as long as marketing and commercialisation manoeuvres around public health regulations. Zhou and colleagues explain that while smoking has decreased considerably in economically developed countries, and that his will translate into a decline in smoking-related lung cancer; there is little evidence of reduction in the upward trend in low-income countries where control is needed and there is limited health care (Zhou et al. 2024).

People who use drugs and those with comorbid mental health conditions have a high prevalence of smoking tobacco products. Consequently, the range of smoking-related health problems is high, as it is with the collateral damage caused by alcohol. These conditions manifest as a wide range of morbid pathologies, including pulmonary and heart disease, but also affect other organs (Gao et al. 2019). As with other observations on the disproportional impact of harmful drug use in low-income populations, the increasing needs of substance use disorder patients as they get older combine with the ability and reluctance to access care, leading to late presentation and premature death. The economic burden and the increased use of emergency services rather than elective or prevention measures is striking (Han et al. 2022, Rodrigues et al. 2025, Scottish Burden of disease 2019).

Among the many challenges that face health care systems are engaging with substance users at an early stage and identifying risk factors for multiple conditions. Health care systems and research establishments are challenged to adjust to managing multiple conditions in the same person rather than the traditional method of identifying and measuring single conditions (Barnett et al. 2012).

As with the multiple risks of infection for people who inject substances, the incidence of disorders reduced during the Covid-19 pandemic which had some impact on the prevalence of substance use. This variation in risks in different communities may be influenced by social and structural factors such as housing and social mixing. As with other observations on prevention, improved social conditions and improved economic situations are likely to reduce the burden of injection-related conditions (Lewer et al. 2023). Many of the harms associated with substance use resonate with lessons from the iconic public health observation first proposed in an essay by Dr Julian Tudor Hart in 1971. Named The Inverse Care Law it postulates that the availability of good medical care tends to vary inversely with the need for it in the population served (Marmot 2018, The Lancet 50 years of the Inverse Care Law Stone 2022).

Assessment and investigations

Crucial to management is the immediate examination of the patient who may draw attention to a specific symptom or complaint but may not understand the full implication. Serious or unresolving injury to skin or infection in tissue surrounding a vein or artery can present as local pain, swelling, warmth and discolouration. Soft tissue infections have been described as a ‘hidden epidemic of suffering’ (Harris et al. 2018) and SSTVIs among injecting drug users may cost the National Health Service, in England, an estimated £47 million per year. Intensive care admission is not uncommon (Hope et al. 2008). Injection sites should be carefully examined for signs of infection, thrombosis or bleeding. Superficial tenderness or redness suggesting inflammation and infection may be trivial or chronic but may indicate emerging problems such as abscess or cellulitis which are among the most common reasons for injecting drug users to contact treatment services (Chambers 2021).

Some of these can be the initial presentation of sepsis that may be caused by lethal infections such as clostridium or anthrax (Brett et al. 2005, McGuigan et al. 2002, Roose et al. 2010, Callahan et al. 1998). Associated with malaise, fever, rigours, nausea, vomiting or pain might indicate deeper infection locally or systemic bacteraemia and sepsis requiring ultrasound or MRI scanning and certainly backed up by blood count and renal and liver function testing. When injecting drugs into the subcutaneous or muscle tissue, "skin popping" infection may be more difficult to detect by simple observation but may be suspected when there is pain over a muscle associated with fever. Injection of medications not prepared for injection such as tablets and capsules is not uncommon (Scott et al. 1992).

The presence of swelling or groin pain in PWIDs raises the clinical suspicion of thrombosis in a femoral vein. The presence of gangrene or deep sepsis may be suspected clinically when crepitus indicates gas under the skin or a characteristic smell is detected. The organism responsible may be identified and confirmed by bacteriological sampling of material at the site or by blood culture.

Examination of the heart and lungs may reveal compromised respiratory function due to a combination of tobacco damage, inhalation of toxins and embolism, and cardiac murmurs may indicate the need to exclude infection and damage to heart valves. Ultrasound and echocardiography and blood cultures are required to exclude endocarditis.

Simple tests should be carried out routinely to detect anaemia, raised white cell count indicating infection, impaired renal or hepatic function. Blood-borne virus screening for HIV and hepatitis B and C is part of any assessment.

Deep vein thrombosis is a common side effect of injecting in the lower limb and will require specialist tests such as a Well's score and D-dimer test followed by venography, ultrasound scanning and intra-vessel angiography. Some success has been reported in the use of antibiotics and low molecular weight anticoagulants (Mackenzie et al. 2000, Sampson et al. 2005). More severe consequences such as critical limb ischaemia from intra-arterial injection may be more common than reported, as are femoral artery aneurysms resulting from damage to the wall of the blood vessel. Symptoms and signs of vascular insufficiency in the lower limb include pain on walking, or even at rest, loss of hair, mottling of the skin, absent pulses and skin ulceration. Urgent assessment by a vascular specialist is required. Acute arterial insufficiency can lead to tissue necrosis and, in extreme cases, gangrene and limb amputation.

Management of poor injecting with simple measures such as hygiene, equipment provison and supervision is clearly not enough and must include many other interventions such as medically assisted pharmaceuticals and support measures to encourage transition from injecting to non injecting drug use (Des Jarlais et al. 2014, Sreathdee et al. 1997, Stone et al. 2021).

Additional and unusual complications of injecting drug use

When assessing injury to people who inject drugs, the obvious symptoms or signs may be all that is required to identify the cause of symptoms and the need for treatment. However, damage to tissues or organs remote from injection sites or not immediately implicated as an explanation for non-specific symptoms such as fever, malaise, weight loss or fatigue should be investigated. Toxicity caused by a toxic substance now not detectable must be considered, as must historic infection from past injecting. Cryptic infections such as endocarditis and deep abscesses may not be immediately obvious, as might inflammatory reactions to chronic low-grade infection.

The introduction of fungal infection to the vascular system has been described several times. This is often associated with contaminated heroin or cocaine which has been mixed with an acidifying agent such as commercial lemon juice (left unrefrigerated and repeatedly used). Widespread candidal infection in organs and skin has been reported and cases of blindness caused by fungal infection in the eye (Collignon and Sorrell 1983, Robertson et al. 2021). Education and supply of acidifying agents such as citric acid along with needles and syringes are likely to make this less common. Overuse of acidifiers has been associated with painful injections and damage to peripheral veins and an increased risk of deep vein thrombis (Harris et al. 2019).

Neurological examination may reveal trauma to peripheral nerves damaged by harmful injecting and central nervous system problems such as embolisation to the brain are unusual events but not unknown (Tunkel Pradhan 2002). Joint or bone pain may indicate osteomyelitis.

Necrotising fasciitis and other necrotising soft tissue infections, although relatively uncommon, have high rates of morbidity and mortality and are medical and surgical emergencies (Chen 2001).

Amyloidosis may be a rarely occurring complication but it may be underdiagnosed. Some suggest that there is a causal relationship between amyloidosis affecting kidney tissue and injecting-related skin and soft tissue infection SSTI (Harris et al. 2018). A simple test for protein in a urine sample may be all that is needed to screen and detect this serious condition (Nayer 2014). There are, of course, individual toxic effects of many drugs. Again, leaving aside the psychological and behavioural disturbances, tissue damage, characteristic syndromes and organ malfunction can be seen in "ketamine bladder". Ketamine is an anaesthetic drug used in veterinary and human medicine. Its use has increased over the last decade in children as young as 13, and among 16–24 year olds, doubling between 2010 and 2020, and its estimated prevalence in 16–59 year olds was estimated to be 2.9% in England and Wales (ACMD 2025).

Ketamine comes in either liquid form or as a crystallised white powder and is most commonly snorted but sometimes swallowed, mixed into a drink, wrapped in cigarette paper (bombed) or put into a gel capsule. It can be injected into a muscle.

It is used as a drug to cause relaxation but also causes euphoria and can be hallucinogenic and induce an out of body experience, a "K hole". In high doses, it can lead to death when associated with other drugs. People can build up a tolerance and can report withdrawal symptoms including cravings, low mood, anxiety, irritability and abdominal pain, as well as mental health problems such as depression, suicidal ideation or psychosis. A recent study of 274 people who identified as having ketamine use disorder found that 60% had experienced bladder problems. Repeated use can lead to serious urinary tract problems (Belal et al. 2024).

As a reminder that injecting contaminated material by injection can result in systemic illness, in the 1930s, there was an outbreak of cases of malaria among people who inject drugs in New York City. The number of cases reported was 200 and the number of deaths, 120. The high mortality was attributed to late presentation and personal neglect (Most 1940). Tetanus has been associated with contaminated injection materials (JAMA 1997, Talan and Moran 1998). In Vietnam a high prevalence of tuberculosis was found in a high risk group with multiple risk factors of injecting drug users indicating the vulnerability to infection in people who inject drugs (Nagot et al. 2021).

Conclusions

There are many morbid and lethal conditions associated with substance use. Some are direct and easily identified and measured, and others are indirect and often not included in the national consciousness as substance-related. The enduring presence of substance use problems in accident and emergency departments is highly visible, as is the overdose rate in wards and intensive care. Less immediately visible is morbidity and mortality due to indirect causes: suicide, neglect, pregnancy complications, violence, etc. Opiate agonist treatment is protective in people who use opiates but not adequate to prevent deaths on its own without additional support services (McAuley et al. 2023).

Although three of the four biggest industrial contributors to worldwide morbidity and mortality are alcohol, tobacco and ultra-processed foods, the fourth being fossil fuels (Gilmore et al. 2023), substance use accounts for considerable morbidity and mortality. Attention to the complexity and range of ever-reported damage caused by injecting requires vigilance and expertise as well as access to modern specialist care facilities.

The marketing and commercial pressures to supply prescription opiates have intensified the urgency to regulate and control the availability of pharmaceutical products and to limit the inappropriate sale of addictive products (Jones et al. 2018). This is further examined in chapter 13.

Complicating a moving target of new substances causing harm are the black market and criminal justice elements of the substance use landscape. Stigma and marginalisation are intimately connected with people who use drugs. An historic lack of engagement by medical research, industry and government has allowed a relative hiatus in our understanding of what we should do to intervene in the, often complex, lives of people who use drugs.

References

ACMD. Updated harms assessment of ketamine: commissioning letter - GOV.UK, 2025.

ACMD: Hidden Harm: Responding to the Needs of Children of Problem Drug Users, report of an inquiry by the Advisory Council on the Misuse of Drugs. Home Office Manning, London, 2003.

Andresz V, Marcantoni N, Binder F, et al. Puffy hand syndrome due to drug addiction: a case-control study of the pathogenesis. *Addiction.* 2006;101:1347–51.

Barnard M, McKeganey N. The impact of parental problem drug use on children: what is the problem and what can be done to help? *Addiction.* 2004;99(5):552–9. https://doi.org/10.1111/j.1360-0443.2003.00664.x.

Barnett K, Mercer SW, Norbury M, Watt G, Wyke S, Guthrie B. Epidemiology of multimorbidity and implications for health care, research, and medical education: a cross-sectional study. *Lancet.* 2012 Jul 7;380(9836):37–43. https://doi.org/10.1016/S0140-6736(12)60240-2.

Bauman ZM, Morizio K, Singer M, et.al. The heroin epidemic in America: a surgeon's perspective. *Surg Infect (Larchmt).* 2019 Jul;20(5):351–8. https://doi.org/10.1089/sur.2019.004.

Belal M, Downey A, Doherty R, et al. British Association of Urological Surgeons Consensus statements on the management of ketamine uropathy. *BJU Int.* 2024 Aug;134(2):148–54. https://doi.org/10.1111/bju.16404.

Best DW, Faulkner N, Gossop M, et al. New estimates of the number of children living with substance misusing parents: results from UK national household surveys. *BMC Public Health.* 2009;9:377. https://doi.org/10.1186/1471-2458-9-377.

Bond M, Buckley, D. Drugs and alcohol in pregnancy: what a paediatrician needs to know, how to ask and why it matters. *J Paediatr Child Health.* 2024; 34(11):430–5. https://doi.org/10.1016/j.paed.2024.08.007.

Brett MM, Hood J, Brazier JS, Duerden BI, Hahné SJ. Soft tissue infections caused by spore-forming bacteria in injecting drug users in the United Kingdom. *Epidemiol Infect.* 2005;133:575–82.

Callahan TE, Schecter WP, Horn JK. Necrotizing soft tissue infection masquerading as cutaneous abscess following illicit drug injection. *Arch Surg.* 1998;133:812–8.

Canfield M, Radcliffe P, Marlow S, Boreham M, Gilchrist G. Maternal substance use and child protection: a rapid evidence assessment of factors associated with loss of child care. *Child Abuse Negl.* 2017;70:11–27. https://doi.org/10.1016/j.chiabu.2017.05.005.

Centers for Disease Control and Prevention (CDC) (2026) Drug Overdose Deaths in the United States, 2023–2024. National Center for Health Statistics. Available at: https://www.cdc.gov/nchs/products/databriefs/db549.htm (Accessed: 4 March 2026).

Chen JL, Fullerton KE, Flynn NM. Necrotizing fasciitis associated with injection drug use. *Clin Infect Dis.* 2001;33(1):6-15. https://doi.org/10.1086/320874

Collignon PJ, Sorrell TC. Disseminated candidiasis: evidence of a distinctive syndrome in heroin abusers. *Br Med J (Clin Res Ed).* 1983 Sep 24;287(6396):861–2. https://doi.org/10.1136/bmj.287.6396.861.

Coughlin PA, Mavor AI. Arterial consequences of recreational drug use. *Eur J Vasc Endovasc Surg* 2006;32:389–96.

CDC. Centers for Disease Control and Prevention. Health Topics - Tobacco - POLARIS. www.cdc.gov. Published October 5, 2021. https://www.cdc.gov/tobacco/about/index.html.

Chambers HF. Skin and soft tissue infections in persons who inject drugs. *Infect Dis Clin North Am.* 2021 Mar;35(1):169–81. https://doi.org/10.1016/j.idc.2020.10.006.

Darke S, Ross J. The use of antidepressants among injecting drug users in Sydney, Australia. *Addiction.* 2000;95:407–17.

Des Jarlais DC, McKnight C, Arasteh K, et al. Transitions from injecting to non-injecting drug use: potential protection against HCV infection. *J Subst Abuse Treat.* 2014;46:325–31.

Felker A, Patel R, Kotnis R, Kenyon S, Knight M (eds.) on behalf of MBRRACE-UK. *Saving Lives, Improving Mothers' Care Compiled Report - Lessons Learned to Inform*

Maternity Care from the UK and Ireland Confidential Enquiries into Maternal Deaths and Morbidity 2021–23. National Perinatal Epidemiology Unit, University of Oxford, Oxford, 2025. https://doi.org/10.5287/ora-4javr692x.

Gao L, Robertson JR, Bird SM, Non drug related and opioid-specific causes of 3262 deaths in Scotland's methadone prescription clients, 2009–2015. *Drug Alcohol Dependence* 2019. Advance online publication. https://doi.org/10.1016/j.drugalcdep.2019.01.019.

Gilmore AB, Fabbri A, Baum F, et al. Defining and conceptualising the commercial determinants of health. *Lancet*. 2023;401(10383):1194–213. https://doi.org/https://doi.org/10.1016/S0140-6736(23)00013-2.

Han BH, Tuazon E, Y Wei M, Paone D. Multimorbidity and Inpatient Utilization Among Older Adults with Opioid Use Disorder in New York City. *J Gen Intern Med*. 2022 May;37(7):1634–40. https://doi.org/10.1007/s11606-021-07130-8..

Harris M, Brathwaite R, McGowan CR, et al. Care and prevent: rationale for investigating skin and soft tissue infections and AA amyloidosis among people who inject drugs in London. *Harm Reduct J*. 2018;15:23.

Harris M, Scott J, Wright T, et al. Injecting-related health harms and overuse of acidifiers among people who inject heroin and crack cocaine in London: a mixed-methods study. *Harm Reduct J*. 2019;16:60.

Hope V, Kimber J, Vickerman P, Hickman M, Ncube F. Frequency, factors and costs associated with injection site infections: findings from a national multi-site survey of injecting drug users in England. *BMC Infect Dis*. 2008;8:120.

Huang MC, Yang SY, Lin SK, et al. Risk of cardiovascular diseases and stroke events in methamphetamine users: a 10-year follow-up study. *J Clin Psych*. 2016;77:1396–403.

JAMA. Tetanus among injecting-drug users—California, 1997. *JAMA*. 1998;279(13):987. https://doi.org/10.1001/jama.279.13.987-JWR0401-2-1.

Jones GH, Bruera E, Abdi S, Kantarjian HM. The opioid epidemic in the United States-overview, origins, and potential solutions. *Cancer*. 2018;124(22):4279–86. https://doi.org/https://doi.org/10.1002/cncr.31713.

Jones CM, Bekheet F, Park JN, Alexander GC. The evolving overdose epidemic: synthetic opioids and rising stimulant-related harms. *Epidemiol Rev*. 2020 Jan 31;42(1):154–66. https://doi.org/10.1093/epirev/mxaa011.

Karimi M, Ghaheri H, Assari S, et al. Drug injection to sites other than arm: a study of Iranian heroin injectors. *Front Psych*. 2014;5:23.

Lewer D, Harris M, Hope V. Opiate injection-associated skin, soft tissue, and vascular infections, England, UK, 1997–2016. *Emerg Infect Dis*. 2017;23:1400–3.

Lappin J. M, Darke S, Farrell M. Stroke and methamphet amine use in young adults: a review. *J Neurol Neurosurg Psych*. 2017;88:1079–91.

Larney S, Peacock A, Mathers B. M, Hickman M, Degenhardt L. A systematic review of injecting-related injury and disease among people who inject drugs. *Drug Alcohol Depend*. 2017;171:39–49.

Lewer D, Brothers TD, Croxford S, Desai M, Emanuel E, Harris M, Hope VD. 2023 Opioid injection-associated bacterial infections in England, 2002–2021: a time series analysis of seasonal variation and the impact of coronavirus disease 2019. *Clin Infect Dis*. 2023 Aug 14;77(3):338–45. https://doi.org/10.1093/cid/ciad144.

McAuley A, Fraser R, Glancy M, et al. Mortality among individuals prescribed opioid-agonist therapy in Scotland, UK, 2011-20: a national retrospective cohort study. *Lancet Public Health*. 2023 Jul;8(7):e484–93. https://doi.org/10.1016/S2468-2667(23)00082-8.

Manning V, Best DW, Faulkner N, Titherington E. New estimates of the number of children living with substance misusing parents: results from UK national household surveys. *BMC Public Health*. 2009;9:377. Published 2009 Oct 8. https://doi.org/10.1186/1471-2458-9-377

Maliphant J, Scott J. Use of the femoral vein ('groin injecting') by a sample of needle exchange clients in Bristol, UK. *Harm Reduct J*. 2005;2:6.

Mackenzie AR, Laing RB, Douglas JG, Greaves M, Smith CC. High prevalence of iliofemoral venous thrombosis with severe groin infection among injecting drug users in north East Scotland: successful use of low molecular weight heparin with antibiotics. *Postgrad Med J.* 2000;76:561–5.

McGuigan CC, Penrice GM, Gruer L, et al. Lethal outbreak of infection with Clostridium novyi type A and other spore-forming organisms in Scottish injecting drug users. *J Med Microbiol.* 2002;51(11):971–7. https://doi.org/10.1099/0022-1317-51-11-971

Murphy EL, DeVita D, Liu H, et al. Risk factors for skin and soft-tissue abscesses among injection drug users: a case-control study. *Clin Infect Dis.* 2001;33:35–40.

Marmot M. An inverse care law for our time. *BMJ.* 2018 Jul 31;362:k3216. https://doi.org/10.1136/bmj.k3216.

Mars SG, Bourgois P, Karandinos G et al. The textures of heroin: user perspectives on "Black tar" and powder heroin in two U.S. cities. *J Psychoactive Drugs.* 2016;48:270–8.

Mars SG, Ondocsin J, Ciccarone D. Toots, tastes and tester shots: user accounts of drug sampling methods for gauging heroin potency. *Harm Reduct J.* 2018;15:26.

Most H. Falciparum Malaria among drug addicts-epidemiologic studies. *Am J Public Health Nations Health.* 1940 Apr;30(4):403–10. https://doi.org/10.2105/ajph.30.4.403.

Nagot N, Hai VV, Dong TTT, et al. Alarming tuberculosis rate among people who inject drugs in Vietnam. *Open Forum Infect Dis.* 2021 Nov 8;9(2):ofab548. https://doi.org/10.1093/ofid/ofab548.

Nayer A. Amyloid A amyloidosis: frequently neglected renal disease in injecting drug users. *J Nephropathol.* 2014;3(1):26-28. doi:10.12860/jnp.2014.06

Ng J, Sutherland C, Kolber MR. Does evidence support supervised injection sites? *Can Fam Physician.* 2017;63:866.

Nair M, Kurinczuk JJ, Brocklehurst P, Sellers S, Lewis G, Knight M. Factors associated with maternal death from direct pregnancy complications: a UK national case–control study. *BJOG.* 2015;122(5):653–62.

Nutt DJ, King LA, Phillips LD. Drug harms in the UK: a multicriteria decision analysis. *Lancet.* 2010;376(9752):1558–65. https://doi.org/10.1016/S0140 6736(10)61462-6.

Phillips KT, Altman JK, Corsi KF, Stein MD. Development of a risk reduction intervention to reduce bacterial and viral infections for injection drug users. *Subst Use Misuse.* 2013;48:54–64.

Reneman L, Habraken JB, Majoie CB, Booij J, den Heeten GJ. MDMA("ecstasy") and its association with cerebrovascular accidents: preliminary findings. *AJNR Am J Neuroradiol.* 2000;21:1001–7.

Robertson R, Broers B, Harris M. Injecting drug use, the skin and vasculature. *Addiction.* 2021 Jul;116(7):1914–24. https://doi.org/10.1111/add.15283..

Rodrigues M, Rosic T, Babe G, et al. Comparative analysis of methods for identifying multimorbidity patterns among people with opioid use disorder: a retrospective single-cohort study. *PLoS One.* 2025 Jun 12;20(6):e0324548. https://doi.org/10.1371/journal.pone.0324548.

Roose Ramsay CN, Stirling A, et al. An outbreak of infection with bacillus anthracis in injecting drug users in Scotland. *Eurosurveillance.* 2010;15:19465.

Ross A, Raab GM, Mok J, Gilkison S, Hamilton B, Johnstone FD. Maternal HIV infection, drug use, and growth of uninfected children in their first 3 years. *Arch Dis Child.* 1995;73(6):490–95. https://doi.org/10.1136/adc.73.6.490.

R J, Hayashi AS, Cunningham CO. Self-management of injection-related wounds among injecting drug users. *J Addict Dis* 2009;28:74–80.

Sampson FC, Goodacre S, Kelly AM, Kerr D. How is deep vein thrombosis diagnosed and managed in UK and Australian emergency departments? *Emerg Med J.* 2005;22:780–2.

Scott RN, Going J, Woodburn KR, et al. Intra-arterial temazepam. *BMJ.* 1992;304:1630.

Scottish Burden of Disease. *Leading Causes of Health Loss (DALY) in Scotland – 2019.* https://scotland.shinyapps.io/phs-local-trends-scottish-burden-diseases.

Siu WT, Yau KK, Cheung HY, et al. Management of brachial artery pseudoaneurysms secondary to drug abuse. *Ann Vasc Surg.* 2005;19:657–1.
Smith ME, Robinowitz N, Chaulk P, Johnson KE. Self-care and risk reduction habits in older injection drug users with chronic wounds: a cross-sectional study. *Harm Reduct J.* 2014;11:28.
Sordo L, Indave BI, Barrio G, Degenhardt L, de la Fuente L, Bravo MJ. Cocaine use and risk of stroke: a systematic review. *Drug Alcohol Depend.* 2014;142:1–13.
Strathdee SA, Patrick DM, Currie SL, et al. Needle exchange is not enough: lessons from the Vancouver injecting drug use study. *AIDS.* 1997;11:F59–65.
Strang J, Volkow ND, Degenhardt L, et al. Opioid use disorder. *Nat Rev Dis Primers.* 2020 Jan 9;6(1):3. https://doi.org/10.1038/s41572-019-0137-5.
Stone J, Artenie A, Hickman M, et al. The contribution of unstable housing to HIV and hepatitis C virus transmission among people who inject drugs globally, regionally, and at country level: a modelling study. *Lancet Public Health.* 2022 Feb;7(2):e136–45. https://doi.org/10.1016/S2468-2667(21)00258-9.
Stone J, Degenhardt L, Grebely J, et al. Modelling the intervention effect of opioid agonist treatment on multiple mortality outcomes in people who inject drugs: a three-setting analysis. *Lancet Psych.* 2021 Apr;8(4):301–9. https://doi.org/10.1016/S2215-0366(20)30538-1.
Summers PJ, Struve IA, Wilkes MS, Rees VW. Injection site vein loss and soft tissue abscesses associated with black tar heroin injection: a cross-sectional study of two distinct populations in USA. *Int J Drug Policy.* 2017;39:21–7.
Talan DA, Moran GJ. Update on emerging infections: news from the centers for disease control and prevention. Tetanus among injecting-drug users--California, 1997. *Ann Emerg Med.* 1998;32(3 Pt 1):385–6.
The Lancet. 50 years of the inverse care law. *Lancet.* 2021 Feb 27;397(10276):767. https://doi.org/10.1016/S0140-6736(21)00505-5.
Tsao JW, Marder SR, Goldstone J, Bloom AI. Presentation, diagnosis, and management of arterial mycotic pseudoaneurysms in injection drug users. *Ann Vasc Surg.* 2002;16:652–62.
Tunkel AR, Pradhan SK. Central nervous system infections in injection drug users. *Infect Dis Clin North Am.* 2002 Sep;16(3):589–605. https://doi.org/10.1016/s0891-5520(02)00015-6.
World Health Organization. (2023). Alcohol and cancer. WHO Regional Office for Europe. Available at: https://www.who.int/europe/news-room/fact-sheets/item/alcohol-and-cancer.
Woodburn KR, Murie JA. Vascular complications of injecting drug misuse. *Br J Surg.* 1996 Oct;83(10):1329–34. https://doi.org/10.1002/bjs.1800831005.
Zhou J, Xu Y, Liu J, Feng L, Yu J, Chen D. 2024 Global burden of lung cancer in 2022 and projections to 2050: Incidence and mortality estimates from GLOBOCAN. *Cancer Epidemiol.* 2024 Dec;93:102693. https://doi.org/10.1016/j.canep.2024.102693.

6 The increasing importance of harm reduction

Background

The concept of harm reduction pervades the realms of policy and political and diplomatic negotiations. The term Principled Pragmatism is discussed by Siemers in his paper discussing the techniques used by Abraham Lincoln in trying to balance many apparently conflicting solutions to complex problems. Siemers concludes that in order to manage and make decisions, Lincoln described several intractable problems and the need to prioritise and "temporarily subordinate" some of the components.

> Each of these contexts led him to reconsider which of his commitments—to universal rights, the law, Union, and popular government—to privilege and which to temporarily subordinate. The result was a highly successful combination of pragmatism and idealism that I label "principled pragmatism.
>
> (Siemers 2004)

In the field of substance use, the term harm reduction is a similar pragmatic concept. Applied to reducing the risks of drug use, it emerged in the 1980s when there was a rapidly increasing number of people using drugs. It may require judgement, but harm reduction requires an estimate in each case of which risks to temporality subordinate in order to minimise the damage. For example, accepting continued drug use but negotiating and supporting a move from injectables to oral medication might be seen as an example of a first step in a recovery journey and a vital harm reduction measure.

Other similar terms are useful in describing the philosophy behind this approach. Damage limitation, risk reduction and harm minimisation are all terms used to define policies and practices which might improve the lives of someone using drugs.

Attempts to separate a policy of abstinence and drug-free recovery from treatment involving continued substance use have impeded progress for some time. Conflicts of interest arise when a purist view of treatment and recovery demands a policy of abstinence from substances and discourages treatment that is prepared to tolerate continued but modified substance use. It is often said that recovery from substance use (and other addictive problems) is a journey, and this prolonged period

DOI: 10.4324/9781003611097-6

in a life needs to be seen as a process during which realignment of priorities is progressive improvement supported by medical, psychological and social supports. The importance of integrating a programme of reducing risks with personalised psychological supports must be viewed as a continuum that may result in rapid benefits and improvement but may last many years (Kelly et al. 2025).

This integrated, multi-agency approach to treatment is increasingly relevant at a time when the substance in common use is changing and the importance of opiate agonist treatment using methadone or buprenorphine is becoming relatively less important in some countries. Increasing cocaine use worldwide and the dominance of methamphetamine and other stimulants challenge a simple framework. Pharmacological interventions remain critically important in countries and regions where heroin, synthetic opiates and drugs such as fentanyl and nitazines remain in the illegal supply chain.

The risks of blood-borne virus infection were perhaps the single most important element of this urgent pressure to change from a policy driven by the need for abstinence and drug-free therapy to a management strategy with multiple approaches. Injecting heroin among young people, the associated rapid increase in hepatitis B (and the yet unknown hepatitis C) and the spectre of an HIV/AIDS epidemic energised change and innovations such as needle and injecting equipment provision, opiate agonist treatment and a wide range of other interventions.

The definition of Harm Reduction is contained in the term and can be as broadly applied as necessary. Anything that makes the likelihood of damage caused by using drugs less might be included. In his excellent article from 1995, Eric Single clarifies the complexity of reducing the harm of drugs and expands the vision and theory behind what is a robust set of policy initiatives.

> Harm reduction attempts to reduce the adverse consequences of drug use among persons who continue to use drugs. It developed in response to the excesses of a "zero tolerance approach". Harm reduction emphasizes practical rather than idealized goals. It has been expanded from illicit drugs to legal drugs and is grounded in the evolving public health and advocacy movements. Harm reduction has proved to be effective, and it has gained increasing official acceptance; for example, it is now the basis of Canada's Drug Strategy. However, the concept is still poorly defined, as virtually any drug policy or programme, even abstinence-oriented programmes, attempt to reduce drug-related harm. The principal feature of harm reduction is the acceptance of the fact that some drug users cannot be expected to cease their drug use at the present time. Harm reduction is neutral about the long term goals of intervention while according a high priority to short-term realizable goals. Harm reduction should be neutral about legalization. The essence of the concept is to ameliorate adverse consequences of drug use while, at least in the short term, drug use continues.
>
> (Single 1995)

The concept of drug use without harms is somewhat contradictory and, to many, complicit with encouraging a damaging behaviour, but an increasing understanding of the nature of addiction/dependency has allowed for mainstream acceptance of a pragmatic and humane approach to drug taking while, at the same time, encouraging transition out of harms way. The value of preventing a lethal injection, the transmission of a virus or bacterium or damage to a vital organ is hard to dispute, and the case for providing clean, sterile injecting equipment might easily be seen as saving lives. The longer vision of transitioning to a controlled and then a drug-free life is in no way a contradiction to harm reduction. The simple and immediate effect of taking away, or minimising, the immediate risk of the next injection forms part of a process and pathways to a more enduring sense of recovery.

Harm reduction, therefore, starts with measures that may be as simple as engaging in discussion leading to a pathway of options such as supported management of drug taking, alternatives to injecting, stability and security of legal alternatives, and a progressive process of social and psychological rehabilitation. The concept of harm reduction also includes the recognition that drug use may continue, sometimes indefinitely, and that progression on any recovery pathway may not be a linear pattern. Stepwise improvement may take time and may halt or suspend at any point. The state of relative safe drug use may be reached and may be an acceptable position for an individual until circumstances change. "Pragmatic" or "pragmatism" are words that resonate throughout the literature and guidance on the management of injecting drug use. The practical application of support, which may seem less than ideal, is offering a realistic intervention in the face of an otherwise insoluble individual or set of risks. This is not to accept the inevitability of injecting drug use but to mitigate the harms at the same time as encouraging safer behaviour and offering a pathway through to a progressively normalised lifestyle. A pragmatic solution may accept partial or slow improvement, understanding limitations without resorting to unnecessary pressure or condemnation.

The progressive implementation of harm reduction as a fundamental paradigm in drug policy has evolved rapidly over the last decade in the light of substantial evidence to support a wide range of interventions that might mitigate the damage done by drugs. Pridgen and colleagues have summarised the situation in the USA in a robust publication,drawing attention to the many interventions that might have been implemented but have not (Pridgen et al. 2025).

Recovery and abstinence are not mutually exclusive. In fact, they are part of the same process of recovery (Hickman et al. 2011).

Signs of stress in injecting communities

It may seem obvious, but harm reduction measures are urgently needed when things go wrong among people who inject drugs. Outbreaks of infections alert public health to an emergency such as clusters of a particular bacterium or virus causing death or illness. Recent episodes of spore-forming bacteria such as *Clostridium botulinum*, *Clostridia novyii* and *Bacillus anthracis* trigger alerts and interventions and demand reviews of policy to prevent recurrence (Trayner et al. 2015, Ramsay et al. 2010, McGuigan et al. 2002). Epidemic hepatitis B or C and HIV have an impact and require immediate and prospective planning and policy change. Urgent situations such as these indicate that there is an infective agent in the circulating drug supply but, importantly, that people are at risk by virtue of sharing substances or equipment.

Increased deaths and overdoses locally or nationally suggest a systemic failure to control substance use and the conditions that support it, whether they are driven by poor economic conditions or an increased risk in the drugs used. A new drug or a more potent variant, an unusual compound, a toxic contaminant or a lethal combination may give rise to increasing fatality rates.

Stress in communities may be apparent from secondary indicators such as homelessness and criminality, increased attendance at support agencies or signs of casual or reckless drug use such as discarded injecting equipment or family concerns.

Whatever the cause, management is the responsibility of everyone from Government to families, statutory health social care agencies and street services. Problems such as these indicate that more support is required or that better delivery of services such as opiate agonist treatment, mental health and psychology assessments and interventions, admission to hospital or residential care, when required, and review of needle and syringe exchange services is required.

Partnership working in communities and across medical and social care organisations has been shown to be the most effective way of engaging and retaining contact with people at risk from drug use. Examples of teams working together are evident in many countries and have lots of different settings and situations, and include various contributing agencies. Linking specialist drug and alcohol services with primary care and general medical practice often includes third sector organisations, pharmacists and laboratory support services.

The legacy of many crises is the lesson that preventing episodes is difficult but that a high level of suspicion is always required and that caring agencies must be vigilant for failures in provision.

The close connection between sudden overdose death and release from custody or after detoxification during hospitalisation remains a problem (Merrall et al. 2010). Provision of naloxone kits and careful briefing on release is not always observed, and preventable deaths continue. Despite the many publications alerting us to the risk of overdose after voluntary or coercive loss of tolerance, systematic provision of education and supply of naloxone remains variable and problematic. In the post-custody scenario, there are numerous difficulties. Discharge from detention is not always planned in advance; release of people on remand from court can be instantaneous, making return to any planning process less likely, and similarly, release from residential situations in hospital or detoxification facilities might be precipitous. Retoxification, the controlled reintroduction of a prescribed opiate to induce tolerance, can be effective but is more than usually not available in busy institutions.

In the clinical situation of stimulant use, the use of prescription stimulants is being considered to avoid the use of more toxic and contaminated illegal supply.

As a harm reduction measure in the face of intensely damaging substance use, this intervention makes much sense and is likely to be of interest to the many clinicians facing an epidemic of cocaine and methylamphetamine use by injection (Fleming et al. 2020).

In a systematic risk reduction plan, this is a critically important challenge to policy and practice.

Paraphernalia provision

The provision of injecting equipment has become standard practice since the HIV/AIDS epidemic of the 1980s (Public Health Scotland 2021). From the early days when a very small number of clinics allowed people to obtain sterile equipment, there are now 89 outlets in the five major cities in Scotland ranging from community pharmacies to specialist clinics with associated other services. Equipment supplied are syringes and needles, individual or in packs, with acidifying agents such as citric acid or vitamin C to improve the solubility of heroin. The syringes are usually one or two mls in size with orange or blue (slightly longer) needles. The package of equipment supplied varies from agency to agency and some allow collection of assorted and varied sizes by choice. Longer needles, for example, may be preferred by people who inject in the femoral (groin) area. The development of "low dead space" needles and syringes is expected to reduce the risk of cross contamination causing blood-borne virus transmission when people share injecting equipment (Zule et al. 2013). A core ambition of the provision of injecting equipment is, however, to discourage sharing of injecting kits, and adequate supplies to allow this to happen are essential (Hussey 2019).

The Scottish Needle Exchange Surveillance Initiative (NESI) is a research programme in Scotland that monitors the prevalence of blood-borne viruses (BBVs) such as hepatitis C (HCV) and HIV. The study reports every two years on this and injecting behaviours such as frequency of injecting and sharing equipment (Public Health Scotland 2022).

In the year 2023, the Scottish Government's department of public health reported that there were 330 outlets (clinics, pharmacies and primary care sites) distributing approximately 2.3 million needles and syringes at 132,447 attendances. The health board area with the greatest supply and demand was the City of Glasgow, where 1 million kits were distributed in 2022/2023. There was reported a gradual decrease in attendances each year since 2014/2015 when there were 4.7 million kits given at 328,329 attendances. Other items of injecting equipment distributed were foil sheets used for smoking instead of injecting drugs such as heroin and crack cocaine, supporting route transition and reducing use of more risky, home-crafted alternatives; citric acid or vitamin C and sterile water for injection, which are used to dissolve drugs (particularly heroin) into an injectable solution, and wipes or swabs. Sharps bins are also provided to allow safe disposal of used equipment.

In different sites, interventions vary. The simple supply of injecting equipment in a package on request may be all that is possible in a pharmacy or mobile unit. Ideally, additional health advice might be given, such as inspecting injection

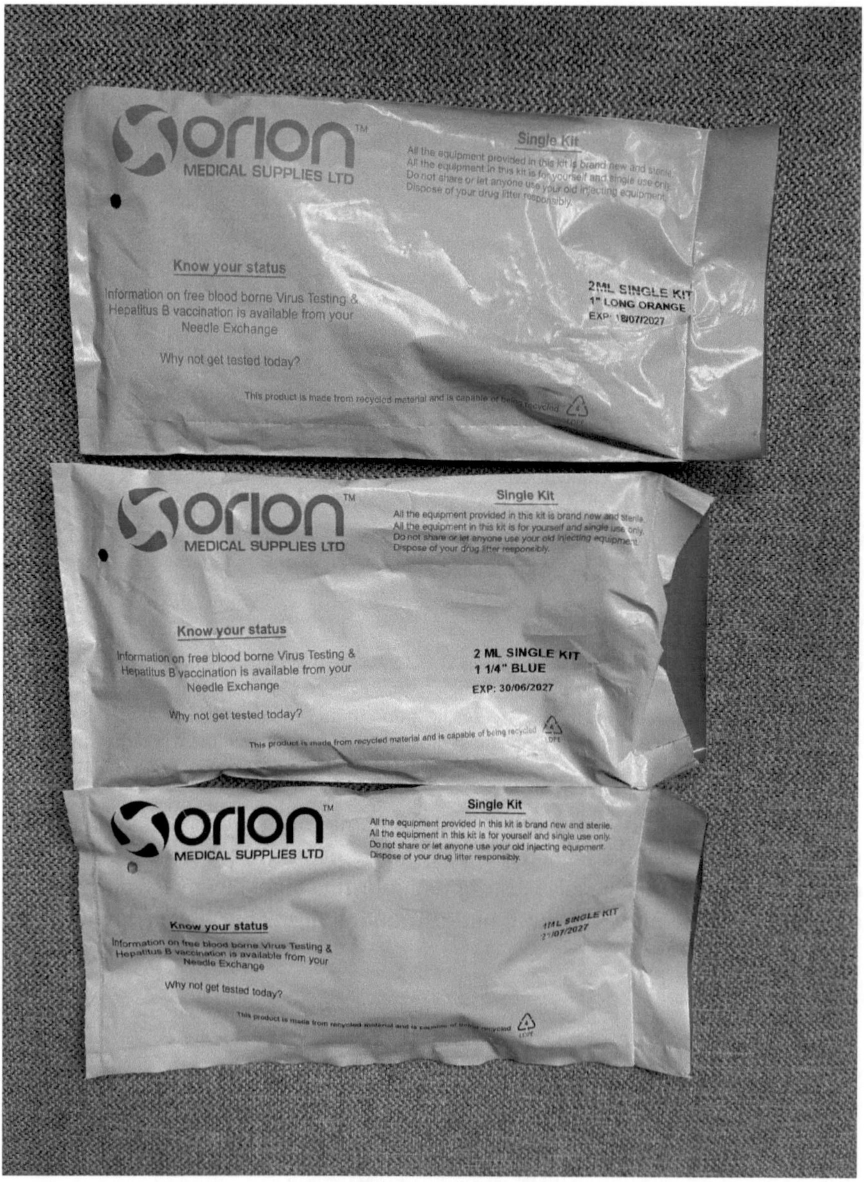

Figure 6.1 Pre-packed injecting equipment with three sizes of needles to allow for preference and varying injection sites.

practices, encouragement to use safer sites and to transition away from femoral vein injecting. A variety of needles and syringe sizes may be made available depending on individual preferences.

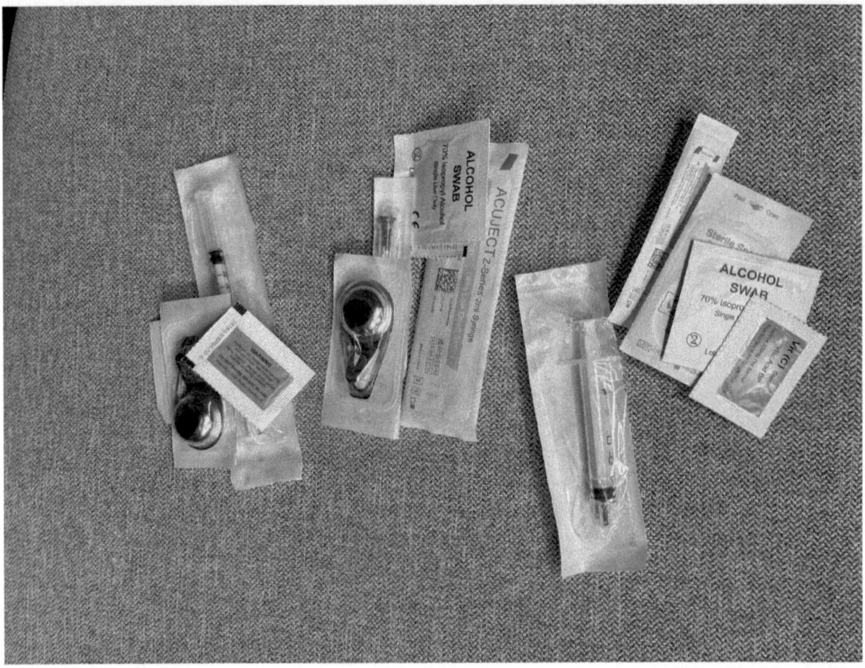

Figure 6.2 In the pack are syringes, needles, a spoon to mix the drug, foil to heat the mixture on, water for injection, sterile swabs and a citric acid sachet to acidify mixture.

Since the COVID-19 epidemic, when the number of needles and syringes distributed per attendance was increased, this has remained much the same (16–17 at each attendance). The agencies distributing injecting equipment vary. Stand-alone agencies were the most common, but distribution at treatment services was also

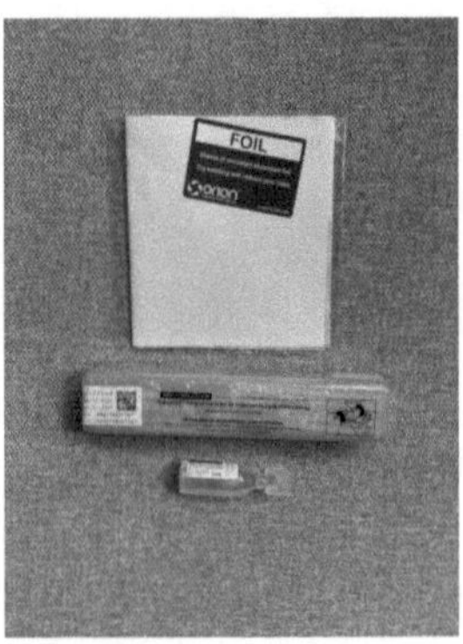

Figure 6.3 Naloxone injection, foil and disposal bin.

Images from equipment used at The Thistle, Glasgow's Safer Consumption Facility.

common. Mobile sites in rural areas, replacement after confiscation and domestic delivery also existed.

The purpose of Injecting Equipment Provision (IEP) is, simply, harm reduction. Minimising the exposure of people who inject drugs to blood-borne virus infection risks is a key objective. The provision of sterile injecting equipment was energised first during the HIV/AIDS epidemics in the 1980s and again after the isolation of the hepatitis C virus in the early 1990s (Jones et al. 2010, Burrows 1998). Originally this intervention was politically highly sensitive and opportunities were limited by strict regulation and by anxiety in treatment services. Experience over many years has clearly identified the need for prevention of harms caused by injection, not just bacterial and virus transmission but the introduction of toxins and damage to vasculature.

The Scottish Government's Sexual Health and Blood-Borne Virus Framework aims to reduce blood-borne virus transmission (Scottish Government 2015). IEP services are known to be effective at reducing higher risk injecting practices in people who inject drugs (European Centre for Disease Control 2011) and have formed a key component of the harm reduction approach adopted by the Scottish Government since the publication of the Hepatitis C Action Plan (Scottish Government 2008). By providing sterile injecting equipment and contributing to wider harm reduction initiatives, IEP services have played a key role in helping to reduce hepatitis C prevalence in Scotland (NESI 2022).

The European Drugs Report recently drew attention to the widening requirements of harm reduction to include the recognition of social inequalities, housing and education and specific interventions beyond opiate agonist treatment and injecting equipment provision. Other essential interventions included in guidance for governments and health and social care services, including custodial situations, include naloxone provision, drug testing facilities and safer consumption rooms. Reducing vulnerability is now recognised as an important harm reduction measure. This includes integrated care with mental health and generic health facilities, improved access to social and health services, housing and supported employment programmes and stigma reduction interventions (European Drugs Report 2024).

In Scotland the recognition of the burden of disease attributable to substance use is considerable. This has considerable implications for the allocation of resources and the focus of treatment (ScotPHO 2023).

In Europe, countries reporting the formal availability of treatments in prison included a wide range of interventions. Some countries provide more comprehensive services on this list than others, with the majority providing a health assessment within 48 hours (26 out of 29 member states, two unknown) and a smaller number providing other interventions such as injecting equipment and naloxone provision (7 out of 28 and 3 out of 29 respectively). In its broadest sense, the term harm reduction can be applied to a wide range of interventions such as:

Health assessment within 48 hours of contact with services
Therapeutic communities
Individual counselling

Group counselling
Peer interventions
Detoxification programmes, drug-free or integrated with pharmacological support
Opiate Substitute Treatments (OST) continued from the community.
OST initiated in prison
OST continuation to the community
HIV, HBV, HCV testing
Vaccination for HBV
HBV/HIV/HCV antiviral therapy
Needle and Syringe Provision
Condom distribution
Naloxone kits (inhalation and injectables available)

Naloxone distribution is of huge international importance, and many countries have included this in their harm reduction measures. The latest findings reported from Public Health Scotland concluded, as the main points in their 2025 report, that in 2022/2023:

- 28,689 Take Home Naloxone (THN) kits were issued in Scotland, which was a 1% decrease compared to 2021/22 (29,075). The annual number of kits supplied in 2021/22 and 2022/23 was substantially higher than in any year up to and including 2020/21 (22,378).
- 22,184 THN kits were issued from community outlets, 1,929 kits were issued in prisons upon release, 3,249 kits were dispensed via community prescription, and 1,225 kits were distributed by the Scottish Ambulance Service (SAS).
- The most common sources of community THN supply were drug treatment services (12,575, 57%), Scottish Families Affected by Alcohol and Drugs (SFAD) (5,042, 23%) and non-drug treatment services (such as homelessness services) (1,581, 7%).
- Of the 28,689 THN kits issued in Scotland, 20,918 (73%) were intramuscular Prenoxad® kits and 7,759 (27%) were intranasal Nyxoid®.
- 7,708 THN kits were distributed as repeat supplies. Of these, 2,013 (26%) were issued because the previous kit was reported as having been used to treat an opioid overdose.
- Of the 2,257 THN kits issued via peer-to-peer supply, 1,453 (64%) were distributed from community outlets and 804 (36%) were distributed from prisons.

At the end of 2022/23:

- A total of 151,944 THN kits had been supplied in Scotland.
- The ‘reach’ of THN (based on the number of people at risk of an opioid overdose supplied with kits between 2011/12 and 2022/23) was estimated to be 705 kits per 1,000 people with problematic drug use.

This is an impressive response to the drug overdose crisis in that country (PHS 2025). Constant attention to these programmes of harm minimisation is essential as routine surveillance demonstrates when decreases in uptake can quickly occur when publicity declines and the services providing support are affected by saving budgets. An example of incomplete implementation is shown in the 2022 survey which found that the majority of participants in the survey (63%) in 2019–2020 had been prescribed a take-home naloxone kit, only 21% were carrying it at the time of interview (Public Health Scotland 2025).

Heroin-assisted treatment and safe injection spaces

In the United Kingdom, there has been a system of heroin prescribing for people who did not tolerate or comply with oral opiate agonist treatments such as methadone. For several decades, a few hundred heroin injectors were prescribed heroin for injection. Some were doctors or nurses and many managed to carry on an otherwise normal life. During the 1960s–1980s, because of a loss of political support, this system was considerably reduced. For a short period in the 1980s and early 1990s, Dr John Marks ran heroin-prescribing clinics in Liverpool, Widnes and Warrington that were controversial. Because of the lack of large-scale trials, only anecdotal evidence existed as to the efficacy of the treatment. This changed in 1994 when Switzerland, faced with one of the largest open drug scenes in Europe at the time, started large-scale trials on the potential use of diamorphine as a maintenance drug. They proved diamorphine to be a viable maintenance drug which has shown equal or better rates of success than methadone in terms of assisting long-term users establish stable, crime-free lives (Strang et al 2010). These results encouraged countries like Germany, Switzerland and the Netherlands to conduct their own trials and finally to include heroin-assisted treatment fully as a part of the national health systems (Perneger 1998, March et al. 2006). A clinic prescribing heroin to a small group of people who inject drugs in Glasgow opened in 2021.

Safer Drug Consumption Facility (SDCF). While drug consumption rooms have become a more accepted harm reduction response, establishing them remains problematic in some countries. In 2023, 10 EU countries and Norway had operational facilities, a total of 78 sites, and in the United Kingdom, one has now opened in Scotland.

Education about injecting technique and suitable sites is available.
Recognition of the burden of mortality in the USA has allowed the development of discussions about safer injecting facilities and overdose prevention centres (Cerdá et al. 2025, Giglio et al. 2023). The rapid increase in drug overdose rates has been due to prescription-related deaths, heroin rates expanding since 2010 and more recently by illegal synthetic opiate ssuch as fentanyl (Spencer et al. 2023). As well as the one million deaths in the last 20 years, injecting drug use has been responsible for epidemics of HIV, hepatitis and sepsis.

Recognizing the impact of safer injecting facilities in Canada and Australia andack nowledging the increasing numbers of these facilities in Europe, the harm reduction impact is increasing, transitioning to policy. Objections such as the belief that these rooms will encourage drug injecting, act as an attraction for people using drugs to vulnerable localities and increase blood-borne virus transmission have, so far, been unsubstantiated (Kennedy et al. 2019, Potier et al. 2014).

Opiate agonist treatment

If the notion of harm reduction remains controversial in some quarters, the use of opiate agonist treatment has become a target in the diverse views on the value of treatment. Possibly because of being uncomfortable with its action to continue dependence on an opiate rather than encouraging abstinence, the word substitute and the practice of daily provision have been associated with disapproval. This is unfortunate, as the balance of research undoubtedly shows the health benefits of treatment with an opiate agonist in reducing harms such as overdose deaths and infectious disease. Added to this, the control regulations associated with pharmaceuticals such as methadone and buprenorphine constrain the supply of these treatments in communities and some custody situations, and in the past, have led to the visible congregation of people in some communities waiting outside pharmacies and clinics, on a daily basis, to receive treatments. Newer formulations of buprenorphine have undoubtedly helped in normalising the access to essential treatments. Opiate treatment is described in detail in Chapter 9.

Benzodiazepines as a coexisting risk

In those countries that compile statistics on drug-related deaths that include comprehensive toxicology results that have been present and may have contributed to the fatal event, benzodiazepines are often present. Conclusions about their role in the causation of death are variable depending upon the other drugs present at post mortem toxicolgy which may have been overwhelmingly toxic and might simply explain the outcome. Often, however, the coexistence of a respiratory depressant such as a benzodiazepine in sufficient quantity is likely to have had a cumulative effect and is therefore included in the certification of causation.

It is important to acknowledge that benzodiazepine prescribing has been controversial since the introduction of these drugs in the 1960s.

Prescribers have been stressed and, to a certain extent, in disagreement about the value of prescribing and evidence of long-term toxicity, where it exists, is limited to relatively small doses and short-term use (Ashton 1994). Lader, for many years the doyen of benzodiazepine research, sums up the lack of evidence in his important paper highlighting the need for further evidence on the efficacy of benzodiazepines when in use for long periods, in this case, a few weeks (Lader 2011). The dangers and damage caused by any use are limited to observation studies involving relatively small doses and often in the elderly population. Most of these studies, and the resulting guidance, don't even begin to assess the damage caused by atypical benzodiazepine drugs and the "mega dosing" commonly seen in communities, bingeing with periodic large intakes of oral tablets and long-term use (Johnson et al. 2016).

For prescribers, the issues are familiar, and practice is driven by pragmatic and basic harm reduction measures based on common sense. Getting people to withdraw from benzodiazepine use is clearly a good objective (except when they are for some evidence-based situations such as epilepsy) but not simple, as dependency is profound.

For those on a legitimate prescription leading to dependency escalation, those doses are a hazard of which prescribers are aware, and most prescribers have a dose tolerance limit based on knowledge of the person involved and local and national guidelines. Some will say never prescribe benzodiazepines, and others will say only prescribe where the clinical situation is short-term or otherwise controlled (for example, occasional predictable situations which cause extreme anxiety).

The difficulty in the current world of drug use is that none of the guidelines or self-imposed practices address the problems now evident with this distinct client group who are more or less dependent/addicted to doses that often wildly exceed any recommended levels and may include drugs that are related to diazepam but have unknown actions and side effects.

For these individuals, many take the view that there is no intervention that is comfortable and therefore they refuse to engage. For those who do engage with this patient group, current interventions have been largely unsuccessful, and suggesting that we try harder or longer with the same treatment options (counselling, information, reduction programmes, etc.) is unhelpful.

Currently being tried in some authorities is replacement maintenance prescribing of diazepam. There is some evidence that this can, like opiate agonist treatment, improve retention in contact with treatment services and reduction of more dangerous illicit use (Matheson 2024). While it may reduce dangerous self-medication, it clearly does not address the common expectation of abstinence and is therefore seen as controversial. More information is required to support and endorse a recommendation for reducing the harm of these drugs by offering a substitute. The recent increase in illegal supply of a range of pharmaceutically prepared and illicit versions of benzodiazepines increases the urgency for a suitable intervention.

Palliative care

Palliative care is a concept not normally associated with the treatment or management of drug dependency, but as the opiate marketplace increases, there are a larger number of people at an end stage of life living with multiple morbidities. Reducing the escalating drug death statistics has become something of a priority in policy, with the responses, understandably, concentrating on education, prevention of harms and assisting recovery in whatever form that takes. Closer scrutiny of those who are included as a drug-related death reveals a spectrum of cases ranging from very young people suffering sudden death from overdose to older people with multimorbid conditions who have accumulated several pathological diseases likely to shorten their lives (Robertson 2021). Preventing death in these cases is important but recognising an adavnced state of illness should trigger a palliative care approach even if the expected death may not be immediate.

The National Institute for Health and Care Excellence defines palliative care as:

> The active holistic care of patients with advanced, progressive illness. Management of pain and other symptoms and provision of psychological, social and spiritual support is paramount. The goal of palliative care is achievement of the best quality of life for patients and their families. Many aspects of palliative care are also applicable earlier in the course of the illness in conjunction with other treatments.
>
> (NICE 2015)

This definition and the extensive guidance from the World Health Organization (WHO 2025) stress the multidisciplinary nature of the palliative care pathways and the alleviation of suffering rather than the shortening of life. One important aspect of the many palliative care guidelines is the early onset of palliative care in chronic conditions causing pain, distress or disability.

The WHO and operational guidelines on hospices and increasingly integrated into clinical services have a wide remit to intervene in cases where death may not be expected in the immediate future, and one definition states that if death might be expected within the next 12 months, then a palliative care approach is appropriate. Knowing what we do about the increased risk of death, especially in multimorbid drug users, this allows for thinking about planning for the eventuality of the end of life.

The World Health Organization, and NICE suggest that providing relief from pain and other distressing symptoms is just one objective of palliative care (WHO 2020, NICE 2015). It is designed to improve the quality of life of patients and their families, to integrate psychological and spiritual aspects of patient care and importantly, in the case of people with a dependency problem, to use a team approach to address the needs of patients alongside any clinical interventions which may be appropriate. Also, a stated benchmark of palliative care is that it intends neither to hasten nor postpone death.

The discussions currently active in UK Parliament as well as the Scottish devolved Parliament on assisted dying legislation have concentrated the minds of health and social care institutions as well as the public on palliative care in the broadest sense. The Isle of Man may be the first UK territory which legalises voluntary dying and there is likely to be change elsewhere soon. This paradigm shift is likely to have the, often stated, effect of enhancing traditional palliative care. Draft legislation concentrates quite rightly on the period immediately prior to the date that the person might be expected to die of whatever condition they are suffering from. Palliative care is, however, a broader concept than just the terminal event and many definitions describe the improvements in quality of life and relief from suffering caused by pain and distress during a time when active treatment for an underlying condition is not with the expectation of cure or reversal of a progressive state. Symptom control, pain management and psychological support might all be part of palliation and form part of a pragmatic approach to management without the expectation of prolonging life. For people with advanced substance use problems with comorbid complications and distress caused by their situation, a compassionate approach to management without the pressure of unrealistic stress on unattainable abstinence goals, and measures to accommodate a stable state which includes prescription drugs seem important. There is great value in removing the threats and stresses of trying to achieve a drug-free state similar to the management of people suffering from advanced cancer or neuropathic pain where the concerns about dependency on opiates are no longer a limiting factor. The challenges may be different in people who have used opiates for many years, but the alternatives for people with substance dependency can be social isolation, loneliness and self-neglect leading to suicide by proxy.

Future direction of harm reduction policies

The advantage of viewing drug problems through a perspective of reducing harms is that policy shifts and practical solutions can be visualised and implemented in line with changing patterns of drug use. The presence of an ageing population of people who have injected drugs in the past and who have multimorbidities demands expansion and reassessment of services and research (Rosen et al. 2011). Degenhardt and colleagues describe the current range of harm minimising interventions and conclude that:

> Despite strong evidence for the effectiveness of a range of interventions to improve the health and wellbeing of people who are dependent on opioids, coverage is low, even in high-income countries. Treatment quality might be less than desirable, and considerable harm might be caused to individuals, society, and the economy by the criminalisation of extramedical opioid use and dependence. Alternative policy frameworks are recommended that adopt an approach based on human rights and public health, do not make drug use a criminal behaviour, and seek to reduce drug-related harm at the population level.
>
> (Degenhardt et al. 2019)

It is disappointing that the most effective evidence-based treatment for opiate use disorder is found to be implemented on an inadequate basis, even in high-income countries, and that policy is slow to follow changing patterns of drug taking. There are many challenges in communities and custodial situations. The constant invention of new drugs and patterns of drug availability and supply chains makes regulation impossible and treatment services difficult.

The concept of palliative care as a relief of suffering rather than treatment aimed at stopping or reversing a disease progression is well-established in the management of end-of-life care, especially when cancer is the underlying condition and the trajectory is clear. The emerging debate and legislative changes endorsing a positive move to end life bring a new perspective to us all. In the context of substance use, there may be features that are singular to people with longstanding drug problems and the collateral damage associated with long-term dependency. Viewed through various lenses, problems and ethical issues abound. People who use drugs may be seen as a psychiatric problem, raising issues of consent and capacity to make decisions; the person with drug problems may be decades younger than most people dying of cancer. The intermittent relapsing and remitting nature of dependency disorders is associated with periods of low self-esteem and extreme lows, or highs. Moods further complicate the wisdom, insight or judgement to make important decisions. A lifetime of adverse events related to substance use may well project an individual to end-of-life decisions where augmented or improved social and medical care might be a better alternative.

Conclusion

The complexity of harm reduction with all the modalities of care and range of services involved demands an acceptance of the concept of reducing a multitude of risks in various ways. Single solutions or models of harm reduction which can be implemented globally are unrealistic as risks and relative risks vary in countries and communities and fromtime to time. There are many models and examples of success as blood-borne virus infection comes under better control, at least in medium and high income countries, and the UNAIDS ambitions progress (UNAIDS 2024, Cranston 2017, Peters 1994).

Emerging problems, such as spreading viral infections or new drugs in a locality, require special urgency and appropriate modelling of interventions. The discovery of epidemic HIV or hepatitis B and C in drug-using communities indicates the need for needle and syringe supplies (Greenwood 1996, Gruer et al. 1993). Various models emerged over the next few years, including vending machines (Stark et al. 1994). The introduction of a new drug such as fentanyl or nitazine into a community is, subsequently, concentrating efforts to prevent overdose events with the upscaling of known interventions and the introduction of innovative solutions (Norton et al. 2024). The increased number of people suffering from opiate overdose in North America and Europe has given rise to many Supervised Injection Sites and Overdose Prevention Sites, which inevitably incorporate a pathway into more measured support services (Wood et al. 2007).

Some principles apply, however, to the delivery of harm reduction. Recognising the variable response required, flexibility and adaptability must be incorporated at strategy and delivery levels. Mutual understanding of and commitment to people who inject (or otherwise use substances in a harmful way) is perhaps one of the most difficult baselines as stigma and territorial funding arrangements conspire to inhibit the sharing of resources. Traditional training models, with specialists becoming increasingly expert in smaller niche areas of scientific and clinical practice, have developed a micro-specialty environment where physicians, surgeons and other clinicians have unique skills rather than a more holistic approach to cases. Even in the potentially ideal and attractive environment of family practice or community care, limited resources of time, trained staff and infrastructure make it easy to see why competition might give rise to excluding cases which seem complex or require additional resources. This is, however, precisely the situation that lends itself to a shared care model which uses multiple expertise and shares the cost. National (United Kingdom) departments of health have espoused the notion of shared care and outline in detail the levels of intervention for different agencies and how joint working and shared responsibility might be to the benefit of all people in care and those who are providing services for management (Clinical Guidelines on Drug Misuse and Dependence Update 2017). Guidelines and arrangements for services require constant revision and updates as new demands emerge.

In a 2011 study, the authors commented on the value of integrating the concepts of recovery, abstinence and harm reduction under a single policy statement:

> Abstinence-oriented treatments, whatever the definition of abstinence, and maintenance-oriented treatment philosophy and practice need to work together to combine the benefits of both. For many with addiction problems, this may affect them for a long period of their life, even though the eventual outcome may be abstinence. Wherever possible, the benefits of interventions should be maximized as early as possible—but this drive must not become dogma and clinicians must not become like Procrustes, forcing their patients to fit the currently fashionable treatments.
>
> (Hickman 2011)

Finally, access to services for people requiring support is essential. Without a patient-centred approach and easy-to-access treatment services the worst harms from substance use will continue to prevail. The "no wrong door" or "universal access" to treatment mantras are short cut terms which usefully suggest that services must be available with minimum obstructions and that, from the service providers' point of view, it is everyone's responsibility to engage with people who need support (NHS Confederation 2022). A single point of care accessible to people of all ages and focusing on continuity of care may seem like an unrealistic expectation but is likely to be cost-effective in saving lives and in reducing burdens, economic and clinical, on services.

Universal approaches remain important due to the "prevention paradox" – proportionately greater health harm may come from the larger group of lower-risk individuals, particularly for the most used substances such as cannabis (Sumnall 2022).

References

ACMD. ACotMo. *Reducing Drug Related Deaths: A Report by the Advisory Council on the Misuse of Drugs: Stationery Office*, London, 2000.

Ashton H. The treatment of benzodiazepine dependence. *Addiction*. 1994;89(11):1535–41. https://doi.org/10.1111/j.1360-0443.1994.tb03755.x.

Burrows D. Injecting equipment provision in Australia: the state of play. *Subst Use Misuse*. 1998;33(5):1113–27. https://doi.org/10.3109/10826089809062210.

Cerdá M, Allen BL, Collins AB, et al. Study assessing the effectiveness of overdose prevention centers through research (SAFER): an overview of the study protocol. *Harm Reduct J.* 2025;22(Suppl 1):76. https://doi.org/10.1186/s12954-025-01211-1-1.

Clinical Guidelines on Drug Misuse and Dependence Update 2017 Independent Expert Working Group. *Drug Misuse and Dependence: UK Guidelines on Clinical Management.* Department of Health, London, 2017.

Cranston K, John B, Fukuda HD, et al. Sustained Reduction in HIV Diagnoses in Massachusetts, 2000–2014. *Am J Public Health.* 2017;107(5):794–9. https://doi.org/10.2105/AJPH.2017.303697.

Degenhardt L, Bucello C, Mathers B, et al. Mortality among regular or dependent users of heroin and other opioids: a systematic review and meta-analysis of cohort studies. *Addiction.* 2011;106(1):32–51.

Degenhardt L, Grebely J, Stone J, et al. Global patterns of opioid use and dependence: harms to populations, interventions, and future action. *Lancet.* 2019 Oct 26;394(10208):1560–79. https://doi.org/10.1016/S0140-6736(19)32229-9.

Dunleavy K, Munro A, Roy K, et al. Spore forming bacteria infections and people who inject drugs: Implications for harm reduction. *Int J Drug Policy.* 2018 Mar;53:45–54. https://doi.org/10.1016/j.drugpo.2017.12.001.

European Centre for Disease Control (2011) Evidence for the effectiveness of interventions to prevent infections among people who inject drugs. Part 1: Needle and syringe programmes and other interventions for preventing hepatitis C, HIV and injecting risk behaviour. http://www.emcdda.europa.eu/attachements.cfm/att_145115_EN_ECDC EMCDDA%20Part%201%20-%20complete%20-%20Web.pdf.

European Drugs Report 2024. Harm reduction – the current situation in Europe (European Drug Report 2024) | www.euda.europa.eu.

Fleming T, Barker A, Ivsins A, Vakharia S, McNeil R.Stimulant safe supply: a potential opportunityto respond to the opioid epidemic. *Harm Reduct J.* 2020 Jan 10;17(1):6. https://doi.org/10.1186/s12954-019-0351-1.)

Fraser R, Yeung A, Glancy M, et al. Suicide in people prescribed opioid-agonist therapy in Scotland, United Kingdom, 2011–2020: a national retrospective cohort study. *Addiction.* 2024. Advance online publication. https://doi.org/10.1111/add.16680.

Greenwood J. Six years' experience of sharing the care of Edinburgh's drug users. *Psych Bull.* 1996;20:8–11.

Gruer L, Cameron J, Elliott L. Building a city wide service for exchanging needles and syringes. *BMJ.* 1993 May 22;306(6889):1394–7. https://doi.org/10.1136/bmj.306.6889.1394.

Giglio RE, Mantha S, Harocopos A, et al. The nation's first publicly recognized overdose prevention centers: lessons learned in New York City. *J Urban Health.* 2023 Apr;100(2):245–54. https://doi.org/10.1007/s11524.

Hickman M, Vickerman P, Robertson R, Macleod J, Strang J. Promoting recovery and preventing drug-related mortality: competing risks? *J Public Health.* 2011;33(3):332–4. https://doi.org/10.1093/pubmed/fdr055

Hussey D, Trinder-Widdess Z, Dee C, Bagnall D, Bojangles T, Kesten JM. Co-design of harm reduction materials for people who inject drugs to implement research findings. *Harm Reduct J.* 2019 Jun 7;16(1):36. https://doi.org/10.1186/s12954-019-0300-z.

Johnson C, Barnsdale L, McAuley A. 2016. https://www.scotpho.org.uk/media/1159/scotpho160209-investigating-the-role-of-benzodiazepines-in-drug-related-mortality.pdf.

Jones L, Pickering L, Sumnall H, McVeigh J, Bellis MA. Optimal provision of needle and syringe programmes for injecting drug users: a systematic review. *Int J Drug Policy.* 2010 Sep;21(5):335–42. https://doi.org/10.1016/j.drugpo.2010.02.001.

Kelly JF, Volkow ND, Koh HK. The changing approach to addiction - from incarceration to treatment and recovery support. *N Engl J Med.* 2025 Feb 27;392(9):833–6. https://doi.org/10.1056/NEJMp2414224.

Kennedy MC, Hayashi K, Milloy MJ, Wood E, Kerr T. Supervised injection facility use and all-cause mortality among people who inject drugs in Vancouver, Canada: a cohort study. *PLoS Med.* 2019 Nov 26;16(11):e1002964. https://doi.org/10.1371/journal.pmed.1002964.

Lader M. Benzodiazepines revisited--will we ever learn?. *Addiction.* 2011;106(12):2086–109. https://doi.org/10.1111/j.1360-0443.2011.03563.

Larney S, Bohnert AS, Ganoczy D, et al. Mortality among older adults with opioid use disorders in the Veteran's Health Administration, 2000–2011. *Drug Alcohol Depend.* 2015 Feb 1;147:32–7. https://doi.org/10.1016/j.drugalcdep.2014.12.019.

Larney S, Tran LT, Leung J, et al. All-cause and cause-specific mortality among people using extramedical opioids: a systematic review and meta-analysis. *JAMA Psych.* 2020 May 1;77(5):493–502. https://doi.org/10.1001/jamapsychiatry.2019.4170.

Larney S, Peacock A, Mathers BM, Hickman M, Degenhardt L. A systematic review of injecting-related injury and disease among people who inject drugs. *Drug Alcohol Depend.* 2017 Feb 1;171:39–49. https://doi.org/10.1016/j.drugalcdep.2016.11.029.

March JC, Oviedo-Joekes E, Perea-Milla E, Carrasco F; PEPSA team. Controlled trial of prescribed heroin in the treatment of opioid addiction. *J Subst Abuse Treat.* 2006;31(2):203-211. doi:10.1016/j.jsat.2006.04.007

Matheson C, Vucic C, Dumbrell J, et al. Clinical Outcomes of Benzodiazepine Prescribing for People Receiving Opioid Agonist Treatment: A Systematic Review of the Evidence. *Pharmacy (Basel).* 2024;12(5):152. Published 2024 Oct 4. doi:10.3390/pharmacy12050152

McCartney G, Bouttell J, Craig N, et al. Explaining trends in alcohol-related harms in Scotland, 1991–2011 (I): the role of incomes, effects of socio-economic and political adversity and demographic change. *Public Health.* 2016;132:13–23.

McCartney G, Collins C, Walsh D, Batty GD. Why the Scots die younger: synthesizing the evidence. *Public Health.* 2012 Jun;126(6):459–70. https://doi.org/10.1016/j.puhe.2012.03.007.

McGuigan CC, Penrice GM, Gruer L, et al. Lethal outbreak of infection with Clostridium novyi type A and other spore-forming organisms in Scottish injecting drug users. *J Med Micro.* 2002; 51(11):971–7.

Merrall EL, Kariminia A, Binswanger IA, et al. Meta-analysis of drug-related deaths soon after release from prison. *Addiction.* 2010 Sep;105(9):1545–54. https://doi.org/10.1111/j.1360-0443.2010.02990.x.

Misuse of Drugs Act 1971. https://www.legislation.gov.uk/ukpga/1971/38#:~:text=Changes%20to%20legislation:,in%20relation%20to%20the%20Council.

NESI 2022. Needle Exchange Surveillance Initiative (NESI), Prevalence of blood-borne viruses and injecting risk behaviours among people who inject drugs attending injecting equipment provision services in Scotland. Available at: Injecting equipment provision in Scotland - 2022 to 2023 - Injecting equipment provision in Scotland - Publications - Public Health Scotland.

NHS Confederation parliamentary briefing (2022) - No wrong door - a ten-year vision for mental health learning disability and autism services.pdf

NICE. *Care of Dying Adults in the Last Days of Life (NICE Guideline).* National Institute for Health and Care Excellence, 2015. http://www.nice.org.uk

Norton A, Ivsins A, Holliday E, Sutherland C, Kerr T, Kennedy MC. A qualitative evaluation of a fentanyl patch safer supply program in Vancouver, Canada. *Int J Drug Policy.* 2024 Sep;131:104547. https://doi.org/10.1016/j.drugpo.2024.104547.

Palmateer NE, Hope VD, Roy K, et al. Infections with spore-forming bacteria in persons who inject drugs, 2000–2009. *Emerg Infect Dis*. 2013 Jan;19(1):29–34. https://doi.org/10.3201/eid1901.120044.

Parkinson J, Minton J, Lewsey J, Bouttell J, McCartney G. Drug-related deaths in Scotland 1979–2013: evidence of a vulnerable cohort of young men living in deprived areas. *BMC Public Health*. 2018 Mar 27;18(1):357. https://doi.org/10.1186/s12889-018-5267-2.

Perneger TV, Giner F, del Rio M, Mino A. Randomised trial of heroin maintenance programme for addicts who fail in conventional drug treatments. *Br Med J*. 1998;317:13–18.

Peters AD, Reid MM, Griffin SG. Edinburgh drug users: are they injecting and sharing less? *AIDS*. 1994 Apr;8(4):521–8.

PHS 2025. National naloxone programme Scotland - monitoring report 2021/22 and 2022/23 - National naloxone programme Scotland: annual - Publications - Public Health Scotland accessed on 09/07/25

Potier C, Laprévote V, Dubois-Arber F, Cottencin O, Rolland B. Supervised injection services: what has been demonstrated? A systematic literature review. *Drug Alcohol Depend*. 2014;145:48–68. https://doi.org/10.1016/j.drugalcdep.2014.10.012.

Pridgen BE, Bontemps AP, Lloyd AR, et al. U.S. substance use harm reduction efforts: a review of the current state of policy, policy barriers, and recommendations. *Harm Reduct J*. 2025;22:101. https://doi.org/10.1186/s12954-025-01238-4.

Public Health Scotland, Glasgow Caledonian University and the West of Scotland Specialist Virology Centre. *The Needle Exchange Surveillance Initiative (NESI): Prevalence of Blood-Borne Viruses and Injecting Risk Behaviours Among People Who Inject Drugs Attending Injecting Equipment Provision Services in Scotland, 2008 to 2020*. Public Health Scotland, Glasgow, March 2022.

Public Health Scotland (2021) Needle Exchange Surveillance Initiative (NESI): prevalence of blood-borne viruses and injecting risk behaviours among people who inject drugs attending injecting equipment provision services in Scotland, 2008–2020. Edinburgh: Public Health Scotland.

Ramsay CN, Stirling A, Smith J, et al. An outbreak of infection with Bacillus anthracis in injecting drug users in Scotland. *Euro Surveill*. 2010 Jan 14;15(2):19465. https://doi.org/10.2807/ese.15.02.19465-en. Erratum in: *Euro Surveill*. 2010;15(3). pii: 19469.

Realistic Medicine 2023- Doing the right thing: Chief Medical Officer annual report 2022 to 2023 - gov.scot

Robertson R, Broers B, Harris M. Injecting drug use, the skin and vasculature. *Addiction*. 2021 Jul;116(7):1914–24. https://doi.org/10.1111/add.15283..

Rosen D, Hunsaker A, Albert SM, Cornelius JR, Reynolds CF 3rd. Characteristics and consequences of heroin use among older adults in the United States: a review of the literature, treatment implications, and recommendations for further research. *Addict Behav*. 2011 Apr;36(4):279–85. https://doi.org/10.1016/j.addbeh.2010.12.012.

ScotPHO. Excess Mortality in Scotland and Glasgow - ScotPHO, 2023. accessed 06/08/25

Scottish Government. Hepatitis C Action Plan, Phase II (May 2008- March 2011), 2008. https://www.webarchive.org.uk/wayback/archive/20170401173122/.

Scottish Government. Sexual Health and Blood Borne Virus Framework 2015–2020 Update, 2015. http://www.gov.scot/Resource/0048/00484414.pdf.

Siemers DJ. Principled pragmatism: Abraham Lincoln's method of political analysis, presidential studies. *Quarterly*. 2004;34(4):804–27.

Single E. Defining harm reduction. *Drug Alcohol Rev*. 1995;14(3):287–90. https://doi.org/10.1080/09595239500185371.

Spencer M, Garnett M, Miniño A. Drug overdose deaths in the United States, 2002–2022 [Internet]. National center for health statistics (U.S.), 2023 Dec. https://stacks.cdc.gov/view/cdc/135849.

Stark K, Leicht A, Müller R. Characteristics of users of syringe vending machines in Berlin. *Soz Praventivmed*. 1994;39(4):209–16. https://doi.org/10.1007/BF01309220.

Strang J, Metrebian N, Lintzeris N, et al. Supervised injectable heroin or injectable methadone versus optimised oral methadone as treatment for chronic heroin addicts in England after persistent failure in orthodox treatment (RIOTT): a randomised trial. *Lancet*. 2010;375:1885–95.

Sumnall HR. Encouraging a 'generational shift' in the UKs relationship with drugs: a commentary on the new UK drug strategy: what can be achieved with drug prevention? *Int J Drug Policy*. 2022;109:103841. https://doi.org/10.1016/j.drugpo.2022.103841.

Trayner KMA, Weir A, McAuley A, et al. A pragmatic harm reduction approach to manage a large outbreak of wound botulism in people who inject drugs, Scotland 2015. *Harm Reduct J.* 2018;15:36. https://doi.org/10.1186/s12954-018-0243-9.

UNAIDS September 2024. Leaders pledge bold action to end AIDS by 2030 | UNAIDS. accessed 25/02/26

van Amsterdam J, van den Brink W, Pierce M. Explaining the differences in opioid overdose deaths between Scotland and England/Wales: implications for European opioid policies. *Eur Addict Res*. 2021;27(6):399–412. https://doi.org/10.1159/000516165.

WHO. World Health Organization. Palliative care. 2020. https://www.who.int/news-room/fact-sheets/detail/palliative-care.

WHO. 2025. http://www.who.int/cancer/palliative/definition/en/ accessed on 25/2/25.

Wood E, Tyndall MW, Zhang R, Montaner JS, Kerr T. Rate of detoxification service use and its impact among a cohort of supervised injecting facility users. *Addiction*. 2007 Jun;102(6):916–9. https://doi.org/10.1111/j.1360-0443.2007.01818.x.

Zule WA, Cross HE, Stover J, Pretorius C. Are major reductions in new HIV infections possible with people who inject drugs? The case for low dead-space syringes in highly affected countries. *Int J Drug Policy*. 2013 Jan;24(1):1–7. https://doi.org/10.1016/j.drugpo.2012.07.002..

7 Anthrax, Clostridium and other infections

Introduction

Injecting drugs is inherently dangerous. Apart from overdose, sudden death and vascular damage, infections are the most commonly experienced side effect. Among the most common uses of emergency departments for people who use drugs are those resulting from infection. The need for secondary care and hospitalisation is not infrequent, and the economic costs are considerable (Kerr et al. 2005, Hope et al. 2008, Lewer et al. 2017).

The nature of drug injecting makes people involved vulnerable to bacterial and viral contaminants. These may be introduced during the many stages of illicit production through to the point of injection. Viral infections remain the most commonly reported (Assoumou et al. 2025). Contamination in countries where drugs are cultivated risks the danger of including spore-forming bacteria caused by animal contact. However, contamination during the passage through many unsterile stages of delivery can easily be the source of infection. At the point of consumption of substances supplied through illicit agents, sharing injecting equipment commonly presents as skin and soft tissue infections such as abscesses and cellulitis caused by staphylococcus and streptococcus. Occasionally, the complication of the diagnosis of debilitating necrotising fasciitis can be life-threatening (Kimura 2004, Chen 2001).

Infection entering the systemic system causes sepsis, endocarditis and infections in bones and joints. Occasionally, infections in organs result from injected material, especially in those substance users with compromised immunity. Rare conditions involving fungal infection or organisms that are not normally highly pathogenic are reported in immunocompromised individuals.

Soft tissue infections, abscesses at injection sites, organ damage such as endocarditis from circulating bacteria, fungi or viruses are all a direct consequence of poor injecting practice and are mostly covered in detail in Chapter 5. Contaminated drugs or infections introduced in cutting agents and solvents used to acidify mixtures to be injected can all introduce infection (Harris et al. 2019). HIV, hepatitis B and C are all described in other chapters. Sepsis, bone and joint infections, and accounts of end organ infections such as embolization of infection to brain tissue are caused by a range of organisms and are common in the medical literature (Attwood et al. 2024, Saldana et al. 2020, Tunkel and Pradhan 2002).

DOI: 10.4324/9781003611097-7

Less usual conditions such as amyloidosis, which can affect several organs, are associated with soft tissue infection (Harris et al. 2018).

In fact, all sorts of infections have been reported either in isolated cases or clusters when a batch of heroin or other drugs is contaminated. Any cryptic illness in an injecting drug user with associated fever and pains should be extensively investigated for a focus of infection.

Endocarditis

Infected heart valves have long been reported as a complication of injecting drugs. When material contaminated with bacteria enters the venous system, it is exposed to infection, and in turbulent areas like the heart valves, infection can lodge and proliferate. Pre-existing valvular abnormality may predispose one to infection. Congenital bicuspid aortic valve, prosthetic valve or valves damaged by rheumatic fever or arteriosclerosis are all likely to increase turbulence and the risk of bacteria lodging. People who inject drugs are more likely to have infection in the right side of the heart, most commonly the tricuspid valve, as the infection travels from the peripheral vein where it is injected to the superior vena cava and into the heart through the tricuspid valve into the right ventricle and the pulmonary circulation. Infection in the mitral and aortic valves does occur, but is more common in non-drug users with endocarditis.

The most common pathogen is staphylococcus, but other organisms such as pseudomonas and streptococcus also occur.

Infectious endocarditis is becoming more common among heroin abusers and usually requires hospitalisation for treatment with intravenous antibiotic administration. In cases in which the endocarditis is severe, cardiac surgery may be required to debride or replace infected valves. Furthermore, infective endocarditis can result in septic embolisation to the lungs, spleen, central nervous system and other organs, resulting in additional morbidity (Saydin et al. 2010). In injection drug users with infective endocarditis, embolisation from infected valvular vegetations may cause cerebral infarction, intracranial haemorrhage and the formation of brain abscess.

Summary findings from five North American and three European studies reported 734 cases among 3,083 cases of infectious endocarditis to be among persons who had injected an illicit substance, making nearly 25% of all cases of endocarditis being caused by contaminated injections. The cases involving the tricuspid valve accounted for 90%, and staphylococcus was the most common pathogen in two-thirds of cases (Crociani 2022). The reasons for the poorer long-term survival among the cases in people who had injected drugs were not completely clear, but this group were more likely to have comorbid hepatitis C and liver damage (Ramadan et al. 2024). Survival after treatment with valve replacement in another comprehensive study was shown to be poorer in people who had been diagnosed with endocarditis due to injecting drug use compared to non-drug user cases. At follow up the commonest cause of death was infection in 66% of cases usually caused by a further episode of infective endocarditis. In one of these studies it was noted that "Surgery conferred no long-term survival advantage, so more efforts are needed to reduce reinfection risks for people who inject drugs PWID" (Straw 2020).

It is suggested that opportunities for psychiatric and substance use disorder treatment are underused in cases before and after surgery and that despite increased evidence for the efficacy of treatment to reduce drug use, opportunities may be lost, leading to increased mortality (Elbatarny et al. 2019). As with other issues involving people who inject drugs, the presence of a multidisciplinary team and joint treatment management is likely to improve outcomes in a condition increasing in frequency due to the North American opioid crisis and with poor short-term and long-term outcomes (Vervoort et al. 2022).

Spore-forming bacteria

In the year 2005, the Food Safety Microbiology Laboratory, Health Protection Agency Specialist and Reference Microbiology Division in London, reported an increase in the number of cases of spore-forming bacterial infections among people who inject drugs.

> Clostridium novyi caused 63 cases of severe illness in 2000 and seven further cases from 2001. Wound botulism first occurred in 2000 (six cases) with 51 further cases to March 2004. Tetanus occurred in 20 cases between late 2003 and March 2004. Infections with C. histolyticum (nine cases), C. sordellii (one case) and Bacillus cereus (one case) were also reported. The reasons for the increase in illness are unclear. The major risk factor was skin- or muscle-popping.
>
> (Brett et al. 2005, Williamson et al. 2001)

The note about skin popping, injecting into subcutaneous or muscle tissue, being an increased risk factor is important. Injecting into muscle or skin tissue as opposed to the venous circulation may allow a longer period in a place conducive to incubation. Where a batch of heroin is contaminated, the heat treatment employed with an acidification compound such as citric acid may well encourage the spores to germinate.

A cluster of cases of *Clostridium novyi* among people who inject drugs was reported in Scotland. In the year 2000, an outbreak among people who inject drugs occurred involving 60 cases: 23 definite and 37 probable. Most had familial or social links with each other, and 50 were from Glasgow. The median age was 30 years, and 31 were female. The majority, especially definite cases, injected heroin with citric acid extravascularly. Of definite cases, 20 died (87% case-fatality rate; 13 after intensive care), 15 had necrotising fasciitis, 22 had injection site oedema and 13 had pleural effusion. The most frequently isolated pathogen among the cases was *Clostridium novyi. T*ransmission was believed to have occurred via a contaminated batch of heroin (McGuigan et al. 2002, Taylor et al. 2005). The clustering of cases suggests a single source, and the mortality among people who injected into soft tissue rather than a free-flowing vein suggests that clostridium survives best and multiplies most efficiently in a relatively low oxygenated tissue.

Between 2009 and 2010, there was an outbreak of anthrax among injecting drug users in Glasgow. By January 2010, there were a total of 14 confirmed cases of anthrax infection, of whom seven had died. Seven confirmed cases in the Glasgow area, four fatal; three cases in Lanarkshire, two fatal cases in Tayside, one fatal case in the Forth Valley area, and one surviving case in Fife (Ramsay 2010).

The outbreak team described the following results in 14 confirmed cases (10 men and four women aged between 27 and 55 years for the men and between 39 and 43 years for the women).

> Generally, the cases have presented with inflammation or abscesses related to sites of heroin injection. Symptoms began between one and two days or longer after injection of heroin and admission to hospital generally followed within four days. Localised lesions developed into necrotising fasciitis in a number of cases, some of whom died. The fatal cases in Glasgow (three men and one woman) died between three and seven days after admission. Cellulitis with very marked oedema has been noted in limbs with infection sites in a number of these cases. In a few cases the presentation has been of patients in advance stages of systemic sepsis some of whom died within hours. At least two cases presented with symptoms thought of at initial assessment as suggestive of a sub-arachnoid haemorrhage or haemorrhagic meningitis. Others presented with relatively localised lesions which have not progressed. The range of presentations is therefore wide and inconsistent.
>
> (Ramsay et al. 2010)

The investigation found no association with sharing injecting equipment, suggesting the contaminated batch of heroin was the source of infection. The investigating team found that some of the infected cases, including one fatal case, were not injectors and concluded that inhalation of anthrax spores was a plausible route of infection. Factors associated with an increased risk of infection included a longer injecting history, receiving opioid substitution therapy and alcohol consumption. Smoking heroin was associated with a lower risk of infection. The association with being a longer-term injecting drug user was thought initially to be that they were more likely to be injecting into soft tissue rather than a vein, but *B. anthracis* is an aerobic organism, so they concluded that other morbidity associated with increased age might be the cofactor. The final number of cases of anthrax in the 2009/10 outbreak was 47 of which 13 were fatal (Palmateer et.al. 2012).

Injection anthrax from heroin often will necessitate surgical debridement because of necrotising soft tissue infections (NSTI). Albeit rare, injection anthrax should be on the differential with heroin use-associated infections given the mortality can be as high as 30% in a cluster of cases in Germany (Grunow et al. 2012).

Conclusion

The hazards of injecting drugs are dominated by overdose and the introduction of infection. Infection is particularly dangerous as covert and unregulated injecting is likely to be contaminated. The second reason why injecting is especially risky from the point of view of infection is the illicit nature of the substance being used. Heroin is imported through complicated supply routes in unsterile conditions from countries where there are no standards of sterile production. Contacts with animals and storage in poor conditions lead to contamination. Cocaine is similarly transported across continents in conditions conducive to the risk of contact with bacteria and toxins. Soft tissue infections involving staphylococcus and streptococcus are a recurring problem for anyone injecting illicit substances and are inevitable considering the conditions in which drugs are used. Soft tissue infections are explored in Chapter 5. Unclear symptoms associated with pain at injecting sites, fever and malaise in a person who has recently injected a substance require urgent investigation.

References

Assoumou SA, Alexander RN, Miller SE. Viral Infections Associated with Injection Drug Use. *JAMA*. 2025;334(15):1386–7. https://doi.org/10.1001/jama.2025.13287.

Attwood LO, O'Keefe D, Higgs P, Vujovic O, Doyle JS, Stewardson AJ. Epidemiology of acute infections in people who inject drugs in Australia. *Drug Alcohol Rev*. 2024 Jan;43(1):304–14. https://doi.org/10.1111/dar.13772.

Brett MM, Hood J, Brazier JS, Duerden BI, Hahné SJ. Soft tissue infections caused by spore-forming bacteria in injecting drug users in the United Kingdom. *Epidemiol Infect*. 2005 Aug;133(4):575–82. https://doi.org/10.1017/s0950268805003845.

Chen JL, Fullerton KE, Flynn NM. Necrotizing fasciitis associated with injection drug use. *Clin Infect Dis*. 2001;33(1):6-15. https://doi.org/10.1086/320874

Crociani P, Schivazappa L. Epidemiologia dell'endocardite infettiva nelle persone che assumono sostanze stupefacenti per via endovenosa [Epidemiology of infective endocarditis in intravenous drug users]. *G Ital Cardiol (Rome)*. 2022;23(11):845–853. doi:10.1714/3900.38824

Elbatarny M, Bahji A, Bisleri G, Hamilton A. Management of endocarditis among persons who inject drugs: A narrative review of surgical and psychiatric approaches and controversies. *Gen Hosp Psychiatry*. 2019 Mar-Apr;57:44–9. https://doi.org/10.1016/j.genhosppsych.2019.01.008.

Grunow R, Verbeek L, Jacob D, et al. Injection anthrax—A new outbreak in heroin users. *Dtsch Arztebl Int.* 2012;109:843–48.

Harris M, Scott J, Wright T, Brathwaite R, Ciccarone D, Hope V. Injecting-related health harms and overuse of acidifiers among people who inject heroin and crack cocaine in London: a mixed-methods study. *Harm Reduct J.* 2019;16:60.

Harris M, Brathwaite R, Scott J, Gilchrist G, Ciccarone D, Hope V, McGowan CR. Drawing attention to a neglected injecting-related harm: a systematic review of AA amyloidosis among people who inject drugs. *Addiction*. 2018 Oct;113(10):1790–801. https://doi.org/10.1111/add.14257.

Hope V, Kimber J, Vickerman P, Hickman M, Ncube F. Frequency, factors and costs associated with injection site infections: findings from a national multi-site survey of injecting drug users in England. *BMC Infect Dis.* 2008;8:120.

Kerr T, Wood E, Grafstein E, Ishida T, Shannon K, Lai C, Montaner J, Tyndall MW. High rates of primary care and emergency department use among injection drug users in Vancouver. *J Public Health (Oxf)*. 2005 Mar;27(1):62–6. https://doi.org/10.1093/pubmed/fdh189.

Kimura A, Higa J, Levin R, et al. Outbreak of necrotizing fasciitis due to Clostridium sordelli among black-tar heroin users. *Clin Infect Dis*. 2004;38:e87–91.

Lewer D, Harris M, Hope V. Opiate injection-associated skin, soft tissue, and vascular infections, England, UK, 1997–2016. *Emerg Infect Dis*. 2017 Aug;23(8):1400–3. https://doi.org/10.3201/eid2308.170439.

McGuigan CC, Penrice GM, Gruer L, et al. Lethal outbreak of infection with Clostridium novyi type A and other spore-forming organisms in Scottish injecting drug users. *J Med Micro*. 2002; 51(11):971–7.

Palmateer NE, Ramsay CN, Browning L, Goldberg DJ, Hutchinson SJ. Anthrax infection among heroin users in Scotland during 2009–2010: a case-control study by linkage to a national drug treatment database. *Clin Infect Dis*. 2012;55(5):706–10. https://doi.org/10.1093/cid/cis511.

Ramadan MS, Bertolino L, Boccia F, et al. Features of infective endocarditis in a contemporary cohort of persons who inject drugs: a matched comparison analysis of long-term prognostic factors. *Intern Emerg Med*. 2024 Mar;19(2):455–64. https://doi.org/10.1007/s11739-023-03502-6.

Ramsay CN, Stirling A, Smith J, et al. An outbreak of infection with Bacillus anthracis in injecting drug users in Scotland. *Euro Surveill*. 2010 Jan 14;15(2):19465. https://doi.org/10.2807/ese.15.02.19465-en. Erratum in: *Euro Surveill*. 2010;15(3). pii: 19469.

Saldana CS, Vyas DA, Wurcel AG. Soft tissue, bone, and joint infections in people who inject drugs. *Infect Dis Clin North Am*. 2020 Sep;34(3):495–509. https://doi.org/10.1016/j.idc.2020.06.007.

Saydin G, Singh J, Dalal B, et al. Outcome of patients with injection drug use-associated endocarditis admitted to an intensive care unit. *J Crit Care* 2010;25:248–53.

Straw S, Baig MW, Gillott R, et al. Long-term outcomes are poor in intravenous drug users following infective endocarditis, even after surgery. *Clin Infect Dis*. 2020 Jul 27;71(3):564–71. https://doi.org/10.1093/cid/ciz869.

Taylor A, Hutchinson S, Lingappa J, et al. Severe illness and death among injecting drug users in Scotland: a case control study. *Epidemiol Infect*. 2005;133(2):193–204.

Tunkel AR, Pradhan SK. Central nervous system infections in injection drug users. *Infect Dis Clin North Am*. 2002 Sep;16(3):589–605. https://doi.org/10.1016/s0891-5520(02)00015-6.

Vervoort D, An KR, Elbatarny M, et al. Dealing with the epidemic of endocarditis in people who inject drugs. *Can J Cardiol*. 2022 Sep;38(9):1406–17. https://doi.org/10.1016/j.cjca.2022.06.004.

Williamson N, Archibald C, Van Vliet JS. Unexplained deaths among injection drug users: a case of probable Clostridium myonecrosis. *CMAJ*. 2001 Sep 4;165(5):609–11.

8 The cases

Case studies and people in a changing landscape

Background

Stories are important in understanding people's lives and influences on their behaviour. In medical practice, great importance is placed on first-hand accounts of symptoms and signs that might indicate a pathological process. Despite modern miracles of scanning and laboratory testing, personal accounts paint a vital insight into disease processes. Interpreting descriptions of feelings and sensations and placing them in a cultural and personal context has always been seen as a skill to be taught and learned from experience by those in a caring role. The advances of data and science still don't detract from the unique value of an individual's account of their experience. Stories of successes are as important, if not more so, than the inevitable tales of relapse and complications. Success can be partial, incomplete or limited to periods in lives otherwise characterised by ongoing substance use. Periods of abstinence or relative abstinence are familiar to anyone who has used substances and vary in quality as well as quantity. Progressive patterns of abstinence from injecting or other use are common as people learn how to be abstinent, understand the triggers leading to relapse and achieve targets which generate confidence in living without drugs. The substance community and the care agencies in support are familiar with the astonishing range of stories of outcomes with or without conventional support systems. The most unlikely events trigger remission and relapse, and spiritual, economic, tragic and unexplained events are all in the recovery journey.

Perhaps the most underdeveloped story is that of spontaneous "recovery" and the reality that this is more common than the pattern most often conveyed in the literature and media. Often portrayed as a relentless and inevitably downward spiral, addiction and substance use is, for many, a short-term experience. The unwritten story of people who use substances to a greater or lesser extent and then stop should be more widely shared.

In recent years, personal testimony, or confessional writing, about drug experience has become a focus of attention for practitioners and policy makers. Lived experience is increasingly valued in formulating appropriate treatment and recovery services and people who are, or have been, in recovery, whatever stage or level of achievement, are often key informants or participants in the design and formulation of service delivery.

DOI: 10.4324/9781003611097-8

Alongside recognising the place lived experience has in directing treatment is the interest in advocacy and stigma. From the consumer perspective, advocacy has, in the past, been viewed as a passive process with the patient or client being the recipient of a benefit delivered by another who is usually in a position of authority or power. Similarly stigma exists with the recipient of negative judgement in a position of weakness and vulnerability brought about by institutional, cultural and populist negative perceptions and rules. These situations are not unique to people who use substances as there are hierarchies of approval and disapproval in many sectors. Stigma can translate into better or worse financial and institutional situations, positive or negative support in mental health, marginalisation for people with other disabilities, minority groups and many more.

People who use drugs are not uniquely disadvantaged but do suffer from multiple difficulties when seeking approval in health social care and inclusion. This is aggravated by the criminal justice and legal position of many of the substances in use and the penalties for possession or distribution. Disclosure of substance use can rapidly lead to threat to employment, restrictions with regard to travel to many countries and exclusion from social circles.

As more people disclose substance use and some legal restrictions change, attitudes to and responsibilities for the welfare of people with substance use issues improve. Recognition of past failures has concentrated governments and other institutions' attention on harms caused by exclusion, punitive policies and stigma, and has shifted responsibility and demonstrated the need for sensitive and evidenced-based care. People who use substances in the modern paradigm may now be seen as victims of a hostile environment rather than through a criminal lens, and as the breadth of substance use increases and decriminalising and reduction in harmful qualities of drug taking become more acceptable, some drugs have become normalised in society.

Case studies and personal stories are an important part of these emerging trends, and examples of individuals and situations are worth considering in order to inform this change. The medical and social care infrastructure has also changed dramatically over the last few decades.

In the immediate aftermath of the HIV testing in 1985/6, interest in the source of these infections was intense. Who was at risk and why? What was the source of the epidemic and when did introduction take place? This was important as the nature of the virus was still unclear and genetic variants were being identified in different countries. Had there been multiple introductions and was there such a thing as an individual with super-infectivity properties? Some of these questions were answered by clinical research and others by listening to those people caught up in a uniquely damaging pattern of behaviour.

Influences in the medical and social care infrastructure of the 1970s until present times

The case of tobacco. Substance use does not exist in isolation from other personal or cultural situations. Over the last century, waves of substance use have affected health and social change. The 20th century has been described as the "cigarette century" (Brandt 2007). As smoking became popular in the early years of the 20th century and the cigarette industry industrialised production, a dramatic number of people became dependent. In the 1950s and early 1960s, the dangers of smoking became apparent and a long slow decline in use began. The connection of tobacco consumption with lung cancer described in the classic papers of Richard Doll and Austin Bradford Hill led to a subsequent paper showing that the number of doctors who smoked tobacco products had dramatically decreased as a result of these findings (Doll 1950, Doll 1964). Subsequent research, of course, revealed the toxic effects on many organs and the multiple cancers and harms attributable to tobacco. By the 1980s, the number of people smoking in the United Kingdom was still high, with between 40–45% of the adult population smoking. This has declined, with bans of smoking in enclosed places, stopping advertising and health promotion policies, to around 12% in 2023 (Office for National Statistics 2024).

Drug treatment emerged slowly. Heroin addiction was unusual in the 1970s in Scotland, the majority of the drug subculture clustering in the Southeast of England, and the majority of people with drug issues lived or had moved towards London where drugs might be more available and any possibility of treatment was more likely. Drug clinics were established in regional centres during the 1960s but experience was limited. The first 100 cases of dependency referred to the Regional Drug Dependency Unit at the Royal Edinburgh Hospital in Edinburgh, for example, were predominantly medical people, nurses or doctors who had become dependent on supplies accessed from medical supplies (Woodside 1973). Other illegal sources came from the Golden Triangle of Burma, Thailand and Afghanistan, but supplies at that time were low-grade heroin and were only available intermittently. This poor supply chain was supplemented from pharmacy shop break-ins when controlled prescription drugs were seized and sold in communities. Highly valued from these pharmacy raids were substances that could be injected such as pethidine and diamorphine ampoules prepared already for injection but also tablets of dipipanone and other opiates which were mixed into a suspension and injected. Medical prescriptions from doctors were accessed under the cover of chronic pain, intractable migraine or other collusions of managing chronic conditions not acknowledged as addiction. This all changed after the Islamic revolution when supplies of high-grade heroin swept into local communities in Western Europe.

Hidden Harm was the title of a government report that was groundbreaking in its exposure, to the authorities and the public, of the full extent of harm done to children because of substance use (ACMD 2003). It drew upon an earlier report which was later published as a paper in the British Journal of Social Work and the research of the committee and others (Forrester and Harwin 2008).

The ACMD document reported details on the "six key findings" that were summarised at the beginning of the document. These findings with background research had a considerable impact on drug policy subsequently and deserve to be reiterated and updated as the impact of substances increases, changes and evolves in complexity.

- We estimate there are between 250,000 and 350,000 children of problem drug users in the United Kingdom—about one for every problem drug user.
- Parental problem drug use can and does cause serious harm to children at every age from conception to adulthood.
- Reducing the harm to children from parental problem drug use should become a main objective of policy and practice.
- Effective treatment of the parent can have major benefits for the child.
- By working together, services can take many practical steps to protect and improve the health and well-being of affected children.
- The number of affected children is only likely to decrease when the number of problem drug users decreases.

Old diseases and new diseases. Tuberculosis, a disease that was prevalent in Edinburgh in the 1950s, was thought to be under control due to the work of Sir John Crofton, who pioneered the use of combinations of drugs rather than single medicines, which rapidly lost efficacy due to the development of resistance by the tuberculosis bacillus. Crofton and colleagues thought that modern approaches like this would eventually eradicate the disease, which had been a scourge since ancient times. Unfortunately, tuberculosis is a worldwide disease and has little respect for national boundaries or small-scale eradication attempts. The hostile Ugandan regime of Idi Amin expelled a large group of Asian Ugandans in an act of ethnic cleansing. This group had a significant prevalence of active tuberculosis (Tuberculosis Among Immigrants in Britain 1978). Subsequent and ongoing population shifts due to conflict, and recently, climate change, have meant tuberculosis is far from eradicated. In a city with a long history of epidemics of infectious disease, past epidemics of plague, cholera and tuberculosis were now apparently facing a new epidemic, AIDS, which, like all emerging crises of this sort, contained the spectre of large population contamination and an unknown burden of disease and death.

Improved medicines. As improvements in pharmaceuticals emerge, old compounds which have more toxicity and are more likely to be used inappropriately are withdrawn. A recent editorial in the Journal of the Royal College of General Practice described medications which were frequently prescribed until their toxicity was shown to cause damage or even fatal overdoses. Diconal (dipipanone), barbiturates, coproxamol, some benzodiazepines such as triazolam, thioridazine and others were withdrawn from manufacture as newer, safer alternatives were produced.

Driving-related consultations. In the daily discussions with people who use drugs, there are recurring themes. Driving a car or other motor vehicle raises issues and concerns. While it may seem clear that driving might be impaired by the association with illegal or legal prescription drugs, the rules are inevitably likely to be interpreted. The United Kingdom Driver and Vehicle Licensing Agency (DVLA) publishes policies designed to prevent accidents arising from drug use. These rules suggest that the agency must be informed if "*you're unfit to do so because you're on legal or illegal drugs*", or "*you have certain levels of illegal drugs in your* *blood (even if they have not affected your* driving)." The agency also gives the advice that, *"legal drugs are prescription or over-the-counter medicines. If you're taking them and not sure if you should drive, talk to your doctor, pharmacist or healthcare professional."*

Both these statements allow for judgement on behalf of the person involved or the doctor, pharmacist or healthcare worker. Assessing the impact of medications for any condition on driving is not necessarily easy and early, and referral to the Agency on trivial examples can lead to prolonged driving suspension and protracted assessments. The Government agency recognises the difficulty in strictly sticking to levels in the blood that result in exclusion from driving, and their expert advisory panel draws attention to the collateral use of alcohol and other drugs in increasing the likelihood of road traffic accidents (DVLA 2014). They do publish levels for various substances but also include the following paragraph in recognition of the variability between cases.

> The government is unable to provide any guidance on what amounts of dosage would equate to being over the specified limits. There are too many variables, such as physical characteristics, where each person will metabolise the drug at different rates. Eating or drinking will also have an effect on the blood concentration.

National guidelines for healthcare workers advising about drugs and eligibility to drive a motor vehicle suggest that, for prescription drugs such as methadone, reassessment should be carried out if the dose changes or tolerance is lost for other reasons (Department of Health 2007).

The rules are specific about some drugs, recommending that if they are prescribed by a healthcare professional, their opinion should be considered. Named drugs include amphetamine, for example, dexamphetamine or selegiline; clonazepam, diazepam, flunitrazepam, lorazepam, methadone, morphine; or opiate and opioid-based drugs, for example, codeine, tramadol, fentanyl, oxazepam and temazepam.

The rules suggest that, "you can drive after taking these drugs if: you've been prescribed them and followed advice on how to take them by a healthcare professional" and that "they are not causing you to be unfit to drive even if you're above the specified limits".

There are also rules about the possibility of roadside drug testing:

> The police can stop you and make you do a "field impairment assessment" if they think you're on drugs. This is a series of tests, for example asking you to walk in a straight line. They can also use a roadside drug kit to screen for cannabis and cocaine. If they think you're unfit to drive because of taking drugs, you'll be arrested and will have to take a blood or urine test at a police station. You could be charged with a crime if the test shows you've taken drugs.

Drug injecting as portrayed in fiction and biographical accounts

Fiction and personal experience play an important part in informing people of real life. Historical accounts by diarists and authors play an enduring role in describing behaviour and personal character traits. Contemporary fiction includes substance use as a staple background to communities and characters. Irvine Welsh tells a story which, for many, was an introduction to drug use that was unknown. Barbara Kingsolver's novel includes vivid description of the degradation and rollercoaster crisis of a personality caught up in the prescription opiate scandal in the USA (Kingsolver 2022).

In Stevenson's case, the dual or multiple personality disorder of Dr Jekyll and Mr Hyde has become synonymous with a "split" personality (Stevenson 1886). However, as one group of authors suggest, "given the extreme rarity of multiple personality disorder, especially in a man compared with the high frequency of a diagnosis of substance dependence, we believe that Jekyll's disordered personality and suffering can be explained by substance dependence" (Altschuler et al. 2000). Literature is full of cases of individuals and situations influenced by intoxication and substances. So much so that stories including descriptions and consequential actions caused by intoxication must be close to the experience of most people.

Sadly, the substance user in fiction is often the criminal or perpetrator of a crime, and sometimes, the presence of a past history of substance use forms part of a character development, implying guilt. People with substance use connections are less likely to be seen as a victim or casualty of financial, social or environmental circumstances.

Some autobiography such as that of the Rolling Stone, Keith Richards, gives fleeting insights into the impact of injecting drugs, and others, such as that of Miles Davis, elaborate further into the community surrounding a particular period and setting for heroin injecting (Davis 1990). Others tell of lives disrupted by the social and medical consequences of substance use but surprisingly, few are able to express the true extent and disastrous damage that might be visible to an intensivist managing a case of overdose, a surgeon amputating an ischaemic limb or a pathologist carrying out post-mortems.

"All the way to the river", a story by Elizabeth Gilbert about personal drug use and the dependence on drugs of her terminally-ill partner, provides an evocative, detailed and at times gruelling account of lives interrupted by drug use Gilbert (2025). The detail and intensity of her writing provide an unusually vivid account of the traumas and psychological roller coaster of a relapsing illness. Insightful recognition of the loss of control over rational judgement during the fugue-like state of a dissociative state and the consequent risks provide an illuminating passage which will resonate with others who have had similar experiences when intoxicated with cocaine and other stimulants. As a compelling read, the book describes short- and long-term harms from drug use better than most.

The extensive account of the partner's terminal illness and circumstances around her death raises all sorts of important questions about capacity to make decisions when under the influence of mind-altering substances and, equally importantly, the correct, or possible, interventions around end-of-life care for people who have a high tolerance to opiates and stimulants and a long history of dependency. As agencies like "dying with dignity" increase and regulations try to accommodate popular demand for legal interventions to end life, the difficulties of drug use will become more apparent. Already, people with advanced addiction problems and related complications are receiving inadequate care when life expectancy is clearly limited. Experience in hospices is limited to a few establishments in the United Kingdom, such as the Mildmay and Milestone House units set up during the days when AIDS was essentially an untreatable condition (McCabe et al. 2022).

Case studies

In a recent review of the role and range of interventions in the management of substance use problems in family practice and primary care there are to several important conclusions. A series of interviews with people who use drugs, their primary care doctors and nurses and family members described the complexity of providing effective care in the community. As well as the inevitable conclusion that financial constraints are damaging service provision, the model of "shared care" among agencies can lead to what one observer called a "collusion of anonymity" resulting from the passing of responsibility from one worker to another, with a resulting lack of individual identity of a key or continuous supporter.

The study however concluded that most carers thought that a shared care model was important and effective when dealing with complex cases often with multimorbidity. There were problems of engagement and retention in services exacerbated by enlarging teams and multiple players with boundaries to their interventions that inhibited holistic functioning. This is by no means exclusive to people who use drugs but has particularly risky consequences in managing a case with all the difficulties associated with a condition excluded from mainstream systems. Grouping service agencies into isolated domains is found to limit effectiveness in a number of ways and suggests that reforms in services and provider training are required (Thom 2025, Pinto et al. 2019).

Blood to blood, the story of the "shooting galleries". The term shooting galleries referred to the meetings of people injecting substance in groups in the USA in the 1950 and onwards. Often in inner cities with heroin on the increase, people congregated to share drugs and injecting equipment. The expansion of heroin and cocaine injecting in the 1980s unfortunately coincided with the arrival in communities of the human immunodeficiency virus. Patterns of drug injecting became of great importance and interest to public health officials investigating hepatitis B (and later, hepatitis C) and, of course, HIV. In Europe, increasing restrictions on injecting equipment was occurring at the same time as heroin supplies soared as a result of geopolitical change in the East. Groups in centres like Glasgow and Edinburgh sourced needles and syringes from reluctant commercial suppliers and disposal containers stolen from accident and emergency departments, and because of limited supply, sharing increased in the 1980s. First-hand accounts of groups of ten or more people in the same room using equipment rented by the session by people also supplying the drugs describe syringes of various sizes being filled with a heroin solution and being used serially by the members of the group. Common practice was to access a vein, draw blood into the syringe to ensure that the needle was in the vein, and then inject some of the solution. As each member of the group did the same, the syringe contained blood from several people along with the heroin. A good way to transmit infection.

Jim Henderson was the owner of a medical supply shop in Bread Street in Edinburgh. In his earlier retail shop in 1972, he had witnessed a few "addicts" asking for injecting equipment, and when he opened his own shop in 1976, he began very tentatively selling needles and syringes to people he knew were injecting drugs, as he saw the state they were in and the desperate use of fabricated equipment. Some people were using contaminated equipment from disposal bins stolen from hospital departments. He increased the sale as he was aware of hepatitis in some people, and by 1977, he was selling 2 ml syringes and orange needles at 5 pence per set, sometimes 10 at a time, every day or every other day. Over the next four years, he sold equipment to 50 or more people and latterly, boxes of 100 per week. He suspected that he was supplying the whole of Edinburgh and Lothian. By 1980, this was affecting his business, and he was being criticised by doctors and the local police drugs squad. He was "interviewed at the local police station". The shop closed in September 1981, and he moved to a job in the pharmaceutical industry. It is no coincidence that the first known positive test for HIV in an injecting drug user was recorded in 1982.

Notes from a GP diary

It is interesting to note that more than half of the cases of people caught up in the disastrous epidemic of HIV among drug users in Edinburgh in the 1980s that remain in my notes are women. This is interesting because most cases in the United Kingdom at that time were men who had become infected during sex with men. I made many entries on a small group of young female patients who became infected circa 1981 and remained with my practice until they died. Case notes, in practices like mine, retained all the primary care consultations dating back in most cases to early childhood, if not birth. Common features include, but not in all cases, difficult parenting problems, family and sibling substance issues, teenage pregnancies and a roller coaster of abstinence periods and episodes of substance use. Treatment was, during the early part of this period, haphazard and minimal with opiate agonist (methadone) dosing which now would be considered subtherapeutic and poor availability of supportive psychological services. As found in other cohorts, those that survived gradually stabilised in their drug injecting, reducing in frequency, sharing equipment with fewer people and living in more stable relationships. There were, of course, many who continued with reckless behaviour throughout. Complications and side effects were common, hepatitis B diagnosed early, HIV when that test became available in 1985 and hepatitis C in 1990.

Donna. was an example. Her case notes go back to 1966 when she was 6 years old and the first few years recorded minimal descriptions of childhood immunisations and minor respiratory infections. Little else was noted until she consulted about her drug use at age 18 when she was working in a local care home as a nursing assistant. This was in March 1983 when she was in “a great state of nerves” and admitted that she had started to use heroin one year previously. The case note entry said that she was spending up to £30 per day and was trying to reduce it. She failed to attend an appointment at the local psychiatric clinic/drug dependency unit. Later that year she said that she had started injecting two years ago, aged about 24 along with her substance-using boyfriend. There followed a number of consultations about losing her job, a short period of custody (shoplifting), boyfriend custody issues and help with regular GP consultations and prescriptions for oral buprenorphine. At that time, buprenorphine was not licensed for the treatment of opiate dependency but methadone was limited in our practice. Later in 1984, a blood test showed past infection with hepatitis B. Notes suggested that she had been abstinent for 8 weeks or more but she was injecting again in October 1985 when the HTLV3 (HIV) test became available. The result was positive. Consulting included discussions about contraception and risk to her sexual partner.

Over the next 12 months, she had 10 GP consultations and in 1987, 35 consultations mostly about prescriptions for opiates but also musculoskeletal pains, cervical cytology and emotional liability. From then until the time of her death, she attended GP consultations at a rate of 15–20 per year. At the same time, she had periodic visits to the specialist HIV clinic and was supported intermittently by mental health psychiatry and nursing colleagues, most of whom were infectious disease specialists and not addiction-trained.

Many of the GP consultations were about her ongoing opiate and benzodiazepine use. Prescriptions were amounts of dihydrocodeine and nighttime sedation. Later that year, she started on methadone which was continuous from then on until converting to morphine in 1997. Weight was low at this time (48 kg), and she pressurised me to prescribe benzodiazepines (on reflection, the problem was that her methadone dose was too small at 50–60 mg per day). Over the next few years, she attended the specialist HIV clinic at the City Hospital and had support from their psychiatrist and also started Zidovudine (AZT) in a clinical trial for the treatment of HIV.

She admitted to being poorly compliant and missing multiple doses, as did her partner. She admitted low mood, family stresses and distress when someone in the street said, “don’t go near them they are junkies. You’ll catch that disease from them”.

At this time, her blood CD4 count was low, indicating progressive disease. In late 1996, she and her partner started the new antiviral chemotherapy with mixed feelings. Compliance was again poor due to low mood, continued opiate use, no injecting for some years by then, and dysfunctional use of prescribed drugs. She talked with her psychiatrist at this time about her mother’s alcohol problems. After stopping methadone, she had become dependent on morphine tablets, which had been started after a severe infection with herpes zoster (shingles). By 1998, her immune function had improved, and she was taking antivirals, slow-release morphine (150 mg per day), benzodiazepines, antidepressants and vitamin supplements. She had a past infection noted with hepatitis C (presumably acquired at the time of her infection with hepatitis B and HIV). There followed a series of admissions to the recently opened hospice at Milestone House and she was requiring treatment for thrombocytopenia, pneumonia, shingles and anxiety (recently diagnosed as obsessive compulsive disorder). She decided to discontinue her antiviral chemotherapy and wasself-medicating with benzodiazepines. In June 2000 she restarted antivirals as symptoms of immunosuppression were evident: thrombocytopenia, neurological symptoms (variously diagnosed as conversion illness and chronic fatigue), weight loss and anxiety.

She was found dead at home by her partner in October 2000. She was 41 years old and had had substance dependency for nearly 20 years and HIV probably since 1982, for 18 years.

Post-mortem examination identified cirrhotic changes in her liver and early brain disease from HIV.

Donnas case was similar in many respects to other people in this cohort and highlights a system struggling to adjust to a combination of substance use and multiple medical problems unfamiliar to the NHS at the time.

John Paul. He was a survivor of multiple problems starting to inject drugs in adolescence at a time when heroin became abundant in his locality. A member of the Trainspotting generation, he had some of the recklessness and attitudes of the classic book and film. Trouble followed, however, and multiple attempts to stop injecting were a failure during his next 30 years. His relationship with a supportive partner gave mutual determination to improve his lifestyle with some success, but it was only with her premature death from a drug overdose that long-term abstinence was replaced by a low-grade dependency on alcohol. Physical problems of hepatitis C, a legacy of injecting, and social isolation resulting in self-neglect and persistent low mood eased in his fifth decade, providing some contentment and resignation to managing a stable state.

Julie. Stigma, implied or real, affected the drug-using community. Julie was a young "drug user" aged twenty-one with liver failure after taking a large quantity of "distalgesic" (a combination of dextropropoxyphene and paracetamol) was turned down to receive a liver transplant in favour of another case who was without the perceived added risk of being dependent on drugs. Liver donations are clearly highly sensitive as the donor case has, in most cases, died in sudden, often tragic, circumstances and liver donations are very few. Receiving a liver donation suitable for transplant is therefore an emotional event for the several families involved and an expensive procedure for the medical establishment. Transplant facilities are few and far between and there is currently only one in Scotland. Decisions about the suitability of the recipient are a judgement taken by multidisciplinary groups of professional surgeons, physicians and scientists. Social, personal and individual health characteristics are obviously considered when decisions are made about the likelihood of the procedure being successful, in the operation and recovery period but also in the longer-term. No one can imagine that deciding who should receive a donation and who will die of liver failure is anything but a hugely complicated set of decisions. Juile died of liver failure.

Peter. travelled extensively with the merchant navy as a deck hand. When interviewed in 1987 about his HIV positive test result, he was 22 years old and talked about travelling regularly to Indonesia, Malaysia, Singapore, Australia and European countries since he was 16 years old. He travelled to the east coast of the USA, Baltimore and New York on the Atlantic Conveyor, which he joined in 1980 (the ship was requisitioned by the Ministry of Defence and struck by two Argentine Exocet missiles in 1982 in the Falklands conflict, leading to its sinking and the loss of 12 lives). Of interest, in tracking a source of his HIV, other than the obvious one in Edinburgh, he said that he had been to Africa in 1982. The trip lasted 6 months, took the crew and cargo to several countries along the western seaboard, ended in the Republic of South Africa. He never injected drugs abroad and denied any sexual contact that might have transmitted the virus. Peter first smoked heroin at the age of 17 and first injected at age 18 or 19; the first time that he used regularly was when he was 20 years old. He used intermittently by injection up until the time of the interview, using heroin before he set out, and had had an episode of hepatitis from which he made an apparently uneventful recovery. He reported injecting heroin in two countries during his travels, but for the most part, was more or less drug-free, returning in better health and with a determination to distance himself from the local drug scene. He had been off heroin for 6 months and out of work for 10 months, but his health was good.

He was found to be HIV positive in 1985, but had probably become infected during the early part of his drug taking when the virus was actively spreading in North West Edinburgh.

He pursued a clinical course resulting in multiple immune deficiency infections and a wasting illness leading to death in hospital in 1992.

Davie. also travelled in Africa as an individual youth explorer trying to get away from a heroin problem that he had embarked on in the late 1970s, a member of an earlier cohort with slightly different personal characteristics from the new wave of heroin injectors of the post-Islamic revolution supply of pure heroin. Davie used drugs in Kenya but had stories of a brutal regime of punishment for drug use in that country. He had been arrested for possession of heroin and had been put in a communal cell with dozens of others on the same or similar charges. When a fight broke out among the men in custody, he suddenly noticed water rising in what turned out to be a sealed room. The water rose to a height of several feet and was left there for most of the day. People in the unit were unable to sit or lie down and there was no escape. The fighting stopped and after several hours, the water level dropped, and the exhausted men collapsed on the floor. He was released and told to leave the country after a few days.

Susie. first used heroin by injection at the age of 18 years. She shared injecting equipment with a small group of friends, and, when first attending her GP, the longest abstinent period since she started was 3–4 weeks. She had been in prison once or twice, the longest sentence being 4 months. She had hepatitis in 1980, subacute endocarditis in 1983, and an eye infection causing blindness in 1983 (caused by a fungal infection from a growth in a lemon juice bottle used for acidifying heroin before injecting). She was found to have HTLV3 (HIV) in

1985. As with many of the cohort, she continued to use heroin with much reduced frequency, less injecting and no sharing of equipment. Oral prescriptions seemed to help, but self-medicating with illegal substances continued as she declined and eventually died of overwhelming lung infections. Causes given on the death certificate included pneumonia, Acquired Immune Deficiency Syndrome and "past drug use".

Adrian. Times changed and the introduction of effective antiviral therapy in 1995 brought about an almost magical return to life for those with advanced or advancing AIDS. Adrian, a long abstinent heroin user, was dying from a combination of a wasting disease caused by advanced AIDS and recurrent infection caused by immunodeficiency. He was started on the new medications in 1996 and, within a few months, was returning to a normal weight and constitution. When last seen, he was working as a social care support worker and was, apart from ongoing medication, leading a normal life.

Ryan. The case of Ryan, a male aged 44, exemplifies the older person still using drugs who has multiple morbid problems. A list taken from contemporary case notes includes eleven serious medical conditions. On the long list of active diagnoses are interventions to support his drug problem including regular repeat prescriptions for opiate agonist treatment (methadone) and diazepam. The hepatitis C condition has been treated successfully and there is now no trace of the active virus in his body but damage caused to his liver has been exacerbated by his chronic alcohol use. The longstanding alcohol intake is also the cause of his early dementia.

The girl from West Virginia. In a remote bunkhouse in the North West of Scotland only accessible by boat from the end of the train line, she was sharing a room with us over a wet weekend. We were hill walking and getting up early to walk and climb two remote peaks. Long days in and out of wet weather and covering 25 km and 4,000 feet of ascent, we were tired by the end of the day. The young woman sharing the dormitory spoke very little until the last night in the local pub/restaurant when she identified herself as a US citizen from West Virginia. I expressed an interest and explained that I had studied the opiate prescribing crisis and West Virginia was a "hot spot" for fatal overdoses. She replied, "that's why I am here, all my friends are dead".

This was reminisent of the scene of Barbara Kingsolver's evocative novel Demon Copperhead. The action is situated in Lee County, Virginia in the USA and describes the prescription opiate epidemic which swept the USA.

This case is one of the astonishing number of people caught up in the marketing and prescription scandal of opiates in the USA (U.S. Department of Justice 2020).

In order to uncover the influence that marketing of opiate products by the pharmaceutical industry had, a study was undertaken using data from the Medicare and Medicaid services in the USA (Hadland et al. 2019). This study examined payments made in "non-research-based opioid marketing" to 67,507 physicians across 22,098 counties in the USA between 2013 and 2015.

The researchers found a clear link between marketing and increased mortality and concluded, rather moderately, that:

> In this study, across US counties, marketing of opioid products to physicians was associated with increased opioid prescribing and, subsequently, with elevated mortality from overdoses. Amid a national opioid overdose crisis, re-examining the influence of the pharmaceutical industry may be warranted.

Terry presents a picture of multimorbidity and high risk of imminent death. Alcohol dependence, cirrhosis of the liver, a dementing process, gastric irritation and accident risk all suggest long-term excessive alcohol consumption and the diagnosis of drug dependence further characterises the commonly occurring dual addictions. Hepatitis C suggests past or present injecting drug use.

A longstanding drug injector and small-scale local supplier of drugs, Terry had multiple problems as evidenced from his "active problems" list in his medical notes (below), a complex list with many conditions strongly linked to drug and alcohol use over many years and dependence on prescribed as well as illicit drugs. His management was constrained by his reluctance to participate in supportive organisations, aggravated by his alcohol-induced dementing process. Drug injecting was primarily into a femoral vein, with the development of a sinus from the groin skin into the major artery from the lower limb to the heart. Any hope of successful intervention might be achieved by a multispecialist team or along a model used in palliative care to provide some control and quality of life without expecting or aiming for an unrealistic cure.

- Alcohol dependence
- Drug dependence
- Korsakoff psychosis
- Hepatitis C
- Iron deficiency anaemia
- Cirrhosis of the liver and Portal Hypertension
- Complex regional pain syndrome
- Gastritis and peptic ulceration
- Accidental falls – into canal
- Asthma
- Coeliac disease

Case notes tell chronological and clinical history, often over years or decades. The following two examples exemplify the seriousness and complexity of the medical background to cases of people who use substances. These are extracted, and anonymised, from primary care records and are the cumulative summary list of clinical conditions over time.

Madelaine is a female who, at the age of 50 years, had a clinical record including ten conditions. As can be seen from the list below, she had multiple pathologies, several including drug dependency with positive ongoing toxicology to show active drug use, hepatitis C, deep vein thrombosis as a result of injecting in lower limb veins and other conditions possibly related to self-neglect. Interestingly, there is no record on the list of formal mental health conditions, but the trauma of a life punctuated by custody, homelessness episodes and debilitating illness suggests considerable misery. In her case, the hepatitis C had not been treated at the time of writing due to difficulty complying with treatment. Recovering from recent cellulitis and community-acquired pneumonia, she resumed her drug injecting shortly after leaving hospital. Reviewing her list of active conditions, it is not hard to see why her life was difficult. A medical list, of course, does not include the coexisting financial and personal problems. Temporary housing, estranged family and struggles with a rigid social welfare system meant that advocacy and support for basic comfort and safety were top priorities. The list of medical conditions indicates multiple areas of self-neglect and the need for a long-term strategy for a range of treatment interventions best delivered in residential care.

- Drug Dependency Methadone 110 mg daily
- Positive toxicology (heroin and cocaine)
- Alcohol problems and heavy smoker
- Hormone replacement for menopausal symptoms
- Deep vein thrombosis
- Hepatitis C – PCR positive
- Gynaecological problems
- Iron deficiency anaemia
- Vitamin D deficiency

Derek. Prior to the discovery of the presence of HIV in the Edinburgh cohort and at the height of the heroin "epidemic", deaths were common in young people. Fatal overdose occurred in houses and flats in the communities of social housing. Derek was using heroin by injection and had had several episodes of remission and relapse. Objectively, his prospects were good. He was young, twenty-seven at the time of his death, clever and motivated to improve his situation. What caused his sudden death was undoubtedly an overdose of strong heroin taken in company one night. He was found by neighbours in the open early one morning. When people injected in a group and succumbed, they were sometimes left out on the stairs or in the open to be found by others in order to avoid police investigation into the use of heroin.

Carol. Individuals caught up in a spiral of drug use are not unusual but provide enormous challenges for families, carers and support services. It is not usual for individuals to escalate substances used over a period of weeks or months, resulting in multiple overdoses and encounters with law enforcement services. Agencies which are able to engage in short-term emergency treatment are limited, especially when it comes to providing essential places of safety. Carol was one of those individuals who was known to multiple services and who found it difficult to sustain contact with any of them. Emergency admissions to a hospital bed were not available, for various capacity reasons, and attendance at accident and emergency departments resulted in referral to community psychiatric and primary care services and a circular pattern of crises and ineffectual interventions. Regrettably, custody resulted from a series of minor offences.

Carol died of a drug (heroin) overdose the day after leaving custody at the only women's prison in Scotland; An occurrence regrettably still not unusual. Death shortly after release from prison was first in the public consciousness when Sid Vicious from the Sex Pistols suffered the same sad fate in 1979 (Sid Vicious 2026). Despite many publications drawing attention to the risk of overdose when tolerance to opiates has been lost during drug-free spells in custody and many attempts to warn of this danger, sudden overdose deaths are common (Favril et al. 2025 in press).

Brian. This man was hard to support as his symptom profile often failed to match any measurable sign of disease and, as time went on, became increasingly fantastic. Matched with unsubstantiated claims of multiple past investigations and treatments, it became unlikely that he had ever injected drugs, although he claimed to have done so for many years. Unlike most cases, he had been reluctant to show physical evidence of injecting (recent injection sites or old scarring over veins). Munchausen's syndrome is a diagnostic eponym now largely replaced by a more descriptive name of factitious disorder imposed on self, or factitious disorder. As is frequently reported in the literature, people approaching treatment centres may not always have a simple story of dependency and a record to support a pathway into substance use or history of past treatments. Validating the requirement for treatment depends on a plausible story and some collateral evidence from family, friends or previous medical professionals. Further evidence of illicit substance use is helpful from toxicology tests. In this case, none of these reassuring signs were present. The patient disappeared without warning.

One of the strengths of the National Health Service is the information held in records in primary care and hospital practice. Almost everyone who has lived in the United Kingdom for any length of time is registered with a medical practice and moving from one to another is associated with the forwarding of these records to the next practice. In the context of substance use treatment, this system makes it difficult to approach serial prescribers for treatment without disclosing past treatments. Private clinics with less formal links to past treatments usually ask new patients for permission to access previous information from NHS staff.

Even in 1988, several years after the test for HIV became available, not all cases of HIV/AIDS were obvious to clinicians. Some positive tests were deliberately concealed or kept in the shadows, and many symptomatic people chose to avoid engagement with supporters or confide in partners or families. Especially in the pre-treatment period, clandestine infection was not uncommon.

Mary. had been using injection drugs for some years before she tested positive for HIV. She had a severely disrupted family life with children in care and others also using injectable heroin. Moving around the country and registering only occasionally with general practitioners, she concealed her diagnosis until presenting to emergency services with abdominal pains, cough, and breathlessness (for about a month), low blood pressure, pyrexia and tachycardia. She deteriorated rapidly in intensive care, where the diagnosis of pneumocystis pneumonia was made, and died shortly thereafter. The death certificate stated the cause of death to be bronchopneumonia, septicaemia and Acquired Immune Deficiency Syndrome.

She had had no treatment for what must have been a slowly progressive immune collapse.

Corrie. was drinking alcohol heavily and smoking cigarettes at the age of 14, had an admission to hospital at age 17 with hepatitis and a positive HIV (HTLV3) test in 1985. She had a baby in 1986, who was not infected with HIV, and was a grandmother at the age of 35. Her substance use continued until her death from multiple conditions, but injecting was not a feature after starting methadone and continuing this at a dose of 120 mg. Multiorgan involvement with amyloidosis, failure of antiviral treatment for immune deficiency, chronic liver failure and bronchiectasis was complicated by a roller coaster of emotional difficulties and relationship problems.

Notes from a general practice diary in 2004 began to notice the complex multimorbidity common in people who have injected drugs, and a sense of hopelessness continued even into the era of effective antiviral chemotherapy for HIV infection.

Polly. had, after many years of injecting off and on, several diagnoses related to infection. In her case summary at the age of 51 years, episodes of confusion, chronic renal failure, cirrhosis secondary to hepatitis C infection, diabetes and AIDS (stage CDC3) were recorded. Her immune system was severely impaired, the most recent CD4 count being 43 cells per cubic (very low indicating advanced immunosuppression). At this time, the confusion was suspected to be due to hepatic encephalopathy resulting from liver failure. Treatment was equally complicated. She was taking 75 mg of methadone per day for her long-term opiate dependency and antiviral therapy (Zidovudine, Lopinavir/Ritonavir and lamivudine). She was also being prescribed Dapsone as an opportunistic infection prophylactic and a combination of other medications for her liver failure (Bumetanide, Spironolactone, alfacalcidol) and treatment for asthma (Beclomethasone inhaler); NovoMix insulin for her diabetes; and amitriptyline, mirtazapine and temazepam for mood and sedation. Compliance with all these drugs was noted to be variable, and during occasional admissions to the Milestone House AIDS hospice, self-harm was contemplated. She was found dead at home shortly later.

A changing community. Early in the 1980s the clinical caseload in local communities in Scotland was different. There was still a cohort of old people who had been born in the 19th century and who had participated in or witnessed World War I. A decreasing number of surviving old ladies described their "sweethearts" going off to the war and not returning and explained that "all the men were gone", leaving them to a life of spinsterhood. One older man who must have been 80 years old by the early 1980s described his memory of the 1918 "Spanish" 'flu epidemic which killed more people than any other pandemic. He remembered waking at night and looking out of the window in the street where he lived. This was a main thoroughfare in Edinburgh. What he saw was a long procession of horse-drawn hearses. The horses' hooves were padded with fabric to deaden the noise and to avoid panicking the public.

Improving medical treatment are changing lives. Medical conditions played out differently in the 1970s and 1980s, and treatments were minimally effective compared to modern management. Rheumatoid arthritis, for example, was a condition which, over many years, resulted in a wasting, crippling disease of contracted muscles and frozen joints, resulting in a dependent, fragile patient in constant pain. An older lady in this state, whose husband was a survivor of working in the Arctic whaling industry of the 1950s, was left to look after her with minimal support. Their children had, like many at the time, emigrated to Australia and, in keeping with the times, were in contact only by very occasional, poor quality and expensive phone calls. Frozen joints and muscles contracted to leave limbs in a fixed situation meant that she was confined to a wheelchair during the day and curled in a fetal position in bed at night. Pain relief was achieved using medications with serious side effects such as nausea, constipation and sedation, often worsening daily living.

Physicians and medical staff with substance use problems

Much of the literature concerning doctor or nurse involvement with substances relates to alcohol dependency and the effect of these difficulties on work, patients and colleagues. For other substances, anaesthetists have been the most frequent sector of the medical establishment to come to the attention of authorities. This has often been attributed to their access to opiates and sedatives in their working day. In early experience of the drug dependency clinics established in the 1960s in the United Kingdom, a large proportion of people being referred worked as medical staff in the National Health Service (Woodside 1973).

Although substance use in the medical population occurs at the same rate as in the general population, it remains difficult to detect on many occasions as this group develops complex strategies to conceal their problems and may only be referred later than would be helpful. Denial, stigma and shame, complicated by workload pressure and low morale, all contribute to concealing the problem, although there is good evidence that once enrolled in prevention and support programmes, their recovery and abstinence record is good. A programme of long-term monitoring, continuing care and follow-up is a model for all treatment of substance use, with up to 80% of dependent physicians in one study remaining sober and fit to return to work in five years time (Srivastava and Gold 2020).

Success stories

Numerous people stop using substances. There are undoubtedly many more people who use substances who never attend the accident and emergency departments or are reported as another statistic in the annual totals of fatalities. Religious conversions, lifestyle changes such as relationships and family events, happy and sad situations are all well recorded as the triggers for abstinences. Progressive recovery is a familiar pattern, and moving from more damaging to less harmful substances or modes of use are all success stories.

In her critically important writings and academic publications Smith describes the journey from dependency to a hugly successful career. Already mentioned in Chapter 1 it is important to again draw attention to her important insights. In the summary of her paper she draws attention to the importance of control being invested in the person with the problem and the limitations that arise from including all sorts of people in a single diagnostic category. Treatment is limited by inflexible models.

"Stigmatization of people with addiction comes from moralizing about drug use but may also originate from well-intended labels. I posit that we should not need labels to care about addicted people and make scientifically informed treatment accessible. Addicted people deserve help because they either need or want it, regardless of labels that presume to describe the etiology or likely trajectory of their problems. I conclude that some labels, even those needed for clinical classification of human behavior, may be pernicious. Clinicians and researchers have an obligation to reflect more deeply on the implications of the disease conceptualization of complex human behaviors such as addiction." Smith 2022).

Milestone House, an AIDS hospice. During the 1980s, up until the introduction of HAART (highly active antiretroviral treatment) in 1996, many of the Edinburgh cases were not so fortunate, and a regular toll of deaths occurred in the community and in the special provision of a new hospice established and designed specifically for people with AIDS. Milestone House had a difficult beginning as it was surrounded by the entrenched stigma and prejudice prevalent around gay people and people who used drugs. Eventually established on a National Health Service site, and incidentally given enthusiastic by the staff and pupils of the local primary school, it was modelled on the Mildmay charity hospice already in operation in London (McCabe et al. 2022).

A place called Severie. Severie is an imaginary name but represents a real place or event described, in their own account of their recovery journey, by most people recovering from substance use. For almost everyone with a substance use experience that is more than transitory, there is a time and a place when their eyes were opened to their situation and insight became clear about the next step in recovery. Often it is a result of a life event, a person they met who inspired them, or an experience shared with others. A period in residential care may not have resulted in lasting abstinence, but something was learned and a new belief that the future holds, sometime for them, recovery. The literature is full of turning points which are unique to the individual, but which had more than just a lesson but a step on a positive pathway. Trying to create a situation where enlightenment happens is notoriously difficult, but this is why some credit the 12-step experience, others recount a personal triumph or tragedy as the turning point and many consider that a formal treatment programme has allowed progress to their version of recovery.

Newspaper headlines

Newspaper and media presentations of substance issues are important for informing public opinion and directly or indirectly influencing policy and practice. The following selected quotes have relevance to ongoing perceptions of substance use but also indicate the stigma and prejudice ever present in reporting. The press tells today's stories and sometimes has historical and social context but more often, poorly expands to convey an in-depth understanding of the problem. Journals, magazines and reflective articles do this better but for immediate impact, breaking stories are highly valued by reporters and editors, and the details can be managed by someone else or at a more leisurely pace.

The media alerts us to emerging crises. These quotes came at a time when AIDS issues were emerging in different populations and with a feeling of something big happening but without a clear bigger picture. The background to these connected but totally different alarm bells was, as we know now, even more alarming than these headlines suggest.

"A killer known as Slim" Thousands of posters plastered throughout Uganda warn people to "Beware of Slim Disease. (Uganda Health Ministry 1986)

Blood supplies hit by fears over AIDS. (Times 19th December 1986)

100,000 may have AIDS" "Paris, Monday – AIDS the disease thought mostly to afflict homosexual men and drug addicts, is crossing all geographical and sociological barriers and may have infected as many as 100,000 people around the World, the Head of the World Health Organization said today. (Scotsman 24th June 1986)

A positive threat to women. (The Guardian 29th May 1990)

Opinions of professionals and others are given viewing in the press

As late as 1987, warnings of ignoring the signs of an emerging crisis were still being issued by people who were seeing cases of AIDS, and influential people in the field had their views offered to the readership:

"Doctor warns against silence on AIDS" Reported in the British Medical Journal 1987

"How can we tackle the drugs menace" Attributed to Mrs Renee Short MP in the GP magazine. She was chair of the House of Commons Social Services Committee.

Commentary by journalists is useful

The value of the press in exploring controversial issues is not to be underestimated and sometimes has the effect of airing in public inconvenient truths. This can have a positive effect in stimulating constructive debate on issues which at first sight have no clear solution. Novel areas of importance can be exposed in the press.

"Free needles for addicts" Andrew Veitch Guardian 19th December 1986

"Study claims more GPs avoid treating addicts" General Practitioner magazine 10th April 1986

"Half of UK prisoners on drugs, officers say" Scotsman 21st July 1986

"Action against AIDS and drugs" A letter to the Scotsman newspaper 25th April 1986 suggesting heroin prescriptions for people addicted to the drug to (36 years before the opening of the first Heroin Assisted Treatment clinic in Glasgow).

Negative and stigmatising information is often portrayed in the press
News headlines reflect popular anxiety,

"You killed your baby with drugs" Daily Record 1st February 1986

"City Junkies in AIDS shock" Daily Record 22nd February 1986

"AIDS rampage in drug city" Daily Mail 22nd February 1986

"Drugs Crisis in Schools" Daily Mail 31st January 1986

"The heartbreak of baby xxxxx. AIDS: An addict mother's tragic story" Today newspaper 12th April 1986

"Wild man of the right leads drive for AIDS apartheid" "known as Proposition 64, thousands of AIDS sufferers could be isolated, quarantined, barred from schools, restaurants, and other public places...." The Observer 31st August 1986

Publicising situations can be educational and, arguably, useful for public health.

"AIDS death sentence. Threat to 100 City addicts" Edinburgh Evening News 21st February 1986

"Drug users 'will die' in Edinburgh AIDS epidemic" Daily Telegraph 22nd February 1986

"AIDS plague terror for Glasgow" Today newspaper 8th April 1986

"The shocking facts about drugs. Children in AIDS nightmare. Early cure unlikely" Edinburgh Evening News 3rd September 1985.

Edinburgh Epidemic City.

The city would like you to remember it as the elegant venue for such glittering public relations exercises as the Commonwealth Games and the International Arts Festival. But no PR executive would dream of handling the account for Edinburgh's newest claim to fame-as the number one centre for AIDS infection in Britain. (New Musical Express April 1986)

Likely limit on free needle scheme "...Ministers remain to be convinced of the effectiveness.....No evidence that the issue of clean needles would affect the rate of contaminated syringes being passed round so-called "shooting galleries". (The Scotsman 13th December 1986)

Figure 8.1 Stigma exists in local communities. This graffiti was on the front of a health clinic.

Lethal virus can pass from mother to breast fed infant. Increase in child AIDS prompts call for screening". (Doctor Magazine 15th January 1987)

Tests cast doubt on lab origin of HIV. (Science, 1986, 234, 746–748)

Time for stark truth over AIDS "Dr Galloway says it's time for doctors to 'come clean' on AIDS". (Doctor Magazine 15th January 1987)

GPs angry over clean needles proposal. (GP News January 1986)

Celebrity endorsement was, as ever, influential and an important event which took place at the Middlesex hospital in April 1987 at the height of anxiety about the potential spread of the virus. Princess Diana attended the opening of a dedicated ward for people who had AIDS and shook hands with a patient. She was not wearing gloves, and this iconic moment signified a turning point in the public perception of the risk of catching from a non-sex or blood-to-blood encounter.

Not just Edinburgh and Scotland, headlines report visions of crises elsewhere

Russia admits to AIDS victims "The Institute of virology in Moscow is currently treating 12 AIDS patients". (Times 26th June 1986)

Drugsville "A world away from the Inner cities: Watlington, the quiet country town with a killer in its midst….heroin*"*. (Daily Express 4th August 1986)

Reagan orders new drug test crackdown…."a spokesman of the American Civil liberties Union denounced the President's move as a flagrant violation of the US Constitution fourth amendment". (The Scotsman 16th September 1986)

Dilemma for doctors over 'clean needle clinic' The plan for Oxford doctors to stop the spread of AIDS by providing a clinic where drug addicts can get clean needs could run into trouble. (Oxford Mail 13th August 1986)

Conclusion

Lived experience in the world of substance use takes on many forms and defies a simple set of descriptions. Even less clear is any guarantee of a successful rule book to define treatment. What is clear is the importance of viglilance by institutions to the risks and dangers of substance use.

References

ACMD. Hidden harm report from the UK Advisory Council on the Misuse of Drugs, 2003. Available at Hidden Harm.

Altschuler EL, Wright D. Dr. Jekyll and Mr. Hyde: a primer on substance dependence. *Am J Psych.* 2000 Mar;157(3):484. https://doi.org/10.1176/appi.ajp.157.3.484.

Brandt AM. *The Cigarette Century: The Rise, Fall, and Deadly Persistence of the Product That Defined America.* Basic Books, New York, 2007.

Davis, M. and Troupe, Q. (1990) Miles: The Autobiography. New York: Simon & Schuster.

Department of Health (England) and the Devolved Administrations. *Drug Misuse and Dependence: UK Guidelines on Clinical Management.* Department of Health (England), the Scottish Government, Welsh Assembly Government and Northern, London, 2007.

Doll R, Hill AB. Smoking and carcinoma of the lung; preliminary report. *Br Med J.* 1950 Sep 30;2(4682):739–48. https://doi.org/10.1136/bmj.2.4682.739.

Doll R, Hill AB. Mortality in relation to smoking: ten years' observations of British doctors. *Br Med J.* 1964 May 30;1(5395):1399–410. https://doi.org/10.1136/bmj.1.5395.1399.

DVLA expert panel. Driving under the influence of drugs. A report from the expert panel, 2014. Driving under the influence of drugs. accessed 17/6/25

Favril L, Strang J, Fazel S. *Drug use among people in prison: a global review of epidemiology, harms, and interventions.* Addiction. In press.

Forrester D, Harwin J. Parental substance misuse and child welfare: outcomes for children two years after referral. *Br J Soc Work.* 2008;38(8):1518–35. http://www.jstor.org/stable/23724026.

Gilbert, E. (2025) All the Way to the River: Love, Loss and Liberation. London: Bloomsbury Publishing.

Hadland SE, Rivera-Aguirre A, Marshall BDL, Cerdá M. Association of pharmaceutical industry marketing of opioid products with mortality from opioid-related overdoses. *JAMA Netw Open.* 2019 Jan 4;2(1):e186007. https://doi.org/10.1001/jamanetworkopen.2018.6007. Erratum in: *JAMA Netw Open.* 2019 Mar 1;2(3):e191625. https://doi.org/10.1001/jamanetworkopen.2019.1625.

Joint Tuberculosis Committee. Tuberculosis among immigrants in Britain: memorandum from the joint tuberculosis committee. *Br Med J.* 1978;1(6119):1038–40. http://www.jstor.org/stable/20418707.

Kingsolver B. Demon Copperhead. Harper 2022.

McCabe R, Richardson A, Taylor D, Robertson R. Milestone house: the story of a hospice for people with HIV/AIDS. *J R Coll Physicians Edinb.* 2022 Mar;52(1):73–9. https://doi.org/10.1177/14782715221088983.

Office for National Statistics (2024) Adult smoking habits in the UK: 2023. Available at: https://www.ons.gov.uk/ accessed 04/03/2026

Pinto RM, Chen Y, Park SE. A client-centered relational framework on barriers to the integration of HIV and substance use services: a systematic review. *Harm Reduct J.* 2019;16:71. https://doi.org/10.1186/s12954-019-0347-x.

Sid Vicious. (2026) Encyclopaedia Britannica. Available at: https://www.britannica.com/biography/Sid-Vicious

Smith KE. Disease and decision. *J Subst Abuse Treat.* 2022 Nov;142:108874. https://doi.org/10.1016/j.jsat.2022.108874.

Srivastava AB, Gold MS. Impaired physicians. In: Sussman S (ed.) *The Cambridge Handbook of Substance and Behavioral Addictions.* Cambridge Handbooks in Psychology. Cambridge University Press, Cambridge; 2020:326–32.

Stevenson RL. The Strange Case of Dr. Jekyll and Mr. Hyde. Longmans, Green, and Co, London, 1886.

Thom B, Whittaker A, O'Gorman A, et al. Preventing drug-related deaths in Scotland: perceptions and experiences of engagement in a 'shared care' model of service delivery. *Drugs Habits Soc Policy.* 2025 (In press).

U.S. Department of Justice (2020) Justice Department announces global resolution of criminal and civil investigations with opioid manufacturer Purdue Pharma. Available at: https://www.justice.gov accessed 02/03/2026

Woodside M. The first 100 referrals to a Scottish drug addiction treatment centre. *Br J Addict Alcohol Other Drugs.* 1973 Oct;68(3):231–41. https://doi.org/10.1111/j.1360-0443.1973.tb01250.x.

9 Treatment including opiate agonist therapy

Background

Terminology reflects fashion in the treatment of opiate use disorder, but opinion remained polarised between pharmaceutical-based treatments and abstinence-oriented interventions. From the early days of methadone treatment, there has been division in popular and political opinion reflecting the stigma associated with heroin use and other substance dependency. Methadone treatment remained controversial in the 1960s and 1970s, and guidelines and formal policy espoused a short-term period of treatment with a slow reduction over several weeks Failure to acknowledge the inadequacy of a short-term "weaning off" dose regime allowed hidden prescribing in many communities. A substantial change took place during the Nixon administration in the USA when "methadone maintenance" treatment was endorsed and escalated in an urgent attempt to address the wave of heroin use and alleged related crime (Raz 2017). As discussed in a previous chapter, the advent of HIV/AIDS in the 1980s further concentrated minds on alternatives to heroin and, more specifically, on reducing injecting. For many years, the belief that substance use and recovery from dependency was under voluntary control and could be encouraged by punitive methods underpinned the "War on Drugs" approach to policy.

Despite this, methadone has remained a divisive treatment and terms like "substitute", "maintenance" and even "long term" have raised conflicts, and in the past, have been specifically excluded from policy documents (Roberts 2012). The preferred terms have moved from Methadone Maintenance Treatment (MMT) to Opiate Substitute Treatment (OST), Opiate Agonist Treatment (OAT), Medically Assisted Treatment (MAT), and Medication Treatment for Opioid Use Disorder (MOUD). Treatment descriptions reflect the need to provide a clinical and scientific intervention rather than to describe the behavioural context. The more recent terms acknowledge the expansion of alternative agonists to include buprenorphine-containing products as well as morphine and, in some jurisdictions, injectables such as hydromorphone and heroin treatment. As these terms are used variably in the historic clinical and research literature and in different jurisdictions there will unfortunately not be one used consistently in this book.

In the United States of America, with the emerging heroin problems of the 1960s and 1970s, attention turned to a medical treatment for opiate dependency.

DOI: 10.4324/9781003611097-9

The pioneering work of the scientist Mary Jeanne Kreek alongside the clinician Vincent Dole and the psychiatrist Marie Nyswander to develop a treatment led to the landmark paper examining the effects of methadone in the treatment of opiate dependency (Dole 1966). Methadone had been originally synthesised as a pain killer for war casualties and had been used for very short-term detoxification programmes in a few clinics, but the research in the 1960s established its importance in the longer-term treatment to prevent relapse rather than just a short-term treatment designed to be an easy pathway to abstinence.

The theoretical basis of the value of methadone, or other opiate agonist treatment, is firmly based in the prevention of harms associated with dependency, relapse prevention and avoiding overdose or other physical damage from injecting or contamination. The logic of continuous treatment emerged from the experience of treatment failure, where short-term withdrawal and abstinence objectives were prioritised.

Prior to the adoption of opiate agonist treatment, opiate dependency was considered to be a problem for the criminal justice system. Rather than a medical problem, it was seen as a voluntary behavioural abnormality best managed by punishment and, at times, incarceration. Much was learned about the nature of addiction from early experimentation in an institution dedicated to the rehabilitation of convicted people who were dependent on drugs in the USA. A prison in Lexington, Kentucky, dedicated to the investigation and rehabilitation of drug-dependent convicts, operated between 1935 and 1975. It was closed after it was judged to be ineffective in delivering enduring abstinece and conducting unethical research on inmates. The research did, however, generate some enduring insights into what was ineffective in "curing" opiate dependency (Kuehn 2005, Winstanley 2020). Perhaps the most important finding from the Lexington studies was that relapse was common after coercive treatment. These findings led to a better understanding that a broad range of interventions (including justice, medical, social, economic and environmental) were likely to be needed in combination to ensure lasting recovery. It was this experience, and particularly the revelations about relapse, which led to the support for methadone treatment. More importantly, the research showed that mortality and relapse were mitigated by longer-term treatment with an opiate agonist like methadone that allowed continuous rather than short-term prescribing. Paradoxically it is the continuity of treatment that is the problem for some opponents of treatment who characterise this as prolonging the dependency disorder rather than achieving the gold standard of abstinence from opiates.

Unfortunately, recovery and rehabilitation facilities have mixed reactions to the provision of opiate agonist treatment alongside other modalities of treatment. One study of 368 treatment centres found that,

> In this national survey of residential programs for opioid use disorder, 29% of programs offered OAT as maintenance therapy, the standard of care for opioid use disorder, while many actively discouraged uses of OAT to callers.

> Thirty-one percent of programs offered OAT only for detoxification, which has worse outcomes compared with OAT maintenance.
>
> (Beetham et al. 2020)

Undertreatment is common in the USA and other countries. One study from the USA concluded that, despite guidelines recommending opiate agonist treatment, approximately only one in five adults with opiate use disorder received any opiate treatment (Jones et al. 2023). In the 2016 UNAIDS report on "The Prevention Gap", the percentage of people who use injection drugs receiving opiate agonist treatment in Asian and African countries varies from virtually zero to less than a quarter (UNAIDS 2016). Increasing evidence indicates the importance of including medical prescriptions in addition to psychosocial support. In this study, relative to patients who initiated treatment with only psychosocial treatment, patients who also initiated treatment with medications for opiate use disorder had a lower risk of having an overdose inpatient or emergency department encounter, a self-harm inpatient or emergency department encounter, and a prescription opioid given to them following treatment initiation. Starting treatment with an opiate agonist was associated with better patient outcomes than initiating treatment with only psychosocial treatment. (Mutter et al. 2023).

In recent guidelines in the USA, harm reduction has become a term popular in the ambitions of treatment. This is important as the traditional models of treatment depended upon a single end point of abstinence from any substance rather than a pragmatic and progressive move away from harm (Lu et al. 2024). Harm Reduction is the focus of chapter 6.

Methadone, however, is well-established on the WHO list of essential treatments and is generally acknowledged as a life-saving medication (WHO 21st WHO Essential Medicines List). Progress in understanding the pharmacology and receptors in the brain has allowed the introduction of buprenorphine and, more recently, different modalities of this drug (in combination with an opiate antagonist such as naloxone and injectable depots to allow monthly or longer periods between dosing).

Tensions have always existed between various views of how best to support people who use opiates and to prevent the adverse social and health consequences of taking a drug with dangerous side effects. A spectrum of opinions is understandable across political and health and social care agencies, and the general public and electorate hold important views which have to be addressed. Controversy didn't go away and the tensions between advocates for abstinence and drug-free treatments remain. Reports from many countries over the intervening periods demonstrate the, sometimes strong, feelings generated in the political and treatment sectors.

Recovery is a word that resonates in the world of management of drug problems. For many, recovery is synonymous with abstinence from all drugs, and the well-established agency Narcotics Anonymous is a great advocate and support for those trying to maintain or maintaining abstinence. For others, recovery is a relative concept based on stability and progressive improvement in the principal measures of risk and potential for harm. The primary metrics of dependency are often described as symptoms such as withdrawal, tolerance and relapse, or situations such as domestic problems, occupational difficulties or mental health issues. Control in these areas of lives are undoubtedly a form of recovery, however incomplete. The exclusion of high-risk behaviours such as sharing injecting equipment and multiple drug use is a step in recovery with immediate impact.

The poor funding of treatment clinics in the USA in the 1970s and 1980s reflected the association of the most damaging manifestations of the drug trade and inner city poverty and the attitudes and stigma associated with drug dependency. Between local and national administrations, support for methadone clinics waxed and waned with crises in heroin use. Notably, a rapid increase in methadone funding occurred in response to the increase in heroin use during the Nixon presidency and again in response to the HIV/AIDS crisis of the 1980s and beyond. In 1974, President Nixon signed the Narcotics Addiction Treatment Act which allowed for the expansion of methadone clinics but only under certain restricted conditions. These limitations disallowed the prescribing of methadone in primary care and mandated frequency of prescribing, limiting the flexibility of those in treatment – restrictions which persist to this time (Joudrey et al. 2020). There is also enormous variation in access to opiate agonist treatments between US states, the most liberal clearly coinciding with the largest concentration of drug use.

Many of these limitations have penetrated the approach to methadone treatment in other countries, although in the United Kingdom, primary care has been effectively used as the focus for methadone and other opiate agonist treatments. In the United Kingdom, methadone treatment was adopted as a policy in the early 1970s after the drug dependency clinics were established throughout the country. Guidelines were, however, clearly oriented toward abstinence with the result that outcomes were similar to those in the USA where relapse became so high that treatment was regarded as failure. By the late 1970s and early 1980s, methadone treatment in this form was increasingly abandoned and people were left to fend for themselves. The UK policy document published in 1982, ironically at the same time that HIV infection was circulating in a cohort of injecting drug users in Edinburgh and Dundee, was firmly based in a non-medical social rehabilitation model (Home Office 1982). Subsequent clinical guidelines for doctors and medical staff in the National Health Service were a response to the Government publication Department of Health and Social Security 1984). These guidelines predate the need for robust evidence and were short, 24 pages and contained only 13 references. They had the merit of stating that it was the responsibility of all doctors to manage people with drug-related problems and outlined the proper (at the time) procedure for assessing and referring to specialist services and community groups. They, however, were most concerned about smoking and inhaling heroin and the problem of barbiturate abuse, and there was amazingly no mention of injecting. Hepatitis was a concern but not HIV. The main message for doctors was about short-term treatment and the expectation that, if methadone had to be prescribed, it would be from an expert rather than a family doctor, and that regimes were short – 2 weeks or, in fewer cases, one month. A suggested treatment for people requiring methadone started with reduction by 5 mg every two days, then by 2 mg every two days to zero after ten days. Longer-term programmes of methadone reduction are described but all require eventual reduction to zero and are described as detoxification rather than "maintenance". Indeed, the word maintenance was actively discouraged from Government policy documents for many years after this.

The only caveat to this in the 1984 guidance was described as "Three to six month detoxification" and:

> For some patients it is useful to maintain and stable dose for or a month or two months to allow them to make and adjustment in their personal life, and to tackle problems related to illicit drug use. This maintenance period should *not be prolonged, and it should be made clear from the outset that it is only a prelude to a detoxification regime such* that prescribing will terminate within a three or six month period.

These guidelines followed the Government in the discouragement of prescribing and were overtaken by events within a short period, but they are typical of the early days of heroin use in the United Kingdom when the background information reported "In 1983 the number of addicts notified to the Chief Medical Officer of the Home Office was about 4200, 50% more than in 1982)".

Events in Scotland revealing a large caseload of injecting drug users and a high prevalence of HIV infection resulted in a report from the Scottish Government quite different from the 1984 version. The MacClelland Report urgently recommended the provision of injection equipment and upscaling opiate agonist treatment (Scottish Government 1986).

The most recent shift in methadone and other opiate agonist treatment provision occurred during the crisis of HIV in the 1980s. The emergence of cases of debilitating and fatal AIDS concentrated minds on prevention, particularly of injecting drug use. The development of a test for HIV in 1985 expanded the need for treating people who were using heroin, and a series of research and policy documents led to a massive increase in treatment clinics in Europe and North America. As the awareness of HIV/AIDS in people who had or still used drugs spread to an increasing number of countries, policy including methadone treatment became established at a variable rate. Some countries adopted methadone treatment programmes quicker than others, and variation persisted in the administrative arrangements. To this day, availability remains more dependent on political support and public opinion than any other evidence-based medical treatment. The research evidence for the benefits of opiate agonist treatment is robust and detailed. Improved survival, reduced morbidity, relapse prevention and improved lifestyle, sociability and integration have all been demonstrated as improvement on treatment with benefits accruing over time (Degenhardt et al. 2011). Crucially good quality treatment has been shown to reduce injecting, equipment sharing, and to enhance engagement with supportive educational and mental health services. If that is not enough, then opiate agonist treatment is convincingly associated with a reduction in acquisitive crime.

The urgency to reduce the risk of spread of HIV infection to domestic and sexual contacts of people infected through drug use further increased the importance of engaging people in treatment (Downs et al. 1996, McClelland Report 1986) although mercifully the transmission by non-sexual domestic contact was shown to be low (Friedland et al. 1986).

Most recently, the crisis of drug-related deaths has driven policy change. In the United Kingdom (particularly Scotland), a rapid increase in drug-related deaths reignited the sector and, paradoxically, the division of opinion between abstinence-oriented and opiate agonist treatments. In the USA, the opiate overdose epidemic was, and is, closely related to prescription opiates and an ongoing scandal of inappropriate marketing and promotion of pharmaceutical opiates required treatment expansion. In the USA and Canada, a crisis of increasing availability of traditional and new synthetic opiates has driven opiate overdose deaths. These crises have again energised the treatment requirements and innovation in preventive measures to divert opiate use. Too many people with substance use disorder continue to have difficultly accessing treatment. A recent study in the USA concluded that, "Despite guidelines recommending medically assisted treatment approximately 1 in 5 adults with past-year opiate use disorder received any medication for opioid use disorder (MOUD). Furthermore, some groups were substantially less likely to receive MOUD, in particular black adults, women, those unemployed, and those in non metropolitan areas. Addressing disparities in MOUD uptake should be prioritized in program, policy, and clinical initiatives" Jones 2021.

An anniversary statement in 2025 from the director of the US National Institute on Drug Abuse outlined some encouraging news but reminded us of the scale of the problem.

> Our 50th year brought hope, as we finally saw evidence of a sustained downturn in drug overdose deaths. From July 2023 to July 2024, the number of fatal overdoses dropped nearly 17 percent, from over 113,000 to 94,000. We still don't know all the factors contributing to this reversal, so investigating the drivers of this decline will be crucial for sustaining and accelerating the downturn. We also need to recognize that the decline is not homogenous across populations: Black and American Indian/Alaskan Native persons continue to die at increased rates. And 94,000 people dying of overdose in a year is still 94,000 too many.
>
> (NIDA 2025)

An update from the United Nations Office on Drugs and Crime (UNODC) — *World Drug Report 2024* further outlined a changing landscape and the international nature of the challenges.

> Demand for opiate treatment services, including for methadone, buprenorphine, and slow-release morphine treatment, may rise, but if these services are insufficient, heroin users may switch to other opioids. Such a switch may pose significant risks to health and lead to an increase in overdoses,

> especially if the alternative opioids include highly potent substances such as some fentanyl analogues or nitazenes that have already emerged in some European countries in recent years (EMCDDA 2024). The impact within Afghanistan will be reflected in rural areas, with farmers struggling to adhere to the drug ban if alternative livelihood opportunities do not emerge. Opiate users may also feel the shortage of opiates and look for alternatives. Moreover, the Afghan drug economy may switch to methamphetamine. It is less clear whether the drug ban announced by the Taliban in April 2022 has also impacted the production of methamphetamine in Afghanistan and exports of the drug. There are indications that the de facto authorities have been targeting methamphetamine manufacture and the collection and sale of the Ephedra plant, which produces ephedrine, a precursor used in the manufacture of methamphetamine. However, seizures of methamphetamine up until the end of 2023 in countries reporting seizures of the drug originating from Afghanistan did not indicate much of a slowdown in methamphetamine trafficking.
>
> (UNODC 2024).

Cascade and tiers of treatment

Various authorities and guidelines stress the need for a treatment hierarchy or cascade of treatment opportunities depending upon various demographic or risk factors. Priority might be given to the very young, the most vulnerable or the people who seem to be at most risk of harm. Triggers for early intervention may be based on age, homelessness, lack of visible support or other social or personal crises. Injury, acute health conditions or unstable mental health may all precipitate admission to care in a hospital or residential support unit. Inevitably, hospital beds are in demand and residential care usually has a long assessment and waiting period; the bar for early admission is high and, in many places, unacceptably high. The presence of injecting drug use, especially as it may be longstanding, is unlikely to trigger a rapid response although, arguably, it represents a critically high risk every time a substance is injected into a vein or beneath the skin into a muscle or subcutaneous tissue. Injecting a known, or frequently unknown, substance carries the risk of overdose, infection, organ or vascular damage at every event. Triage at street clinics, primary care or specialist units attempts to place the patient in the most appropriate situation to reduce acute risk and to enter a pathway designed to lead to a stable and progressively risk-free future. Drug workers and clinicians are required to make judgements in every case and on every presentation about how to pursue these objectives but are always aware that, with the rare exception of involuntary detention of a seriously psychotic person, under a protective mental health protocol, treatment is voluntary, and the choice belongs to the individual. It doesn't take much experience of the difficulties and constraints of being dependent on an illegal substance to know that progress has to be measured carefully, interventions have to be personalised and timed to suit, and that the seriously dependent person may have adapted to a lifestyle including drugs that is, in the short-term, more comfortable than the challenge demanded by most treatment options.

The decision for a person using a substance to confide in a healthcare or other drug management agency is an enormous change and requires acknowledging the presence of a problem. Choosing who to trust with such a personal problem is another hurdle familiar to health and social care workers, and many people live with a serious drug problem for many years before asking for help. Some never ask for assistance, and projects and facilities have to try hard to be approachable and accessible, as well as carefully designed to retain people in contact over time.

The UK clinical guidelines for the management of people with drug use stress the assessment process as being a critically important step in the management (Clinical Guidelines on Drug Misuse and Dependence Update 2017) and acknowledge the gaps in care provison. This is not just a UK problem with local and international examples of the difficulty in providing comprehensive support services (Arwady et al. 2024)

Project worker whether medical or nursing staff or otherwise trained are a key element in the success of treatment. The core skills required for project workers are identified as needing to:

- identify and manage drug (and alcohol) dependence
- identify and manage
- identify and manage coexisting physical health, mental health and social problems
- deliver effective harm reduction interventions
- support psychosocial interventions and effective prescribing
- deliver holistic, person-centred treatment and recovery care planning.

Once contact has been made, then the range of treatment options needs to be available and tailored for the individual who may enter the treatment pathway at any stage depending upon past experience and suitability for the intervention. The general headings for treatment identified in the guidelines include assessment of general health, assessment for psychosocial interventions, assessment for initiating opioid substitution treatment, assessment for opioid detoxification, assessment within the criminal justice system, assessment of opioid-dependent patients within general hospital settings and assessment of young people.

In all these areas, structures are recommended and complexities are examined within the guidelines as they are in the many national, regional and local management structures.

Injecting drug users have a special place for any agency or health and social care system interacting with people who have this problem. As was examined in detail in chapter 5 the hazards for people who inject drugs might be seen as the top of a hierarchy of risk and therefore a top priority for support. Thc awareness of blood-borne viruses, bacterial infections and sudden deaths from overdose, all considered in detail in earlier chapters, has concentrated minds on the importance of specialised interventions. Funding expensive treatments requires overcoming the public and institutionalised stigma associated with drug problems, but the realisation that the consequences of increasing drug-using populations costs governments enormous amounts in health and criminal justice services has allowed some progress. The additional recognition of the collateral damage to children and families and the potential for sexually transmitted infections to the non-drug-using population further encourages innovation in care.

Models of opiate agonist treatment

Over the last few decades, with increasing numbers of people using heroin and, more recently, an increasing range of synthetic opiates, the approach to using agonist compounds has evolved. Methadone was first synthesised in Germany in 1937 and developed as a synthetic alternative to morphine, which was in short supply. It was later introduced to the United States after World War II, where it was given the name methadone. It became widely used in the nineteen sixties in the United States as part of opioid addiction treatment programmes, especially as a maintenance therapy for heroin dependence, following research by Drs. Vincent Dole and Marie Nyswander.

Since then, it has been the standard treatment for opiate dependency when a pharmacological option is requested. In the early days, the treatment was increasingly used in large doses with the expectation that “narcotic blockade” required increased quantities to eliminate the urge to supplement with heroin. More recently, it is recognised that tolerance can increase with the dose and optimal therapeutic responses need not necessarily be achieved by an increased dose.

Both prescribed and “bring your own” injectables have been recognised as important interventions in many countries. Consultation with people who inject drugs has been an important part of the development of this additional method of reducing the harm accruing from injecting. In an insightful series of interviews with people who inject drugs, Salisbury and colleagues concluded that the international evidence supported safer injecting spaces and that the interviewees recognised the value for their own safety and the protection of the immediate environment (Salisbury and Hill 2024). Objections to opening a safer injecting facility have been economic and political and there is anxiety about the risks to public health. Worries that this might encourage increased drug use, or have a detrimental effect on the local environment, have been largely outweighed by evidence that there is a reduction in blood-borne virus transmission, a reduction in overdose deaths, an increase in the uptake of primary care support and a decrease in public injecting and discarded needles and syringes (ACMD 2016, EMCDDA 2017, Vecino et al. 2013, Salmon et al. 2010). In Canada and Australia, convincing evidence has shown that on-site resuscitation facilities, access and recruitment to opiate agonist treatment, and normalisation of behaviour have all contributed to reducing harms (Kerr et al. 2006, Kennedy et al. 2018). Other countries in Europe have developed different models of safer injecting facilities; some in Switzerland and Germany have coexisting support services to address welfare rights, homelessness, mental and physical health issues and are often staffed by a variety of clinical and non-medical people with lived experience.

Heroin prescribing has been researched for safety and economic viability in several European countries (Strang et al. 2010, Strang 2002, Rehm et al. 2001, van den Brink et al. 2003). Initially experimentally and later as part of routine services, the concept of safer injecting locations has been implemented in several countries, including Switzerland, the Netherlands and, most recently, in the United Kingdom (Scotland). Alternative injectables such as hydromorphone have been used in Australia when heroin is not allowed (Rodgers et al. 2024).

A model safe consumption facility

The Glasgow clinic opened in January 2025 after careful political and local planning and consultation. Features of this clinic are in many ways unique to the requirements of the local population and result from pressure arising from the widespread street use of injecting drugs and the high rate of death from overdose (Drug-related Deaths in Scotland in 2023).

The new clinic is located in central Glasgow on the same site as the Heroin Assisted Treatment clinic, which opened a few years earlier. Facilities include a reception area and assessment room, injecting space, recovery room, and separate lounge areas (described below), outside smoking area, admin and storage, shower and washing rooms, toilets and a store of clothing if required. Blood testing for viral infections on site is available, and supplies of injecting equipment are supplied for use in the clinic and/or to take away (described in chapter 6–). In the first 8 weeks, 160 people made contact, not all of whom used the injecting space.

The majority are cocaine users (80%), representing the changing drug supply in the city. This is reflected in surveillance data suggesting an increase in cocaine injecting across Scotland.

"While heroin continues to be the most prevalent drug injected, cocaine injecting has increased in recent years, with 37% of those who had injected in the past six months reporting using it in 2019–20" (Public Health Scotland 2022).

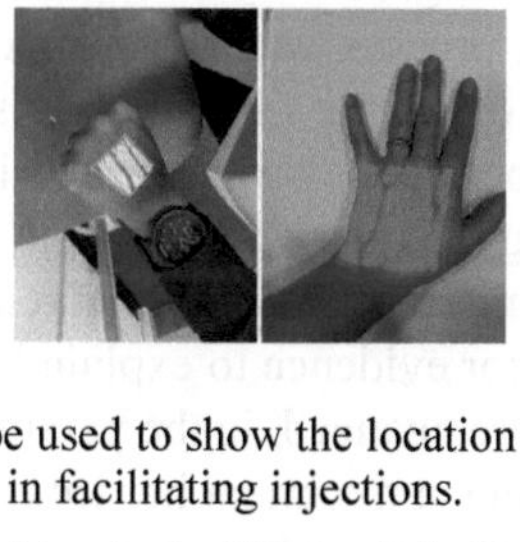

Figure 9.1 These devices can be used to show the location of superficial veins beneath the skin and are helpful in facilitating injections.

Supplied by NHS practitioners working in the Thistle clinic Glasgow and neonatal unit Kirkcaldy hospital, with thanks.

The remaining are heroin users or both, sometimes injecting combined heroin and cocaine (snowball). Some super strong heroin recently with a green appearance has caused overdose events requiring resuscitation (15 events in the last month).

Additional add-on services available or planned include social work and housing support, drug testing facilities, virology specialist clinics and medical clinics.

Not included in the present set up is space for smoking heroin or cocaine. The health and safety requirements for smoking booths are under discussion and ventilation to a required specification is already installed.

It is noted that the model described here is different and might be considered superior to the Swiss and other European clinics. The clientele in Geneva is older and often employed. The Dutch clinics are more economical in the sense that staffing is less and services available are less comprehensive. In a developing field, different models are tried. Smoking heroin rooms have the disadvantage of the technical arrangements required to avoid contamination and inhalation by staff, and injecting supervision can occur at various levels with support from medical and nursing staff needed in case of overdose or vascular damage. Political interventions impose constraints, and prioritising this relatively expensive intervention has to compete with other important treatments.

The prospects and further innovations for the future are being considered. Linking with other specialists is likely; a General Practitioner service with prescribing capacity would be an additional advantage.

Evidence for the benefits of Opiate Agonist treatment

The controversial nature of drug use for politicians, the public and the academic and health and social care establishments has meant that the need for evidence to support policy actions is intense. More than most areas of public health care, addictions and dependencies suffer from an institutionalised stigma that penetrates all levels of the establishment and results in poor investments in treatments and a bias towards non-medical interventions such as residential rehabilitation, with an emphasis on abstinence. At times there is a default to a punitive solution through the criminal justice system. The urgency for research into the benefits, risks and outcomes of opiate agonist treatment has been a priority for several decades. Support and crucial funding have been driven by a narrow view of what is expected of treatment, and the nature of research has been guided by a limited vision of what the nature of addiction means. A learning process was most importantly demonstrated in the experimental nature of the work at the Lexington prison, otherwise known as the "Narcotics Farm". These experiments have resulted in revelations that for many, drug use is part of a relapsing disorder with multiple factors influencing initiation into drug use, episodes of remission and causes of relapse. Research has therefore become wider, in the search for evidence to explain behaviour leading to all these elements of drug use, and more nuanced, in the parameters studied.

The simplest way of looking at treatment benefits is to follow the life course of people receiving therapy. Outcomes and consequently treatment policy guidelines followed the outcomes of short-term opiate treatments. The disappointing results seemed to demonstrate that the treatment was a failure and policy in the late 1960s through to the 1980s was driven away from methadone treatment towards drug-free behavioural treatments. Limited designs of studies endorse this belief and the presence of a caseload of people who had recovered from heroin use and were now abstinent and living stable lives encouraged the belief that this was possible for everyone. The Lexington experience and the follow-up research that followed the inmates seemed to endorse the view that the treatment had been unsuccessful as many of the people had relapsed or died shortly after release (Vaillant 1970). Subsequent follow-up studies reported conflicting results over relatively short-term follow-up (Maddux et al. 1992) but longer-term studies began to demonstrate a different picture. Most long-term outcomes showed a high mortality rate compared to the non-drug-using population and increasingly demonstrated the variation in demographic and situation of cases and the variable rate of any stable recovery (Rounsaville et al. 1982, Joe et al. 1982). Relating this to treatment took some time to become clear as short-term treatment was more commonly associated with relapse and longer-term treatment was complicated by the presence of other variables and coexisting conditions such as infectious diseases and alcohol use (Grella et al. 2011). Equally important were the complicating factors of other lifestyles and the morbidity associated with violent incidents, comorbid psychiatric and social problems. When treatment outcomes were increasingly measured in the longer-term, the cumulative benefits of "maintenance" opiate agonist treatment became apparent (Hser et al. 2001, Darke et al. 2007, Vaillant 1988). More detailed studies relating treatment to survival clearly show a positive relationship with the length of opiate agonist treatment and survival (Xia et al. 2015).

Studies were, and are, still flawed. Most are dominated by men and many of the groups studied are from socially disadvantaged backgrounds. Associated family and adverse early life experiences play important roles in the genesis of dependency, and current social situations, homelessness, poverty and mental health conditions exacerbate use and lead to relapsing outcomes and treatment "failure." Treatments themselves are flawed, being less supportive than they might be and being limited in their vision. The failure to supply additional treatments such as housing and financial interventions and psychological therapies is inevitably increasing the expectations of treatment failure.

Recent studies of opiate overdoses and the relative benefits of residential care compared to outpatient opiate agonist treatment have concluded that "relative to outpatient treatment, residential treatment was not associated with reductions in opioid overdose or opioid-related emergency department encounters/hospitalizations. Regardless of setting, MOUD (medications for opioid use disorders) use was associated with a significant reduction in opioid overdose risk" (Hartung et al. 2022).

All this is complicated by associated additional drug use. In many treatment programmes, the dominant drug of use may not be an opiate. The presence of stimulants such as cocaine and methylamphetamine is a crucially important complicating factor in opiate agonist treatment programmes, as is the co-use of benzodiazepines, alcohol and drugs such as ketamine and synthetic cannabinoids.

It is an obvious observation that the treatment group with the most complex interactions of situations and least "social and personal capital" is likely to fare least well, and the opposite profile is likely to allow recovery by whatever measure that is applied. It is easy therefore to point to the happy outcome of treatment where family support, past high educational standards and financial security provide a route out of drug use.

Treatment, in the form of opiate, therefore, is a programme of interventions which depend upon having a range of treatments delivered by a collection of agencies over a longer period of time.

Treatment, in the broadest sense of the term, encompasses personal, social and health areas of the individual's life and a pragmatic appraisal of what might be possible to achieve over an expected time period. Starting with addressing the immediate risks to life and the situation causing most distress and pain, resources must be targeted in the most pragmatic way. Priorities such as reducing injecting of drugs and, at the very least, stopping using contaminated equipment may take away the immediate risk of infection, and stopping injecting completely by moving to an oral substitute will enormously reduce the risk of sudden fatal overdose. Assessments of mental state and capacity, providing emergency accommodation and supporting negotiations with the penal system might all provide the immediate comfort to allow a planned series of interventions building a stable recovery platform. Opiate agonist treatment is an essential early step on this pathway and, carefully tailored to the needs of the individual, might remove the hazards of obtaining illegal drugs and running the risk of contaminated products of unknown toxicity. Stability leads to the many benefits of rehabilitation and social integration. Many years of experience of ongoing opiate agonist treatment have shown that, combined with financial, social and educational support programmes as well as employment and independent living opportunities, it is compatible with a secure and stable lifestyle. The often forgotten "British system" of long-term supplies of diamorphine to people with opiate dependency was associated with an otherwise "normal" lifestyle (Spear and Mott 1993). In view of the apparent success of this intervention, the possibility of heroin prescribing was considered by US Congress in the early 1970s as an addition to methadone prescriptions (Koran 1973). After a successful visit to the United Kingdom by a representative of the Bureau of Narcotics and Dangerous Drugs, it was concluded that there should be support for a similar trial in the United States (Lewis 1973). This never happened and an upscaling of methadone treatment continued. The prescribing of heroin and injectable methadone in the United Kingdom remained controversial and the need for long-term evaluation of its effectiveness was observed by several investigators (Zador 2001, Lader 2001) but vigorously defended by others (Carnwath 2001, Jones 2002). Concluding his contribution, a addiction specialist reported that

> I would be happy to defend my practice if required in court. In spite of the anxieties expressed by Lader (2001), I believe that there is sufficient evidence of efficacy and safety to justify the prescription of diamorphine in a situation where all other standard treatments have failed, and the patient's

> health is seriously at risk. I cannot believe that courts would find this practice un-reasonable, considering also that it has been sanctioned for 80 years in British practice, it is licensed by the Home Office with support from the Department of Health and it is the subject of scientific trials in at least five countries.
>
> (Johns 2002)

Policy eventually moved in the direction of supervised heroin clinics.

Protocols for opiate treatment

Managing a caseload of people who have dependency problems is complicated and has to take into account individual circumstances, physical and mental health comorbid diagnoses and a past history of successes or failures in interventions. Circumstances which will enhance recovery include the support available from family and local organisations and the absence of complications like involvement in criminal or civil court proceedings. Perhaps most critically important is the willingness and favourable circumstances associated with the individual.

Prescribing an opiate agonist as a treatment is an important decision for the substance user and requires careful briefing. Selection of the appropriate opiate is important, as is careful induction and supervision of what is potentially a drug with serious harms associated with it. A range of opiates – oral opiate tablets such as dihydrocodeine and codeine derivatives – have been used in the past, but the favoured option in the last fifty years has been methadone mixture in an oral solution, the usual preparation being a green coloured solution containing 1 mg methadone per ml solution. Methadone is also available in 10 mg/ml and 20 mg/ml solutions and as oral 5 mg tablets and an injectable solution or suppository, but these preparations are less commonly prescribed and require special precautions. The oral mixture is commonly introduced under some supervision and protocol, and guidance for daily doses, degree of supervision and progressive titration to reach optimal therapeutic effect are included in national and local guidance documents. Supervision can take place in the clinic where the prescription is issued, but more commonly in many countries, including the United Kingdom, this is undertaken by a pharmacist on a hospital or local site or in a community setting. Local protocols will usually start with close observation of ingestion of methadone prescriptions on a daily basis, followed by assessments of the efficacy and need for increased or decreased doses. As stability is achieved, allowing increasing independence means dispensing doses to take away and to be ingested at home. Most clinics combine these treatment protocols with urine sample testing to ensure compliance. In stable cases with longstanding compliance, occasional supervision and toxicology testing are demanded. Buprenorphine preparations have similar protocols but come in different preparations. Preparations may be in the form of oral tablets which dissolve in the mouth or a film lyophilisate with a quicker absorption rate.

British National Formulary suggests dosing schedules for the sublingual tablet including "Initially 2 mg daily, followed by 2–4 mg if required on day one, adjusted in steps of 2–6 mg daily if required, maximum 18 mg per day".

More recent development of an injectable buprenorphine preparation has introduced an exciting alternative to the daily routine of MAT and the requirement for close supervision for safety and security. As a novel alternative to the well-established opiate agonist treatment, the long-acting preparation offers more than just an equivalent benefit to traditional oral treatments. Early studies have been encouraging in identifying the benefits of the periodicity of treatment compared to the once-daily regime familiar with methadone and, relatively, short-acting modalities (Rutrick et al. 2023). Some of these benefits are the added value of prolonged abstinence, the accessibility of this treatmentand the important opportunity it creates to allow employment. (Martin et al. 2022).

There are two long-acting injectable formulations of buprenorphine licensed in the United Kingdom – the Camurus product (Buvidal) and the one developed by Indivior (branded Subutex prolonged-release in the United Kingdom and parts of Europe / the Nordics, and Sublocade in the US and Australia). Buvidal has been available in the United Kingdom since 2019 and, although there is a Marketing Authorisation in place, Indivior has not launched its product in the United Kingdom.

Long-acting injectable buprenorphine (LAIB) for opioid dependence treatment guidelines from New South Wales gave a comprehensive treatment protocol using Buvidal and Sublocade, demonstrating considerable prospect for using a depot formulation to control symptoms. These guidelines recognise the imperfection included in all pharmaceutical treatments for substance use disorder but indicate a significant development of a formulation that can make substantial differences to the lifestyle of people using substances and the associated prospects for normalising behaviour. Acknowledgement is made of continual use of illicit opiates while on treatment and helpful advice about topping up doses of LAIB to try to help with this (Lintzeris et al. 2024). With the extended fentanyl crisis in North America, LAIB has been shown to be a useful additional therapeutic option (Nunes et al. 2024).

A summary of inhibiting and enhancing factors may include some of the following enhancing and enabling features and possible actions include the following positive and negative features. These observations are especially relevant for people receiving a prescribed dose of methadone. Similar criteria are, however, relevant for people taking a buprenorphine-containing prescription even if the risk of fatal overdose is reduced.

The table indicates favourable features in opiate agonist treatment situations

Indicators of stability	Possible actions
Stable dose of methadone in the region of 100mls (1mg/ml)	Careful monitoring
History of recent compliance with treatment and regular attendance at clinic appointments	Suitable interval prescribing and dispensing

Toxicology tests indicating compliance and absence of undisclosed drugs	Community care support
Stable housing and family/friendships	Contact available, if necessary, with family doctor or mental health worker
Vison of recovery plan and direction	
Absence of unstable mental health	

The following table illustrates situations which may indicate risk to stability or safety of prescribing and possible actions.

Poor engagement with specialist clinic

Indicators of instability and unfavourable features	Possible actions
Higher doses of methadone (greater than 120mg)	Consider increasing supervision of methadone or other opiate agonist treatment. May need ECG to detect QT interval defect.
Coexisting mental health problems	Joint working with psychiatric specialist services.
Additional prescriptions which may exacerbate sedation (For example, antipsychotics, benzodiazepines,SSRIs or GABA analogues)	Consider modifications in opiate agonist treatment, especially when inititaing new medications which could cause sedation.
Inconsistent toxicology results	Discuss with patient to investigate possible irregular substance use
High-risk behaviours such as transactional sex or criminality and poor attendance record for review appointments	This is a case for a multidicplinary meeting with specialist and social work colleagues.
Multimorbidity (COPD, Cardiac or Liver disease)	Joint working with liver, respiratory or other specialists.

Side effects of methadone (and other opiates on prescription)

Any opiate carries with it a risk of unwanted or dangerous side effects. Methadone is a strong opiate with a non-linear dose equivalence ratio depending upon the dose and the individual's tolerance and experience with the drug. The strength compared to morphine increases disproportionately with larger doses, although the majority of opiate agonist treatment is in a range of 50–150 mg with a dose equivalent between three and five times that of morphine. At a starting dose below 100 mg, methadone is roughly three times stronger than morphine. This is important as the single most important side effect of any opiate is respiratory depression leading to asphyxia and death when tolerance is exceeded. Common side effects of methadone (and other opiates), listed in the British National Formulary, include drowsiness, nausea, dry mouth, vomiting, constipation, sweating and itching. Dental decay is frequently blamed on methadone mixture, and this may be due to poor dental hygiene and the frequent ingestion of a sugary mixture. Less common is urinary retention and dizziness.

The most serious side effects are respiratory depression and prolonged QT interval on ECG. Recording leads rarely to cardiac arrhythmia and possible cardiac arrest. These risks must be weighed up when considering dosage (risks increase with dose) and the possible increased danger when other drugs are being prescribed or self-administered. In a series of drug-related deaths, the presence of multiple drugs is frequently cited as the cause of death.

Buprenorphine has a similar range of side effects, but being a partial agonist, it is safer than full agonists like methadone, morphine and heroin. It does have the additional side effect of inducing withdrawal when taken by an individual who has recently had a dose of a full agonist.

Extended and adjunctive treatments

Obviously, opiate agonist treatment does not exist in isolation. Individuals in this therapy are subject to personal and individual influences in their day-to-day lives, many of which have a critical place in the success or failure of treatments. Most guidelines on any prescription medication for drug dependency treatment include a wide range of psychological options, acknowledging the importance of addressing all the requirements to build recovery. Opiate agonist treatments have never existed in isolation, usually being supported by generalist or specialist doctors or nurses, but increasingly used in conjunction with behavioural treatments such as cognitive behavioural therapy, family therapy, motivational interviewing, 12-step facilitation therapy, contingency management. These are often used in combination with Opiate Agonist Treatment OAT treatment at the same time or as serial interventions.

In a recent paper, the value of contingency management, including in digital formats, was explored by Getty and colleagues. In the introduction, an explanation of the definition of contingency management was offered (Getty et al. 2025).

Contingency Management is an intervention which is an adjunct to other treatments and as such a useful way of encouraging engagement or promoting consistency and adherence to whatever treatment is being offered.

> Contingency management (CM) is a behavioural intervention involving the adjunctive application of positive reinforcement (e.g. monetary incentives) contingent upon evidence of positive behaviour change. CM is based on the theoretical principles of operant conditioning and is among the most efficacious psychosocial interventions in promoting substance use-related behaviours, including abstinence from smoking, alcohol and illicit drugs, medication adherence, vaccination uptake and attendance.
>
> (Getty et al. 2025)

CM has been in use for some time, but models change, and the metrics included have an influence on effectiveness. For example, the magnitude of the effect declined over time and CM was more effective for opiate and cocaine use than tobacco or multiple drug use. Maybe unsurprisingly, a larger effect size in one meta-study was found to be associated with higher researcher involvement (Prendergast et al. 2006).

Interventions using CM are likely to become increasingly mainstream in the management of people trying to abstain from opiates (Metrebian et al. 2021).

The wide range of treatment modalities again stresses the complexity of drug dependency and the need for individual portfolios of treatment not just at any point in time but over as long a term as is necessary.

Conclusion

Opiate agonist treatment is well-established and there is a good evidence base supporting treatment for people who inject substances that are opiate-based. There are risks of overdose, particularly with unregulated methadone, and protocols and guidelines are detailed in their inclusion of ways to prevent the harm from toxicity, acknowledging the dangers of cumulative toxicity when taken with other substances. Evidence suggests that the results of MOUD are best when opiate agonist treatment is combined with holistic personal care and the provision of strategies to support homelessness, mental health problems and difficult social and financial conditions. The added benefits of treatment with a prescribed opiate are access to other harm reduction interventions such as the provision of sterile injecting equipment, testing for blood-borne infections and specialist care for comorbid liver or other diseases. As a short-term emergency management of high-risk opiate injecting, MOUD has a critically important place. Medium to long-term management with MOUD can be combined effectively with interventions to support the medical and social multimorbidity often associated with substance use. As a pathway to stable living, MOUD is completely compatible with eventual abstinence from all substances.

References

Advisory Council on the Misuse of Drugs (ACMD). *Reducing Opioid-Related Deaths in the UK*. ACMD, London, 2016.

Arwady MA, Delphin-Rittmon M, Volkow ND. Major gaps in the cascade of care for opioid use disorder: implications for clinical practice. *JAMA*. 2024 Sep 3;332(9):701–2. https://doi.org/10.1001/jama.2024.11977.

Beetham T, Saloner B, Gaye M, et al. Therapies offered at residential addiction treatment programs in the United States. *JAMA*. 2020;324(8):804–6. https://doi.org/10.1001/jama.2020.8969.

Carnwath T. In defence of the British system of injectable diamorphine prescription. *Addiction*. 2001 Oct;96(10):1405–7. https://doi.org/10.1046/j.1360-0443.2001.961014054.x.

Darke S, Ross J, Teesson M. The Australian Treatment Outcome Study (ATOS): what have we learnt about treatment for heroin dependence? *Drug Alcohol Rev*. 2007 Jan;26(1):49–54. https://doi.org/10.1080/09595230601036986.

Department of Health and Social Security. *Guidelines of Good Clinical Practice in the Treatment of Drug Misuse*. DHSS, London, 1984.

Downs AM, de Vincenzi I. Probability of heterosexual transmission of hiv: relationship to the number of unprotected sexual contacts. *J Acquir Immune Defic Syndr Hum Retrovirol*. 1996;11:388–95.

Drug-related Deaths in Scotland in 2023 | National Records of Scotland (nrscotland.gov.uk) drug-related-deaths-23-report.pdf.

Degenhardt l, Brucello C, Mathers B, et al. mortality among regular or dependent users of heroin and other opioids: a systematic review and meta-analysis of cohort studies. *Addiction*. 2011;106:32–51.

Dole VP, Nyswander ME, Kreek MJ. Narcotic blockade. *Arch Intern Med.* 1966;118(4):304–9.

EMCDDA. Perspectives on drugs. Drug consumption rooms: an overview of provision and evidence, 2017. https://www.euda.europa.eu/topics/pods/drug-consumption-rooms_en.

EMCDDA. European Monitoring Centre for Drugs and Drug Addiction (2024). *European Drug Report 2024: Trends and Developments*, 2024. https://www.emcdda.europa.eu/publications/european-drug-report/2024_en.

Friedland GH, Saltzman BR, Rogers MF, et al. lack of transmission of HTLV3/LAV infection to household contacts of patients with aids or aids-related complex with oral candidiasis. *N Engl J Med*. 1986;314:344–9.

Getty CA, Metrebian N, Neale J, Weaver T, Strang J. Addiction specialists' perspectives on digital contingency management and its role within UK drug and alcohol services: a qualitative exploration. *Drug Alcohol Rev*. 2025 May;44(4):946–60. https://doi.org/10.1111/dar.14046.

Grella CE, Lovinger K. 30-year trajectories of heroin and other drug use among men and women sampled from methadone treatment in California. *Drug Alcohol Depend*. 2011 Nov 1;118(2–3):251–8. https://doi.org/10.1016/j.drugalcdep.2011.04.004.

Clinical Guidelines on Drug Misuse and Dependence Update 2017 Independent Expert Working Group. *Drug Misuse and Dependence: UK Guidelines on Clinical Management*. Department of Health, London, 2017.

Home Office 1982 Treatment and Rehabilitation. *Report from the Advisory Council on the Misuse of Drugs*. Home Office, London, 1982.

Hartung DM, Markwardt S, Johnston K, et al. Association between treatment setting and outcomes among oregon medicaid patients with opioid use disorder: a retrospective cohort study. *Addict Sci Clin Pract*. 2022 Aug 19;17(1):45. https://doi.org/10.1186/s13722-022-00318-1.

Hser YI, Hoffman V, Grella CE, Anglin MD. A 33-year follow-up of narcotics addicts. *Arch Gen Psychiatry*. 2001 May;58(5):503–8. https://doi.org/10.1001/archpsyc.58.5.503.

Joe GW, Lehman W, Simpson DD. Addict death rates during a four-year posttreatment follow-up. *Am J Public Health*. 1982 Jul;72(7):703–9. https://doi.org/10.2105/ajph.72.7.703.

Johns, A. (2002) Prescribing heroin: a defence. The British Journal of Psychiatry, 180, pp. 198–199.

Jones CM, Han B, Baldwin GT, Einstein EB, Compton WM. Use of medication for opioid use disorder among adults with past-year opioid use disorder in the US, 202. *JAMA Netw Open*. 2023;6(8):e2327488. https://doi.org/10.1001/jamanetworkopen.2023.27488

Joudrey PJ, Edelman EJ, Wang EA. Methadone for opioid use disorder-decades of effectiveness but still miles away in the US. *JAMA Psych*. 2020 Nov 1;77(11):1105–6. https://doi.org/10.1001/jamapsychiatry.2020.1511.

Kuehn BM. Methadone treatment marks 40 years. *JAMA*. 2005;294(8):887–9. https://doi.org/10.1001/jama.294.8.887.

Koran LM. Heroin maintenance for heroin addicts: issues and evidence. *N Engl J Med*. 1973 Mar 29;288(13):654–60. https://doi.org/10.1056/NEJM197303292881305.

Kennedy MC, Scheim A, Rachlis B, et al. Willingness to use drug checking within future supervised injection services among people who inject drugs in a mid-sized Canadian city. *Drug Alcohol Depend.* 2018;185:248–52.

Kerr T, Stoltz JA, Tyndall M, et al. Impact of a medically supervised safer injection facility on community drug use patterns: a before and after study. *BMJ.* 2006;332(7535):220–2.

Lader M. Injectable opiate maintenance in the United Kingdom–within a medicines act perspective. *Addiction.* 2001 Apr;96(4):555–7; discussion 564–5. https://doi.org/10.1080/09652140020031601.

Lewis E Jr. A heroin maintenance program in the United States? *JAMA.* 1973 Jan 29;223(5):539–46.

Lintzeris N, Dunlop A, Schulz M. *Long-Acting Injectable Buprenorphine (LAIB) for Opioid Dependence Treatment: Brief Guide*, 2nd edn, NSW Ministry of Health, 2024. https://www.health.nsw.gov.au/aod/Publications/buprenorphine-brief-guide.pdf.

Lu T, Whitley SD, Wiegand TJ, et al. *Treatment of Opioid Use Disorder* [Internet]. Johns Hopkins University, Baltimore, 2024 Feb. https://www.ncbi.nlm.nih.gov/books/NBK558319/.

McClelland Report 1986. Edinburgh: Scottish home and health department. 15 Johnson am, Petherick a, Davidson S.J et al Transmission of HIV to heterosexual partners of infected men and women. *AIDS* 1989; 3: 367–72.

Maddux JF, Desmond DP. Ten-year follow-up after admission to methadone maintenance. *Am J Drug Alcohol Abuse.* 1992;18(3):289–303. https://doi.org/10.3109/00952999209026068.

Martin E, Maher H, McKeon G, Patterson S, Blake J, Chen KY. Long-acting injectable buprenorphine for opioid use disorder: A systematic review of impact of use on social determinants of health. *J Subst Abuse Treat.* 2022 Aug;139:108776. https://doi.org/10.1016/j.jsat.2022.108776.

Metrebian N, Weaver T, Goldsmith K, et al. Using a pragmatically adapted, low-cost contingency management intervention to promote heroin abstinence in individuals undergoing treatment for heroin use disorder in UK drug services (PRAISE): a cluster randomised trial. *BMJ Open.* 2021 Jul 1;11(7):e046371. https://doi.org/10.1136/bmjopen-2020-046371.

Mutter R, Spencer D, McPheeters J. Outcomes associated with treatment with and without medications for opioid use disorder. *J Behav Health Serv Res.* 2023;50(4):524–39. https://doi.org/10.1007/s11414-023-09841-8.

NIDA. Reflecting on NIDA's 50th year and looking to 2025, 2025, Jan 8. https://nida.nih.gov/about-nida/noras-blog/2025/01/reflecting-nidas-50th-year-looking-to-2025

Nunes EV, Comer SD, Lofwall MR, et al. Extended-release injection vs sublingual buprenorphine for opioid use disorder with fentanyl use: a post hoc analysis of a randomized clinical trial. *JAMA Netw Open.* 2024 Jun 3;7(6):e2417377. https://doi.org/10.1001/jamanetworkopen.2024.17377.

Prendergast M, Podus D, Finney J, Greenwell L, Roll J. Contingency management for treatment of substance use disorders: a meta-analysis. *Addiction.* 2006 Nov;101(11):1546–60. https://doi.org/10.1111/j.1360-0443.2006.01581.x.

Raz M. Treating addiction or reducing crime? Methadone maintenance and drug policy under the nixon administration. *J Policy His.* 2017;29(1):58–86. https://doi.org/10.1017/S089803061600035X.

Rehm J, Gschwend P, Steffen T, Gutzwiller F, Dobler-Mikola A, Uchtenhagen A. Feasibility, safety, and efficacy of injectable heroin prescription for refractory opioid addicts: a follow-up study. *Lancet.* 2001;358(9291):1417–23.

Rounsaville BJ, Weissman MM, Kleber H, Wilber C. Heterogeneity of psychiatric diagnosis in treated opiate addicts. *Arch Gen Psych.* 1982 Feb;39(2):161–8. https://doi.org/10.1001/archpsyc.1982.04290020027006.

Roberts S. "Rehabilitation" as boundary object: medicalization, local activism, and narcotics addiction policy in New York City, 1951–62. *Bull His Med.* 2012;91(3):586–623.

Rutrick D, Learned SM, Boyett B, Hassman D, Shinde S, Zhao Y. 18-Month efficacy and safety analysis of monthly subcutaneous buprenorphine injection for opioid use disorder: Integrated analysis of phase 3 studies. *J Subst Use Addict Treat.* 2023;154:209155. https://doi.org/10.1016/j.josat.2023.209155.

Salmon A, Van Beek I, Amin J, et al. The impact of supervised injecting facility on ambulance call-outs in Sydney, Australia. *Addiction.* 2010;105:676–83.

Rodgers C, Siefried KJ, Ritter A, et al. Implementation of time-limited parenteral hydromorphone in people with treatment-resistant injecting opioid use disorder: a protocol for a single-site, uncontrolled, open-label study to assess feasibility, safety and cost. *BMJ Open.* 2024 Aug 3;14(8): e082553. https://doi.org/10.1136/bmjopen-2023-082553.

Salisbury P, Hill D. Who's asking me? Service user perspectives on safer injecting facilities. *Drug Sci Policy Law.* 2024;10. https://doi.org/10.1177/20503245241308745.

Sarfraz A, Alcorn RJ. Injectable methadone prescribing in the United Kingdom--current practice and future policy guidelines. *Subst Use Mis.* 1999;34(12):1709–21. https://doi.org/10.3109/10826089909039423.

Scottish Government 1986. *HIV infection in Scotland: Report of the Scottish Committee on HIV Infection and Intravenous Drug Misuse.* Scottish Home & Health Department, Edinburgh, 1986.

Spear HB, Mott J. Cocaine and crack within the "British system": A history of control. in: Bean P (ed.) *Cocaine and Crack: Supply and Use.* The Macmillan Press, London, 1993.

Strang, J. (2002). Prescribing heroin: what is the real issue?British Journal of Psychiatry, 180(3), 197–198.

Strang J, Groshkova T, Uchtenhagen A, et al. Heroin on trial: systematic review and meta-analysis of randomised trials of diamorphine-prescribing as treatment for refractory heroin addiction. *Br J Psych.* 2015;207(1):5–14.

Strang J, Metrebian N, Lintzeris N, et al. Supervised injectable heroin or injectable methadone versus optimised oral methadone as treatment for chronic heroin addicts in England after persistent failure in orthodox treatment (RIOTT): a randomised trial. *Lancet.* 2010 May 29;375(9729):1885–95. https://doi.org/10.1016/S0140-6736(10)60349-2.

Strang J, Groshkova T, Uchtenhagen A, et al. Heroin on trial: systematic review and meta-analysis of randomised trials of diamorphine-prescribing as treatment for refractory heroin addiction. *Br J Psych.* 2015;207:5–14. https://doi.org/10.1192/bjp.bp.114.149195

UNAIDS. *Prevention Gap Report 2016.* UNAIDS, Geneva, 2016. https://www.unaids.org/sites/default/files/media_asset/2016-prevention-gap-report_en.pdf..

UNODC. World Drugs Report 2024. WDR24_Key_findings_and_conclusions.pdf.

Vaillant GE. The natural history of narcotic drug addiction. *Semin Psych.* 1970 Nov;2(4):486–98.

Vaillant GE. What can long-term follow-up teach us about relapse and prevention of relapse in addiction? *Br J Addict.* 1988;83(10):1147–57. https://doi.org/10.1111/j.1360-0443.1988.tb03021.x.

Vecino V, Villalbi J, Guitart A, et al. Safe injecting rooms and police crackdowns in areas with heavy drug dealing: evaluation by counting discarded syringes collected from public spaces. *Adicciones.* 2013;25(4):333–8.

van den Brink W, Hendriks VM, Blanken P, et al. Medical prescription of heroin to treatment resistant heroin addicts: two randomised controlled trials. *BMJ.* 2003;327:310.

WHO. 21st WHO Essential Medicines List (EML). WHO Model List of Essential Medicines. https://www.who.int/groups/expert-committee-on-selection-and-use-of-essential-medicines/essential-medicines-lists (World Health Organization, 2019)

Winstanley EL. The bell tolls for thee & thine: compassion fatigue & the overdose epidemic. *Inter J Drug Policy.* 2020;85:102796. https://doi.org/10.1016/j.drugpo.2020.102796.

Xia Y, Seaman S, Hickman M, et al. Factors affecting repeated cessations of injecting drug use and relapses during the entire injecting career among the Edinburgh Addiction Cohort. *Drug Alcohol Depend.* 2015 Jun 1;151:76–83. https://doi.org/10.1016/j.drugalcdep.2015.03.005.

Zador D. Injectable opiate maintenance in the UK: is it good clinical practice? *Addiction.* 2001 Apr;96(4):547–53. https://doi.org/10.1046/j.1360-0443.2001.9645473.x.

10 International comparisons

Background

In the complex world of drug control sometimes characterised as the "War on Drugs", there are increasingly tortuous arguments in the debate about reducing penalties for the use of drugs and reformulating regulations. In the last two decades, experimentation and research in individual countries has allowed for new evidence informing rational debate on how best to protect people from the undoubted harms connected with various substances at the same time as allowing for personal choices. As developments rapidly move forward in challenging the United Nations Conventions on drug control, it is worth looking in detail at the movements in member states in the move towards reduced control of psychoactive substances. Cannabis, in many ways, was the defining drug of the 1940s and 1950s. Although its long-term traditional use in many countries was obvious, the increase in cannabis during this period ignited a moral anxiety about its effect on the younger population in the USA and, to a lesser extent, in Europe. In current times, cannabis for personal recreational use has become the lever driving control reform and challenging the UN Conventions. Actions to reduce control of cannabis taken by several countries and individual US states provide increasing evidence and experience that should inform future change. These changes have implications for other substance control and therefore on the use of substances by injection.

Since the United Nations Convention on drugs in 1961, known as the Single Convention, member states have been prohibited from cultivating, manufacturing, selling or possessing drugs controlled under the convention. It was named the Single Convention because it merged pre-existing laws into a single set of rules. Previous international agreements such as the International Opium Convention, which was passed in 1912 and revised in 1925 and 1931, and the Convention for the Suppression of the Illicit Traffic in Dangerous Drugs, which came into force in 1936, were passed under the framework of the League of Nations in the Hague, the predecessor of the United Nations, which came into existence in 1946. The Single Convention has remained the most important international mechanism for restricting drug use.

The 1961 convention took a hard line on controlling drugs, which were assumed at the outset to be harmful rather than having any benefit for non-medical use. After a decade of debate about cannabis, this drug was included in the convention despite

DOI: 10.4324/9781003611097-10

the protests from the Indian Government and others about the traditional use of cannabis in many "non-Western" cultures (Mills 2016). Interestingly, despite the recent relaxation on control in some states and countries, the value of cannabis as a medically useful therapeutic agent remains controversial. The place of cocaine has been equally confusing when it comes to control and legislation. In India, for example, its use in remedies and medicines became popular in the post-colonial era, and the position of this and other drugs in recent history is instructive in understanding the complexity of substance control worldwide (Mills 2007).

Member states which are signatory to the Convention are bound to adhere to the rules by including them in their own, domestic legislation. Among the many member states, the United States ratified the 1961 Convention and is legally bound to implement its provisions through domestic law (for example, the Controlled Substances Act in the USA which was signed into law in 1971). In the same year, the United Kingdom instituted their own drug control law, the Misuse of Drugs Act. Like legislation in other member states, these defined what was a "controlled drug" and restricted trade and supply of these substances as well as specifying penalties for breaching the law.

The UN Convention has resulted in restrictions on research and experimentation with alternative methods of controlling use. After Uruguay (in 2013) and Canada (in 2018), Malta became the third sovereign State, in late 2021, to legalise cannabis for non-medical purposes. In recent years, countries such as some US member states, Canada, and increasing numbers of European countries have used changes in domestic advice to law enforcement agencies to reduce penalties and minimise prosecutions (Blickman 2022, Boister et al. 2018). More dramatic changes in the control of cannabis use in the US and Canada have resulted in decriminalisation and subsequent marketisation of this drug. Canada did recognise in their legislation Bill C-45 that they were contravening the regulation Article 4(c) in the UN Charter. Article 4(c) reads:

> The parties shall take such legislative and administrative measures as may be necessary……subject to the provisions of this Convention, to limit exclusively to medical and scientific purposes the production, manufacture, export, import, distribution of, trade in, use and possession of drugs.

The intriguing phrase "respectful noncompliance" referring to the departure from UN regulations on cannabis encapsulates the experimental nature of this departure from the long-held Convention (Hoffman 2018).

The Maltese legislation uses another article in the Convention to justify their decriminalisation of cannabis, recognising a responsibility to control illegal use and, interestingly, the need to reduce the harm caused by illicit cannabis use.

As of 2025, 24 UK states have legalised the recreational use of cannabis, and forty have allowed medical use of the drug.

In his book entitled High Compliance Riboulet-Zemouli. explores the legal framework and interpretation of the Single Convention (Riboulet-Zemouli 2022). He makes the point that "the Convention is not a prohibition treaty, but a framework convention on the control of some medicines within the medical and pharmaceutical sectors". The convention is almost silent on recreational use and interpretations of some paragraphs lead governments to believe that in advocating and mandating control over recreational use and reducing the harmful use allows the rules to be in line with the intentions of the convention. A benevolent and benign domestic law can therefore encourage a positive and creative landscape without being in conflict with international obligations.

There are, of course, alternative arguments which suggest that these interpretations risk a "house of cards" situation leading to increased drug availability and use and consequent harm and that instead of looking for new interpretations of the legal text of the Convention, a new framework is required.

Several groups and individual commentators acknowledge the complexity and contradictory nature of the legal situation in the modern era. Relying on legal gymnastics to allow liberalisation is against the good faith of conventions which are designed to provide international consensus while at the same time respecting diversity. Several states including India and Nepal in the case of cannabis and Bolivia in the case of coca leaf were given exemptions, with a time limit in the original 1961 Act in recognition of the traditional use of these drugs. Fragmentation and disorder of the international treaties is further seen in the progressive marketisation in the USA and Canada of cannabis at the same time as pressure is exerted on countries like Nepal to control use. In the EU, progressive legalisation of cannabis in Malta, Germany and Luxembourg conflicts with trade and membership of the EU. The coffee shop scenario in the Netherlands has never attracted a sanction from the EU using the argument that under Article 2(2) of the Treaty the initiative "exclusively intended to provide for their personal use as defined by national law".

Individual countries take different approaches

The influence of local policy initiatives in influencing national change cannot be overemphasised. Frequently, practice is in advance of political decision and, for much of the progress, the success of local initiatives can drive improvements. There are many examples in the substance field of clinical and social change starting as a voluntary sector project or a medical service pragmatic response to a problematic situation. Research underpins policy but can also influence decisions in novel areas and warn of problems in policy ambitions (McCartney et al. 2025).

By the mid-1980s, the Netherlands, with its 14 million inhabitants, had possibly between 15,000 and 20,000 heroin addicts. According to the authorities at the time, the number of heroin addicts appeared to be stabilising, but certain shifts in the population of drug addicts were distinguished. An increasing number of addicts were of non-Dutch origin, and more than 50% of all addicts resided in Amsterdam, Rotterdam, The Hague and Utrecht. By far, the greatest number, between 4,000 and 7,000, live in the capital city. The number of addicts among persons of Surinam origin (180,000) and among persons with a Moluccan background (30,000) is estimated to be 2%. Like the UK experience until the mid-1960s, drug use was confined to certain small groups of doctors and artists. The small Chinese colony in

Amsterdam used opium, which was permitted through "connivance". Toward the end of the Vietnam War, a new outlet for drug traffickers led to the appearance of heroin on the market in Amsterdam in 1972. At present, much heroin is imported from Iran, Afghanistan and Pakistan.

Drugs and the Law

In 1919, the first Opium Act was enacted in Holland. This law has been changed a number of times, with the most recent alteration in 1976. The drug policy of the government, however, not only consists of the tracing and prosecution of punishable facts; relief work and prevention also play an important role. Internationally speaking, Holland had ratified the 1961 Single Convention on Narcotic Drugs of New York. The Convention stipulates the taking of effective measures against the abuse of narcotics. The possession of narcotics has to be limited to medical and scientific purposes. The Dutch legal system takes as a starting point the prevention and alleviation of the individual as well as the social risks involved in the use of drugs. In 1976, a distinction was made between high-risk drugs and drugs with lower risk, such as cannabis. This distinction is not made in the neighbouring countries. The penal provisions for drugs with an unacceptable risk have been more rigidly enforced since 1976. The following distinction has been made for punishable behaviours, namely the possession or presence of drugs and the import and export of drugs (van de Wijngaart 1986).

The Dutch experience over the next two decades was in many ways a model of management in Europe (de Vries HJ et al. 1997). Ethnic minorities were recognised as having special requirements. Policy, especially in the major centres of Rotterdam and Amsterdam, was geared towards prevention. Adoption of low-threshold easy-access methadone was piloted by street and self-help agencies. Early adoption of equipment, syringes and injecting paraphernalia was encouraged at a time when most other countries were opposed to this intervention along with studies to demonstrate the value of this activity and absence of risk of encouraging new users (van den Hoek et al. 1989).

In their paper on the Portugal situation, Hughes and Sevens define the terms as follows: legalisation is defined as the complete removal of sanctions, making a certain behaviour legal and applying no criminal or administrative penalty; decriminaliaation is defined as the removal of sanctions under the criminal law, with optional use of administrative sanctions (e.g. provision of civil fines or court-ordered therapeutic responses); and depenalisation is the decision in practice not to criminally penalise offenders, such as non-prosecution or non-arrest (Hughes and Stevens 2010).

The importance of the Portuguese experience is that it applies to all drugs where other countries have concentrated on cannabis alone. The outcome is equally important. The common argument for not reducing penalties is that there will be an increase in drug use. This was not the result of the comprehensive package of changes implemented with the decriminalisation legislation where only a small increase in drug use was observed and a reduction in harm such as infectious diseases was recorded. The additional inclusion of methods to "dissuade" drug use and to provide increased access to treatment is considered to contribute to these outcomes. There has also been a measurable reduction in cost to the criminal justice system.

The United Kingdom has, in comparison, been slow to change to modern requirements or to follow the international trend of reducing penalties for drug use or possession. The devolved Government in Scotland has responded to the exceptionally high rate of drug-related deaths by proposing change and implementing some fascinating projects. With some exceptions, the jurisdiction on drug policy is a power "reserved" to the UK Westminster Government, and the parliament in Scotland is limited in making wholesale changes. There has, however, been the possibility to reduce the harm, and hopefully drug-related deaths, by implementing a raft of changes to education and treatment systems. Included in these changes and recommendations are a leading project on naloxone provision, upscaling opiate agonist treatment clinics, the first UK heroin-assisted treatment clinic, and the groundbreaking, safe injecting facility in the area of highest drug-related problems. The impact of these changes on the rate of drug-related deaths (the highest in Europe) remains to be seen, but the rate of increase has slowed, and there may well be a plateauing of the numbers in recent years. Some of the problems are the legacy of a rapid increase in drug use in the 1980s. Recent figures suggest a decrease in the numbers of younger drug users appearing in the death statistics. The fatigue in UK Government drug innovation undoubtedly continues to contribute to the lack of progress in modernising drug policy (Robertson and McCartney 2025, Norman et al. 2011).

The key UK regulation controlling the legal supply of drugs is the Misuse of Drugs Act 1971. This piece of legislation made it unlawful to possess or supply a controlled drug unless an exception or exemption applied. Several specific offences were created, such as unlawful possession of a controlled drug and unlawful possession of a controlled drug with intent to supply to another person. In Schedule 2 of the Act, drugs are divided into classes A, B and C, where the severity of the penalty could be imposed for an infringement of the Act. Drugs such as heroin and cocaine are classified as A, and cannabis and amphetamine as class B. Class C contains drugs seen as less harmful, such as benzodiazepines. The Act then contains various schedules which deal with the rules governing who can prescribe and supply the drugs for legal health care purposes and under what conditions they must be stored.

During the "Shipman Inquiry", which investigated the actions of the Manchester GP who killed more than 200 of his patients, it was noted that he legally obtained vast quantities of diamorphine (heroin) from the local pharmacist before his crimes were detected.

The police inspection officer who was responsible for checking pharmacy records of controlled drugs at the time of Shipman's activities failed to note the unusual nature of the records, which showed, for example, that on one occasion, the Controlled Drug Register at the Market Street pharmacy in Manchester showed that the doctor asked for and was supplied 12 prescriptions for 30mg ampoules of diamorphine for several separate patients. Why he did not alert others to this and why the pharmacist did not recognise the irregularity was one of the important discussions of the Inquiry. An expert witness at the Inquiry stated that the usual dose to relieve pain in a community setting was likely to be 2.5mg and that during her career as a General Practitioner, she had never used or asked for supplies of 30mg ampoules. This is in line with the British National Formulary (Joint formulary committee 1993) guidance which read that for acute pain 5mg subcutaneously or intramuscularly (or by slow intravenous injection half that dose) might be administered, and for acute cardiac pain or pulmonary oedema, a similar dose was recommended. The judge, Dame Janet Smith, concluded on this point that "it is clear that during that year (1993), Shipman used these single 30mg ampoules of diamorphine to kill patients" (Shipman Inquiry 2004).

It was clear to the Inquiry that the main interpretation of the Inspectorate at that time was to obtain the names of "drug addicts" so that these could be reported to the Home Office where a list of people was recorded on the "Addicts Index".

Amongst the many other findings of the inquiry was the lack of regulations controlling the use of drugs such as strong opiates once they had been supplied to a patient.

The United States of America possibly best demonstrates all the tensions and fault lines in drug policy. Driven by successive waves of drug problems and mortality and morbidity on a greater scale than almost any other country, successive governments have struggled to define a coherent and consistent approach. From the defining moments of the cocaine and cannabis "problems" of the 1940s to the 1960s, the Single Convention of 1961 has guided, and many would say, prevented progressive policy. The injecting drug use that led to the catastrophic HIV/AIDS mortality of the 1980s, until the introduction of HAART antiviral chemotherapy, never resulted in the adoption of harm reduction as a policy ideology, and injecting equipment suppliers and agencies remain, in many states, problematic. Opiate agonist treatment, as in many countries, remains, for many policymakers, controversial despite copious evidence of its efficacy. The 'brain disease model of addiction' has gained widespread acceptance in the field of neuroscience as the dominant paradigmatic understanding of addiction (Volkow et al. 2016, Matano and Wanat 2000). The contest between the view that persistent and continuous use of substances of addictive nature leads to irreversible changes in brain structure and subsequent function and the behavioural and environmental paradigm has had some modification by the inclusion of comorbidity with other mental, genetic and behavioural disorders into the generally accepted view of the addiction model (Hall et al. 2015, Volkow and Koob 2015). This is reminiscent of the apparent opposition between harm reduction and abstinence-based recovery movements. Unlike the conceptualisation of other diseases, the "cause and effect" discussion, progression in drug treatment seems to be obstructed by ideological competition. This unfortunately frequently transmits into policy silos. The presentation of addiction as a disease and explanation of everything including compulsion as caused by brain damage is convenient for those requiring a simple explanation and allows that people with this degree of dependency have no control over their behaviour.

Inevitably, controversy in models of dependency will result in competition for resources both in the research and development of a pharmaceutical model of treatment and the behavioural and environmental set of interventions.

More recently, the National Institute on Drug Abuse and other commentators have embraced a wider view and encompassed the importance of prevention and harm reduction policies. Important publications have drawn attention to gaps in care for people who use drugs, both in communities and in custody situations and, in New York, demonstating the value of overdose prevention centres in the light of increasing drug related deaths and increase in fentanyl and other synthetic opiates (Arwady et al. 2024, Kelly et al. 2025, Cerdá et al. 2025, Frost et al. 2022).

Injecting stimulants such as methamphetamine

Harms caused by stimulant injecting are in many ways similar to opiates. Sharing injecting equipment, skin infections and the introduction of blood-borne viruses or bacterial contaminants are the same as with any illicit and unsupervised injecting. Injecting methylamphetamine is increasing in some countries, significantly Australia and Canada, Iran and other countries (Fairbairn et al. 2007, Mansoori et al. 2020). Estimates from the Illicit Drug Reporting System (IDRS) in Sydney show that methamphetamine continues to be the most common drug of choice among people who inject drugs, after surpassing heroin in 2021 for the first time since monitoring began. During the same period, the number of people injecting heroin decreased considerably (Sutherland et al. 2024).

New psychoactive substances

A record-breaking 688 new psychoactive substances (NPS) were reported worldwide in 2024 – the highest number ever recorded by UNODC's Early Warning Advisory (EWA 2025).

As of 10 October 2025, a total of 1,396 unique new psychoactive substances have been reported to UNODC EWA by 153 countries and territories worldwide. The annual number of unique NPS reported in 2024 reached a record level of 688 NPS, marking the highest number reported in a single year so far. This figure may continue to rise as data collection continues. In addition, 101 distinct and new substances were reported by 45 countries in the

he year 2025 (United Nations Office on Drugs and Crime (2025). The Vienna based UN group further reported that stimulants remained the largest category of NPS reported globally in 2024, constituting 33% of the total, followed by synthetic cannabinoid receptor agonists (24%) and classic hallucinogens (14%). Synthetic opioids and unassigned NPS accounted for 9% each, sedatives/hypnotics for 7% and dissociatives for 4%.

The synthetic opiates and stimulants are the groups most frequently injected, but other groups, such as sedatives, are occasionally injected when regular supplies are disrupted.

Conclusion

The control and regulation of psychoactive substances are always under review despite the overarching United Nations agreements. Evolution, by popular demand, is driving change, and liberal policies are allowing increased numbers of countries to legalise cannabis and to reduce penalties for possession of other substances. Ironically, as the West reduces tariffs on drug control and moves in many states to a market economy, restrictions are still enforced in countries where cannabis has been a traditional drug for centuries. In the past, arguments in support of decriminalisation have centred around the concern of a cascade effect leading to a progressive loss of control of all substances.

Use of substances varies from country to country and evolves at different rates depending upon illicit supply networks and chains. Injecting heroin, so prevalent in the USA and Western Europe and Australia in the 1980s and 1990s, has given way to a mixed drug culture with increasing amounts of stimulants, cocaine in Europe and methamphetamine in Australia. In many Asian countries, the common drug of injection is heroin due to its local or regional cultivation, but the increase in injecting stimulants has been considerable in South East Asia. In Africa, the common drug of injection remains heroin, although, like other countries, there is variation and a mixed economy of drugs are available including cocaine and pharmaceuticals such as buprenorphine, tramadol and ketamine, which are sometimes crushed and injected. In many countries, the injecting substance use problem remains inextricably linked to the spread of HIV/AIDS (UNODC 2023). According to the report, "of the estimated 980,000 persons who inject drugs in Africa, over 100,000 (11.3%) are living with HIV". Statistics and prevalence rates for some countries are hard to quantify. The Global Burden of Disease Study 2017 shows that "among age groups, the under-5 age group experienced huge reductions in mortality between 1950 and 2017, while adults have made much less progress, particularly adult males (Global Burden of Disease 2017)" Substance use has a significant place to play in morbidity and mortality.

References

Arwady MA, Delphin-Rittmon M, Volkow ND. Major gaps in the cascade of care for opioid use disorder: implications for clinical practice. *JAMA*. 2024 Sep 3;332(9):701–2. https://doi.org/10.1001/jama.2024.11977.

Blickman, T. (2022) Cannabis regulation and the international and European frameworks. Presentation at the side event 'The green wave hits Europe: Recent cannabis regulation initiatives in Europe', 65th session of the Commission on Narcotic Drugs, Vienna, 15 March. Transnational Institute.

Boister N, Bewley-Taylor D, Fitzmaurice M, Jelsma M, Walsh J. *Balancing Treaty Stability and Change, Inter se Modification of the UN Drug Control Conventions to Facilitate Cannabis Regulation.* TNI/WOLA/GDPO, 15 March 2018. https://www.tni.org/en/publication/balancing-treaty-stability-and-change.

Hughes CE, Stevens A. What can we learn from the Portuguese decriminalization of illicit drugs? Br J Criminol. 2010;50(6):999–1022. https://doi.org/10.1093/bjc/azq038.

Cerdá M, Allen BL, Collins AB, et al. Study assessing the effectiveness of overdose prevention centers through evaluation research (SAFER): an overview of the study protocol. *Harm Reduct J.* 2025;22(Suppl 1):76. https://doi.org/10.1186/s12954-025-01211-1.

EWA. United Nations, UNODC, Early warning Advisor on New psychoactive substances (EWA) database, 2025. UNODC Early Warning Advisory (EWA) on New Psychoactive Substances (NPS) accessed 22/10/25

Fairbairn N, Kerr T, Buxton JA, Li K, Montaner JS, Wood E. Increasing use and associated harms of crystal methamphetamine injection in a Canadian setting. *Drug Alcohol Depend.* 2007 May 11;88(2–3):313–6. https://doi.org/10.1016/j.drugalcdep.2006.10.019.

Frost MC, Austin EJ, Corcorran MA, et al. Responding to a surge in overdose deaths: perspectives from US syringe services programs. *Harm Reduct J.* 2022 Jul 19;19(1):79. https://doi.org/10.1186/s12954-022-00664-y.

Global Burden of Disease 2017. Institute for Health Metrics and Evaluation (IHME). Findings from the Global Burden of Disease Study 2017. Seattle, WA: IHME, 2018.

Hall W, Carter A, Forlini C. The brain disease model of addiction: is it supported by the evidence and has it delivered on its promises? *Lancet Psych.* 2015 Jan;2(1):105–10. https://doi.org/10.1016/S2215-0366(14)00126-6.

Hoffman, S.J. et al. (2018) The legalization of cannabis in Canada and international drug control treaties. American Journal of International Law Unbound, 112, pp. 298–303.

Joint Formulary Committee (1993) British National Formulary. No. 25. London: Pharmaceutical Press

Kelly JF, Volkow ND, Koh HK. The changing approach to addiction - From incarceration to treatment and recovery support. *N Engl J Med.* 2025 Feb 27;392(9):833–6. https://doi.org/10.1056/NEJMp2414224.

McCartney G, Hiam L, Smith KE, Walsh D. UK welfare reforms threaten health of the most vulnerable. *BMJ.* 2025 Mar 25;388: r593. https://doi.org/10.1136/bmj. r593. Erratum in: *BMJ.* 2025 Apr 2;389:r660. https://doi.org/10.1136/bmj.r660.

Mansoori Y, Mehmandoost S, Khezri M, et al. Methamphetamine use and associated factors among people who inject drugs in Iran 2020. *Subst Abuse Treat Prev Policy* 2025;20:19. https://doi.org/10.1186/s13011-025-00645-x

Matano RA, Wanat SF. Addiction is a treatable disease, not a moral failing. *West J Med.* 2000 Jan;172(1):63. https://doi.org/10.1136/ewjm.172.1.63.

Mills JH. The IHO as actor: the case of cannabis and the Single Convention on Narcotic Drugs 1961. *Hygiea Int.* 2016 Dec 7;13(1):95–115. https://doi.org/10.3384/hygiea.1403-8668.1613195.

Mills JH. Drugs, consumption and supply in Asia: the case of cocaine in colonial India. *J Asian Stud.* 2007;66(2):345–62. https://doi.org/10.1017/S0021911807000587.

Norman P, Boyle P, Exeter D, Feng Z, Popham F. Rising premature mortality in the UK's persistently deprived areas: Only a Scottish phenomenon? *Soc Sci Med.* 2011;73:1575–84. https://doi.org/10.1016/j.socscimed.2011.09.034

Robertson R, McCartney G. Learning from HIV and drug policy failures: reflections from clinical practice and research in Edinburgh. *Drugs, Habits and Social Policy.* 2025. https://doi.org/10.1108/DHS-09-2024 0031.

Shipman Inquiry. Fourth report – The Regulation of Controlled Drugs in the Community. Presented to Parliament by the Secretary of State for the Home Department and the Secretary of State of Health July, 2004.

Sutherland R, Karlsson A, Uporova J, et al. *Australian Drug Trends 2024: Key Findings from the National Illicit Drug Reporting System (IDRS) Interviews.* National Drug and Alcohol Research Centre, UNSW Sydney, Sydney, 2024. https://doi.org/10.26190/unsworks/30464.

United Nations Office on Drugs and Crime (2025) Record high of 688 individual new psychoactive substances reported worldwide in 2024. Vienna: UNODC Early Warning Advisory on New Psychoactive Substances

UNODC. United Nations Office on Drugs and Crime. *World Drug Report 2023*. UNODC, Vienna, 2023.

van de Wijngaart GF. Heroin addiction in the Netherlands. in: Carmi A, Schneider S. (eds.) *Drugs and Alcohol. Medicolegal Library*, vol 6. Springer, Berlin, Heidelberg, 1986. https://doi.org/10.1007/978-3-642-82595-8_8

van den Hoek JA, van Haastrecht HJ, Coutinho RA. Risk reduction among intravenous drug users in Amsterdam under the influence of AIDS. *Am J Public Health*. 1989 Oct;79(10):1355–7. https://doi.org/10.2105/ajph.79.10.1355.

de Vries HJ, van Brussel GH, Kanhai K. More of the Surinam and Antilles drug addicts involved in the GG&GD (Community Medical and Health Service) methadone program in Amsterdam should be referred to the family physician for their methadone maintenance. *Ned Tijdschr Geneeskd*. 1997 Feb 8;141(6):288–91.

Riboulet-Zemouli K. (2022). High compliance, a lex lata legalization for the non-medical cannabis industry: How to regulate recreational cannabis in accordance with the Single Convention on narcotic drugs, 1961. FAAAT editions, Paris and Washington, DC. https://ssrn.com/abstract=4057428

Volkow ND, Koob GF, McLellan AT. Neurobiologic advances from the brain disease model of addiction. *N Engl J Med*. 2016 Jan 28;374(4):363–71. https://doi.org/10.1056/NEJMra1511480.

Volkow ND, Koob G. Brain disease model of addiction: why is it so controversial? *Lancet Psych*. 2015 Aug;2(8):677–9. https://doi.org/10.1016/S2215-0366(15)00236-9.

11 Social determinants of drug taking

Edinburgh as case study

Background

Although drugs and alcohol are used by all sectors of society and in all communities, the association of inequalities and poverty with the most visibly damaging outcomes of drug use has long been recognised. Studies of multimorbidity almost always cite drug use as a significant factor in the impact and severity of diseases associated with substance use. The statistics of years of life lost due to drugs and the disability preventing work or social engagement show that, in most tables, drug use accounts for one of the highest numbers of people dying prematurely or being unable to function normally (Smyth et al. 2007). Premature death caused by substance use is second only to cardiovascular and malignant conditions. As a cause of loss of ability to achieve employment, only musculoskeletal conditions account for a greater impact than the effects of substance use (Wyper et al. 2022).

Separating physical medical and mental health diagnoses in these broad categories of health harms due to drugs is more complicated. The additional factors of inequality of resources and opportunity add a further dimension to the measurements and quantification of harms.

Understanding the interaction between poverty and brain development may provide a better insight into the prevention of pathways into addiction. At least one study has shown some improvement in brain capacity when some of the impact of poverty was minimised (Brody et al. 2017). Crucially, the intergenerational effects of harms done by poverty might be ameliorated by interventions to improve inequality (Hill et al. 2020).

Young people are particularly vulnerable to the dangers of drug use as they are to other manifestations of risk taking. The importance of the vulnerability of young people is emphasised by progression in our understanding of brain development, particularly the frontal cortex, which, among other things, governs decision making, planning and impulse control. Neuroimaging studies support the finding that structural changes in the frontal and limbic circuitry during adolescence are associated with a heightened sensitivity to motivational cues and immediate rewards, as well as an increased likelihood of engaging in behavioural risks, including substance use, reckless driving or other risky activities. The onset of drug use might, therefore, result in a transitory flirt with substances in adolescence, a temporary lifestyle choice or more serious dependency and comorbid damage, complicated by

DOI: 10.4324/9781003611097-11

custody, serial relapse and progression to a lifetime of problems (Lin et al. 2024). Risks and protective factors are context dependent and operate on people taking drugs for a variety of reasons.

The complexity of engaging people who use or have used drugs in the past is well known, and many strategies are adopted to encourage attendance at clinics and agencies offering help. The multidimensional nature of substance use means that a range of interventions are required at the outset, but as part of a long-term support and recovery service. Community-based, local access, medical and social facilities combined with welfare rights, advocacy and the need for continuity are all elements of a recovery service and inevitably require cooperation between sectors. Primary care in the United Kingdom and elsewhere can act as a hub with confidential resources for data and allow sharing and referral to a wide range of services (Thom et al. 2025). Increasingly, the need for multi-agency collaboration is written into drug strategies.

Edinburgh past and present

In his book "Edinburgh" the author explains the reason for the emergence of cramped housing in the city after the disastrous defeat at the Battle of Flodden in 1513 (Scott-Montcrieff 1947).

> The Flodden Wall is important in the history of Edinburgh, for long defining the city boundary. Nor for 250 years did the people risk building houses outside it, but instead as the population increased, piled story upon story to a height that made Edinburgh unique among cities in Europe: the skyscraper community of the day. They reached eventually nine or ten stories, and some of the "lands" may have had up to fourteen from the lower levels of the back lanes from which their wall towered up to 180 feet in height.

The "Old Town" of Edinburgh dates back many centuries and the landscape of the Royal Mile from the Castle to the Palace of Holyroodhouse resonates with history in the closes, alleyways and cellars of the old city. The close by, so-called, "New Town" was built in stages between 1760 and 1890 and itself has been host to illustrious residents, and not so distinguished residents.

In the ancient parts of the city, tourists can visit "plague streets" in cellars and underground caverns beneath the City Chambers and the several generations of buildings constructed above. Mary King's Close is full of descriptions of plague victims and haunting stories from the epidemics of the mid-18th century.

Not far behind the scenes is the old medical school resonating with stories of Dr Robert Knox and the "body snatchers" Burke and Hare. The anatomy museum, at the University of Edinburgh, contains William Burke's skeleton. This is described in the following paragraphs.

> William Burke (1792–1829) was an Irish navvy (a manual labourer) who came to Scotland to work on the Union Canal in the 1820s. When the work was finished, he moved into a lodging house near the Grassmarket, owned

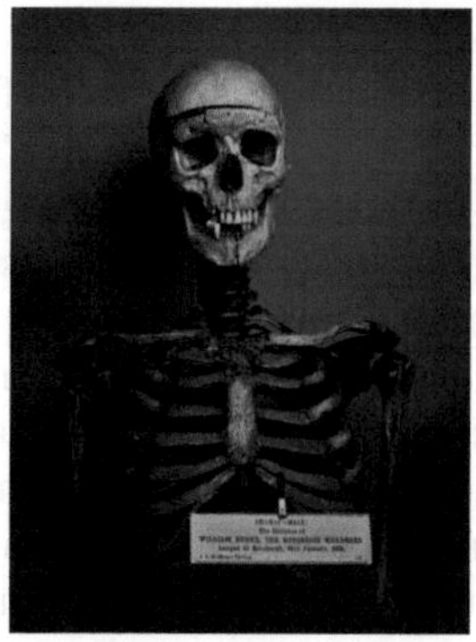

Figure 11.1 Serial killer hanged in 1829 for his part in the West Port murders.
Reproduced with permission of the Department of Anatomy Edinburgh University.

by William Hare and his wife. A short while after this, a fellow lodger died owing Hare some rent. To recoup his losses, Hare decided to sell the body to Dr Robert Knox, a freelance anatomy teacher who had set up private classes in Surgeons Square in direct competition with those run by the University.

After receiving about £8 from Knox, they decided not to wait for lodgers dying from natural causes but to murder them instead, by pinching the nose and lying on the chest to cause suffocation, which meant that there were no marks on the body. This became known as "Burking".

Many of their victims (chosen due to lack of friends) were lured to the lodging house, plied with drink and then suffocated. They killed at least 16 people. Their last victim was found dead under a bed, and they were reported to the police, and the pair were arrested. However, as there was insufficient evidence, Hare was persuaded to give evidence against Burke and allowed to flee.

Burke was found guilty of the murder on 25th December 1828 and hanged in the Lawnmarket on 28th January 1829, his sentence being that he be hanged and publicly dissected. It is not known what became of Hare.

Source (with permissions): Anatomy Collection,
University of Edinburgh

Edinburgh resonates with its illustrious literary heritage. Robert Burns, Walter Scott, Robert Louis Stevenson, Thomas De Quincey, James Boswell and Arthur Conan Doyle at some time all inhabited the society of the Old Town, and their accounts of places and people have left an indelible mark on our understanding of drugs. Traces of their influence can be found in modern policy approaches. With all their shared experiences, the differences are striking and remind us how dependency and addiction are phenomena with many manifestations.

The eighteenth-century writers frequently allude to opium, laudanum and the effects of these opiates and sometimes derive much of their timeless interest from describing the popularity of these drugs. Stevenson's creation of the split personality of Jekyll and Hyde suggests strongly a drug-related origin, at least one observer noting that Jekyll fulfils many of the diagnostic criteria for drug dependence (Altschuler et al. 2000). De Quincey eloquently describes the experience of opiate intoxication; Boswell used laudanum, like many people in the period, for pain control and probably emotional support. Burns and Boswell were undoubtedly heavy drinkers, often in a social context, but with damaging effects. Whether Conan Doyle used cocaine or opium is unclear, but his fictional character Sherlock Holmes presented an interesting caricature of a drug user that persists to this day (Pearce et al. 1994).

In modern times the mystique of the effects of drugs ranges from their destructive qualities to their popular use embedded increasingly alongside alcohol as a recreational choice. This will undoubtedly increase as the contagion of cannabis decriminalisation and legalisation spreads. Strong narratives around the situation of deaths of people in popular culture arouse conspiracy theories largely derived from lack of exposure to the actual facts, and cases like those of the singer-songwriter Sandy Denny, the celebrated jazz musician Miles Davis and the musician Jimi Hendrix are only illuminated when autobiographies or responsible biographies are published. Unfortunately, many remain, for understandable reasons, private and therefore subjects of speculation, rumour and intrigue.

In contemporary literature, Alexander McCall-Smith, Val McDiarmid, Ian Rankin and Irvine Welsh draw heavily on Edinburgh as a background to stories, plots and characters. In the case of McDiarmid and Rankin's detective Rebus, plots include drug scenarios and situations. Welsh has an important part to play in exposing a drug-related lifestyle and by exploring a contemporary drug culture did a great service in humanising and consequently destigmatising substance use. In the American counterculture of the 1960s, William Burroughs describes the darker side of addiction and coined some of the early descriptions of "Junkies", which remain a historical landmark in popularising drug use. Despite his involvement in drug injecting, Burroughs lived to be 84 years old, representing the ability of people who inject drugs to survive (Burroughs 1953, 1959).

More recently, another crisis involving infectious disease was causing problems in Edinburgh. The extent of the high prevalence of tuberculosis in residents of the city is described in the memoirs of Sir John Crofton, an illustrious physician, author and President of the Royal College of Physicians (Edinburgh). Deaths had dropped since their peak in the late 19th century, but in the 1950s, Scotland was the only country in Europe, apart from Portugal, where new cases of TB were continuing to rise unchecked. A local campaign encouraged residents of the city to attend for a chest X-ray. It unearthed a surprising number of cases. A close link was established between the overcrowded and insanitary conditions of the older streets of the city and increased numbers of cases. Crofton managed to get the epidemic under control within a few years, having originally predicted that it would take 20 years. This was done by the revolutionary practice of using three drugs instead of

Figure 11.2 Despite his well-publicised substance use, he lived to a good age.

Reproduced with permission from the Visual Materials Collections, Wisconsin Historical Society.

one at a time, which resulted in managing the difficulties of resistance to antibiotics and consequent treatment failure. This approach quickly became standard treatment and saved many lives. It was hoped at the time that tuberculosis would become a disease of the past, but this was unfortunately not the experience of subsequent decades. Among other problems, the pandemic of HIV in the 1980s gave rise to a disastrous combination of an ancient disease active in a modern condition characterised by vulnerability to infection. Interestingly, John Crofton was actively involved as a volunteer during his retirement in the HIV epidemic in Edinburgh and provided a useful link between the activist agencies in North West Edinburgh and the establishment in the Scottish Government (Royal College of Physicians Edinburgh).

As recently as the post-war period and up until the early 1960s, poor housing and post-war economies meant that the central areas of Edinburgh around the "Old Town" accommodated families in historic tenement properties, like other cities such as Glasgow, which had escaped the damage caused by wartime bombing of many UK city centres. The Old Town is relevant to our story as the impoverished moved to the greenfield sites of North Edinburgh. Rebuilding and remodelling of the expanding city meant that families moved from cramped, squalid flats in stairs with shared toilets to large housing estates built on greenfield sites to the north of the city near the river Forth estuary and the south side towards the Scottish Border hills. The new tower blocks were characterised as a new way of living and a more adventuristic experiments as "cities in the sky", with social engineering of older people in ground floor flats and younger families and single people at higher levels. This was later described as the "brutalist" concrete design of the Balfron and Trellick towers in London popularised by the Hungarian architect Erno Goldfinger and others (Banham 2020, Dobraszczyk 2025).

Enormous changes occurred in Edinburgh in the 1960s; new housing on the periphery of the city allowed people to be decanted from the older parts of the city, where tenements and stairways had been neglected and were outdated, with small, cramped houses in tall buildings often many centuries old. Shared toilets were not uncommon. The advantage of new buildings on greenfield sites with local amenities seemed obvious, and the modern style houses were lighter and relatively spacious. The architecture of the 1970s and the "streets in the sky" visions of a new way of living were not yet discredited.

Initial enthusiasm was palpable; families previously sharing living and sleeping space, as well as toilet facilities, had a self-contained space with access to local shopping and recreational facilities. Individual stories included that of an old lady whose "sweetheart" had never returned from World War I was rehoused in her own, immaculate, flat on the ground floor. Another mother of four children who had moved from a small, overcrowded city centre flat remembered being amazed that the whole three-bedroomed house was all for her family. This was contrasted with the lady who remembered there being nothing but cornfields between the city and the river estuary. Loss of green space and encroachment of the city into farmland and the previous rural habitat was mitigated by potential for new young communities and better public health after post-war polio and tuberculosis outbreaks. Enthusiasm was understandable.

By the 1980s, things had changed. Years of neglect and local authority indecision and funding cuts meant that the housing environment had deteriorated. This was an era predating universal central heating, when houses were poorly insulated and heated from coal fires. Hypothermia in winter months was underestimated as a cause of morbidity and even death in older people living on their own.

Edinburgh has a history of public health crises, many of which are due to infectious diseases, but the interaction of poverty and difficult social circumstances has many of the markers associated with damaging drug problems. The circumstances in Edinburgh giving rise to an internationally recognised "drugs problem" in the 1980s and beyond did not come out of nowhere. It is worth taking a brief view at the history of the housing and social environment in Edinburgh over the last few hundred years leading up to the drug crisis. The multimorbid nature of drug problems has an origin and interaction between poverty and lack of opportunity.

Economies rise and fall, and deindustrialisation and capitalisation were to have a devastating effect in reversing the benefits of these modernisations and over the next two decades, inner city decline and poverty became outer city decay, and along with it came a rise in social disorder and a deterioration in the life of residents. By the late 1970s and early 1980s, these estates had been neglected to an extraordinary state of disorder. Local amenities had not yet benefitted from the provision of modern shopping centres, household heating still depended on coal, open fires and poorly maintained insulation. House fires with associated fatalities were distressingly common and often attributed to inflammable furniture being ignited by burning cigarettes. Medical emergencies which are less common today such as hypothermia in old people, sudden infant deaths and cases where cancer had been concealed until very advanced stages were not unusual as were emerging concerns about covert violence within the family. Injured children were increasingly defined as a medical syndrome, initially with the dramatic name of the "battered baby syndrome" and later as part of a pattern of neglect (Caffey 1965, Griffiths and

Moynihan 1963). Although the 1960s had seen the opening up of medical interest in child neglect arising from the early work of the radiologists in the United Kingdom and USA and the observation of Griffiths and colleagues in 1963 that they (the radiologists) wanted 'to give publicity to a syndrome which we think commoner than is usually believed', child protection was still in its developmental stages and exploration of the wider field emerging. The diagnosis of Munchausen's by Proxy, later renamed, Factitious disorder imposed on another (FDIA), saw the linking of mental health disorders in adults as a cause of injury to children.

Recreational areas were increasingly used for poor housing, filling spaces initially reserved for leisure. The visual environment was of smoky streets, few car owners, shabby gardens and feral dogs. Pigeon huts in small backyards were still common. The poor quality of the interior of houses was testament to a low-wage economy and was cold and reminiscent of the older generation of city centre grimness. Small-scale crime prospered, and the large blocks of housing became unsafe, threatening and miserable. The local housing authority planned and redeveloped on a crisis-to-crisis basis, condemning some blocks and decanting families piecemeal, resulting in an increasing number of empty flats and houses and remaining people surrounded by further deterioration.

In his book *A Medical Tour* through the whole island of Great Britain, Louis Appleby describes the scene he encountered in the late 1980s. Later, Sir Louis and, amongst other things in a stellar career, was appointed the UK Government's first National Director for Mental Health ('mental health tsar') from 2000 to 2010, then the first National Clinical Director for Health and Criminal Justice from 2010 until 2014.

> This part of Pilton looks like a ghost town, and I had expected to see tumbleweed blowing towards me across the concrete. Most of it is boarded up. Only one in ten of the windows shows any sign of life inside and only the odd balcony is strung with washing. The walls are filthy, and their numerous cracks have been cemented over in a way that makes them more obvious, in fact so striking are they that from a distance they give the impression of being an unusual mosaic, though certainly one that has gone wrong. The conventional form of urban art, graffiti, is abundant, though largely mysterious much of it consisting of words and symbols I couldn't decipher. The rest reports on the details of local romance but there is one wall where someone with a sense of humour has painted what appears to be sunflowers and another that sports the words EAT THE RICH.

Environmental degradation was palpable, and visual housing stock was neglected, with heating deepening upon open fires burning coal. The streets were neglected; cars were few, but weekend abandoned vehicles, sometimes burnt out, suggested an undercurrent of disorder. Gardens were full of debris and decay. Pigeon huts in back gardens were common until the 1990s, when a generation of enthusiasts was replaced by a more restless youth seeking excitement elsewhere.

The medical estate and public services accommodation was still poor in the 1970s. Crumbling Victorian hospitals with generations of cheap and fragile additions were known to require modernisation but remained that way during the worst period of transmission, having been neglected pending wholesale demolition and replacement. Other public services were in a similar state of decline, social work being housed in temporary buildings past their expected termination dates and police and prison accommodation in a Dickensian condition. The police custody cells remained in the High Street of Edinburgh and were dungeons several metres beneath the ancient, cobbled streets until the late 1980s. The city mortuary, where pathological examinations are still conducted in 2025, was and remains, in accommodation primitive by modern standards, in the Cowgate alongside the glitzy tourist attractions of the old city.

The UK Government of the 1980s failed completely to reverse this declining estate. The legacy of the Thatcher government between 1979 and 1990 and her successor John Major, until the landslide Labour victory of 1997, will be interpreted differently by different sectors of the economy, health and social infrastructure, but swinging cuts in health and social care and a drive that generated economic inequalities on a scale not seen since Edwardian times led to inner city unrest and social disorder. The feverish activity in the international move towards private investment and sale of national companies and assets failed to deliver benefits to local inner city environments.

Social disorder resulted. Riots in local communities, the largest of which were in Brixton and Toxteth, were cause for alarm if not a warning of something bad happening. With the economy in recession and unemployment at a 50-year high, tensions between groups and the police were high. The Scarman report commissioned in 1981 after the Brixton riots highlighted racial and poverty tensions as the cause of riots in England, but the forces behind the stresses in Scotland were driven by institutional neglect of a sector of the population in sink estates (Scarman 1981).

This combination of events and politics provided a setting for trouble, and this came in the form of an unprecedented supply of cheap and exceptionally pure heroin. The events of the Russian invasion of Afghanistan and the fall of the Shah of Iran unleashed a trade in illicit opiates resulting in availability to young people in cities across Western Europe. Harms from drugs resulting from these epidemics of injecting are described in the subsequent chapter but the series of events from 1980 until the present include a landslide of deaths increasing over four decades, a stream of trauma-led disease associated with injecting illicit heroin and a lasting intergenerational impact of social and health disorders. The human immunodeficiency virus explosion in the East of Scotland is described in detail in Chapter 3 and the roller coaster of blood-borne virus and bacterial outbreaks in Chapters 6 and 7.

Analysis of these events addresses some of the causes and effects, the political climate, the social factors in Scotland and the feeling of hopelessness and the toll in terms of premature deaths (McCartney 2017, Parkinson et al. 2018).

Extract from GP diary

> Until recently medical emergency night time consultations in peoples' homes were done solo and were taken in turn with partners in our GP practice These visits were continuous with day duties and the doctor on call may have had several trips through the night returning to daytime work with no break. Touring the area, which comprised the geographical locality of responsibly, looking for the household with a medical emergency was usually required three or four times between 6pm when the surgery doors closed and 8 am when the day team arrived. Navigating difficult locations, dogs and intoxicated people added to hazards and stress of arriving at a home where someone was in need of help and often in distress. Common conditions were minor injuries, chronic pain from ongoing serious conditions like cancer, acute pains such a migraine and the suspicion of an emerging crisis such as stroke, chest pain suggesting heart problems or uncertain acute pain elsewhere. Deaths were a not unusual reason for a call. Some were sudden involving police and others were not unexpected as a result of preexisting known condition. These required confirmation and later formal certification. Listening to "Sailing by", the UK shipping forecast on the car radio and late night news was part of a familiar routine. Then the morning radio started up with a medley of tunes. These included, Early One Morning, Men of Harlech (Wales), Rule Britannia (England), Danny Boy (Ireland), Annie Laurie (Scotland), What Shall We Do with the Drunken Sailor? (Royal Navy), Scotland the Brave and "Greensleeves" to satisfy all 4 nations.

The war on drugs and its impact on drug policy

In a key publication, the impact of a punitive and outdated system of control is described as having a wide range of damaging effects in the United States of America. Three key points highlight the adversity of these policies and how responses might mitigate these problems (Cohen et al. 2022):

> A *drug war logic* that prioritises and justifies drug prohibition, criminalisation, and punishment has fuelled the expansion of drug surveillance and control mechanisms in numerous facets of everyday life in the United States negatively impacting key social determinants of health, including housing, education, income, and employment.
>
> The U.S. drug war's frontline enforcers are no longer police alone but now include physicians, nurses, teachers, neighbours, social workers, employers, landlords, and others.
>
> Physicians and healthcare providers can play a significant role in promoting individual and community health by reducing the impact of criminalisation upon healthcare service provision and engaging in policy reform.

The social and economic costs of substance use

Evidence from Scotland in 2011 suggests that the total social and economic cost of illicit drug use is just under £3.56 billion (around £61,000 per problem drug user). Estimated costs of crime are reduced significantly for individuals in treatment from £12,713 for individuals with no intervention in place to £1,536 for those in treatment for more than one year (Scottish Centre for Crime and Justice Research 2011).Custody and maintaining the criminal justice system and the prison estate is enormous. As well as the impact on the economy of this, the custody and incarceration situation risk an increase in the resulting harms for people who use drugs. There are many ways in which custody and criminalisation of drugs cause harm, outlined in previous chapters. Individuals may also choose a more harmful pattern of use in prison by altering their route of administration. In order to avoid detection, people may shift from a drug such as cannabis, which can be detected several days after ingestion, to one such as an opiate or cocaine, which is less likely to be detected on routine mandatory drug testing. Injecting may be more likely to maximise the use of expensive drugs that are hard to access. There is also an increased risk of using shared injecting equipment in a custody situation where needles and syringes are in short supply.

Conclusion

The explosion of heroin availability in communities such as those described in Edinburgh came at a time when drug use in smaller cities had been relatively small and was largely a satellite of London and some European capitals although similar things were happening in the USA (O'Kelly 2012, Joe et al. 1982, Joe and Simpson 1987). Attention to the need to reform was slow and only energised by the arrival of HIV/AIDS. The dynamic forces of the sexual activists who had a history of lobbying and negotiating, and a membership with influence within establishment figures, were not reflected in the drug-using community who were historically outsiders and regarded as among the criminal class. Institutions such as the criminal justice system were poorly prepared for the arrival of large numbers of young people charged with possession of personal supplies of a Class A drug. Rapid modernisation was also required in the Health Service which, after years of disinvesting in infectious diseases specialist care, was confronted with a disorder associated with terminal illness but also the spectre of a range of unfamiliar infections and conditions such as dementia, resurgent tuberculosis, systemic fungal infections and opportunistic microorganisms in multiple organs. Managing these disabling conditions in people who had serious addiction problems with the coexisting criminal convictions and fractured social support was, to say the least, challenging. Attributing blame for a crisis is fraught with difficulties. In this case, considerable harms came about as a result of missed opportunities to recognise the warning signs of increasing drug use in Scotland. Indicators of rising numbers of people injecting heroin were present in the late 1970s and were either ignored or managed wrongly. Coexisting policy directions in housing and inequalities clearly linked with an institutional stigma towards drug users created the perfect environment for hepatitis and HIV transmission, drug-related mortality and morbidity caused by direct drug toxicity and the indirect traumas for drug users, their families and their communities (Salisbury 2024). Scotland had a particular vulnerability to the changing context of the 1980s, in particular relating to the high levels of industrial and public sector employment, council housing and historical urban planning decisions (Walsh et al. 2021). The Thatcher government exposed these vulnerabilities leading to a rapid worsening of mortality inequalities, with mortality worsening in absolute terms in some Scottish deprived areas (Scott-Samuel 2014; Walsh et al. 2021). Drug misuse quickly became endemic in poorer communities in the face of rising unemployment, poor-quality housing, rising poverty and political disenfranchisement (Collins and McCartney 2011). HIV and hepatitis B and C infections spread quickly in this context, adding a deadly element to the already toxic mix of poverty and drug use. Stigmatisation of HIV as being prevalent only in people who use and inject drugs and homosexual men led to delays in research, clinical and policy action. It was only the spread to the heterosexual population and uncertainties over whether the wider (and more affluent population) might get infected that led to concerted action.

A legacy of drug-related deaths can be tracked back to poor investment in prevention policies. There was also recognition of the legacy of blood- borne virus transmission to the current problem but a failure to recognise that the cumulative total of drug-related deaths is greater than that reported. The officially reported deaths attributed to drug use are all because of overdose and do not include the mortality connected to legacy blood-borne virus infections and other causes. This increased burden of disease caused by drug use is hard to quantify but modelling has estimated that for every overdose death reported in the official figures from the Office of National Statistics in England and Wales and the National Records for Scotland, there are at least an additional two deaths attributable to drugs. These include violent trauma, suicide, vascular and infectious diseases such

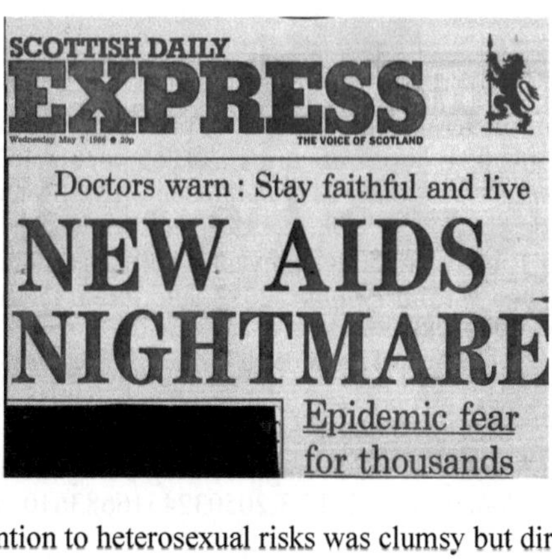

Figure 11.3 Press attention to heterosexual risks was clumsy but direct, in 1986.
Scottish Daily Express front page 7th May 1986. Permission from Reach plc.

as HIV/AIDS, hepatitis B and C and clusters of blood-borne virus infections such as clostridium and anthrax (Degenhardt et al. 2014). Policy directions and lessons from the Edinburgh case study have resonance today. Drug use is a symptom of another greater societal malaise and policy confusion. Availability of heroin and other illicit drugs is, thus, reliant on an illegal but industrial scale supply chain. The widespread damage caused by this criminal supply chain, and the clear inability of policing to stop this, suggests that decriminalisation and bringing the supply of drugs into a regulated and legal environment has substantial potential to radically reduce individual, community and societal harms (Cabral 2017, Hughes and Stevens 2010). The apparently relentless increase in overdose deaths over the last 20 years has paradoxically resulted in a normalisation of a shocking set of statistics and a compassion fatigue in communities and institutions. What would have previously been seen as shocking and an alert to action has become normal and expected. The risk of overdose compassion fatigue is that it could have negative consequences by eroding support for evidence-based services and fuelling driven policies that blame people who use drugs (Winstanley 2020).

The social and environmental issues that determine, initiate and sustain substance use are well documented and, for many, are the key factor in the mission to reduce substance misuse and their harmful consequences. Many factors are involved and therefore prevention is not just a political but a whole societal challenge (Freudenberg 2022). Homelessness, inequalities and poverty undoubtedly have a close relationship with drug use and many of the harms are connected with the criminal statuses of some drugs (Galea and Vlahov 2002, Caruso 2017, Hughes et al. 2020). Solutions are complex, multidimensional and inevitably face the opposition of many opinions and agencies. The risk of looking to find which piece of the jigsaw is the most important is a pointless exercise and interventions which might help are variable and people are individual in their requirements.

Bureaucratic and institutional inertia conspire to limit or obstruct change. Progress is likely in some areas and knowledge and research, when funding is available, is opening avenues and changing opinions.

References

Altschuler EL, Wright D. Dr. Jekyll and Mr. Hyde: a primer on substance dependence. *Am J Psych.* 2000 Mar;157(3):484. https://doi.org/10.1176/appi.ajp.157.3.484.

Banham R. *Megastructure: Urban Futures of the Recent Past.* Monacelli Press, New York, 2020.

Brody GH, Gray JC, Yu T, et al. Protective prevention effects on the association of poverty with brain development. *JAMA Pediatr.* 2017 Jan 1;171(1):46–52. https://doi.org/10.1001/jamapediatrics.2016.2988.

Burroughs, William S. *Junkie: Confessions of an Unredeemed Drug Addict.* Ace Books, New York, 1953.

Burroughs WS. *Naked Lunch.* Grove Press, New York, 1959.

Cabral TS. The 15th anniversary of the Portuguese drug policy: its history, its success and its future. *Drug Sci. Policy Law.* 2017;3:2050324516683640. https://doi.org/10.1177/2050324516683640.

Caffey J. Significance of the history in the diagnosis of traumatic injury to children. *J Pediat.* 1965;67(5): 1009.

Caruso GD. *Public Health and Safety: The Social Determinants of Health and Criminal Behavior*. Researchers Links Books, London, 2017.

Cohen A, Vakharia SP, Netherland J, Frederique K. How the war on drugs impacts social determinants of health beyond the criminal legal system. *Ann Med.* 2022;54(1):2024–38. https://doi.org/10.1080/07853890.2022.2100926

Collins C, McCartney G. The impact of neoliberal 'political attack' on health: the case of the 'Scottish effect. Int J Health Ser. 2011;41(3):501–23. https://doi.org/10.2190/ HS.41.3.f.

Degenhardt L, Larney S, Randall D, Burns L, Hall W. Causes of death in a cohort treated for opioid dependence between 1985 and 2005. *Addiction.* 2014;109(1):90–9.

Dobraszczyk P. *Vertical Urbanism and the Fantasy of the Sky City*. Reaktion Books, London, 2025.

Freudenberg N. Integrating social, political and commercial determinants of health frameworks to advance public health in the twenty-first century. *Int J Health Serv.* 2022 Sep 15:207314221125151. https://doi.org/10.1177/00207314221125151.

Galea S, Vlahov D. Social determinants and the health of drug users: socioeconomic status, homelessness, and incarceration. *Public Health Rep.* 2002;117:S135–45.

Griffiths DL, Moynihan FJ. Multiple epiphysial injuries in babies ('Battered Baby' Syndrome). *Br Med J.* 1963;21:1558–61.

Hill KG, Bailey JA, Steeger CM, et al. Outcomes of childhood preventive intervention across 2 generations: a nonrandomized controlled trial. *JAMA Pediatr.* 2020 Aug 1;174(8):764–71. https://doi.org/10.1001/jamapediatrics.2020.1310.

Hughes N, Ungar M, Fagan A, et al. Health determinants of adolescent criminalisation. *Lancet Child Adolesc.* 2020;4:151–62.

Hughes CE, Stevens A. What can we learn from the Portuguese decriminalization of illicit drugs? *Br J Criminol.* 2010;50(6):999–1022. https://doi.org/10.1093/bjc/azq038.

Joe GW, Simpson DD. Mortality rates among opioid addicts in a longitudinal study. *Am J Public Health.* 1987 Mar;77(3):347–8. https://doi.org/10.2105/ajph.77.3.347.

Joe GW, Lehman W, Simpson DD. Addict death rates during a four-year posttreatment follow-up. *Am J Public Health.* 1982 Jul;72(7):703–9. https://doi.org/10.2105/ajph.72.7.703.

Lin CQ, Cousins SJ, Zhu YH, et al. A scoping review of social determinants of health's impact on substance use disorders over the life course. *J Subst Use Addict T.* 2024;166:209358.

McCartney G, Popham F, Katikireddi SV, Walsh D, Schofield L. How do trends in mortality inequalities by deprivation and education in Scotland and England & Wales compare? A repeat cross-sectional study. *BMJ Open.* 2017;7(7):e017590. https://doi.org/10.1136/bmjopen-2017017590.

O'Kelly FD, O'Kelly CM. The natural history of injecting drug use: a 25-year longitudinal study of a cohort of injecting drug users in inner city Dublin. *Ir J Med Sci.* 2012 Dec;181(4):541–8. https://doi.org/10.1007/s11845-012-0814-9.

Parkinson, J., Minton, J., Lewsey, J., Bouttell, J. and McCartney, G., 2018. Drug-related deaths in Scotland 1979–2013: evidence of a vulnerable cohort of young men living in deprived areas. BMC Public Health, 18, p.357.

Pearce DN. Sherlock Holmes, Conan Doyle and cocaine. *J Hist Neurosci.* 1994 Oct;3(4):227–32. https://doi.org/10.1080/09647049409525615.

Royal College of Physicians of Edinburgh. Sir John Wenman Crofton Hon FRCP Edin. Available at: https://www.rcpe.ac.uk/heritage/heritage-obit/sir-john-wenman-crofton-hon-frcp-edin (Accessed: 27 February 2026).

Salisbury P, Hill D. Who's asking me? Service user perspectives on safer injecting facilities. *Drug Sci Policy Law.* 2024;10:20503245241234567. https://doi.org/10.1177/20503245241308745

Scarman, L. (1981) The Brixton disorders 10–12 April 1981: Report of an inquiry by the Rt. Hon. the Lord Scarman, OBE. London: HMSO.

Scott-Moncrieff G. *The Old Town.* Scribner's Sons, London, 1947:40–61.

Scottish Centre for Crime and Justice Research. Interventions for Drug Users in the Criminal Justice System: Scottish Review. Research Report No.05/2011 Interventions for Drug Users in the Criminal Justice System: Scottish Review Margaret Malloch (SCCJR, University of Stirling) November 2011 www.sccjr.ac.uk. http://sccjr.ac.uk/wp-content/uploads/2012/11/SCCJR_REVIEW_OF_EFFECTIVENESS.pdf.

Scott-Samuel A, Bambra C, Collins C, Hunter DJ, McCartney G, Smith K. The impact of Thatcherism on health and well-being in Britain. *Int J Health Ser.* 2014;44(1):53–71. https://doi.org/10.2190/HS.44.1.d.

Smyth B, Hoffman V, Fan J, Hser YI. Years of potential life lost among heroin addicts 33 years after treatment. *Prev Med.* 2007 Apr;44(4):369–74. https://doi.org/10.1016/j.ypmed.2006.10.003.

Thom B, Whittaker A, O'Gorman A, et al. Preventing drug-related deaths in Scotland: perceptions and experiences of engagement in a "shared care" model of service delivery. *Drugs Habits Soc Policy.* 2025. ahead-of-print. https://doi.org/10.1108/DHS-04-2025-0020.

Walsh D, McCartney G, Minton J, Parkinson J, Shipton D, Whyte B. Deaths from 'diseases of despair' in Britain: comparing suicide, alcohol-related and drug-related mortality for birth cohorts in Scotland, England and Wales, and selected cities. *J Epidemiol Community Health.* 2021;75:1195. https://doi.org/10.1136/jech-2020-216220.

Winstanley EL. The bell tolls for thee & thine: compassion fatigue & the overdose epidemic. *Int J Drug Policy.* 2020;85:102796. https://doi.org/10.1016/j.drugpo.2020.102796.

Wyper G, Fletcher E, Grant I, et al. Widening of inequalities in COVID-19 years of life lost from 2020 to 2021: a Scottish Burden of Disease Study. *J Epidemiol Comm Health.* 2022. http://dx.doi.org/10.1136/jech-2022-219090.

12 Social and environmental impact resulting from injecting drug use

Long-term outcomes of substance use

What happens to people who inject a substance is a frequently asked question. Many might assume that something with such dramatic associations with sudden death, serious infection, chronic addiction or dysfunctional lifestyle is inevitably going to shorten the life of the person involved. Although on first look it seems an obvious question with a hopefully simple answer, there are reasons why the trajectory and outcome of lives affected by substances are less clear.

Perhaps most obvious is the difficulty of defining, accessing and studying a representative sample of people affected. Defining a suitable cohort or group of people affected requires definition of a case. If substance use has been a one-off experiment or extended only over a short period in someone's life, then it may not be appropriate to include them in a study of the consequences of drug use. It could, however, be that a single shot of heroin could be fatal and that exclusion of this case would ignore an important outcome. Are we trying to study a group with a passing contact with a substance or a cohort with a clinically important dependency problem? What, for that matter, constitutes a dependency state? Drugs are often used in combination or serially over months or years, and knowing that dependency is characterised by periods of heavy use and episodes of abstinence makes outcomes uncertain at any point in time.

We know from personal testimony and case reports that short-term drug use is not uncommon. This applies to many casual experimentations, especially in younger people. The presence of injecting might therefore be a useful distinction in any project attempting to measure the impact of substance use. Casual and transitory use of stimulants such as ecstasy or less immediately toxic drugs such as cannabis should be considered for their adverse consequences separately.

Most studies, therefore, are drawn from groups attending a clinic or programme offering help, and inclusion of the "casual" user comes from anonymous or opportunistic surveys, which tell us little about the outcomes of dependent use. The samples, therefore, from clinics or rehabilitation programmes are responsible for most of the research evidence about the course of a life affected by heroin and other drugs.

These samples create difficulties of their own. Are those who are available for follow-up representative of the whole group, and is the source a group that has

DOI: 10.4324/9781003611097-12

special qualities such as cultural identities, geographical characteristics or unique situations brought about by the way the group is formed? Are those in the sample, in general terms, representative of people elsewhere who use heroin? For example, is a study recruiting people from social housing in England the same as one from Amsterdam, New York, California or Mexico?

The answer is clearly that regional, cultural, social and economic differences are likely to have a huge influence on the outcome for people using drugs. The influence of coexisting psychiatric disorders and childhood adversity are increasingly recognised as influential in determining recovery (Grella and Lovinger 2011), and new discoveries in genetics and the influence of the environment on genetic expression, may well reveal vulnerabilities to dependency and inhibitors to recovery (Bevilacqua and Goldman 2009, Goldman et al. 2005). The common neurological pathways for the addiction process of rewards and subsequent behaviour make the study of heredity in outcomes more important but may have less of an influence on treatment. For many observers, these critically important factors have as much influence on how to manage policy as the dependency itself. Solving an economic crisis, providing safe accommodation, resolving criminal justice issues and offering career opportunities have, arguably, influence in stimulating recovery as much as giving specific attention to drug use. This is important when considering interventions.

The so-called "natural history" of drug use, particularly heroin, has been discussed at length and it is increasingly recognised that early research failed to acknowledge the variation in use over time. It seems obvious now that most people who use a drug like heroin have periods of greater or relatively less intake of the drug. There are, in addition, many people who use in a "controlled" intermittent or episodic fashion and who may be regarded using a term such as recreational users. For most longer-term users, there are periods of remission and relapse and might reflect on periods of little or no use extending from days to years. Measuring intake or current use after a period may therefore not take enough account of periods of abstinence and recovery. Most people who use drugs, including alcohol and cannabis, will recognise factors triggering remission or relapse and influences in their lives that enhance resistance or encourage continuing episodes. The challenge for individuals and for families and treatment agencies is therefore to maximise the opportunities for stability and building confidence.

Bearing in mind all these additional factors, it is useful to study the lives of people who use heroin over a longer time period and to consider what we do know about survival and quality of life of groups affected.

Several major longitudinal studies of heroin users have been conducted over periods of 10 to 33 years. (Hser et al. 2021, Maddux and Desmond 1992, O'Donnell 1964, Simpson et al. 1986, van Santen et al. 2021, Vaillant 1970, Xia et al. 2015). Some of these studies have included a majority of male cases, precluding analyses of gender differences; others have specific geographical situations or are located in a time when heroin use was epidemic. Others fail to include or consider demographic, family and environmental, cultural or criminal justice influences. Drug "careers" are considered in more detail by others (Anglin et al. 2001).

The answer to the initial question of what happens to people who use heroin is therefore complicated, and the results of research have to be put in the context of the individual's characteristics and the environment surrounding her/him.

What is consistent in the limited research is that mortality is high, collateral damage is enormous and outcomes in terms of abstinence have only been accurately measured at a point in time. A useful measure of the total number of days or years of use during a follow-up period is harder to define as prospective records are hard to compile and retrospective estimates based on memory are less accurate.

In one study of 914 people who had been recruited from a methadone programme in the USA, 428 (46.8%) were dead after a follow-up time of 25 years. Of the remaining 486 people, some were interviewed and their trajectory over the years analysed. In a similar fashion to other studies, the influences of background childhood disorders, environment, alcohol and other drugs complicated the findings and again stressed the importance of a combination of factors influencing survival and drug use outcomes (Grella and Lovinger 2011). Most studies have shown that after time, death rates increase and are associated with alcohol and other drug use. As might be expected from the research, where most people are in or have been in prolonged treatment with opiate agonists (mostly methadone), the correlation between staying in the programme and survival is significant and can be measured positively with length of time in treatment (Xia et al. 2015).

Drug use may persist into middle age and older age, and as early as 1975, the National Institute for Drugs in the USA convened a meeting to discuss older drug users (NIDA 1975). A more recent review of the literature showed that studies of older drug users were infrequent and that while they indicated the ongoing needs of people in the older age group, in this case, over 50 years old, the persistence of mental health problems indicated the need for ongoing treatment and support. One study showed that admission to a treatment programme for heroin users, aged 65 years or older, between 1992 and 2008 increased from 7.2% to 16% (Rosen et al. 2011).

In another important study involving a review of 58 prospective studies, the conclusions were clear. "*Mortality among opioid-dependent users varies across countries and populations. Treatment is clearly protective against mortality even in non-randomized observational studies. Study characteristics predict mortality levels; these should be taken into account in future studies*" (Degenhardt et al. 2011).

Most of these research projects fail to identify the important factor of injecting or to measure the frequency trajectory of injections. Assuming that among those who are survivors reduce the harms they are exposed to, sharing less and with a smaller peer group, then one might also expect that injecting frequency deteriorates with time. There are qualitative studies and case reports that support this view. As expected, however, the balance of information supports the morbidity in older drug users sometimes as a direct result of heroin use but also collateral damage from lifestyle issues, alcohol and tobacco use and an increased burden of mental health problems.

Most studies conclude that, for many people, opiate dependency and use is a lifelong problem despite treatment interventions and is associated with multimorbidity of physical and mental health burdens.

The impact on families of injecting drug use

Trying to quantify the cost to close relatives and families resulting from substance use is almost impossible. The emotional, structural and financial burdens are limitless and are responsible for short-term pain and anxiety and often long-term separation, isolation and estrangement. Families may be causal in some way but are almost certainly an insight into the social and psychological state of the substance user. They hold vital opportunities for treatment and care. Close family groups can determine outcomes for substance users, and people with substance use problems have effects on children varying from significant in their upbringing to disastrous for their future (Lander et al. 2013). Perhaps because of the stigma, and at times cryptic nature of substance use, studies of the impact on children are relatively few (Mardani et al. 2023). This lack of attention to families and children in favour of the substance-using individual is frequently present even when the dependent patient's treatment involves the family. Undoubtedly, the family of an addicted person suffers pressures that result in negative consequences on social, economic and social aspects of their lives. The impact on children described in the government report entitled Hidden Harm outlines the magnitude and extent to which children are at risk and suffer damage in connection to the proximity of parents and families who use substances (ACMD 2003).

Enduring a behaviour disorder characterised by intensity of emotion and frequent crises can drain all the resources of the most robust family, and in progressive cases where physical decline demands care and commitment to managing medical and psychiatric complications, resources can be stretched beyond capacity. Support groups beyond the usual interventions by statutory medical and social care services are frequent in communities but depend on short-term funding and goodwill of volunteers.

Stigma of people who use drugs pervades beyond the inadequate funding in the competition with other health funding into everyday acts of social harm that becomes normalised (Addison 2023). The compassion fatige described in communities may have a impact on reducing empathy and evidence based policies and encouraging stigma driven practice (Winstanley 2020). By association stigma extends beyond the individual substance user to family, friends and others. Arguably this prejudicial narrative involves the health and care establishment which is considerably under resourced in manpower and infrastucture. It is easy relate poor outcomes of treatment and education in the substance use sector to marginalisation in the ever present competiton for funding. The term vicariou traumatisation is a psycholgical description of the outcome of stress experienced by staff managing the very difficult social and health demands of an already traumatised caseload (Ewer 2015, Annunziata 2025).

Evidence accumulated from research and other findings in the last few years indicate that the incorporation of family members in the treatment of substance use produces benefits by diminishing consumption and improving family functioning (Esteban et al. 2023). Family therapy is not new, and various formats have been proposed and implemented from support to the closest and most resourceful family member to radical family restructuring (Kaufman 1985).

Economic costs

People who use drugs can have costs to themselves, their families and communities and also to national economies and infrastructure. It isn't hard to see the damage caused to an individual and, to add in, the impact on health with subsequent costs to health care organisations. The criminal justice cost, police, court time and custody in prison are considerable as are the costs to welfare.

The National Institute of Drug Abuse estimates costs in the USA to be in the hundreds of billions of dollars and divides these into three areas he estimates cover three primary areas. Productivity losses can be due to loss of earnings, reduced work productivity and custody-related loss of earnings and productivity. The second area of economic impact is loss due to heathcare requirements, which include hospital, drug treatment and the health consequences of drug use (infectious diseases, suicide, liver disorders and mental health effects). The third area is that of the criminal justice system (law enforcement, court and custody costs) (NIDA).

The multiple causes of costs to many countries have been observed for many years and continue to grow. The long-term observations from countries such as Canada have been exacerbated in recent years by waves of new drugs such as fentanyl and other synthetic opiates (Single et al. 1992) and the "Opiate crisis" in the USA caused by aggressive marketing has reached a new level of opiate-related deaths and associated costs (CDC 2024). The combination of a market-driven healthcare system and a predatory policy to target a vulnerable population caused a national scandal which still resonates. The ultimate cost will be impossible to measure.

In a recent study of the use of health care settings, patients who use illicit opiates in England appear to access health services more often than those who do not. The difference between the two groups is most significant for emergency care, which, the authors reflect, is due to "episodic illness and decompensation of long term conditions."

In this study, there was an increase in emergency hospital admissions and diagnoses, with the most excess admissions being drug-related and respiratory conditions. Those with the highest rate were personality and behaviour drug-related and chronic obstructive pulmonary disease (van Hest et al. 2024).

References

ACMD. Hidden harm report from the UK Advisory Council on the Misuse of Drugs, 2003. Hidden Harm.

Addison, M. (2023). Framing stigma as an avoidable social harm that widens inequality. *The Sociological Review*, *71*(2), 296–314.

Anglin MD, Hser YI, Grella CE, Longshore D, Prendergast ML. Drug treatment careers: conceptual overview and clinical, research, and policy applications. In: Tims FM, Leukefeld CG, Platt JJ (eds.) *Relapse and Recovery in Addictions*. Yale University Press, New Haven and London, 2001:18–39.

Annunziata KN, Curtis EA, Comiskey CM. A Literature Review and Narrative Synthesis of Vicarious Trauma Findings Among Nurses Working in Addiction Services. *J Addict Nurs*. 2025;36(1):53–60. doi:10.1097/JAN.0000000000000609

Bevilacqua L, Goldman D. Genes and addictions. *Clin Pharmacol Ther*. 2009 Apr;85(4):359–61. https://doi.org/10.1038/clpt.2009.6.

CDC. 2024. Understanding the Opioid Overdose Epidemic | Overdose Prevention | CDC accessed 24/5/25.

Degenhardt L, Bucello C, Mathers B, Briegleb C, Ali H, Hickman M, McLaren J. Mortality among regular or dependent users of heroin and other opioids: a systematic review and meta-analysis of cohort studies. *Addiction*. 2011 Jan;106(1):32–51. https://doi.org/10.1111/j.1360-0443.2010.03140.x.

Esteban J, Suárez-Relinque C, Jiménez TI. Effects of family therapy for substance abuse: a systematic review of recent research. *Fam Process*. 2023 Mar;62(1):49–73. https://doi.org/10.1111/famp.12841.

Ewer PL, Teesson M, Sannibale C, Roche A, Mills KL. The prevalence and correlates of secondary traumatic stress among alcohol and other drug workers in Australia. *Drug Alcohol Rev*. 2015;34(3):252-258. doi:10.1111/dar.12204

Goldman D, Oroszi G, Ducci F. The genetics of addictions: uncovering the genes. *Nat Rev Genet*. 2005 Jul;6(7):521–32. https://doi.org/10.1038/nrg1635.

Grella CE, Lovinger K. 30-year trajectories of heroin and other drug use among men and women sampled from methadone treatment in California. *Drug Alcohol Depend*. 2011 Nov 1;118(2–3):251–8. https://doi.org/10.1016/j.drugalcdep.2011.04.004.

Hser YI, Hoffman V, Grella CE, Anglin MD. A 33-year follow-up of narcotics addicts. *Arch Gen Psych*. 2001;58:503–8.

Kaufman E. Family systems and family therapy of substance abuse: an overview of two decades of research and clinical experience. *Int J Addict*. 1985 Jun-Jul;20(6–7):897–916. https://doi.org/10.3109/10826088509047758.

Lander L, Howsare J, Byrne M. The impact of substance use disorders on families and children: from theory to practice. *Soc Work Public Health*. 2013;28(3–4):194–205. https://doi.org/10.1080/19371918.2013.759005.

Maddux JF, Desmond DP. Ten-year follow-up after admission to methadone maintenance. *Am J Drug Alcohol Abuse*. 1992;18:289–303.

Mardani M, Alipour F, Rafiey H, Fallahi-Khoshknab M, Arshi M. Challenges in addiction-affected families: a systematic review of qualitative studies. *BMC Psych*. 2023 Jun 16;23(1):439. https://doi.org/10.1186/s12888-023-04927-1.

NIDA. Conference on Drugs and the Elderly (1975): Chevy Chase, M., National Institute on Drug Abuse. Division of Resource Development, National Institute for Drug Programs. *Drug Use and the Elderly: Perspectives and Issues.* National Institute on Drug Abuse, Rockville, 1975.

O'Donnell JA. A follow-up of narcotic addicts: morality, relapse and abstinence. *Am J Orthopsych*. 1964;34:948–54.

Rosen D, Hunsaker A, Albert SM, Cornelius JR, Reynolds CF 3rd. Characteristics and consequences of heroin use among older adults in the United States: a review of the literature, treatment implications, and recommendations for further research. *Addict Behav*. 2011 Apr;36(4):279–85. https://doi.org/10.1016/j.addbeh.2010.12.012.

Simpson DD, Joe GW, Lehman WE, Sells SB. Addiction careers: etiology, treatment, and 12-year follow-up outcomes. *J Drug Issues*. 1986;16:107–22.

Single E, Robson L, Xie X, Rehm J. The economic costs of alcohol, tobacco and illicit drugs in Canada, 1992. *Addiction*. 1998 Jul;93(7):991–1006. https://doi.org/10.1046/j.1360-0443.1998.9379914.x.

Vaillant GE. The natural history of narcotic drug addiction. *Semin Psych*. 1970;2:486–98.

van Hest N, Brothers TD, Williamson A, Lewer D. Health-care resource use among patients who use illicit opioids in England, 2010–20: a descriptive matched cohort study. *Addiction*. 2024 Apr;119(4):730–40. https://doi.org/10.1111/add.16401.

van Santen DK, Coutinho RA, van den Hoek A, van Brussel G, Buster M, Prins M. Lessons learned from the Amsterdam Cohort Studies among people who use drugs: a historical perspective. *Harm Reduct J*. 2021 Jan 6;18(1):2. https://doi.org/10.1186/s12954-020-00444-6.

Winstanley EL. The Bell Tolls for Thee & Thine: Compassion Fatigue & the Overdose Epidemic. *Int J Drug Policy*. 2020;85:102796. https://doi.org/10.1016/j.drugpo.2020.102796

Xia Y, Seaman S, Hickman M, Macleod J, Robertson R, Copeland L, McKenzie J, De Angelis D. Factors affecting repeated cessations of injecting drug use and relapses during the entire injecting career among the Edinburgh Addiction Cohort. *Drug Alcohol Depend*. 2015 Jun 1;151:76–83. https://doi.org/10.1016/j.drugalcdep.2015.03.005.

13 Political and commercial determinants of health

Edinburgh as a case study

Political influence

One of the singular features of the substance use sector is the politicalisation of policy and practice. The urgency to control psychoactive substances has existed since the 1940s and became a priority in the 1950s when substances such as cannabis and cocaine became widely used in western countries, most obviously in the United States of America. Legislation in the USA and the United Kingdom became crystallised under the aegis of the United Nations in the 1961 "Single" Convention which has dominated the international policy stage since that time. The restrictions of the convention, and modifications included in updates, and its influence on national domestic laws have prevented evolution in control and sentencing policy until recent years. This is particularly unfortunate for health and criminal justice sectors which have struggled to develop a humanitarian and compassionate response to damaging effects inflicted by dependency.

Worldwide substance use policy ranges in different countries from hostile and punitive suppression of substance use to a more enlightened but still constrained development of support and understanding. In some countries, the role of religion is dominant in condemnation of substance use and in others, the legacy of religious judgement remains thinly disguised as dogmatic programmes conceptualised in a spiritual context. In many countries, the enduring optimism of recovery framed as an abstinence from all substances is the single ambition. Enforced by epiphanies and idealised descriptions of personal recoveries, the funding of policy initiatives remains dominated by optimistic thinking about models of care aspiring to cure a condition that is more enduring for many people.

At local and national levels, guidelines proliferate as much to reassure changing administrations and rotating Ministers as with the expectation that their conclusion is the final word. Political expediency demands a response to a crisis, and substance use creates frequent crises in which the electorate and populist views require answers. Unfortunately, a vote-winning response is not usually to invest in support and public investment so much as an attractive short-term solution. The associations with substance use, mental health, inequalities and multimorbidity conspire to increase the unpopularity of research and infrastructural change. Substance use issues frequently create new problems for policy not least in the expanding consituency of people with substance problems. New approaches are required in more

DOI: 10.4324/9781003611097-13

than just young people as an older caseload with substance use issues or a legasy of past behaviour emerges and expectation evolve (Cheng 2017, Macleod 1967).

Avoiding the existential questions of the nature of addiction/dependency, the morality of substitute opiate prescriptions versus the high ground of abstinence has become a political imperative. The rising numbers of deaths, particularly in the USA and Canada in the wake of serial crises, with prescribing scandals and the advent of large illegal supplies of fentanyl, have projected harm reduction practice to the forefront of policy. Simplistic solutions based on the single outcome of abstinence from substances have, for many, been moulded into a collection of interventions. Treatment and support have become a project which must be managed over a time period in the life of a substance user. Treatment is no longer restricted to reduction targets as treatment providers recognize the periodicity of dependency over time and the cumulative benefits of positive experiences and building of resilience. Partial "recovery" and incremental improvements are associated with secure housing, stable relationships and a learning process about avoiding the triggers leading to relapse. Promoting recovery and preventing drug-related mortality needn't be seen as competing risks (Hickman 2010).

As ever, evidential trials and research must underpin policy. In a policy zone where public opinion and individual personal testimony are in danger of replacing science with wishful thinking and marginalised treatment options, the outcome of robust research is critical. Studies showing counterintuitive outcomes and suggesting some interventions may cause harm rather than benefits are uncomfortable but instructive. An example of this is a study suggesting that residential rehabilitation with abstinence from pharmaceuticals may be responsible for more deaths than those getting no treatment at all. Despite these findings UK and other countries persisted for many years with a single strategy of treatment based on abstinece until the rising tide of drug realted harms demaded reconsideration (Heimer 2024, , ACMD 1982, Home Office 1985).

There are increasing pressures on governments and health care institutions to consider influences on health that are described as social and commercial determinants of health. The World Health Organization (WHO) defines social determinants of health as "the conditions in which people are born, grow, work, live, and age, the systems put in place to deal with illness, and the wider set of forces and systems shaping the conditions of daily life." Commercial influences on health are not new, but the globalisation of marketing and the opportunities for influencing behaviours that might have a negative influence on health increase all the time running the risk of gaps in care for marginalised or unpopular conditions such as mental health and substance use (Kickbusch et al. 2016, Gilmore et al. 2023, Arwady 2024). The WHO identifies the many aspects of life affected by commercialisation including many diect and indirect influences on health (WHO 2023).

The impact of negative influences on health is further magnified in vulnerable populations, and this is nowhere more significant than in groups of people who use drugs. In his paper on hepatitis C and the urgency of action to implement treatment in populations of people who have contracted this infection through injecting drugs, Joseph Amon draws attention to the problem of discrimination against minorities, in this case, people who use drugs. "Drug users around the World face stigma, discrimination, mistreatment, and the systematic violation of their human rights" (Amon 2012). The human rights of people who use drugs has become a rallying call not just from activists recognising individual harms but among more forward-looking policymakers and some governments. Defining rights and enshrining them in policy is complicated and requires strategies for implementation and regulation. Bold statements or legal interventions need to be integrated into policy and delivery areas, and the inevitable competition between rights for one group must be measured against the rights for others.

Action demanded by Amon and others, in the case of hepatitis C, was helped by the development of effective drugs to treat this disease which allowed the conventional mainstream of health care to intervene. Inevitably, the limiting factors became capacity in health care systems, training of medical specialists and nurses and paying for the cost of expensive drugs. A cartoon in a medical journal depicted the doctor talking to the patient about treatment for their hepatitis C, saying, "there is a side effect of this drug, the NHS goes bankrupt". As ever, the need to overcome the funding and technical treatment problems emerged, complicated only by the underlying recurrent problems of engaging a diverse, disorganised and at times, distrusting caseload and a residual institutionalised stigma in the health care system.

The recognition that there was a rights deficit, in the case of hepatitis C, might have been less complicated if it had been recognised that an identical problem of implementing care for those people who had become infected with human immunodeficiency virus had occurred twenty years earlier (Gottlieb 1981). The evolving case definition and the emergence of antiviral chemotherapy for HIV in 1995 ushered in a revolution in treatment for HIV/AIDS and has continued to be a triumph of pharmaceutical invention and allowed controlling this disease and a vision of eradicating new infections of HIV infection worldwide by 2030 (AIDS 1987, Goldman 2014, Ho 1995, United Nations 2023, Berridge 1996). This is an ambitious target and already, with just 4 years to go (at the time of writing), the interim target in the United Kingdom, of a reduction of new infections by 80% by 2025, is likely to be missed.

There are clearly lessons to be learned from these experiences. It takes a crisis to energise political and economic systems, and when solutions become available, then there can be considerable energy applied to support an intervention. The management of substance use required substantial change from government action to implementation of a harm reduction policy agenda with radical interventions to prevent virus transmission in the UK and elsewhere, such as Portugal, where drug policy had been in the doldrums (Kalk et al. 2017, Berridge 1991, Berridge 2005, Cabral 2017, Hughes 2010). New situations require investment in science, research and policy and a change in approach to interpreting epidemiology and causation was on the agenda (Krieger 1994). A drug or a vaccine to treat or prevent a disease or condition would be ideal allowing a plan to be developed, and negotiations to begin to allow realistic costing to the health care systems and funding arrangements but this takes time. Treatment of conditions like HIV/AIDS and hepatitis C, and vaccination programmes for hepatitis B, have been spectacularly effective in countries where resources are available, and in disadvantaged areas, a project and a process that can be used to generate actions. Action plans and implementation strategies are evident in statutory organisations and in the voluntary and charitable sectors, hopefully complementing each other. Governments and institutions like a simple plan as it can be delegated and implemented as part of a global programme, and even when budgets are limited, it is possible to measure success and reach targets, even if speed is less than ideal.

Other examples of tangible and manageable projects are easy to find where a policy and technical solution to one or other element of the harms done by drugs becomes available. Closing outlets supplying damaging products is a good example of a practical solution to a direct harm and was effective in stopping the supply of a drug which became available in Edinburgh in the early 2000s, and which caused fatalities and multiple morbidities when injected. This drug, ethylphenedate, was technically legal and was sold in retail outlets until banned using local public health laws. Rescheduling pharmaceutically available drugs to a more restrictive category or withdrawing them from prescribing local or national pharmacopoeia is effective in cutting supplies of drugs found to cause harms by misuse. Over the past few decades in the United Kingdom, debate and actions to control certain classes of drugs have withdrawn some found to be more toxic and limited the availability of others to allow prescription for specific conditions only. The availability of informed and appropriate media and communications provides a channel for transfer of positive messages (Davies 1988, Hansen 1985, Mold 2021, Wakefield 2010).

Preventing overdoses by making antagonists such as naloxone available has generated much activity, and supplying injecting equipment has become mainstream in most western countries. The global economic costs of the multimorbidity and mortality associated with injecting drug use is extraordinary and is one of the crucial drivers of policy change (Piot 2001, Degenhardt 2010, Degenhardt 2014, Sweeney 2009). The burden of disease and associated costs are increasingly identified as the drivers of substance use policy. Mental health in many forms, homelessness, crime, and dometic violence are in many situations interlinked with substance and alcohol use (Tweed 2022).

Why then is progress slow on human rights, political consensus on treatment and allocation of resources to manage the drug problem? These difficulties might be seen as falling into several categories creating problems of who claims ownership and responsibility. Areas of conflicting interests might be seen as political and ideological, multifactorial (drug legislation crosses several boundaries and jurisdictions such as criminal justice, health and social care) and financial. Far from being separate in their interests, there is an inherent conflict immediately apparent in trying to change patterns of drug availability and consumption. At the same time as border controls are trying to minimise imports, the demand increases, and as legal restrictions try to reduce availability, there are strong advocates for reducing control for drugs like psychedelics and cannabis. Further debates on the value of some drugs for personal use are conflated with scientific and medical research to evaluate potential treatments using the same compounds. It is easy to see why governments and ministers read carefully, or in many cases avoid the issues completely, when dealing with conflicting interests. There are very few votes to be gained in anything other than marginal changes.

There is evidence of the harmful effects of marketing cannabis in the USA and Canada where legalisation has occurred widely (NIDA 2024). The marketing to children in colourful packages and the advertising of therapeutic benefits of cannabis has increased consumption. The fastest growing group in one study is the over 65 age group (Han 2020). As expected, the expanded use of cannabis and the higher doses used have resulted in an increase in the number of individuals suffering from adverse health consequences from these exposures.

Marginal and incremental change has been the most likely way forward for many issues connected with drug use and the harms arising from it in the past. However, seismic changes in cannabis regulations in North America, Canada and some European countries have rapidly redrawn the landscape. It remains to be seen how commercialisation and marketing of cannabis products affect health and whether this represents a model for control of other drugs. Inconsistency among UN member countries is stark. At the same time as the USA and Europe are loosening controls on cannabis, countries like Nepal, where cannabis has been a traditional drug of use for centuries, are facing stringent controls imposed by western states who happily market damaging alcohol products.

A report in March 2025 from the London Drugs Commission "The Cannabis Conundrum: a way forward for London" had many findings but summarised its main recommendations in five points.

- Cannabis can be addictive, and more explicit provision of services focused on problematic use and addiction to the drug is needed, alongside greater join-up across health services.
- Possible gains from legalisation, including tax revenues and reduction in criminalisation, can be realised early. However, the extent of harms, particularly with respect to public health as well as personal and societal costs, takes longer to emerge and are not yet well understood.
- Inclusion of cannabis as a Class B drug in the Misuse of Drugs Act is disproportionate to the harms it can pose relative to other drugs controlled by the Act. The sentencing options currently available, especially for personal possession, cannot be justified when balanced against the longer-term impacts of experience of the justice system, including stop and search, or of serving a criminal sentence can have on a person.
- Cannabis policing continues to focus on particular ethnic communities, creating damaging, long-lasting consequences for individuals, wider society and police-community relations.
- The content and timing of education about cannabis and its use, for both young people and healthcare professionals, is inadequate. It fails to acknowledge drivers of use and, in school settings, is often led by providers who lack sufficient credibility and insight.

In his appreciation of Brandt's book on the cigarette industry in the 20th century, Packard, Professor of the History of Medicine at Johns Hopkins University, comments, "Brandt's long awaited history of the cigarette in America uncovers the extraordinary lengths to which the tobacco industry has gone to hide the health consequences of smoking" (Brandt 2007, Matthes 2023). The global increase in lung cancer, just one of the serious morbidities caused by tobacco, is charted by scientists who predict a massive rise in smoking-related lung cancer over the next 25 years, encouraged by aggressive marketing, lobbying against control measures and targeting women and vulnerable groups. With a strong social gradient and cases increasing in China and Asia and low- and middle-income countries, lung cancer is the leading cancer worldwide, and the current incidence of 2.4 million cases and 1.8 million deaths in 2022 may rise to 4.6 million cases and 3.55 million deaths by 2050 (Zhou et al. 2022).

As well as the relentless advertising and sale of tobacco and alcohol, the current marketing of ultra-processed foods has similarly been shown to cause harms (Moodie et al. 2013). This will inevitably add to the multimorbidity disproportionately affecting the least well off in society and has been shown to contribute to multiple diseases. The conclusion of a recent study was that "The totality of the evidence supports the thesis that displacement of long-established dietary patterns by ultra-processed foods is a key driver of the escalating global burden of multiple diet-related chronic diseases" (Monteiro et al. 2025).

At the heart of contemporary theory about addictive issues are sociological observations based on gambling as a paradigm of the expansion of marketing and commercialism. While gambling is seen as the most obvious and intrusive example of industrialisation of addiction, this is easily seen in other areas such as sport, the fast food industry and exercise, where the same neurological pathways are active.

In the arena of gambling, Reith argues that:

> gambling is a paradigmatic form of consumption that captures the intensified logic at the heart of late modern capitalist societies. As well as a site of intensified consumption, it claims that gambling has also become the location of what has been described as a new form of "social pathology" related to excess play.
>
> ...It also reveals the existence of a geo-political dispersal of 'harms', conceived as deteriorations of financial, temporal and social relationships, which disproportionately affect vulnerable social groups.
>
> (Reith 2013)

Others have investigated the methods and practices of the gambling industry and its "turbo charged" activity on the Internet (Schor 2008). Extending this to other activities, speculation about sport and other activities as an opportunity for profit and the manipulation of addictive behaviours, the future seems full of risks for the unwary, unlucky and the vulnerable (Guillou-Landreat et al. 2021).

In an earlier book (*The McDonaldization of Society*), George Ritzer describes the methods of the fast food industry in introducing speed over quality, standardisation and efficiency to maximise profits and, amongst other things, control, using non-human technologies to replace humans.

The direction of travel is easy to see, and the pace of change is penetrating everyday activity, communications and heavily associated with dependency, addiction and the neurological basis of rewards and pleasures.

Activists and advocacy

Representation on behalf of people who use drugs may be divided into categories. People with lived experience are an obvious force for supporting change and diversity in policy. Individuals may represent themselves in the public domain and support may come from professional groups or organisations.

Persuasive arguments exist for policies advocating abstinence from drugs as the gold standard of successful therapy, whereas others regard success as gradual, cumulative and sometimes partial, with modified drug use removing the most harmful excesses as the outcome deserving a description of success (Atkinson et al. 2019).

The mechanism of support or advocacy may come in various forms; membership of groups, committees or policy agencies may be more effective in generating progress than solo efforts, and publication in peer-reviewed journals might be a more enduring way to entrench messages than on the more ephemeral news reports or publications. All these interventions are, however, important and can surprise in drawing attention to cases or situations.

Equally important is the value in countering inaccurate or damaging information when presented in the public sector. The contemporary problem of checking the accuracy of facts presented online or in other media outlets is, in some ways, familiar in the world of drug use, as the whole sector has been demonised and misrepresented in film, news reports and other sources of information. Personal accounts of drug use, the nature and effects of drugs and the association with crime and social disorder have led to serious misunderstandings about people who use drugs, why they do use them and what effects this has on the individual and their environment. Depending upon their sources of information and their personal situations, a wide variety of views, opinions and interpretations of "facts" has given rise to wildly varying attitudes and policies. Truth is hard to establish in an arena where cannabis can be in the same category as opiates, taking tablets carries the same tariffs as injecting and outcomes of treatment require nuanced measures over many years.

Motives vary according to the agency concerned. Law enforcement and criminal justice systems may, and do, interpret information differently. Rising numbers of people using cocaine, for example, will generate anxieties among the people responsible for trafficking and supply but also for those with a mandate for treating those who come to harm from the drug.

Role models and examples of successful advocacy are important. The AIDS Coalition to Unleash Power (ACT UP) is perhaps one of the best-known activist organisations founded in 1987 and known for its publicity stunts to bring awareness of the emerging AIDS crisis, civil disobedience demonstrations, but also its science group which advocated for research and a better understanding of the disorder. The group spawned many international branches developing similar methods of awareness campaigning. The London chapter was founded in 1989 and carried out public awareness campaigns in the United Kingdom. In her account of the group "Let the Record Show: A Political History of ACT UP New York, 1987–1993", Sarah Schulman records interviews with people affected by HIV/AIDS and the background to the organisation. The "call to arms" encourages future actions and notes the ever-widening need for change.

Philanthrocapitalism

Warning about the influence of uncontrolled philanthropy is clear. Preference for subjects chosen for support is based on personal beliefs and bias, and democratic selection is eliminated. Mental health and drug use are in a world of investment and favouritism for technology, and the development of novel therapy is likely to be low on the list of projects funded. Similarly, primary care and social support are less attractive to those wishing for visible results (Clark and McGoey 2016).

The history of international humanitarian aid is alarmingly political. The AIDS pandemic saw extraordinary confusion and divisive political interventions from the outright denial of the US President Reagan administration when the unfolding epidemic in the US gay population was systematically ignored. Subsequent administrations were constrained by the Christian Right lobby. The second Bush administration increased aid massively to support the treatment of people with HIV/AIDS but could not accept the harm reduction and barrier contraception in favour of a policy of abstain from sex and you will be safe. This was copied in the UK AIDS education campaign which led with a headline of "Stay faithful and live" a thinly veiled mirror of the American abstentionist programme outlined in the excellent book *Body Count* (Gill 2006). Most recently, an ideologically driven withdrawal of support across all sectors of overseas aid has seen the collapse of prevention programmes in low-income countries.

The Edinburgh hepatitis and human immunodeficiency virus epidemics

Transmission of these three viruses came at a time of political change and the instability associated with economic transition. After decades of consensus and stability in the National Health Service, established in the Post-War Settlement, the Thatcher government presided over a profound political revolution introducing a free market economy and associated tightening of public sector funding (Beveridge 1942, Tomlinson 2000). This had an immediate effect on health service and social care services, making swinging cuts and freezing spending plans for development. Privatisation of public services, cuts in taxes for higher earners, deregulation of financial markets and cuts in public services were quickly implemented with devastating consequences (Collins and McCartney 2011). Rapid increases in unemployment, poverty and income inequality combined with fraying public services and disinvestment in what has subsequently been described as the 'foundational economy' (Foundational Economy Collective 2018). The net health impacts were predictable; inequalities in health widened quickly while mortality rates in the poorest areas increased including the devastation of HIV/AIDS (McCartney2017, Scott-Samuel 2014, Norman 2011, Robertson 2007, Brettle 1996, Coyle 2008). In Scotland, the wholescale adoption of the neoliberal economic agenda exposed particular vulnerabilities in historical urban and housing policy, leading to much higher mortality than the rest of the United Kingdom even after accounting for the higher levels of multiple deprivation (Walsh et al. 2017, Schofield et al. 2016). Although the mortality impacts were seen across causes of death, the impacts on suicide, homicide, alcohol-related and drug-related deaths were particularly pronounced, some characterised as deaths of despair(Copeland 2012, Schofield. 2016, Walsh 2021).

Since the "neoliberal" policies of the 1980s, successive UK Governments have allowed the commercialisation and competition to proliferate, and for practitioners to behave more like employees in a company than independent clinicians. Administration outside academic and professional organisations encourage compliance with loyalty and conformity to questionable standards and to be directly vulnerable to economic pressures.

The introduction of heroin into these socioeconomic circumstances led to an explosion in use amongst young adults, who were naïve to the risks and hazards of injecting and the dangers of a toxic commodity. Indeed, this cohort would go on to experience high levels of drug-related deaths, compared to the generations before or after, for the following 40 years (ACMD 2000, Parkinson et al. 2018; Walsh et al. 2021; Lewer et al. 2022).

Multiple systems were unprepared for the management of a new set of risks to health, family services, education and the criminal justice systems. Political levers and funding streams were attuned to traditional patterns and with economic restraints currently the zeitgeist, and institutional stigma towards drugs and drug-using communities, any chance to innovate was problematic. Control remained the pattern in public discourse, and rather than accommodating a research agenda, the punitive approach prevailed. Guidance for general practitioners and specialists relied upon outdated evidence from projects in the 1960s and 1970s already known to be flawed and misinterpreted. Projects and research from the USA had largely been driven by the penal system and by most accounts, have demonstrated the failure of coercive "treatments" to achieve abstinence in heroin-dependent people. Rather than looking for the reasons for relapse into drug use after what was clearly inadequate treatment, cases were either abandoned or referred for custodial or other punitive disposals. The urgency of the Nixon administration to increase methadone prescribing was largely driven by the real, or imaginged, connection of drugs with social disorder (Raz 2017).

However, things were rapidly changing in the understanding of the nature of recovery and the phenomenon of relapse after treatment. Never had the social, political and even commercial determinants of health been more clearly displayed.

The need for recognition of a new perspective on managing health was emerging (Gilmore 2023, Freudenberg 2022). Politicians in Europe, where new cohorts of heroin-dependent people were emerging, and in the USA, where existing norms for what constituted best treatment were being challenged, were struggling to reconcile radical change with popularity at the polls.

Research, however, was delivering new insight into the nature of addiction; the drivers to sustain dependency and to trigger relapse were illuminated by research into the longer-term outcomes of heroin use. The associations of problematic drug use with inequalities and adverse childhood experiences made it easier to understand the enduring difficulties faced by people who inject or otherwise use drugs over long periods. The recognition that drug problems were linked to other health problems and the negative impact these have on recovery further helped understanding how treatment programmes might accommodate a range of factors (Barnett et al. 2012). Guidelines, all of a sudden, included the need to understand longer-term treatments with opiate agonist drugs, but not only that; the treatment had to include psychological assessments and treatments, help with accommodation, housing and social situations and the need to recognise the role of the family. From the programmes of a few weeks of opiate substitute leading to a rapid weaning off all drugs, the new approach adopted a longer-term treatment engagement. This unfortunately met with resistance. The belief that long-term treatment might lead to unregulated commitments by treatment agencies raised concerns, and worse than that, the charge that people with drug problems were locked into a managed lifestyle which, rather than improving the situation, perpetuated addiction unnecessarily. For several decades, polarisation of views has inhibited a progressive improvement in policy. Health authorities are limited by the usual constraints of funding and other practical prioritisation. The legal framework around substances in domestic and international organisations is complex. This may not be surprising in view of the risks to life of opiates and other potentially harmful drugs, but regulations, statutory authorities and politicians have a difficult balancing act when trying to prevent access to drugs and when loosening controls to allow a more humanitarian approach to treatment. There are many examples of the need for control to be exerted in clinical practice. The inappropriate use of opiates by clinical practitioners is well recorded, and some outstanding examples of loss of control over access to pharmaceuticals have taken the government by surprise and required revisions of documentation and control mechanisms. Unfortunately, for clinical and research into novel treatment scandals like the case of Dr Harold Shipman, in England, who was able to access extraordinary quantities of diamorphine through legitimate channels to kill between 200 and 250 patients (Holden and O'Donnell 2004).

This was dwarfed by the opioid prescribing crisis in the USA, the implications of which still resonate on policy, control, legal and clinical practice domains (Makary et al. 2017). The blame is levelled at the marketing policy of pharmaceutical companies, the poor state of dependency services in the United States, and the government's lack of control. Solutions, inevitably, advise a wide restructuring of policy and implementation of treatment and harm reduction practices in communities (Kolodny et al. 2015). All this had political and economic consequences. Despite the evidence for in-depth, long-term, multidimensional interventions, political resistance continued.

Political requirements dominate both clinical and public health interventions. Unlike most other areas of public health and medical treatment, political constraints exist to exert a level of control, and at times prohibition, of treatment options that in other areas of health might be the concern of medical staff only.

The role of representation by people who have used substances

The involvement of lived experience and personal testimony has increased over the years as an important part of developing policy and clinical interventions. The National Institute for Health and Care Excellence issues periodic guidance in the United Kingdom for topics such as opiate agonist treatment and psychosocial interventions. The latter iteration includes advice and evidence for the importance and effectiveness of surveys and information groups featuring people with personal experience of substance use (NICE 2007).

The longest-running agencies representing self-help and personal support are probably Alcoholics Anonymous (AA) and Narcotics Anonymous (NA). AA was founded in the United States in 1935 and the United Kingdom in 1947, and NA in 1953 and 1980 (White 2000). The "fellowships" or 12-step models of self-awareness and recovery remain central to the treatment of people with dependency problems, and while they previously maintained a separation from the wider service models of care and treatment, they are now seen as an integral part of a portfolio of "treatments" that can and should be accessed by people with dependency issues. The importance of these interventions and the benefits are not disputed, and the benefits for non-religious as well as religious participants are acknowledged, as are the benefits for women as well as men. Follow-up and rigorous outcome measures are hampered by high dropout rates and discontinued treatment, and the recognition of recovery journeys as non-linear and treatment as opportunistic, cumulative over time, and successful even in partial measures makes defining the impact of self-referral and self-help agencies difficult (Kelly 2003). The fellowships are user-led organisations and provide a pathway to "recovery" either on their own or as an adjunct to more formal treatments. As members inevitably come into direct contact with people who are actively using drugs, there is concern that there is an increased potential for relapse.

Rehabilitation centres have evolved over time and with changing attitudes to drug dependency. The early "concept houses" arose out of Alcoholics Anonymous and were characterised as demanding and rigorous in their acceptance policy and conditions for inclusion, as well as their intensity of programming. Modern models have developed a more inclusive and sympathetic range of support systems but remain, in most cases, with the requirement for pre-admission abstinence from medicated treatments and aim to progress treatment in a drug-free environment (National Collaborating Centre for Mental Health 2008). The inclusion of other modalities of support has become integral to most rehabilitation units, including social welfare and housing support and reintegration pathways to family and communities (Austin and Boyd 2021).

The complicated role of user involvement and the boundaries between non-user professional players is important and not always clear. User involvement requires a better definition and a recognition that there are power struggles and hierarchies in the treatment landscape. One multi-publication review points to ambiguous and fluid understandings of user involvement and a lack of consensus on the definition of user involvement. The awareness that user involvement is understood in different ways influences how best to understand and evaluate the effectiveness of user involvement in treatment (Selseng et al. 2021).

The development of harm reduction as a core strategy arose from the twin epidemics of hepatitis B and HIV of the early 1980s. Prior to this, in the United Kingdom and other countries, treatments were variable and depended on detoxification programmes, sometimes involving quickly reducing doses of methadone over a short number of days or weeks. Inevitably, relapse was the usual outcome. Methadone maintenance was, for the majority, unavailable. A small residual group from the early days of heroin prescribing remained in treatment in London and Manchester (Mars 2003). The pre-AIDS policy agenda was highly politicised, and prosecutions for what was thought to be inappropriate functioned as a deterrent to most of the medical profession (Mars 2012).

Role models for drug dependency treatment advocacy

Addressing the many barriers to treatment among people who inject drugs has been problematic for politicians and the electorate. Things are changing, however, and recognition of basic human rights in managing the complexity of marginalised diseases and social conditions has given rise to pressure groups and advocacy organisations. Medical crises such as the rapid increase in drug-related deaths in Scotland have political backing for institutional change. The development of a "Charter of Rights for People Affected by Substance Use" was supported by the Parliament and the First Minister (Scottish Government 2024). While this is not a legal document, it provides a powerful guideline and statement of intention by the institution to protect the interests of a vulnerable group.

Personal contributions to the development of a rational and humane policy for people who use drugs are many, but some serve as useful examples of valuable models of care.

Robert Newman was a physician and public health official in New York who, with the backing of the Rothschild Foundation, travelled worldwide to advocate for numerous institutions to introduce methadone therapy. As an assistant health commissioner for the city, he devoted his career to destigmatising opioid addiction and treatment (Roberts 2018, Schumaker 2018). He also served as president of Beth Israel Medical Center, where he presided over its partnership with St. Luke's-Roosevelt Hospital Center and other institutions in 1997 to form Continuum Health Partners. Under his leadership, Beth Israel became the world's largest provider of methadone, with about 8,000 patients by the time he retired from Continuum in

2001. From then until 2013, he directed the Baron Edmond de Rothschild Chemical Dependency Institute at Mount Sinai Beth Israel. (It has since been disbanded).

Newman's philosophy was simple. His view about heroin dependency was that it is a medical problem – for which a treatment exists, but for which, at the moment, a cure does not. He continuously emphasised the humanitarian aspects of dealing with the drug-dependent patients and he went on to create the world's largest methadone maintenance programme, establishing it in New York City under Mayor John V. Lindsay in 1970. He also advocated needle exchanges for addicts long before the AIDS outbreak generated broader support for such controversial programmes. He also opened an AIDS outpatient clinic, honoured do-not-resuscitate requests when the patients' rights movement was still nascent and set up one clinic that served gay women.

In 2011, he predicted two consequences of the emerging widespread abuse of prescription opioids.

Despite decades of scientific evidence showing that methadone is an effective treatment for heroin addiction, Newman faced opposition from abstinence and 12-step proponents throughout his career, as well as from policymakers like New York Mayor Rudy Giuliani, who tried to shut down New York's methadone programme in 1998 on the grounds that methadone was substituting one addiction for another.

Newman's response to Giuliani's short-lived crusade against methadone was characteristically diplomatic. In interviews, he stressed that methadone treatment allows people with addiction to lead productive lives and wrote emails to friends saying that arguing with the mayor wouldn't accomplish anything.

By 2011, as the modern opioid epidemic picked up steam, Newman forecasted the future of his decades' work de-stigmatising addiction.

"I'm hoping that pragmatism will win out," he said:

> "As more and more Congresspeople, people in the general community and physicians have children who develop a problem with prescription drug use and can't get treatment for it, I think it will make people more receptive to opening doors to treatment".

Still, he noted, it was a tragedy that so much suffering had to happen and lives had to be lost in the learning process. "I'm afraid that that may, in fact, be necessary if there's going to be a change in orientation."

Although many drug users who want medication-assisted treatment are still unable to get it, mainstream support for addiction medicines has grown amid the destruction left by the opioid epidemic. In April 2018 , the Food and Drug Administration Commissioner Dr. Scott Gottlieb matter-of-factly called methadone and related drugs buprenorphine and naltrexone "safe and effective".

That patient-centred ethos was a tenet of Newman's own practice, said Lynn Paltrow, executive director of National Advocates for Pregnant Women. Early in Paltrow's career, Newman sent her a letter complimenting a talk she had given on pregnant women and drug use. He would go on to advocate and fundraise for

NAPW, including calling officials, writing letters and travelling to testify in person for women who were in danger of being incarcerated or losing their children because they were in methadone treatment.

Despite his roles as a city employee and hospital executive, Newman wasn't afraid of unorthodox solutions to ensure patients had access to addiction treatment. When a private methadone clinic in New York City shut down in 1972, Newman started a methadone programme on an out-of-use Staten Island Ferry boat, shuttling methadone back and forth to the ad hoc unit using his 1-year-old son's stroller.

Decades later, he described the ferryboat clinic as crucial to the eventual success of the city's programme and one of the highlights of his professional career.

> Advocacy by research, clinical practice and teachingDr Selwyn's advocasy and interventions in the clinical and teaching arena has already been acknowledged and his insightful, and at times emotional accounts deserve wide interest for everyone involved with caring for others (Selwyn 1999, Selwyn 2014). Dr. Selwyn has spent nearly his entire career at Montefiore and Einstein, where he is a professor of family and social medicine, of epidemiology & population health, of medicine and of psychiatry and behavioral sciences; chair of family and social medicine; and director of the Palliative Care Program at Montefiore.

Sam Friedman, Don Des Jarlais and many colleagues have contributed more than almost any epidemiologists and observers of drug damage and policy initiatives worldwide, to our understanding of harm reduction and of the epidemiology and prevention of HIV/AIDS and other infections among people who use drugs. From the early days of the pandemic their contributions to understanding the epidemiology and clinical implications of HIV to the economic and political costs across the planet have been extaordinary (Des Jarlais 1987, Des Jarlais 2020, Des Jarlais 2021, Marmor 1984).

Friedman, now at the Centre for Opioid Epidemiology and Policy at NYC Langone, continues to provide crucial evidence that guides policy. His past and ongoing research has focused on the social epidemiology and social network aspects of drug use and infectious diseases. His macro and micro projects span the globe and aspects of drug use from political perspectives, local initiatives, personal harms and prevention to treatments and the social and economic structures and processes that drive overdoses and deaths (Rivera and Friedman 2024). His collaboration with colleagues in genetics and related science has used phylogenetic techniques to track viruses in communities and across countries. His papers on political and philosophical realities contribute much to understanding why substance use is so intractable in the USA and western countries. He uses the term "structural racism" to define the sort of institutional problems that perpetuate substance use harms in people marginalised by race, gender and economic factors. The paper analyses, among other factors, "the history of racism; how racial oppression, class, gender and other intersectional divisions interact to create health inequities; and how structural racism is institutionalized in ways that contribute to disease disparitics among people who use drugs and other people" (Friedman et al. 2022).

Health economics

Global studies of people using injection drugs show a link between city living and national income and age, and an association between the relative youth of the drug injecting population and poor supply of treatment services, including injecting equipment (Hines et al. 2020). Middle- and low-income countries now contribute the most growth in global population, and an increasing number of people who inject drugs are from Asia, Africa and South America, where the provision of policies and treatments is inadequate or non-existent. The potential for the spread of blood-borne infections is considerable. The other marker of injecting drug use, where control and treatment services are poor, is hepatitis C (Luhmann et al. 2015).

The role of gender in the economics of the HIV epidemic is important, and one recent study found that:

> 53% of the 37.7 million people living with HIV globally are women and girls. In sub-Saharan Africa, six out of seven new HIV infections among 15- to 19-year-olds are among girls. Around 4200 women aged 15–24 years in sub-Saharan Africa acquired HIV every week in 2020.
>
> (Tariq and Kasadha 2022)

Evidence from Scotland suggests that the total social and economic cost of illicit drug use is just under £3.56 billion (around £61,000 per problem drug user). The Interventions for Drug Users in the Criminal Justice System: Scottish Review estimated costs of crime are reduced significantly for individuals in treatment (from £12,713 for individuals with no intervention in place to £1,536 for those in treatment for more than one year) (SCCJR 2011).

Conclusions

The HIV/AIDS pandemic had a seismic effect on substance use policy as it did on aspects of human rights, inequalities and, crucially, the economy of health care well beyond infectious disases. Political systems had to adjust to a new reality of ownership of data and participation in decisions to do with health. Increased substance use in the UK, Europe and North America and the connected morbidity and mortality had dramatic consequences still not played out. Isolated and local examples are consideed here as local epidemics are useful to inform a wider constituency (Robertson 2007, Lazzarin 1985, O'Kelly 2012, Leen 1997). A whole system approach is the current zeitgeist for strategy managers at local and Government levels (ACMD 2025). This, like other drug strategies over many decades, has the attraction of involving multiple systems and integrating clinical and social care with public participation. In an all-encompassing policy strategy like this, there is something in it for everyone, and people who use substances can be, partially, reassured that their voice is being heard. The risk, as ever, is that responsibility is shared but not allocated to a single or easily identified agency or organisation. The consequence might be that resources are shared but are less concentrated, and individual interests and requirements are pursued in different localities. Financial resources, or lack thereof, is always the limiting factor in any policy, and projects succeed or fail when funding is limited in scale or time, and pressure from emerging trends and fashions in substance use tests the limits of any sector.

References

ACMD. Advisory Council on the Misuse of Drugs. *A Whole-System Response to Drug Prevention in the UK* [Internet]. GOV.UK, London, 2025. https://www.gov.uk/government/publications/a-whole-system-response-to-drug-prevention-in-the-uk.

Addison M. Framing stigma as an avoidable social harm that widens inequality. *Sociol Rev.* 2023;71:296–314. https://doi.org/10.1177/00380261221150080.

Advisory Council on the Misuse of Drugs. *Treatment and Rehabilitation.* HMSO, London, 1982.

Advisory Council on the Misuse of Drugs. Report. Home_Office_Reducing_drug_related_deaths_2000.pdf. (drugsandalcohol.ie) accessed 22/5/24.

AIDS: 1987 revision of CDC/WHO case definition. *Bull WHO.* 1988;66:259–63.

Amon JJ. Hepatitis in drug users: time for attention, time for action. *Lancet.* 2011 Aug 13;378(9791):543–4. https://doi.org/10.1016/S0140-6736(11)61132-X.

Amon JJ, Baral SD, Beyrer C, Kass N (2012) Human Rights Research and Ethics Review: Protecting Individuals or Protecting the State? PLoS Med 9(10): e1001325. https://doi.org/10.1371/journal.pmed.1001325

Arwady MA, Delphin-Rittmon M, Volkow ND. Major gaps in the cascade of care for opioid use disorder: implications for clinical practice. *JAMA*. 2024 Sep 3;332(9):701–2. https://doi.org/10.1001/jama.2024.11977.

Atkinson AM, McAuley A, Trayner KMA, Sumnall HR. 'We are still obsessed by this idea of abstinence': A critical analysis of UK news media representations of proposals to introduce drug consumption rooms in Glasgow, UK. *Int J Drug Policy*. 2019;68:62–74. https://doi.org/10.1016/j.drugpo.2019.03.010.

Austin T, Boyd J. Having a voice and saving lives: a qualitative survey on employment impacts of people with lived experience of drug use working in harm reduction. *Harm Reduct J.* 2021;18:1. https://doi.org/10.1186/s12954-020-00453-5.

Bacchi C. Problematizations in alcohol policy: WHO's "alcohol problems". *Contem Drug Prob.* 2015;42(2):130–47.

Barnett K, Mercer SW, Norbury M, Watt G, Wyke S, Guthrie B. Epidemiology of multimorbidity and implications for health care, research, and medical education: a cross sectional study. *Lancet.* 2012 Jul 7;380(9836):37–43. https://doi.org/10.1016/S0140-6736(12)60240-2.

Berridge, V. (1996) 1986: The drugs issue: AIDS rises up the policy agenda. In: Berridge, V., AIDS in the UK: The Making of Policy, 1981–1994. Oxford: Oxford University Press, pp. 81–99.

Berridge V. AIDS and British drug policy: history repeats itself…? in: Whynes DK, Bean PT (eds.) *Policing and Prescribing: The British System of Drug Control.* Palgrave Macmillan, London, 1991:176–99. https://doi.org/10.1007/978-1-349-11451-1_10.

Berridge, V. (2005) 'The "British system" and its history: myth and reality', in J. Strang and M. Gossop (eds) Heroin addiction and the British system, Abingdon: Routledge, pp 7-16.

Beveridge, W. (1942) *Social Insurance and Allied Services (The Beveridge Report).* Cmd. 6404. London: His Majesty's Stationery Office (HMSO).

Brandt AM. *The Cigarette Century. The Rise, Fall and Deadly Persistence of the Product That Defined America.* Basic Books, New York, 2007.

Brettle RP. Clinical features of drug use and drug use related HIV. Int J STD AIDS. 1996 May-Jun;7(3):151–65. https://doi.org/10.1258/0956462961917483.

Broz D, Carnes N, Chapin-Bardales J, et al. Syringe services programs' role in ending the HIV epidemic in the US: why we cannot do it without them. *Am J Prev Med.* 2021 Nov;61(5 Suppl 1):S118–29. https://doi.org/10.1016/j.amepre.2021.05.044.

Cabral TS. The 15th anniversary of the Portuguese drug policy: Its history, its success and its future. *Drug Sci Policy Law.* 2017;3:2050324516683640. https://doi.org/10.1177/2050324516683640

Cheng S, Siddiqui TG, Gossop M, Wyller TB, Kristoffersen ES, Lundqvist C. 2021. The patterns and burden of multimorbidity in geriatric patients with prolonged use of addictive medications. *Aging Clin Experiment Res.* 2017;33:2857–64. https://doi.org/10.1007/s40520-021-01791-5

Clark J, McGoey L. The black box warning on philanthrocapitalism. *Lancet.* 2016 Nov 19;388(10059):2457–59. https://doi.org/10.1016/S0140-6736(16)32184-5.

Collins C, McCartney G. The impact of neoliberal "political attack" on health: the case of the "scottish effect." *Int J Health Serv.* 201141:501–23. https://doi.org/10.2190/HS.41.3.f.

Copeland L, Robertson J, Mckenzie J, et al. Premature mortality in Scottish injecting drug users: a life-history approach. *Scott Med J.* 2012;57:38–42. https://doi.org/10.1258/smj.2011.011289.

Coyle H. *A Tale of One City - A History of HIV/AIDS policy making in Edinburgh.* University of Edinburgh, Edinburgh, 2008.

Davies, J. K. (1988). Mass media and the prevention of illicit drug use in Scotland. *Health Education Journal, 47*(1), 23-25. https://doi.org/10.1177/001789698804700109 (Original work published 1988)

Des Jarlais DC, Friedman SR. HIV infection among intravenous drug users: epidemiology and risk reduction. *AIDS.* 1987 Jul;1(2):67–76.

Des Jarlais DC, Feelemyer J, LaKosky P, Szymanowski K, Arasteh K. Expansion of syringe service programs in the United States, 2015–2018. *Am J Public Health.* 2020 Apr;110(4):517–519. https://doi.org/10.2105/AJPH.2019.305515.

Des Jarlais DC, Feelemyer J, McKnight C, Knudtson K, Glick SN. Is your syringe services program cost-saving to society? A methodological case study. *Harm Reduct J.* 2021 Dec 7;18(1):126. https://doi.org/10.1186/s12954-021-00575-4.

Degenhardt L, Larney S, Randall D, Burns L, Hall W. Causes of death in a cohort treated for opioid dependence between 1985 and 2005. *Addiction.* 2014;1091:90–9.

Degenhardt L, Bucello C, Mathers B, et al. Mortality among regular or dependent users of heroin and other opioids: a systematic review and meta-analysis of cohort studies. *Addiction.* 2010;106:32–51.

Foundational Economy Collective, Froud, J, Johal, S, Moran, M, Salento, A & Williams, K 2018, Foundational Economy: The Infrastructure of Everyday Life. Manchester Capitalism, Manchester University Press, Manchester.

Freudenberg N. Integrating social, political and commercial determinants of health frameworks to advance public health in the twenty-first century. *Int J Health Serv.* 2022 Sep 15:207314221125151. https://doi.org/10.1177/00207314221125151.

Friedman SR, Williams LD, Jordan AE, et al. Toward a theory of the underpinnings and vulnerabilities of structural racism: looking upstream from disease inequities among people who use drugs. *Int J Environ Res Public Health.* 2022 Jun 17;19(12):7453. https://doi.org/10.3390/ijerph19127453.

Friel S, Collin J, Daube M, et al. Commercial determinants of health: future directions. *Lancet.* 2023 Apr 8;401(10383):1229–40. https://doi.org/10.1016/S0140-6736(23)00011-9.

Goldman DP, Juday T, Linthicum MT, Rosenblatt L, Seekins D. The prospect of a generation free of HIV may be within reach if the right policy decisions are made. *Health Aff (Millwood).* 2014 Mar;33(3):428–33. https://doi.org/10.1377/hlthaff.2013.1280.

Gill, P. *Body Count. How They Turned AIDS into a Catastrophe.* Profile Books, London, 2006.

Gilmore AB, Fabbri A, Baum F, et al. Defining and conceptualising the commercial determinants of health. *Lancet.* 2023;401(10383):1194–213. https://doi.org/https://doi.org/10.1016/S0140-6736(23)00013-2

Gottlieb MS, Schanker HM, Fan PT, Saxon A, Weisman JD. Pneumocystis Pneumonia - Los Angeles MS Gottlieb, MD, HM Schanker, MD, PT Fan, MD, A Saxon, MD, JD Weisman. Morbidity and Mortality Weekly Report (MMWR). 1981;30:250–2.

Guillou-Landreat M, Gallopel-Morvan K, Lever D, Le Goff D, Le Reste JY. Gambling marketing strategies and the internet: what do we know? A systematic review. *Front Psych.* 2021 Feb 26;12:583817. https://doi.org/10.3389/fpsyt.2021.583817.

Han BH, Palamar JJ. Trends in cannabis use among older adults in the United States, 2015–2018. *JAMA Intern Med.* 2020;180(4):609–611. https://doi.org/10.1001/jamainternmed.2019.7517.

Hansen A. Will the government's mass media campaign on drugs work? *Br Med J.* 1985;6:1054–5. https://doi.org/10.1136/bmj.290.6474.1054

Heimer R, Black AC, Lin H, et al. Receipt of opioid use disorder treatments prior to fatal overdoses and comparison to no treatment in Connecticut, 2016-17. *Drug Alcohol Depend.* 2024;254:111040. doi:10.1016/j.drugalcdep.2023.111040

Hickman M, Vickerman P, Robertson R, Macleod J, Strang J. Promoting recovery and preventing drug-related mortality: competing risks? *J Public Health (Oxf).* 2011 Sep;33(3):332–4. https://doi.org/10.1093/pubmed/fdr055.

Hines LA, Trickey A, Leung J, et al. Associations between national development indicators and the age profile of people who inject drugs: results from a global systematic review and meta-analysis. *Lancet Glob Health.* 2020 Jan;8(1):e76–91. https://doi.org/10.1016/S2214-109X(19)30462-0. Erratum in: *Lancet Glob Health.* 2020 Apr;8(4):e487. https://doi.org/10.1016/S2214-109X(20)30047-4.

Ho DD. Time to hit HIV, early and hard. *N Engl J Med.* 1995;333(7):450-451. doi:10.1056/NEJM199508173330710

Holden J, O'Donnell S. The shipman inquiry. *Br J Gen Pract.* 2004 May;54(502):389.

Home Office. 1985. *Tackling Drug Misuse: A Summary of the Government's Strategy.* Home Office, London, 1985.help_outline

Hughes CE, Stevens A. What can we learn from the portuguese decriminalization of illicit drugs? *Br J Criminol.* 2010;50:999–1022. https://doi.org/10.1093/bjc/azq038.

Kalk NJ, Robertson JR, Kidd B, Day E, Kelleher MJ, Gilvarry E, Strang J. Treatment and intervention for opiate dependence in the United Kingdom: lessons from triumph and failure. 2017. https://doi.org/10.1007/s10610-017-9364-z.

Kelly JF. Self-help for substance-use disorders: history, effectiveness, knowledge gaps, and research opportunities. *Clin Psychol Rev.* 2003 Oct;23(5):639–63. https://doi.org/10.1016/s0272-7358(03)00053-9.

Kickbusch I, Allen L, Franz C. The commercial determinants of health. *Lancet Global Health.* 2016;4(12):e895–6. https://doi.org/https://doi.org/10.1016/s2214-109x(16)30217-0.

Kolodny A, Courtwright DT, Hwang CS, Kreiner P, Eadie JL, Clark TW, Alexander GC. The prescription opioid and heroin crisis: a public health approach to an epidemic of addiction. *Annu Rev Public Health.* 2015 Mar 18;36:559–74. https://doi.org/10.1146/annurev-publhealth-031914-122957.

Krieger N. Epidemiology and the web of causation: has anyone seen the spider? *Soc Sci Med.* 1994;39:887–903. https://doi.org/10.1016/0277-9536(94)90202-X.

Lazzarin A, Galli M, Geroldi D, Zanetti A, Crocchiolo P, Aiuti F, Moroni M. Epidemic of LAV/HTLV III infection in drug addicts in Milan: serological survey and clinical follow-up. *Infection.* 1985 Sep-Oct;13(5):216–8. https://doi.org/10.1007/BF01667214.

Leen CS, McMenamin J, McMillan A, et al. The molecular epidemiology of human immunodeficiency virus type 1 in six cities in Britain and Ireland. *Virology.* 1997;235:166–77. https://doi.org/10.1006/viro.1997.8656.

Lewer D, Brothers TD, Van Hest N, et al. Causes of death among people who used illicit opioids in England, 2001–18: a matched cohort study. *Lancet Public Health.* 2022;7:e126–35. https://doi.org/10.1016/S2468-2667(21)00254-1.

Luhmann N, Champagnat J, Golovin S, et al. Access to hepatitis C treatment for people who inject drugs in low and middle income settings: Evidence from 5 countries in Eastern Europe and Asia. *Int J Drug Policy.* 2015 Nov;26(11):1081–7. https://doi.org/10.1016/j.drugpo.2015.07.016.

Macleod RM. The edge of hope: social policy and chronic alcoholism 1870–1900. *J Hist Med Allied Sci.* 1967;XXII:215–45. https://doi.org/10.1093/jhmas/XXII.3.215

Mars S. Heroin addiction care and control: the British system 1916 to 1984. *J R Soc Med.* 2003 Feb;96(2):99–100.

McCartney G, Popham F, Katikireddi SV, Walsh D, Schofield L, How do trends in mortality inequalities by deprivation and education in Scotland and England & Wales compare? A repeat cross-sectional study. *BMJ Open.* 2017;7:e017590. https://doi.org/10.1136/bmjopen-2017-017590.

Makary MA, Overton HN, Wang P. Overprescribing is major contributor to opioid crisis. *BMJ.* 2017 Oct 19;359:j4792. https://doi.org/10.1136/bmj.j4792.

Mars SG. Ambiguous justice: the general medical council and dr ann dally. In: *The Politics of Addiction. Science, Technology and Medicine in Modern History.* Palgrave Macmillan, London, 2012. https://doi.org/10.1057/9781137272218_5.

Mathers BM, Degenhardt L, Phillips B. Global epidemiology of injecting drug use and HIV among people who inject drugs: a systematic review. *Lancet.* 2008;372:1733–45. https://doi.org/10.1016/S0140-6736(08)61311-2.

Matthes BK, Alebshehy R, Gilmore AB. “They try to suppress us, but we should be louder”: a qualitative exploration of intimidation in tobacco control. *Global Health.* 2023 Nov 16;19(1):88. https://doi.org/10.1186/s12992-023-00991-0.

Matthes BK, Kumar P, Dance S, Hird T, Carriedo Lutzenkirchen A, Gilmore AB. Advocacy counterstrategies to tobacco industry interference in policymaking: a scoping review of peer-reviewed literature. *Global Health.* 2023 Jun 21;19(1):42. https://doi.org/10.1186/s12992-023-00936-7.

Marmor M, Des Jarlais DC, Friedman SR, Lyden M, el-Sadr W. The epidemic of acquired immunodeficiency syndrome (AIDS) and suggestions for its control in drug abusers. *J Subst Abuse Treat.* 1984;1(4):237–47. https://doi.org/10.1016/0740-5472(84)90002-3.

Mold A. Just say know: drug education and its publics in 1980s Britain. *Int J Drug Policy.* 2021;88:103029. https://doi.org/10.1016/j.drugpo.2020.103029.

Monteiro CA, Cannon G, Levy RB, et al. Ultra-processed foods and human health: the main thesis and the evidence. *Lancet.* 2025;0(0).

Moodie R, Stuckler D, Monteiro C, et al. Profits and pandemics: prevention of harmful effects of tobacco, alcohol, and ultra-processed food and drink industries. *Lancet.* 2013;381(9867):670–9. https://doi.org/10.1016/S0140-6736(12)62089-3.

NCCMH. National Collaborating Centre for Mental Health (UK). *Drug Misuse: Psychosocial Interventions.* British Psychological Society, Leicester, 2008.

NICE. Overview | Drug misuse in over 16s: psychosocial interventions | Guidance | NICE, 2007.

NIDA. Commercial interests contribute to drug use and addiction, 2024, Sep 26. https://nida.nih.gov/about-nida/noras-blog/2024/09/commercial-interests-contribute-to-drug-use-addiction.

Norman P, Boyle P, Exeter D, Feng Z, Popham F. 2011. Rising premature mortality in the UK’s persistently deprived areas: only a Scottish phenomenon? *Soc Sci Med.* 2011;73:1575–84. https://doi.org/10.1016/j.socscimed.2011.09.034.

O'Kelly FD, O'Kelly CM. The natural history of injecting drug use: a 25-year longitudinal study of a cohort of injecting drug users in inner city Dublin. *Ir J Med Sci.* 2012 Dec;181(4):541–8. https://doi.org/10.1007/s11845-012-0814-9.

Parkinson J, Minton J, Lewsey J, Bouttell J, McCartney G. Drug-related deaths in Scotland 1979–2013: evidence of a vulnerable cohort of young men living in deprived areas. *BMC Public Health*. 2018;18:357. https://doi.org/10.1186/s12889-018-5267-2.

Piot P, Bartos M, Ghys PD, Walker N, Schwartländer B. The global impact of HIV/AIDS. *Nature*. 2001;410:968–73. https://doi.org/10.1038/35073639

Raz M. Treating addiction or reducing crime? Methadone maintenance and drug policy under the nixon administration. *J Policy Hist*. 2017;29(1):58–86. https://doi.org/10.1017/S089803061600035X.

Reith G. Techno economic systems and excessive consumption: a political economy of 'pathological' gambling. *Br J Sociol*. 2013 Dec;64(4):717–38. https://doi.org/10.1111/1468-4446.12050.

Rivera BD, Friedman SR. What would it really take to solve the overdose epidemic in the United States? *Int J Drug Policy*. 2001;128(2024):n.p.

Roberts S. Obituary: Dr. Robert Newman, apostle of methadone treatment, dies at 80. *New York Times*, 2018.

Robertson R, Richardson A. Heroin injecting and the introduction of HIV/AIDS into a Scottish city. *J R Soc Med*. 2007;100:491–4.

SCCJR. Research Report No.05/2011 Interventions for Drug Users in the Criminal Justice System: Scottish Review Margaret Malloch (SCCJR, University of Stirling) November 2011 www.sccjr.ac.uk. The Scottish Centre for Crime and Justice Research, 2011. http://sccjr.ac.uk/wp-content/uploads/2012/11/SCCJR_REVIEW_OF_EFFECTIVENESS.pdf.

Scottish Government. Charter of Rights for People Affected by Substance Use, 2024. gov.scot accessed 13/06/25.

Schofield L, Walsh D, Munoz-Arroyo R, et al. Dying younger in Scotland: trends in mortality and deprivation relative to England and Wales, 1981–2011. *Health Place*. 2016;40:106–15. https://doi.org/10.1016/j.healthplace.2016.05.007.

Schor J. Tackling turbo consumption. *Cult Stud*. 2008;22(5):588–98.

Schumaker E. New York's 'methadone pope' fought for addiction treatment decades ahead of his time. *HuffPost*. 2018.

Scott-Samuel A, Bambra C, Collins C, Hunter DJ, McCartney G, Smith K. The impact of thatcherism on health and well-being in Britain. *Int J Health Serv*. 2014;44:53–71. https://doi.org/10.2190/HS.44.1.d

Selseng LB, Follevåg BM, Aaslund H. How people with lived experiences of substance use understand and experience user involvement in substance use care: a synthesis of qualitative studies. *Int J Environ Res Public Health*. 2021 Sep 28;18(19):10219. https://doi.org/10.3390/ijerph181910219.

Selwyn PA. Surviving the fall: an AIDS caregiver's journey. *AIDS Patient Care STDS*. 1999 Aug;13(8):453–7. https://doi.org/10.1089/108729199318174.

Selwyn P. Dancing with life and death: Peter Selywn, M.D, M.P.H. | Einstein Magazine, 2014. accessed 26/01/2025.

Sweeney R, Conroy AB, Dwyer R, Aitken CK. The economic burden to the public health system of treating non-viral injecting-related injury and disease in Australia (a cost of illness analysis). *Aust N Z J Public Health*. 2009 Aug;33(4):352–7. https://doi.org/10.1111/j.1753-6405.2009.00407.x.

Tariq S, Kasadha B. HIV and women's health: where are we now? *Womens Health (Lond)*. 2022 Jan-Dec;18:17455065221076341. https://doi.org/10.1177/17455065221076341.

Tomlinson J. *The Politics of Decline: Understanding Post-war Britain*. Pearson Longman, London, 2000.

Tweed EJ, Leyland AH, Morrison D, Katikireddi SV. Premature mortality in people affected by co-occurring homelessness, justice involvement, opioid dependence, and psychosis: a retrospective cohort study using linked administrative data. *Lancet Public Health*. 2022;7:e733–43. https://doi.org/10.1016/S2468-2667(22)00159-1.

United Nations report. The path that ends AIDS. 2023. https://www.unaids.org/en/resources/presscentre/pressreleaseandstatementarchive/2023/july/unaids-global-aids-update.

van Santen DK, Coutinho RA, van den Hoek A, van Brussel G, Buster M, Prins M. Lessons learned from the Amsterdam Cohort Studies among people who use drugs: a historical perspective. *Harm Red J.* 2021;18:2. https://doi.org/10.1186/s12954-020-00444-6.

Wakefield MA, Loken B, Hornik RC. Use of mass media campaigns to change health behaviour. *Lancet.* 2010;376:1261–71. https://doi.org/10.1016/S0140-6736(10)60809-4.

Walsh D, McCartney G, Collins C, Taulbut M, Batty GD. History, politics and vulnerability: explaining excess mortality in Scotland and Glasgow. *Public Health.* 2017;151:1–12. https://doi.org/10.1016/j.puhe.2017.05.016.

Walsh D, McCartney G, Minton J, Parkinson J, Shipton D, Whyte B. Deaths from 'diseases of despair' in Britain: comparing suicide, alcohol-related and drug-related mortality for birth cohorts in Scotland, England and Wales, and selected cities. *J Epidemiol Community Health.* 2021;75:1195. https://doi.org/10.1136/jech-2020-216220.

Watts, G. Robert Gabriel Newman. *Lancet.* 2018;392(10152):1008.

White WL. *Toward a New Recovery Movement: Historical Reflections on Recovery, Treatment and Advocacy*. Center for Substance Abuse Treatment, Arlington, 2000.

Winstanley EL. The bell tolls for thee & thine: compassion fatigue & the overdose epidemic. *Int J Drug Policy.* 2020;85:102796. https://doi.org/10.1016/j.drugpo.2020.102796

World Health Organization. Commercial determinants of health. www.who.int. Published March 21, 2023. https://www.who.int/news-room/fact-sheets/detail/commercial-determinants-of-health.

Zhou J, Xu Y, Liu J, Feng L, Yu J, Chen D. Global burden of lung cancer in 2022 and projections to 2050: Incidence and mortality estimates from GLOBOCAN. *Cancer Epidemiol.* 2024 Dec;93:102693. https://doi.org/10.1016/j.canep.2024.102693.

14 Research and education

The importance and value of research

There is an urgent need for research and evidence in the management of substance dependency and related problems. Historically, injecting drug use has been difficult to investigate in detail for several reasons. As substance use is stigmatised in public and political discourse, outlawed in most countries and demonised in communities, research has been difficult to fund, and access to caseloads and research materials to study is problematic. Without structure including academic infrastructure, adequate funding, and access to a caseload to interrogate, projects have often relied on case reports, observational studies, surveys and second-hand reports, all of which have immense value but sometimes lack the in-depth findings of more formal projects. People who inject drugs are inevitably reserved, secretive and suspicious, and are reluctant, for obvious reasons, to trust authorities or to believe that it is in their interest to participate in research.

Changes brought about by digital datasets and opportunities to access information on a regional and national scale have improved research oppportunities dramatically. Although, at an early stage, the possibility to interrogate sources of information from medical records and police files and to match these with social services data and other sources makes research possible on a new scale. Limitations are many however and access to data governed by ethical and privatisation regulations remains a barrier. Organising and programming data and ensuring that the relevant data points are present in the first place all limit the current extent of research in this format. Some areas are more likely to be accessible than others, and sensitive, unusual and technical elements which require studies might not be available at all or only in limited numbers as they are not necessarily gathered in routine data sets.

The broader landscape of research covers a multitude of disciplines and topics too wide to summarise in one document. Substance use comes into the vision of law and criminal justice, medicine (public health and clinical practice), education at all levels, psychology, psychiatry, sociology and many other academic disciplines. Short-term inquiries are required as new issues arise, and longer-term projects and analyses are essential to measure and judge policy and practice successes and failures.

DOI: 10.4324/9781003611097-14

In the everlasting debate on the value and success of treatment interventions, it is clear that policy is at risk of being driven by personal views and entrenched positions, and global policy must balance complex and sometimes conflicting demands and priorities when making judgements that sometimes seem counterintuitive (Zullino 2024). In most national economies, judgement is required to spend money effectively and to the advantage of all. Affordability in the budget for managing substance use problems must make difficult decisions about the relative importance of research compared to direct interventions and treatments, and decisions based on intuition and dogma might allow for funding of less than ideal interventions. Research agendas must convince stretched funding agencies of their importance, and sometimes, it is only in times of crisis that funding is diverted to problematic areas such as substance use. Examples of these crises are the HV/AIDS epidemics seen in several countries since the 1980s, drug-related deaths which are rising as injecting populations age, epidemics including hepatitis C and those of other blood-borne pathogens (Kalk et al. 2017, World Drugs report 2024, WHO 2024, Brett et al. 2005, CDC 2024). Adding to these crises are the simple statistics from survey data on substance use, demonstrating an evolution in substance use from heroin and cocaine to synthetic opiates and other psychoactive drugs.

What might seem to be desirable in treatment and support systems for people with substance use problems is not necessarily the same as what works, and treatment should always remain substantiated by evidence and robust independent research. Finance and policy essentially require evidence in order to be credible and ultimately sustainable.

A recurring theme in recent medical literature is medical mistakes leading to harms and deaths. Startling statistics with headlines like "Medical error – the third leading cause of death in the US" raise alarm and must influence policy in education and health care delivery. Systems for coding diseases systematically miss many diagnoses and gathering and interpreting information may encourage minimalising the effect of medical mistakes (Makary and Daniel 2016). These findings are also familiar in the experience in completing substance use data and the systems that underestimate morbidity and mortality. This is explored in further detail in the chapter 4 on drug-related deaths.

As with any scientific enquiry, research is cumulative and progresses in stages. The urgency to carry out research into drug and substance use has been driven by a public health and political requirement to respond to emerging trends, medical crises and public awareness. The early research into the heroin expansion in the 1940s and 1950s in the USA has been described in Chapter 9, starting with large-scale government-driven initiatives to find a cure for the addiction "disease". Punitive and coercive treatments emerged at the same time as self-help organisations. Initially arising from the evangelical Christian organisations of late Victorian and Edwardian England and the evangelical movements in the United States, and later expanding after prohibition in the USA the "higher life movement" message of the Oxford Group evolved into the Alcoholics Anonymous organisation (Alcoholics Anonymous 2026). Subscribing to benchmark mantras such as the five C's (Confidence, Confession, Conviction, Conversion, Continuance), AA got its ideas of self-examination, acknowledgement of character defects, restitution for harm done, and working with others as a result of the work of the Oxford Group. Eventually becoming the Twelve-Step movement familiar today, with an increasing academic credential, it is one of the major players in the recovery agenda, with eighty years of experience and millions of members attending for treatment that is free at the point of access. There is now high-quality evidence that the standardised interventions of AA are as, if not more, effective than other psychological therapies, such as Cognitive Behaviour Therapy, for increasing abstinence (Kelly et al. 2020). Similar results and outcomes are less well-researched for Narcotics Anonymous, but can be imputed from the alcohol experience.

Inequality and social marginalisation and other gaps in the research literature

Increasingly, attention has been drawn to minority groups and people with special interests who also have substance use issues. The coexistence of mental health problems and a range of other medical problems predating the onset of substance use or having some causal link can add to the complexity of treatment and the need for multidisciplinary teamwork.

Special topics which might influence the requirements of an individual might be dependence on an unusual drug or combination of drugs. Some drugs have special therapeutic requirements either as targeted treatment such as opiate agonist therapy, and others may require special interventions such as hydroxocobalamin (vitamin B12) replacement for depletion of this vitamin in people linked to nitrous oxide misuse or thiamine replacement in chronic alcohol dependency.

The intersection of LGBTQ+ identity with substance use is an area with less clarity and requires considerable research attention. Minority groups requiring special consideration include people with mental health problems. As discussed in the aetiology of substance use, the link with a large range of mental health issues is clear. Causation or association are both likely to be important, and it is not difficult to imagine the inevitable problems of anxiety and depression, as well as the more enduring psychotic illnesses, existing alongside substance use (Turner et al. 2018). Self-medicating, with alcohol and benzodiazepines for coexisting problems such as anxiety, depression, pain, trauma or other emotional situations, is a frequent factor in people who are in therapy for substance use problems and is recognised as important in assessment (Vojt et al. 2025). Substance use among deaf and hard of hearing populations and those with learning difficulties is a neglected area of research.

The importance of inequalities and poverty in generating and sustaining the worse manifestations of addiction is increasingly recognised in literature and in clinical practice. Frustration with the lack of progress in reducing drug-related deaths and other harms caused by substances has been expressed at the intractable problems of poverty and lack of opportunity for large parts of the population. This frustration can be framed as purely political, or a consequence of economies starved of resources to improve public health and education, or as an ideological resistance to address the increasing divide in western economies between the rich and those at the lower end of the economic and social scale. The health impact of inequalities is often referred to as based on inequity of provision or the "Inverse Care Law" originally outlined by the Welsh GP, Dr Julian Tudor Hart. The Lancet publication in 1971 outlined the Inverse Care Law as follows.

> **The availability of good medical care tends to vary inversely with the need for it in the population served.** This inverse care law operates more completely where medical care is most exposed to market forces, and less so where such exposure is reduced. The market distribution of medical care is a primitive and historically outdated social form, and any return to it would further exaggerate the maldistribution of medical resources.
>
> (Tudor Hart 1971)

This maxim has been adopted in many expressions and publications designed to generate change or funding and support at all levels from governments to local departments, principally in health care provision, although the concept of uneven distribution of wealth is evident elsewhere. A recent report from two Scottish universities drew attention to the needs of primary care and general medical practice to address the problems of disproportionality in funding for health care (Tackling the inverse care law in Scottish general practice 2025)

The key points of the report relate to the failure of a national (Scottish) health service to implement corrective changes and were summarised as follows.

> The "inverse care law" describes how people who most need health care are least likely to receive it. Research shows it applies to general practice in both Scotland and England.
>
> This report explores the inverse care law in Scottish general practice. It analyses policies and interventions in Scotland since 2000 and presents the latest available data. It also draws on insights about the Scottish Deep End project – a collaboration between academic and front-line GPs working in the most deprived areas.
>
> Since Scottish devolution in 1999, there have been numerous policy commitments to strengthening general practice in deprived areas. However, there remains a major implementation gap between policy ambitions to address health inequalities and sustainable delivery on the ground. Of the 20 interventions identified, few have received sustained investment. Only two – Community Link Workers and Welfare Advice and Health Partnerships – have been rolled out nationally in Scotland, but their future remains uncertain.
>
> General practice funding per patient in the most deprived areas of Scotland is roughly equal to the least deprived areas, despite much higher levels of need. The most deprived areas also have both a smaller number of GPs and general practice workforce overall.
>
> Interviews with stakeholders highlighted concerns that the current Scottish General Medical Services (GMS) contract – introduced in 2018

> – insufficiently accounts for patient complexity and workload in deprived areas. Interviewees emphasised the important role of the Scottish Deep End Project in advocating for patients and providing a collective voice.
>
> Policymakers in Scotland need to take steps ensure practices in more deprived areas are resourced in proportion to the needs of patients. Where interventions are working well, policymakers need to ensure long-term sustainable funding. The upcoming second phase of the 2018 GMS contract is an important opportunity to take lessons forward.

Morale and resilience in the medical workforce are critical in areas of multimorbidity, both in the resources required to address the increased workload that attends poverty and inequalities, and the structural resources in personnel, facilities and accommodation. The relatively poor income for medical practitioners in areas of multiple deprivation is a longstanding structural fault line visible in most western health care organisations (Anderson et al. 2025). This economic disincentive to working adds to the problems of people who use substances, and leads to stigma in the caseload and burnout in the workforce.

Epidemiology and survey data

The global prevalence of injecting drug use is of huge importance and for many countries and this is increasing. Consequences for blood-borne virus transmission are obvious, especially in low-income and middle-income countries and areas where policy is directed by governments towards people who use drugs. What data is available from African countries suggest an increase in the poor availability of treatment and supply of injecting equipment, Prevalence rates for HIV infection in the countries where injecting is the most prevalent vary from mid-estimates of HIV prevalence among injectors of 12%, 16%, and 37% in China, the USA and Russia respectively. HIV prevalence among injecting drug users was 20–40% in five countries and over 40% in nine countries in the same study (Mathers et al. 2008). In Europe, the distribution and prevalence of HIV among people who inject drugs is not even, the Eastern regions being worse affected (Jolley et al. 2012).

It isn't just in drugs and blood-borne virus research where women are under represented, but it is a frequently observed case that women injectors seem to evade research and treatment more often compared to men. A study of HIV and women's health found that "under representation is most marked among key populations including women who inject drugs, a growing population who encounter gender-related barriers to harm reduction services and research participation" (Hedge 2021, Shirley-Bevan 2020). Strategies are required to address these gender-related problems and to ensure that appropriate interventions are adjusted to accommodate all groups. This study goes further into advocating for women who inject drugs.

"To address these needs, we advocate for women-specific thinking and approaches that consider the social, micro, and macro contexts of women's lives. We present a women specific risk environment framework that reflects the unique lives and contexts of women who use drugs and provide a call to action for intervention, prevention, and policies" (El Bassel and Strathdee 2015).

Drug-related deaths

Risk factors for drug deaths are many and indicate the areas that require illumination and research. Much of this has been covered in Chapter 11, but areas where research has been either effective, less than effective or non-existent are worth discussion. Deaths in specific populations lend themselves to studies by virtue of being a visible and obvious end point. In most countries, there are systems to record deaths in some database format, and although analysis is variable, outcomes can be studied. There are systematic and cultural limitations, however, and interpretation of data is not always compatible between administrations. Further limitations include the format of these data, how they are storied and the variations between administrations. Not all deaths are attributed to substance use when the outcome is clearly related to the cause. Examples of this are the delayed impact of blood-borne viruses, the trauma which might not be attributed to substances and the organ damage resulting from past drug ingestion. Numbers of drug-related deaths must be interpreted carefully, allowing for limitations in research design and reach.

Having said that, epidemiological data from national and international datasets has been enormously influential in altering the course of treatments and in driving policy (EMCDDA 2024, Larney et al. 2016). Other studies have pointed towards the wider range of drug-related deaths and the conditions associated with drug use that contribute directly or indirectly to a fatal outcome (Gao et al. 2013). Research has endorsed policy and has confirmed the empirical clinical experiences in treatment in areas such as medically assisted treatment for opiate dependency. Refining the research to better understand the components of treatment packages is critical in providing better treatment. Rather than a simple study of the survival outcome for people who have had MOUD treatment, understanding the quality of life of someone in treatment is important, as is the added value, if any, of accompanying treatments such as psychological support, social benefits such as housing and environmental improvements and relationship and social benefits.

Recognising missing information is an important driver for research. Gaps in knowledge can be identified by policy makers, public health officials, clinicians or lived experience and family observers.

Custody and imprisonment require investigation

Deaths post custody have been researched for many years, most reports indicating the vulnerability of people in the first two weeks (Merrall et al. 2010). In a seminal study of over 30,000 people released from Washington State prisons, the risk of dying from drug overdose within two weeks post-release was over 100 times higher compared with their general population counterparts (Binswanger et al. 2007). Research like this would seem to be an obvious trigger for change and improvement in custody systems but not always so. Recent studies have suggested that despite the evidence, prison and custody establishments have great difficulties in translating research findings into practice (Favril et al. 2026). Even a simple intervention like the supply of opiate antagonist naloxone on release, a well-researched intervention, is found to be compromised by compliance in many custody authorities and in the recipient of the product. Even with a sound evidence base for the feasibility of a practical implementation policy, the translation of evidence into practice requires a combination of will to achieve the desired result and cooperation between delivery and enthusiasm for receiving the treatment (Parmar et al. 2017, Strang et al. 1996, Seaman et al. 1998). Other interventions, such as medically assisted treatment, are researched in a limited way but show signs of effectiveness in preventing blood-borne virus transmission and effective ways of engaging people in treatment, but other interventions such as needle and syringe provisions are less well-researched (Favril et al. 2026).

Delivering a wider range of treatments to people with drug problems in prison has similar difficulties (McIntosh 2006). This is partly resulting from the usual problems of time pressures, inappropriate staffing, rapid turnover of people in short-term sentences and disagreement about the value of differing treatment options. The prevalence of people who have used, or continue to use, drugs in prison, is ten times greater than in the general population and mental health problems are so common as to be the norm (Favril et al. 2024, Austin et al. 2023). The figures for women are higher, with a large number of women in custody reaching the criteria for a substance use diagnosis (van den Bergh et al. 2011).

Research in prisons therefore has many difficulties. Accessing people in a stressed environment, with a focus on incarceration rather than therapy, is associated with institutional distrust and suspicion, rapid turnover and difficulty in finding follow-up informant and contact. The problem for research is not just the transition of findings into policy but of designing studies that are appropriate for the situation in the real world of a stressed prison sector.

Evidence from diversion schemes show similar opportunities for preventing the hazards of custody and the risks when returning to a community life. Drug courts and other diversion schemes involving reducing police interventions for minor offences and alternative sentencing to custody have shown economic and harm reduction benefits (Blais et al. 2022, Virtanen et al. 2024, Bernard et al. 2020).

Policy, public health and politics

During the rapid period of change in the substance use sector, policymakers of the 1970s and early 1980s relied on information which was inevitably flawed, inaccurate or just out of date. Research was only just beginning to measure the benefits of treatments such as methadone, and there was only a poor understanding of the causal factors and the pathways to recovery. Studies involving homogeneous cohorts of people using substances were hard to establish, and follow-up over periods of time was difficult. Groundbreaking studies over the next two decades gradually painted a clearer picture of survival, remitting and relapsing lifestyles and the benefits of treatments. Giving clearer pictures of long-term outcomes and the persistence of substance use with or without treatment, several longitudinal studies had a profound effect on treatment policy (Valliant 1973, Stimson et al. 1978, Hser et al. 2001).

The next generation of research was tasked with identifying the complexities of factors contributing to drug use, the influences and benefits of various treatments and the outcomes over a lifespan. This turned out to be considerably more complicated than expected and essentially remains a work in progress despite the identification of the many factors involved. Factors such as those leading to substance use include social inequity, homelessness, adverse childhood experiences, coexisting mental health problems and other less clear reasons for experimenting with substances (Amaro et al. 2021, Lin et al. 2024). Similarly, projects have been examining the reasons why some people manage to stop using substances while others become apparently locked in to long-term use (Manhica et al. 2021). A further area of useful research has been concerning the impact and protective effect of pharmacologically based treatments (Xia et al. 2015, Degenhardt et al. 2019). For many practical reasons, the research into the benefits and outcomes of residential treatment programmes has been difficult. Issues such as defining recovery, selecting people with similar backgrounds and characteristics, and follow-up after treatment have hampered research in this area, although more recent studies have added to the knowledge of what types of programmes have the best results and for which people.

Most recently, research has turned to examine the factors that inhibit recovery and those that maximise the benefits of treatment, whatever modality is employed. Conclusions include that despite the undoubted benefits of treatment, medical or social reintegration programmes, the criminalisation of substances and substance use is inhibiting progress and that alternative policy frameworks are recommended and that harm reduction measures adopt an approach based on human rights and public health. The benefits of decriminalisation of substance use are gaining traction and research is increasingly focused on assessing the outcomes of reducing penalties for possession and use and normalising drug use behaviour. The impact of stigma associted with all aspects of alcohol and substance use remains a defining factor in inhibiting rational and progressive public policy. Research into the causes and enhancing factors that sustain stigmatisation are complex but some progress is being made (Hedge 2021 UNESCO 2022). Further studies to illuminate institutional stigma whch inhibit investment and promotion of substance use agendas are slow to emerge and methods of education which are effective in reducing stigma are limited in their scope.

The urgency to rationalise treatment is based on clinical outcomes and success of models of management. Economic pressures are inevitably a consideration when it comes to expensive plans such as residential care. The importance of reaching the most at-risk population makes access to treatment an imperative and compliance and completion essential. The apparent high failure rate of some treatments needs to be judged from a long-term perspective as recovery is incremental and cumulative rather than immediate. The population presenting for support is far from homogeneous and treatments must be targeted and personally selected. Research needs, therefore, to be nuanced, and outcomes assessed with the expectation that there is no single magic treatment. Having said that, unless resources are used carefully and selectively, opportunities are missed and harm can be inflicted rather than benefits gained (Heimer 2024).

Conclusions

Better research is the usual recommendation at the end of even the best constructed study. The need to improve is never more evident than when practice changes in the drugs being consumed, the combinations being taken or the demographic of the consumer population changes. Identifying gaps in the literature is a skill in itself and designing a study that adequately addresses an important question requires skill and resources. Increasingly, people work in teams, across disciplines and in national and international collaborations. The requirements for high-quality research with results that answer important questions lead to greater expenses requested from funding agencies. Funds from government and foundations are spread across the statutory and non-statutory sectors, and types of studies and interests of those applicants range from short-term surveys and small case studies to formal trials. Large trials can last from a few to many years between conception; raising funds; employing research workers, data analysts and statisticians, to the final preparation of results and presentation of conclusions. Risks in these projects are many; disappointing recruitment of study cases is frequently an unexpected limitation, as is the retention in whatever the study requires to observe. The project may fail for many reasons and not infrequently, may find outcomes that don't support the hypothesis.

Most projects, however, inform the next stage, and even a poor outcome can give direction to future studies. Things that need to be researched increase all the time and projects have to be repeated over time to replicate results and to study changes.

At present, research into substance use and injecting drug use in particular is a neglected area of academic and clinical practice for all the reasons outlined above. Funding and energy in the research sector are most commonly driven by crisis and outbreaks of infection among people who use drugs. Clusters and outbreaks of HIV, hepatitis and other infections have increased research funding but tend to be time-limited and specific rather than examining the complex interactions that lead to harms.

The possibilities for research into populations using linked datasets are unlimited and very exciting. It depends on quality information being included in records and fields that are relevant to the questions being asked. At present, adequate technology is available only in high-income countries, but this is rapidly changing. For research into injecting drug use, the importance of studies in middle- to low-income countries is increasingly important as the balance of frequency shifts.

Research into the extensive landscape of substance use impacts on an unlimited number of disciplines and the range of possibilities is endless. The educational establishment needs to know about best practice in the prevailing culture, the justice system urgently requires information to make appropriate decisions about sentencing and management of custody and every branch of the humanities and medicine requires an understanding of contemporary substance use. The limits for research are endless.

It hardly needs to be said that education is a critical element of preventing drug use and injecting. Educating children about the risks and harms of substances is central to most policy initiatives. The complexity of this area requires specialist study and trials by teachers and educationalists and is beyond the scope of this book. Secondary education of those already involved with drug use is integrated into treatment programmes. An essential part of limiting the damage of substance use is related to the supply of information and the capacity to engage in less harmful activity. The supply of injecting equipment, access to drug testing facilities and suitable venues for safe drug use are all part of educating individuals and communities to reduce the risks.

References

Alcoholics Anonymous. (2026) History of AA. Available at: https://alcoholics-anonymous.eu/about-aa/history-of-c-e-r/ (Accessed: 3 March 2026).

Amaro H, Sanchez M, Bautista T, Cox R. Social vulnerabilities for substance use: stressors, socially toxic environments, and discrimination and racism. *Neuropharmacology*. 2021;188:108518. https://doi.org/10.1016/j.neuropharm.2021.108518

Anderson M, Gibson J, Walker B, Hutchinson J, Checkland K, Sutton M. Deprivation and general practitioners' working lives: Repeated cross-sectional study. *J R Soc Med*. 2025 May;118(5):157–66. https://doi.org/10.1177/01410768251330076.

Austin A, Favril L, Craft S, Thliveri P, Freeman TP. Factors associated with drug use in prison: a systematic review of quantitative and qualitative evidence. *Int J Drug Policy*. 2023;122:104248.

Binswanger IA, Stern MF, Deyo RA, et al. Release from prison—A high risk of death for former inmates. *New Engl J Med*. 2007;356:157–65.

Bernard CL, Rao IJ, Robison KK, Brandeau ML. Health outcomes and cost-effectiveness of diversion programs for low-level drug offenders: a model-based analysis. *Plos Med*. 2020;17:e1003239.

Blais E, Brisson J, Gagnon F, Lemay SA. Diverting people who use drugs from the criminal justice system: a systematic review of police-based diversion measures. *Int J Drug Policy*. 2022;105:103697.

Brett MM, Hood J, Brazier JS, Duerden BI, Hahné SJ. Soft tissue infections caused by spore-forming bacteria in injecting drug users in the United Kingdom. *Epidemiol Infect*. 2005 Aug;133(4):575–82. https://doi.org/10.1017/s0950268805003845.

CDC. Centre for Disease Control, 2024. Understanding the Opioid Overdose Epidemic | Overdose Prevention | CDC accessed on 25/5/2025.

Degenhardt L, Grebely J, Stone J, et al. Global patterns of opioid use and dependence: harms to populations, interventions, and future action. *Lancet*. 2019;394(10208):1560–79. https://doi.org/10.1016/S0140-6736(19)32229-9.

El-Bassel N, Strathdee SA. Women who use or inject drugs: an action agenda for women-specific, multilevel, and combination HIV prevention and research. *J Acquir Immune Defic Syndr*. 2015 Jun 1;69(Suppl 2):S182–90. https://doi.org/10.1097/QAI.0000000000000628.

EMCDDA. European Monitoring Centre for Drugs and Drug Addiction. *European Drug Report 2024: Trends and Developments*, 2024. https://www.emcdda.europa.eu/publications/european-drug-report/2024_en.

Favril L, Strang J, Fazel S. Drug use among people in prison: A global review of epidemiology, harms and interventions. Addiction. 2026;121(4):749–764. https://doi.org/10.1111/add.70245

Favril L, Rich JD, Hard J, Fazel S. Mental and physical health morbidity among people in prisons: an umbrella review. *Lancet Public Health.* 2024;9:e250–60.

Hedge B, Devan K, Catalan J, Cheshire A, Ridge D. HIV-related stigma in the UK then and now: to what extent are we on track to eliminate stigma? A qualitative investigation. BMC Public Health. 2021 May 30;21(1):1022. doi: 10.1186/s12889-021-11000-7. PMID: 34053441; PMCID: PMC8166014.

Heimer R, Black AC, Lin H, et al. Receipt of opioid use disorder treatments prior to fatal overdoses and comparison to no treatment in Connecticut, 2016-17. *Drug Alcohol Depend.* 2024;254:111040. doi:10.1016/j.drugalcdep.2023.111040

Hser YI, Hoffman V, Grella CE, Anglin MD. A 33-year follow-up of narcotics addicts. *Arch Gen Psych.* 2001;58(5):503–8. https://doi.org/10.1001/archpsyc.58.5.503.

Jolley E, Rhodes T, Platt L, Hope V, Latypov A, Donoghoe M, Wilson D. HIV among people who inject drugs in Central and Eastern Europe and Central Asia: a systematic review with implications for policy. *BMJ Open.* 2012 Oct 18;2(5):e001465. https://doi.org/10.1136/bmjopen-2012-001465.

Kalk NJ, Robertson JR, Kidd B, et al. Treatment and intervention for opiate dependence in the United Kingdom: lessons from Triumph and Failure, 2017. https://doi.org/10.1007/s10610-017-9364-z.

Kelly JF, Humphreys K, Ferri M. Alcoholics Anonymous and other 12-step programs for alcohol use disorder. *Cochrane Database Syst Rev.* 2020(3): Article No. CD012880. https://doi.org/10.1002/14651858.CD012880.pub2.

Larney S, Peacock A, Mathers BM, Hickman M, Degenhardt L. A systematic review of injecting-related injury and disease among people who inject drugs. *Drug Alcohol Depend.* 2017 Feb 1;171:39–49. https://doi.org/10.1016/j.drugalcdep.2016.11.029.

Lin C, Cousins SJ, Zhu Y, et al. A scoping review of social determinants of health's impact on substance use disorders over the life course. *J Subst Use Addict Treat.* 2024;166:209484. https://doi.org/10.1016/j.josat.2024.209484.

Makary MA, Daniel M. Medical error-the third leading cause of death in the US. *BMJ.* 2016 May 3;353:i2139. https://doi.org/10.1136/bmj.i2139.

Manhica H, Straatmann VS, Lundin A, Agardh E, Danielsson AK. Association between poverty exposure during childhood and adolescence, and drug use disorders and drug-related crimes later in life. *Addiction.* 2021;116(7):1747–56. https://doi.org/10.1111/add.15336.

Mathers BM, Degenhardt L, Phillips B, et al. Reference Group to the UN on HIV and injecting drug use. Global epidemiology of injecting drug use and HIV among people who inject drugs: a systematic review. *Lancet.* 2008 Nov 15;372(9651):1733–45. https://doi.org/10.1016/S0140-6736(08)61311-2.

Merrall EL, Kariminia A, Binswanger IA, et al. Meta-analysis of drug-related deaths soon after release from prison. *Addiction.* 2010 Sep;105(9):1545–54. https://doi.org/10.1111/j.1360-0443.2010.02990.x.

McIntosh J, Saville E. The challenges associated with drug treatment in prison. *Probat J* 2006;53:230–47.

Parmar MK, Strang J, Choo L, Meade AM, Bird SM. Randomized controlled pilot trial of naloxone-on-release to prevent post-prison opioid overdose deaths. *Addiction.* 2017 Mar;112(3):502–15. https://doi.org/10.1111/add.13668.

Seaman SR, Brettle RP, Gore SM. Mortality from overdose among injecting drug users recently released from prison: database linkage study. *BMJ.* 1998 Feb 7;316(7129):426–8. https://doi.org/10.1136/bmj.316.7129.426.

Shirley-Beavan S, Roig A, Burke-Shyne N, Daniels C, Csak R. Women and barriers to harm reduction services: a literature review and initial findings from a qualitative study in Barcelona, Spain. *Harm Reduct J.* 2020 Oct 19;17(1):78. https://doi.org/10.1186/s12954-020-00429-5.

Strang J, Darke S, Hall W, Farrell M, Ali R. Heroin overdose: the case for take-home naloxone. *BMJ.* 1996 Jun 8;312(7044):1435–6. https://doi.org/10.1136/bmj.312.7044.1435.

Stimson GV, Oppenheimer E, Thorley A. Seven-year follow-up of heroin addicts: drug use and outcome. *Br Med J.* 1978;1(6121):1190–2. https://doi.org/10.1136/bmj.1.6121.1190.

Tackling the inverse care law in Scottish general practice 2025. A report from the universities of Edinburgh and Glasgow. https://www.health.org.uk/reports-and-analysis/reports/tackling-the-inverse-care-law-in-scottish-general-practice. Accessed 02/07/2025.

Tudor Hart J. The inverse care law. *Lancet.* 1971 Feb 27;297(7696):405–12.

Turner S, Mota N, Bolton J, Sareen J. Self-medication with alcohol or drugs for mood and anxiety disorders: a narrative review of the epidemiological literature. *Depress Anxiety.* 2018;35(9):851–60. https://doi.org/10.1002/da.22771.

UNESCO (2022) The power of education to end HIV-related stigma and discrimination. Paris: United Nations Educational, Scientific and Cultural Organization, 7 July. Available at: The power of education to end HIV-related stigma and discrimination. accessed 28/02/2026

Vaillant GE. A 20-year follow-up of New York narcotic addicts. *Arch Gen Psych.* 1973;29(2):237–41. https://doi.org/10.1001/archpsyc.1973.04200020065009.

van den Bergh BJ, Gatherer A, Fraser A, Moller L. Imprisonment and women's health: concerns about gender sensitivity, human rights and public health. *B World Health Organ.* 2011;89:689–94.

World Drugs Report 2024. WDR24_Key_findings_and_conclusions.pdf.

WHO. World Health Organisation. 2024. https://www.who.int/health-topics/hepatitis.

Xia Y, Seaman S, Hickman M, et al. Factors affecting repeated cessations of injecting drug use and relapses during the entire injecting career among the Edinburgh Addiction Cohort. *Drug Alcohol Depend.* 2015;151:76–83. https://doi.org/10.1016/j.drugalcdep.2015.03.005.

Zullino D. Do not conflate debates on regulating therapeutic use of psychotropic substances with those on the legalization of their non-therapeutic use. *Addiction.* 2024. https://doi.org/10.1111/add.16667.

Virtanen S, Aaltonen M, Latvala A, Forsman M, Lichtenstein P, Chang Z. Effectiveness of substance use disorder treatment as an alternative to imprisonment. *Bmc Psych.* 2024;24:260.

Vojt G, Family HE, Poulter H, et al. Motivations underlying co-use of benzodiazepines and opioids in the UK: a qualitative study. *Harm Reduct J.* 2025;22(1):152. https://doi.org/10.1186/s12954-025-01312-x.

Index

Note: Page numbers in *italics* indicate figures.